Clean Cabbage
in the Bucket

and Other Tales from the Irish Music Trenches

*By Frank Emerson, Seamus Kennedy,
Robbie O'Connell, Harry O'Donoghue,
Dennis O'Rourke*

Edited by Dennis O'Rourke

Llumina Press

ISBN: 978-1-59526-991-1

Printed in the United States of America by Llumina Press

Library of Congress Control Number: 2007900775

I am Raftery the Poet

I am Raftery the poet
Full of hope and love
My eyes without sight
My mind without torment
Going west on my journey
By the light of my heart
Tired and weary
To the end of the road
Behold me now
With my back to the wall
Playing music
To empty pockets.

Anthony Raftery
Born: Killeadan, County Mayo

Translated from the Irish by James Stephens

INTRODUCTION

One afternoon, in the summer of 2001, I was rolling across Florida's Alligator Alley to a gig in Fort Myers, daydreaming of nights, days, and seasons gone by—and where I might be if I hadn't picked the life of a road musician. I was in the twenty-fifth year of my career, and things were getting bleak. Irish pubs were springing up everywhere, it seemed, but they were relying less on live entertainment. Some of the best clubs had closed; others were struggling, staying afloat by cutting back on expenses, which usually meant paring down the entertainment. Irish pubs were never that lucrative, but I could make a living, and it was fun—great fun. Now it was a struggle to get by, and it was growing tougher to get an audience to pay any attention. Twenty-five years, I thought. How did I get here?

***

I learned to play the guitar because I loved music, I wanted to meet girls, and I couldn't dance. Someday, I was going to write songs and a few good novels. There would be no nine-to-five job for me. That determination was burned into my heart when I was fifteen and working a summer job that I would hold through my last two years in high school and my first year of college.

I worked in a factory—a sweatshop—that produced phonebook covers out of vinyl. My task was to sit at a table at the back of a machine that pulled in a roll of vinyl, silk-screened it with ad copy, and then perforated an outer ridge with a heat sealer. Hour after hour, I sat there, "pulling covers," watching for the odd glitch, smudge, or off-center stamp in ads for clothing stores, restaurants, dry cleaners, and sub shops. Sales representatives had convinced retailers to pay to have their logos, addresses, and phone numbers inked on hundreds, sometimes thousands of covers tailored to fit their local phone directories. They were mailed for free to residents of small, wooded, country burgs in Pennsylvania or Maryland, farm towns in Iowa, or perhaps a dying manufacturing hamlet in New England, where "Sal's Little Sicily Pizzeria" gave the local teenagers a sanctuary in which to hang out long after dark on school nights; a place to come in out of a steel-cold rain on an unforgiving, melancholy, Saturday afternoon in November. That's how I saw it in my head when I read the ads.

***

In 1964, I was a high school kid playing in a folk-duo with Rob Morelli. We called ourselves the Wandering Brothers. Then we formed a rock and roll band. By the time I discovered the Clancy Brothers and Tommy Makem, I was already deep into Irish history. In college, I was devoted to James Joyce. *Ulysses* was my bible. It naturally followed that I would buy every record the Clancys and Makem put out and learn the songs. In the beginning, I tried to sing like Makem.

My decision not to be trapped in an ordinary day job, or an ordinary life, for that matter, took me to sea for a couple of years. I sailed in the Merchant Marine—on oil tankers and freighters—a couple of them to the Far East. By the early seventies, the Irish folk boom was in full swing in America, and I wanted to play that music on stage. I felt my time at sea had given me the right, the integrity, to sing chanteys and sea-songs, even though the music aboard an oil tanker usually came from a sailor's tape player, and more often than not was George Jones or Johnny Cash. Performing Irish material was another matter. Most of the pub entertainers in America then were Irish-born. Since it had always been my desire to live in Ireland, I decided now was the time. It would go a long way to legitimizing my ambitions. In 1974, I set up shop in Dublin for eighteen months, acquiring dual citizenship. I played wherever I could and satisfied my writer's urge by reviewing books in the *Hibernian Fortnightly*, a publication of the *Irish Times*. (I began a novel that stumbled forward for a few hundred pages and then ground to a halt. The second was a fantasy/occult tale that I did finish, though it has never seen the light of day.)

I returned to the States. A week before St. Patrick's Day in '76, I got a call from a friend who knew an agent looking for acts to work on the big day. The agent's name was Billy Carson, an entertainer himself. He was a stocky Scotsman from Glasgow with a happy demeanor and a soaring voice. He had a gig for me at a restaurant. I was to walk around the tables, strumming, and singing. This was not what I had been expecting, but I couldn't turn it down. I felt silly, the diners studiously averted their eyes, and I swore I would never again do one of these strolling minstrel bits.

"Don't look at him, Millie. He'll come this way."

After an hour of this, a manager asked if I would come into the bar and play, and I quickly agreed. A nice little group gathered 'round, and I had such a good time I played two hours longer than scheduled. At the end of the night, I was elated; I was also hooked—very hooked.

Billy Carson was my agent for a while. I worked as an EKG technician in a hospital and did the gigs on the weekends. Then he offered me an entire month at a club in Chicago. There it was. I was a working road musician, at last. I went to part-time at the hospital and finally quit.

After a year, I had established myself. I had safely skirted the deadly maw of a regular day job, and I was doing something I loved. I was on my own, and to a certain extent, was my own boss. The years roared by 'til I found myself on Alligator Alley, wondering where the time had gone and what I was going to do next. Where was the road taking me now?

I made a stab at a novel based on my experiences as an Irish pub singer, but after a hundred pages, I realized I was writing nothing more than a series of anecdotes. This led me to consider a non-fiction work, but there was a problem there, too. While I had some interesting stories, there was not quite enough to justify a book. The solution to this came quickly.

One of the more enjoyable aspects of my life as an entertainer was sharing experiences with friends—my peers in the business. Along with exchanging information about equipment, guitars, and new clubs, we regaled one another with our adventures on the road. Over a jar, we would catch up, laugh, commiserate, and sometimes lament. The idea for the book took hold. Late in that summer of 2001, I decided to give it a go. All I had to do was pick my collaborators.

I met Robbie O'Connell in the late seventies. A nephew of the Clancy Brothers, his musical pedigree was unimpeachable. I spent a good deal of time at his house, where we sat and talked about music, listened to it, and played it. He had a sunny nature, and he loved to laugh. I loved to make him laugh and sometimes play the odd trick on him. He had two children then, and I would get down on the floor with them and play. Robbie and his wife Roxanne would hover and remark how wonderful Dennis was with kids. We'd have a riotous time, and then I would say goodnight. Of course, I had the kids so wound up by then it took an hour to settle them down and get them into bed. Robbie didn't make the connection for a long time, until one night, I was set for a romp with them and the light of realization illuminated his face. He grabbed me by the shoulders and forced me to the door. "Get out of here, you bastard. I'm on to you now."

Once, we were working separate clubs in DC, and we shared a by-the-week flat in Arlington, Virginia. It wasn't in the best of areas and we were a bit nervous about break-ins. When we left, Robbie would lean through the door and shout into the empty room, loud enough for the whole building to hear, "Remember to feed the dogs, darlin'. You know how vicious they can get."

Seamus Kennedy. He was one of the most colorful characters I have ever seen on stage. He played and sang beautifully, and his wit was quick and acerbic. Hecklers had no chance. I went to his gigs at Liam's and stood in awe at his ability to work a crowd. One night, I watched him do a ninety-minute set in front of a packed house. It was masterful. One of the bar regulars standing beside me said, "Are you watching this? He's got them in the palm of his hand."

"I'm watching," I replied, "and I'm taking notes."

Frank Emerson was the most intense guy I'd ever seen on stage. He'd close his eyes and sing in his rich baritone, and be in another world. I used to see him a lot when he partnered with Tony O'Riordan, a gas character in his own right. Over the years, performing solo, Frank developed an amazing repertoire. He was a walking jukebox, and he put stirring shows together for special occasions—the Easter Rebellion in Dublin in 1916 and notably, American holidays, like the Fourth of July and Veteran's Day. Songs, stories, and poems of the valor of the American soldier in war would fill the room, thrilling the audience, often bringing them to tears.

I didn't meet Harry O'Donoghue until the late eighties, although I knew him by reputation. I saw him perform at the Kevin Barry Pub in Savannah. He was an all-around good entertainer. Like Seamus, he could stop the music, and one joke after another would roll off his tongue. His sometimes dry, sardonic take on life's irregularities was comfortably aligned with a compassion and romanticism that shone in his stage shows and original songs. He could tell a story, so I figured he could write one as well.

***

For four years, between gigs, tours, and personal travails, we followed a literary road and wrote these stories. (I spent a year in the Caribbean entertaining on cruise ships; in Cozumel or St. Martin, I went to Internet cafes and downloaded their new material.) My collaborators approached the project with enthusiasm. Stories are told in the third person, in dialogue, in play form and a few nice takes on Damon Runyon. I interviewed each of them and dropped the best bits into the text under the heading "Stray Chats." The stories are grouped according to subject matter or other commonalities.

***

How do things stand now? Where am I, five years after that epiphany on Alligator Alley? Well, the music business, all facets of it, is just as tough as ever. It's a scramble for gigs, but I'm still at it. I ruminated for a time on what other work I might take on to carry me through the rest of the sojourn, but never too seriously. I perform where I can, and I write songs. I have a book I can look to—no small accomplishment—put together with four good friends, and I'm proud of it. We all are. We're still out there, on the road, in the musical trenches. Look for us.

Dennis O'Rourke
October 2006

TABLE OF CONTENTS

Clean Cabbage in the Bucket

and Other Tales from the Irish Music Trenches

OTHER MUSICIANS, OR FELLOW TRAVELERS GUILTY OF COMMITTING MUSIC

The Best Feet in the Business

Frank Emerson

One evening, I am taking a busman's holiday at the bar of the Dubliner, which is close by Union Station in Washington, DC. It is a very successful establishment with a hotel above it, in case anyone is in need of forty winks. The newspaper scribes say that the Dubliner is where you will see many Capitol Hill "staffers." Now, I would not know a "staffer" from a "staffee." And, personally, I never see any staffing going on in the Dubliner, so they are probably making mountains out of molehills.

At this time, I am enjoying the company of Bill Whitman, a flute player in various traditional Irish bands and a regular Joe. He does not look much like a flute player. He looks more like a college wrestler or a furniture stripper. Coincidentally, this is what he is before he gets tired of wrestling and stripping and decides to get into the flute-playing racket. Anyway, we are having a couple of cocktails, talking about this and that, and listening to the group Celtic Thunder, which is holding forth on the stage.

Celtic Thunder is a five-piece, traditional Irish band. Just fitting them all on stage at the Dubliner is a good trick, what with the fact that they all play several instruments that they squeeze on stage with them. The band is made up of the Winch brothers—Terry and Jesse, Nita Connolly, and Linda and Steve Hickman. Linda and Steve are married up with each other more or less, but remain good friends all the same. Like most traditional bands, they play old jigs, reels, airs, and what not, but they also sing strong harmonies. They are very good and easy on the ears. That is to say, there are hardly any bum notes to speak of.

Now, over the years, I am noting that by and large, traditional musicians sit down when they play. This happens not only at sessions—which are informal gatherings around somebody's kitchen table, where it is only polite to sit down, but also at official performances such as on stage at the Dubliner. In fact, at this moment, the members of Celtic Thunder are all sitting in chairs, which they pilfer from some of the audience tables and lug onto the stage. I have to admit they appear comfortable enough with the whole set up. I am curious about this. I venture a question to Bill, who I figure would be in the know, about this business of sitting down on the job. Bill says to me as follows:

"Yes, that is pretty much the standard with 'trad-types.'" "Trad-types" being shorthand for traditional musicians—a very hip way of referring to them. "They always sit down on stage. And do you know why?"

"Well, no," I say. "That is just why I ask you."

Bill glances left and right over his shoulders. He then looks at me square on with an expression that makes me figure he is about to let me in on the real skinny. He leans into me, and with a nod toward Celtic Thunder, he says, "Do you see how at ease they seem to be?"

I look, and I nod to say, "Yes, I do."

"Well," he says, "here is the thing. They are really only about half at ease. If the truth be told, trad-types sit on stage only because the management frowns on it if they lie down."

I let this steep for a minute or so as he turns back to his glass and downs it. I cannot tell if he is serious, but I reason that Bill has no call to hand me a whopper, so I accept this as a fact.

"I guess that makes sense," I say.

"I will tell you another thing," Bill says, "and it is something very unique, indeed. But first, we will need another cocktail."

It is really Bill's turn to buy a round, but I am not above paying for information, particularly unique information. So I call for two more of the same. The cocktails arrive. Bill takes a big slug and continues.

"Take another gander at Celtic Thunder as they play this tune. It is a reel. Tell me, what do you notice?"

"They are all sitting down," I say.

Bill gives me the look a teacher gives to a slow pupil. "Yes, I believe we have established that," says he.

I am quick to defend myself.

"Hold on, hold on. I am not done. I also notice that none of members of Celtic Thunder is a slave to fashion."

I feel safe in this statement and am proud of myself, even though it is fairly common knowledge that traditional musicians do not usually go in much for duds from Armani or Dior.

"You are right at that," says Bill. "But look harder. Look at how they are playing."

I concentrate. They are wailing away on a tune called "The Thunder Reel." It is an excellent number, written by Terry Winch, who is playing the lead lines on his button accordion, which is named PJ Conway. The whole band is carrying on with great enthusiasm—their knees just bouncing away. I mention these very things to Bill.

"Right again! Very good!" he says. "You are getting warmer. Look at their feet."

One thing that hits me right off the bat is that some of their feet are very large. Specifically, the Winch brothers are in possession of regular gunboats. This aside, what else grabs me is that the collective feet of Celtic Thunder are slapping the stage "Ker-plap! Ker-plap!" in unison, as steady as clockwork, in time with the beat of "The Thunder Reel."

Bill seems to read my mind on this discovery.

"That is it, right there! That is why Celtic Thunder has steady work. They play all sorts of tunes like a house on fire, but so do other traditional bands. They are in demand for another reason—none other than the fact that they are known far and wide as having the best feet in the business!"

Bill nods at me as if to say "and now you know." Then he takes another slug of his cocktail.

Now I have not just fallen off some turnip truck. I have been around, see, so I am dubious. I tell Bill this.

"Oh, yes? Is that right?" Bill asks. "Well you just wait a bit. Give a listen more to the tune."

I have no problem with this suggestion, as I am enjoying the tune, for as I say, it is a very good tune at that.

All of a sudden, Bill says to me, "Okay, now. Take a look at your own feet."

I look down and sure enough, my feet are going "Ker-plap! Ker-plap!" —right along with the feet of Celtic Thunder. I am surprised, as I did not even realize my feet are doing this!

Bill smiles and says, "That is what I am talking about! They do that to people!"

I glance around the room, and I see straight away that everyone's feet are going "Ker-plap! Ker-plap!"

"No one knows how they do it, but the music goes right from the feet of Celtic Thunder to your feet. Why, even I am not immune to this sorcery," says Bill, his feet ker-plapping away like I don't know what. "What's more—if you weren't sitting down right now, you would be leaping around. You wouldn't be able to help yourself. That is why I say they have the best feet in the business. No other trad band in the world has this talent! It's spooky, if you think about it. But it's kind of fun, don't you think? How about another cocktail?"

As I call for another cocktail, I realize that I do indeed think. It's both spooky and kind of fun, and as it turns out, I have to agree with Bill even further. You see, from that day to this, I hear a good number of Irish traditional bands at sessions and performances. Some of them set me to nodding along or even tapping along to their music. But I will tell you this, and you can bank on it—not one of them holds a candle to the feet of Celtic Thunder.

ೞ೪ಬ

STRAY CHAT/FRANK

DOR: You partnered with Tony O'Riordan for a while as Ourselves Alone.

FE: Yeah.

DOR: What was it like working with Tony, for however many years that was?

FE: I think it was about five years, and I don't see how I could have asked for a better partner. He was always cooperative, always wanted to push and to learn more, and get better and better and better, and was not afraid to try things—very daring onstage, with an absolute love of performing. He didn't take himself particularly seriously, but he took what he did for a living very seriously, and I appreciated that more and more as I worked with him. Then it was just time for a change. There were no hard feelings involved; he went on and is still working with different people. But I know if he walked in the room now it would be like a conversation we just had yesterday. Just pick up and start talking again.

DOR: How did you adjust to going solo? What did you miss?

FE: Well, there was nobody to share the good times with, but nobody to share the blame with, either. But nobody to share the— If you did good, you could have it all to yourself. You didn't have to share that with anybody. That sounds a little self-serving, and I suppose it is, but that's the deal; that's what it is when you work alone. You're out there naked. It's your fault, your blame, or your laurels.

DOR: Tony played mandolin and banjo. You must have missed the backing he gave you, the harmonies—

FE: Absolutely.

DOR: And the material—did it change the material?

FE: Well, one time I was late for work when I was with Tony, and the way we did many tunes was to alternate verses. So, Tony knew verses one, three, and five, and I knew verses two, four, and six. So, he got through a whole bunch of material in a very short time that night because everything was cut in half. (Laughs) What it forces you to do, certainly, is to learn the lyrics, learn more stuff, and try to play a little more carefully. There's no place to hide. You're out there, and you're playing, and you try to play better.

᎙᎚Ꮄ

Remembering Johnny Cunningham

Robbie O'Connell

The great Scottish fiddler, Johnny Cunningham, was well known for his sense of humor. He always had a joke to tell, but it was his playfulness on stage that I enjoyed most. Johnny began his career with the seminal Scots band Silly Wizard, but over the years, he played in several other groups. In the 1980s, he toured with Relativity, which included his brother, Phil, and Triona and Michail O'Domhnall from Ireland.

I saw them at the Somerville Theatre in Massachusetts one night. About fifteen minutes into the show, Johnny made a little speech. They had just come back from a tour in California, and he wanted to tell us about the latest craze out there—hugging. He readily acknowledged that, at first, he hadn't liked it, but gradually he had gotten used to it. Now that they were back in the East, he had begun to miss it. He claimed it was very therapeutic and urged us all to try it. Then he announced that he was going to come down and hug everyone in the front row. The audience grew uneasy. People wondered if he had flipped his lid, particularly as the other band members looked embarrassed. But down he came, sauntering along the front row, hugging everyone as he went. Some people were laughing; others were confused. What was the point of all this? When the hugging was over, he climbed back onstage and to the great relief of the audience, the band launched into a set of reels.

About twenty minutes later, Phil asked Johnny to play the new tune they had rehearsed. Johnny protested a bit, saying he hadn't really gotten it down yet, but Phil persisted, and Johnny finally agreed, on the condition that he could read the chart, which he had brought with him. Then he began to empty his pockets onto a chair beside him, searching, so we thought, for the sheet music. One by one, he pulled out several watches and wallets, pieces of jewelry, and packs of cigarettes. Slowly the audience began to titter. It looked like he had picked the pockets of all the people he had hugged. It took a few seconds to sink in, but we all realized that we had been set up. He had brought the stuff with him. It took about five minutes for the laughter to stop and the show to continue.

Another night, Johnny and I were splitting a bill at the Cape Cod Theatre in Dennis, Massachusetts. Six nights a week during the summer, the theatre presented a play, so we performed on what is called the actors' "dark night." When we arrived at the theatre, we discovered that the set for the current play, a combination kitchen and living room, had to be left on the stage. I could see the glint in Johnny's eyes as he looked around at the props. During our sound-check in the afternoon, he poked around the set trying to find some way to incorporate it into the show. A big refrigerator stood on one side of the stage, and Johnny honed in on it. He opened the large lower door and peered inside. It did not inspire him. He then tried the smaller freezer door on the top. Realizing that the fridge was not plugged in, he removed his fiddle from its case and placed it in the freezer. I had no idea what he had in mind. We went in search of a bite to eat and a few drinks before the show. It was a hot, muggy night, and the theatre was full when we got back. Johnny was the first on stage to open the show.

"Ladies and gentlemen, please give a big Cape Cod welcome to Johnny Cunningham."

Johnny walked out with a big smile and greeted the audience. He turned to where he expected to find his fiddle, or so he pretended. His face registered the shock of seeing nothing there. He searched around the stage in a panic, looking behind the couch, under chairs, lifting cushions. Then he crossed the stage to the fridge. He opened the lower door wide, as if he was certain the instrument was there. Miming a great look of disappointment, he closed it again. The audience was bewildered. He grabbed the handle of the freezer door, and with a look of wide-eyed expectation, he turned towards the audience. Slowly he pulled back the freezer door to reveal his fiddle, and with a flourish, removed it. He walked up to the microphone, paused a moment, and said, "Ah! You can't beat a cool fiddle on a hot night." He had the audience in the palm of his hand for the rest of the night.

ೞ೩೦

STRAY CHAT/ROBBIE

DOR: Who has influenced you as a songwriter?

ROC: That's a tough one because there's so many, you know, different— I think Ewan MacColl would be right up there. John Prine. Paul Simon. It's hard to—I like story songs. Harry Chapin. I loved his stuff. I grew up with the old ballads that tell stories. I like songs that do that. I think of songs as short stories, the way Harry Chapin did. People like Bob Dylan wouldn't have been much of an influence on me. I mean, I like several Bob Dylan songs, but I find an awful lot of his stuff pretentious, and just stylized to the point where I don't think they'll really last; whereas I think John Prine, you know, a song like "Hello in There," is just like a beautiful little movie, and I think that song will outlive— Do you know what I mean? Songs that tap into little slices of real life, the way a short story does. Those are the kind of things I'm drawn to. So anybody who wrote in that style—I listened a lot to Donovan when I was growing up, but now I listen to it and wonder what I really saw in it. It was more that it was guitar and singing and melodic, and I've always been drawn to a strong melody.

ೞ೩೦

Well, Har-Dee-Har-Har

Dennis O'Rourke

Leo Egan and I had been a duo for a year. We had contracted with a company in the mid-west that owned several different theme restaurants— Irish pubs being one part of the organization. We'd been signed for six gigs, two weeks each, over the course of several months, at four different locations. We had been a bit uneasy about the lack of an audience in the first club. Not only were they not coming to hear us, they were spurning the four-star restaurant, and it so happened that the food was *very* good. The manager assured us that we were doing a terrific job and that the lack of business was just growing pains. In time, they would come. I wasn't so sure. It had been my experience that when a new restaurant and pub opened, especially one as elegant as this, it was packed from the get-go. Everyone wanted to be first to try it. This was not the case here.

As it turned out, the second gig, in a different state, was at a pub actually doing some business, and it happened to be within walking distance of one of the company's other ethnic theme restaurants. Leo and I had heard that the entertainer at the other joint—call him Bubba—was a gas character. We went over during one of our breaks to catch his act. He was indeed a great deal of fun, a good guitar player with a decent voice and a big and boisterous laugh. We deemed it proper to introduce ourselves. We agreed to meet later that night at a local Denny's or some-such. Backgrounds and war stories were exchanged. Leo was especially taken by the guy—there was that laugh. He dropped in on one of our gigs, and a mutual admiration society developed, camaraderie between working road musicians.

Over the next few nights, we learned that Bubba was being paid less than we were on an individual basis and had to provide his own accommodation. He was lamenting this fact over his eggs, and Leo and I exchanged looks.

"Tell him, Den," Leo said. I was only too happy, and after extracting a promise that the source of the information I was about to reveal should remain anonymous, I told him the deal we had received from the company. This was information we routinely passed among ourselves on the Irish circuit. Now, this guy was not on that circuit and we didn't know him. But he seemed such a good fella we took the chance. He displayed mild surprise and interest, but otherwise appeared fairly unruffled. We had been complimenting him right along about his show and urged him then to press for the extra dough. And again, we reminded him not to use our names in any negotiation of demands. He fell all over himself promising he would not do that to us. His gig ended, and he hit the road. We bade him good-bye and good luck. What a nice guy, we agreed.

As our run continued, we heard rumors from the staff that a shake-up was coming because the Irish pub part of the organization was not generating enough money to suit the company. Undoubtedly, the bean counters had suggested the cutbacks in cash outlay for all the entertainers. Our first gig had included round-trip airfare. That had been scratched, and we had driven out for the second. Instead of separate hotel rooms, we were given one.

Food and booze allowance was severely curtailed. Indeed, our welcome at the next club was cool and curt. The manager let us know that as far as he was concerned we were no different from the other employees. We wondered if the aim was to make things so uncomfortable for us we would quit. Removal of perks notwithstanding, the money was still good, and we had six more weeks booked. We had no intention of quitting or doing anything that would get us fired, and we performed to generally enthusiastic audiences. Unlike the first club, this one appeared to have hit the ground running.

On the final day of that gig, a call came to our hotel room from the corporate office. It was a woman who had greeted us at the first restaurant and expressed delight in our show. She had bad news. She was calling to tell us that our remaining gigs had been cancelled. More to the point, we had been fired. They had found a reason to terminate us, and the reason was Bubba. He had made his way to the corporate office and shouted and bawled about unfair and unequal treatment. He demanded more money and accommodations. Why should he be paid less than O'Rourke or Egan? He was every bit as good.

The expression on my face alerted Leo to the fact that something catastrophic was occurring. He sat on the bed opposite me. "You can't be serious," I said to the woman. "Just because he used our names *we're* fired?"

Leo looked stricken.

"I'm afraid so," she said. "He was loud and obnoxious, and he used your names so many times that when he finally left, my boss told me to call and tell you that you had been cancelled. I'm sorry, I really am. You guys are great, but there's nothing I can do. If it's any consolation to you, though, Bubba didn't get the raise."

The financial loss to us was in the thousands. Suing them was not something we thought seriously about. Contract or no, neither of us had any desire to get involved with courts and lawyers. We drove back in a gloom, wondering how we were going to fill those dates on such short notice. What bothered us most, especially Leo, was Bubba's infamy— his betrayal of a confidence. Leo was always a good judge of character, but his instincts had failed him this time.

When we got home, I wrote Bubba a short note, as we had exchanged addresses early on. I asked him to explain himself. I marked out all the dates he had cost us and the money involved. I told him that

that big laugh of his was ringing hollow in our ears. Not surprisingly, he didn't have the guts to write back. I spent a few days earnestly praying that he might meet the wrong woman someday and spend a week pissing red-hot, rusty fishhooks.

STRAY CHAT/HARRY

DOR: Can you think of the worst moment you've had onstage?

HOD: Well, no, I can't remember the worst moment (Laughing) because I was comatose. I fell off the stool one night, which wasn't a good moment. It all had to do with—this should really be a story. It all had to do with a newspaper interview set up by my partner Trish. It was Tuesday night, and we only had two nights off, playing here at Kevin Barry's. I was dating Traci at the time—she's now my wife—so I said, "Well, Trish, it's Tuesday night, and we're going to a movie. Why don't you do the interview?" Anyway, she did the interview, and everything was fine. This thing came out in the newspaper, and the way it read was like, "Terra Nova was Trish Rogers and Trish Rogers; and Trish Rogers and Trish Rogers and Trish Rogers; and by the way, Harry O'Donoghue sings a couple of songs.

Vic called me up and he said, on the phone, he says, "Have you read this thing?" I said, "No." So he read out parts of it to me, and I wasn't particularly happy. So anyway, I go down to meet him in the Hyatt, and we start drinking. It was early Saturday afternoon, and the more drink we got the more we decided Trish was the "star," and I was the "kid."

What we did was we got well liquored-up. We came back to Kevin Barry's and took the two stools off the stage and put her stool in the middle; moved all the lights to shine on her stool, and then put a small chair beside it with a microphone so "the kid" could sit in the chair. Then we had more drinks, and he had the idea—he said, "Well, look, you know, seeing as you're going to be a kid, you're not the main part of the act—why don't you put on a pair of shorts?" So I put on a pair of shorts, and he had an old skullcap, you know those—skull caps like we wore at school.

I proceeded to put these on, and we continued drinking in the River House right next door to Kevin Barry's. This is all afternoon. When Trish came to the gig that evening, we were sitting at the end of the bar—me wearing, you know. And she was sensitive to the fact that the interview was out, and she knew she'd fucked up. So she took a look down the bar and said, "For fuck's sake. You're not going on like that."

I said, "I am."

So we had the bar clientele decide, and they were unanimous that I would indeed go on dressed like that. (Laughing) She went out to tune her guitar on the stage, saw how we had arranged it, and came back in livid. "Bastard."

And, of course, Vic was now disowning me completely. She talked me into putting a pair of pants on. Got on the stage. I was playing bass guitar, and the bar was now having bets with the bartender, Jimmy Anderson, on how long I would last. Midway through the first set, I fell backwards into the Red Hand of Ulster. (Laughs)

DOR: The big mural on the wall behind the stage.

HOD: Yeah—mouth and nose. Anyway, I headed for the bathroom, and you know, the usual—in a quandary, not knowing whether to kneel or sit. Just wasn't good. And Trish, in the meantime, was talking to Vic at the bar, saying, "I'm going home. I'm not doing the gig."

Vic said, "What would your father do?"

Her father's a great character, a proud Irishman with divilment in his eyes. "Go and do the fucking gig."

So he talked—she had a few drinks herself—he talked her into getting back on the stage. She made huge apologies, profuse and profound apologies about her partner who was sick, and said she was going to continue on her own.

Thunderous round of applause from the audience. She was on her second song when I got my second wind. I came to the entrance at the archway to a standing ovation. (Laughing) I mean it's not really a bad moment onstage; I don't remember that much of it. We played the rest of the night, until two-thirty, and nobody left. By the end of the night, I was drinking pints of bourbon and ginger, and she was drinking pints of screwdrivers. And Vic was on his knees under the archway (laughing), drunk as a lord. Great night.

CREO

When the Months Turn to Years

Frank Emerson

Some time ago, I had this pal in Chicago, another player. His name was George, and he was from County Clare. Still is, I suppose, on both counts—although I haven't seen him in a while. George was one of those fellows who not only loved life, but was thrilled to be doing what he did for a living. The whole idea of playing music tickled him pink. He couldn't believe he could be so lucky. As a result, he really applied himself to the trade. He wanted to be as good as it was possible for him to be. Well, it worked. He was good—very good. In fact, in a short time, he had developed a decent following in and around the Windy City.

It was a quirk of the business in those days that how good you were didn't necessarily have a lot of influence on how well you were paid. This was particularly true around Chicago. Lots of short arms and deep pockets. Ask anyone. Sometimes it still works that way—and not just around Chicago, either. Anyway, at the time in question, George was not knocking down a lot of dough.

So George figures that if he has a record, he could push it at his shows. This will certainly help bolster his money situation. He is bound to sell a lot since his crowd loves him.

Now making a record on your own can run into some serious cash. You had best have all your I's dotted and T's crossed before you step into that studio because this is where time really is money. George knows this. Consequently, he is well rehearsed, fully prepared, confident, and absolutely determined as he heads into the studio to cut his first album.

He is intense and totally driven as he records a whole slew of standard covers. His session men are prepared, and he cuts costs by doing many of the songs in one take. He is flying.

Now he makes a fateful decision. He is going to record a number that he has just started doing on stage. It is a new one by Johnny McEvoy called "Long Before Your Time." It is around the same time Bobby Goldsboro is hitting home runs with the likes of "Honey" and "Watching Scotty Grow." McEvoy's tune is a similar theme—bittersweet heartbreak where the wife dies, the kid lives, and is raised by the old man, who cries and talks in rhyme about his dead wife a lot. You know—real happy-go-lucky stuff.

People just eat this up with a spoon—crying their eyes out. McEvoy is doing real well with the tune, but George is resolved to give him a run for his money. He is determined to have people sobbing before he gets through eight bars.

I must admit that George succeeds in making a terrific recording of the song. He emotes like crazy. He is dripping sentiment, and the session men are right there with him. It is just wonderful except for one little thing.

There is a line in the song—the most important line, since it sets up the payoff where the wife craps out. The singer is explaining the wife's death to the daughter. The line is:

"For nine long months she carried you,
But in the end she died."

What George sang, just as beautiful as I don't know what, is:

"For nine long **years** *she carried you."*

The thing is—everyone was so intent on the emotional content, nobody noticed the flub. Not the engineer, not the session men, and certainly not George. These were men on a mission. Mission accomplished.

After George gets the records back from the company, he has a listen. *Now* he hears it. He is stunned. He can't believe it. He figures maybe no one will pick up on it. Everything else is so damned poignant, after all. Yeah, right.

He sells a few dozen, and word gets around. George is mortified. He has to put up with comments every night like, "Oh, that poor woman!" "She probably died of exhaustion, is what she died of." "How about that gestation period, huh? How about it?"

The records start selling like mad. Collector's items, don't you know. George figures he will soon have enough to get back to the studio, make the correction, and re-cut the track. He mentions this to some fans. No dice. It has to be "nine years," or forget it.

George might be from Clare, but he did not just fall off the turnip truck. Art takes a back seat. He goes through at least four more pressings of the thing before it becomes a glut on the market. By this time, he has long since cut a new track of the song, but the Bobby Goldsboro stuff is now passé, and disco is coming on strong. That's another reason to cry. But hopefully not for "nine long years."

Inspector Clouseau Sings "Danny Boy"

Dennis O'Rourke

Attending a Seamus Kennedy performance is a journey into the delightfully unknown. Those who know him expect the unexpected; those who know him well are very much aware that Seamus does not need a spotlight or a stage to gambol through the comedy arena.

The Eagle Brook Saloon. In 1982, it was a new club in Norfolk, Massachusetts, and Leo and I had become the house band. We loved the place. They treated us royally. I got Seamus a gig. I was there his first night, and he was brilliant. This was a Western-style saloon and Seamus obliged with the occasional Slim Whitman—yodel and all. Owners Dave Kelley, John McTernan, and manager Chuck Horne were tickled.

We sat at the end of the bar after hours. The bar was littered with beer bottles, pints, glasses, and ashtrays. Seated on a stool, Seamus announced he was going to do Inspector Clouseau singing "Danny Boy." He began to sing, instantly nailing that perfectly perplexing accent of Peter Sellers' bumbling policeman. As he began the second verse, he rose slowly and dramatically from the stool, but caught his foot in the lower rung. He fell down. When he tried to stand, his leg was caught between two rungs. He tried to shake it loose. He stood and hit his head on the bar. He ignored all, still singing and stepping forward a few feet, dragging the stool with him. He reached the end of the song—the big last line—and the highest note on the word "here." *"And all my grave will warmer sweeter be—"* He stretched his arms out, his left arm hovering over the bar, and leaned forward. *"I'll be heeeeerrrre—"* He flung both arms back, and of course the left one swept through the glass. Bottles, glasses, and ashtrays flew off the bar and landed on both sides of it, most shattering. Everyone dove out of harm's way, and Seamus sang the last lines *sotto voce.* Any apprehension I had about how this would be received was quickly dispelled; the laughter was immediate and uproarious. And Seamus was booked again, on the spot.

☙❧

STRAY CHAT/SEAMUS

DOR: Was there an entertainer you saw when you were young, and you said, "I want to do that"?

SK: Tommy Makem. First and foremost. I first saw the Clancy Brothers and Tommy Makem in the Ulster Hall in Belfast in 1964. There was an album recorded of that show, and I'm in the photograph on the album cover. Ulster Hall was so full they had to put some of the audience onstage in bleacher seats at the back, behind them, and I was in those bleacher seats. And I just saw Makem do his thing. The other guys were great, but Makem was the one who grabbed me. I loved his delivery. I loved the songs he wrote. I loved how he worked an audience. I loved how he injected humor into everything. You know, if this sounds like a paean to Tommy Makem, so be it.

ଓଃନ

It's All in the Shwett

Frank Emerson

Michael Coyne was a decent looking fellow, so the girls all said. And he thought so, too. He had Dennis Morgan-type wavy hair, twinkling eyes, and pretty much all of his teeth, which he liked to show off.

Because he was from County Cork, he used to bill himself as "The Roving Cork Boy." In my opinion, from the way he leapt around on stage, "The Bobbing Cork Boy" would have been more like it.

Believe you me—this guy would have St. Vitus tied to a post. With disregard for his own safety, Mike would fling himself from one side of the stage to the other, hopping up and down, turning around, slapping at his guitar, and singing away at the microphone, which was pitching and rolling on its stand. Of course, this was only during up-tempo numbers. During ballads, Michael struck tableaus, which he abruptly and dramatically changed to increase the impact of the song's lyrics. The whole thing was really something to see, if not to hear. It took your attention away from the music, which was probably a good thing.

I have to explain. I'm not telling tales out of school when I say that Michael had an impressive and extensive collection of song titles. Unfortunately, his grasp of lyrics lagged somewhat behind the titles. In addition, his vocal range was rather succinct. His notes were all in the same neighborhood, on the same block, within three or four houses of each other. But this was okay because his guitar playing covered about

16

the same number of chords—except for the ones he made up, which weren't really chords, anyway.

Don't get me wrong; Michael changed keys occasionally, but only with his voice. This was probably okay, too, since the last time his guitar was in tune was when it was in the store, so it wouldn't have made much difference. The truth be told, I am not altogether certain his key changes were always planned. Now and then, he got this real surprised look on his kisser. I'm thinking that maybe that was when he just happened to be playing and singing in the same key. It didn't come about very often, and of course, it threw him. He would jump back from the microphone, roll his eyes, shake his head, and smile his killer smile. All in all, Michael's act was quite remarkable.

You might think from all of this—and it's all true, so help me—that Michael didn't work much. Well, you're way off. Mike always had more work than he could handle. He was what you call "in demand." I realize that doesn't add up, but here is how it worked.

Michael had the whole thing down to a science. He made no bones about where his talent lay. It wasn't as a singer and certainly not as a player, even if he did use a very, very expensive Martin D-45 that made you or me cry at what he did to it. No, neither of those. His talent wasn't in his good looks, either. There were plenty of guys in the business even prettier than Michael was—plenty of guys. Never mind that he didn't think so, there just were.

No, what Michael did better than anybody was sweat. Stage lights, as you probably know, are hot sons of guns, anyway. They would make you perspire even if you were as unflappable as Perry Como. Couple the lights with Mike's perpetual motion and the five or six pints he'd toss down before and during a set and we're talking major league perspiration here.

The sweat just leapt off him. It was Jersey Joe Wolcott-Getting-Smacked-by-Rocky Marciano-flying-sweat. Why there were rainbows all around his big old head, for crying out loud! It was a regular Aurora Borealis! As if this weren't enough to get your attention, Michael's clothes, in particular his shirt became absolutely sodden. He always wore quiana, silk, or some such fabric that changed color as it got wet and shimmered—sort of like a hologram. I don't know what might have been going on in his trousers. I don't like to think about it.

With an impressive looking, but thumpy-sounding, flourish on his guitar, Mike would finish a song and hold a pose for a few beats—his chest heaving. Then he would step to the microphone to announce his next song, and he would be just glistening. His wavy hair a mass of kiss curls, his face aglow, his eyes blinking, dewy with sweat and tears, a Jack Nicholson smile on his puss, Michael just reeked of sincerity. The girls were riveted. And there you have it. That was the payoff of Michael's talent: the girls. Did I say girls? Not just girls—lots of girls! All shapes, sizes and ages—glued to this sweaty Corkman. It was unbelievable. I just didn't get it.

One night after his show, Michael took me aside. At a far corner of the bar, we hunched over a couple of pints. In that unique Cork accent, with its sing-song lilt, and the "sh's" left over from the Gaelic, he laid out the whole thing to me. It was so simple.

"You know what it is, Frankie? You know what it is?"

"No, Michael, what is it?"

"It's all in the shwett, is what it is—it's all in the shwett."

"What do you mean?" I asked. I thought I was justified in this follow up.

"Look. You see me up there. I'm a shwetting maniac! Right?"

"Right," I said.

"Right as rain," says he. "I'm up there shwetting my liver out, and the girls—lots of girls—come in to watch me shwett."

"Yeah?" says I. "So?"

"Well, guess who comes in where there's lot's of girls?"

"Who?"

"The bhoys! Lots of bhoys. They watch the girls watching me shwett. They get thirsty. They buy drinks for the girls and for themselves and sometimes for me! They make the register ring! And that, Frankie, is the boss's favorite music. He don't care what I sound like as long as I bring the punters in, and the way I do it is with the ould shwett. I figger if I ever shtop shwetting, I'm shcrewed!"

He grabbed a beer, wiped his brow, winked, and wandered off to the end of the bar toward some girls who couldn't take their eyes off him.

Time went by and I lost track of Michael. He knocked around for a while, soaking stages right and left. One day I heard he had moved back to Cork due to a little set-to with Immigration about the questionable existence of his green card. It was probably all right with him, though. He'd made a bit of cash and developed a good name as a moneymaker. Now he was going to do the same thing at home. As Michael would say, "It was no shwett. No shwett at all!"

THERE ARE RISKS, BUT IT'S
BETTER THAN PLAYING IN THE
PIRANHA POOL...SORT OF.

The Tornado

Seamus Kennedy

Sunday, Memorial Day Weekend, 2001. It's just after five pm, and I'm on stage for the second set of my three-set show at the Jack Frost Mountain Irish Festival in the Pennsylvania Poconos. The three hundred-foot-long tent is divided into two sections—vendor's booths at one end, and the stage and audience area at the other. Vendors are doing brisk business hawking various Hibernian wares, and the audience is having a fine old time listening to my jokes and songs while helping themselves to pitchers of beer of the Yuengling and Guinness variety.

I had just finished telling a series of jokes about New Jersey and New Jersey girls, such as:

"What's the difference between a New Jersey girl and a catfish? One's slimy with whiskers, and the other's a fish!"

Or

"Why are all the ballparks in New Jersey covered with Astroturf? To keep the cheerleaders from grazing!"

Or

"What's the difference between a New Jersey girl and a parrot? A parrot can say no!"

Or

"What's the difference between a New Jersey girl and garbage? Garbage gets picked up and taken out!"

Or

"What's the difference between a New Jersey girl and a Rolls Royce? Not everyone's been in a Rolls Royce!"

I'm singing "The New Jersey Turnpike Song," a parody of John Denver's "Country Roads," when suddenly there's a loud drumming on the tent; hailstones are nearly keeping time with the music. The sky is getting very dark. A huge gust of wind blows through the tent, causing it to billow upwards like an opening parachute, and lift off its poles.

"Jesus," I think. "That was one helluva gust. Nearly took the tent with it." But I continue with the song.

෴

Concrete Road

J. Denver, B. Danoff, T. Nivert Danoff, Cherry Lane Music Pub.
New Lyrics: C. Goff, S. Kennedy

Almost fatal, north New Jersey,
Newark Airport, Pulaski skyway.
Pollution's old there,
Killed off all the trees,
Trash piled up in mountains,
Blowing in the breeze.

Chorus: *Concrete Road, take me home*
To the place I belong,
Jersey City, Bayonne Mama,
Take me home, Concrete Road.

All the horseflies gather 'round her,
Refinery lady, stranger to clean water;
Dark and dirty,
Floating in the sky,
Disgusting smell of sewage,
Cinders in your eye.

Chorus:

I hear her voice,
From the cheap motel, she calls me.
Sirens remind me
That the cops aren't far away.
And drivin' down the road
I get the feelin'
I ain't got the toll
Again today, again today...

Chorus:

Molly Pitcher, Richard Stockton,
Vince Lombardi, Admiral William Halsey,
Clara Barton, Woodrow Wilson, too.
J. Fenimore Cooper, John Fenwick,
Joyce Kilmer, I love you,
And old Walt Whitman, too,
Grover Cleveland, too, Alexander Hamilton, too,
And Thomas A. Edison, too.
And when Bruce Springsteen dies,
He'll have a rest area named after him, too—
(In the end zone, next to Jimmy Hoffa.)

Another gust arrives, and this one is packing a punch. The tent lifts off the poles in front of the stage and begins to rip. The four-foot tent pegs, which have been sledge-hammered into the ground by muscular youths, are pulled free as easily as you would extract a needle from a pin cushion, and whip wildly around at the end of their ropes. People are struck. One man has his leg broken, a little girl suffers a neck injury, and a fellow who tries to hold down a flying guy-rope is flung aloft.

Folks scream and start to run out of the tent. Others dive under the picnic tables, which are inexplicably stationary.

I'm still singing.

I look up through the huge tear in the tent, and there, swirling in the dark sky, I see vendors' merchandise, posters, flyers, beer pitchers, and bales of hay.

A tornado.

The top of the tent is torn away from the main pole, and the pole begins to tilt and sway 'til it catches a side of the tent and leans there like a drunk against a wall. People are well and truly panicked now, pushing and clambering over each other towards a shredded opening on one side.

It's time to stop singing.

The first thing I think of is my guitar, so I take it off and head towards an opening and my car. I stow it safely and turn back to see if I can help. Pat O'Kane, the leader of the next act, Gael Force (believe it or not), shouts from the rear of the tent. "Seamus, get back on the microphone and get some of them to come this way! They'll trample each other!"

He's right. They're all trying to get out one way. I jump back on the stage, grab the mike, and direct them to where Pat is holding open a tent flap, all the while telling them to stay calm. It works. The rear of the crowd hears me and heads towards Pat. Everyone gets out safely, and seconds later, the tornado is gone.

As tornadoes go, it was fairly small, but it wrought havoc, nonetheless, and it frightened the hell out of all present and injured a few, though none critically, I'm glad to say.

By then, most everyone had retreated to the ski lodge; the ground crew came out to help the vendors and musicians gather their gear and break down what's left of the tent.

I wish I had a dollar for every person who later said to me, "Seamus, you really brought the house down today, didn't ya?" or "That'll teach you to make fun of New Jersey. God is from New Jersey, and that was his revenge."

Oh, there's a hook for a song if ever I heard one…

I'm standing there, watching the clean up, when a member of Pat's band Gael Force drives up. This guy has just driven in from New Jersey, and he's missed it all. He gets out of his van and starts to unload his stuff, then stops and looks around, a little puzzled.

"What the fuck happened here?" he says. "It looks like a tornado hit this place."

ೞೕ

God is from New Jersey
(The Tornado Song)

Seamus Kennedy, Gransha Music

I am a wandering minstrel,
And I travel 'round the land,
With lots of silly stories
And songs to beat the band
Some folks say I'm irreverent
Because of all my jokes,
But I was there at Jack Frost
When the Almighty spoke.
(Repeat)

God is from New Jersey,
He brought the whole house down.
West Virginia's almost heaven,
But Bayonne's God's hometown.

I was poking fun at Jersey
And girls who can't say no,
When suddenly the sky turned black
And the wind began to blow.
I was singing about the Turnpike,
And the rest stops on the way
When the Lord said, "That ain't funny."
So he blew the tent away.
(Repeat)

God is from New Jersey,
He made it very clear.
He tore the tent to pieces,
And he sucked up all the beer.

Now, I can pick on Pottsville,
And no one really cares,
'Cause I saw cans of Yuengling
Go swirling through the air.
And the moral of the story
That I have learned is this:
Thou shalt not pick on Jersey,
'Cause the Lord gets really pissed!
(Repeat)

God is from New Jersey,
He brought the whole house down.
West Virginia's almost heaven,
But Bayonne's God's hometown.

ക്ഷ

Tinted Windows

Dennis O'Rourke

I worked the Village Coach House in Brookline Village, Boston fairly regularly back in the late seventies. It was owned by the Varien family, from County Cork. A railroad bar, one of those laid out straight to the back places, longer than it is wide—an old brick wall on the one side, the bar on the other. A little stage, but decent lights.

The audience was always good on the weekends—big, well behaved, and often attentive. Weeknights were hit or miss: no apparent reason why there would be a crowd one Wednesday, and nothing much the next. When it did fill during the week, it was often with hospital workers just off their shifts—nurses, technicians, a doc or two—perhaps some office personnel who'd been working late, students, and of course, the regulars. It was that kind of neighborhood. I'd make a small effort to rope them into the music, but they were usually more interested in talking for its own sake. I never pushed them because I didn't want them going elsewhere for their nightcap and chat. Henry Varien had said to me, "I love the sound of the music, Dennis," and then he pointed to the cash register. "But I love the sound of that even better." So I kept my volume at a decent level. Indeed, I'd discovered long ago that when you pushed up the volume because a crowd was noisy, they just got noisier. At the Coach House, we'd compromise. I'd play quietly, and they'd talk quietly, at least until the booze warmed them to their subject. There was no holding them back then, so I'd concentrate on the ones still listening.

Well, it was a weeknight and a likeable crowd, but nothing memorable. I sang the last tune, had a couple of pints at the bar, and left about two in the morning. I was on the deserted, tree-lined VFW Parkway in West Roxbury, headed home, when a car fell in behind me. In a bit of a reverie, with the moon and the warm evening and all, I slowed to encourage it to pass in the other lane, but it didn't. It slowed with me. I speeded up a tad, and it did the same. I slowed again, well below the speed limit, and it followed suit. This was annoying. Up ahead was a red traffic light. The car pulled around me. Now, I thought, now I'll get a look at this jerk. He came up beside me—and I believe it was the first time in my life—I found myself looking at tinted windows. I could not see into the car.

The light turned, and I took off at a good clip. He fell in behind me. Now I was a little concerned. It was after two in the morning, and it seemed I was being followed by a person or persons unknown. I thought back to the gig. Had I shot out some zingy little rejoinder to someone in the crowd and pissed them off? This was one of those times I cursed myself for my careful cultivation of an acid tongue. Sometimes it has to be done cautiously—something to shut a heckler up, but not enrage him to the point he's charging the stage, waiting for you outside, or following you in a car with tinted windows. But I couldn't recall any such exchange, nor could I conjure a face in the audience that had seemed to bear malevolent will towards me. Nevertheless, I couldn't shake the feeling that it *was* someone from the bar.

A rotary loomed ahead, and I decided to find out for sure if I was truly being followed. You may well ask what more evidence I needed. Blame it on human nature. We've all seen movies where a character, alone in a house on the infamous "dark and stormy night," hears a noise in the attic or the cellar and just has to find out what it is. I was hoping I was wrong. Instead of bearing off halfway around the rotary, I continued on, full circle. The car stayed right behind me. I went around it again, with the same result: anonymous and now threatening headlights in the rearview mirror. It was time for evasive action. I left the rotary, gunned the engine down the parkway, and put a bit of distance betwixt me and my pursuer. To either side of the parkway were little residential streets, and I turned suddenly left onto one of them and went as fast as I safely could for a quarter-mile. I looked into the mirror, and there he was, turning down the same street, still coming after me.

In that instant, rising fear turned to real anger. I'd had enough. My eye caught the crook lock lying on the floor beside me. It was an iron bar, an anti-theft device with a hook at either end, meant to go around the steering wheel and the brake. I stopped the car with a squeal, grabbed the crook lock, and jumped out the door. On he came, barreling down the little street. I raised the crook lock over my head and brandished it. He slowed about fifteen yards before me. I took two steps into the road. We were between streetlights, so I still could not see a face. But my intention to shatter his windshield was manifest. The car shot past me and down the street.

I threw my weapon into the front seat, jumped in after it, made the tightest, speediest three-point turn on record, and roared back towards the parkway. In the rearview, I saw his brake lights come on, and I was sure he was turning to resume pursuit, so when I got back on the main road, I floored it, and as I picked up speed, I began to howl—the adrenaline firing me up. If he caught up with me again, I was determined to engage him in some way other than the crook lock—though I wasn't sure what form such a confrontation would take. I took side streets and back roads to my apartment, all the while checking behind me.

I'd lost him.

When I got home, I poured myself a very large tumbler of scotch, and sat there for a long time. I kept asking myself, "Who *was* that and what the hell was it all about?"

I never found out. I finished the week at the Coach House without incident. I scanned the crowd from the stage and saw nothing but happy, or at worst, bored faces. No one ever came forward admitting to it, to say it had been a joke, or that they knew who had done it and why, or to express such dislike for me and my act as to cause me to think it had been them driving the shadow car. It was a mystery then and remains one today, twenty-some years later.

I had the opportunity, a while back, to relate this story to Frank Emerson. I told him of my suspicion that it had been someone in the audience. When I had finished, he thought a moment and said, "Maybe it was a music critic."

CRSO

The Shift Drink

Seamus Kennedy

The two guys had been needling each other all night.

I had started singing at nine o'clock on the little fenced-in stage at Ireland's Own. There's a lovely mural of an Irish rustic scene on the wall behind me. Painted by the very talented musician and artist, Brendan Sheridan, it depicts an elderly farmer in a cloth cap outside his thatched cottage, putting his donkey into harness between the shafts of a little cart. He's standing at the donkey's left hindquarter with his back

28

to the viewer, and is in the act of cinching the girth-strap, which to the uninitiated, looks like he's peeing. I get a big laugh every night when I point out the picture to the audience and tell them it's entitled, "Irish Farmer Takes Leak against Donkey's Back Leg." But I digress.

The two guys were still needling each other. They were with two different groups of about twelve men apiece, at adjacent tables, sitting back to back. What had started out as an "Oh, yeah? Well, up yours, buddy!" kind of thing was slowly escalating. I don't know what caused the beef between them, but the other fellas in each group were not amused. "Cut it out, you assholes!" "Why don't you two give it a rest?" "Listen, dickheads, take it outside!"

There were a few periods of truce when nothing was said, and I continued my songs and extremely witty patter, much to the delight and amusement of the assemblage. Considering the unfolding drama in front of me, the night went pretty smoothly. No one in the audience outside of the two groups knew what was going on, but the exchange almost came to a head just before the start of my last set. I heard, "Well, fuck you! Let's go!" and both guys stood up, turned around, and faced each other, ready to square off. But cooler heads in the groups did as cooler heads are wont to do—they prevailed. "Come on, guys, sit down!" "Jesus Christ! You're acting like a pair of kids!" "Knock it off!" And the bar got another reprieve.

The other men were genuinely embarrassed at their colleagues' behavior, and apologized to each other across the tables. "Shit. We're sorry about this. We don't know what's gotten into him. He's not usually like this. Sorry!" Mutual nods of commiseration abounded, but the antagonists continued to glare at each other. Finally, the entertainment was over; I finished my show as well. I sang "The Parting Glass," thanked the audience for coming, reminded them to tip their waiters, waitresses, and bartenders, admonished them to drive home safely, and placed my guitar on its stand. The audience started to filter out slowly as I repaired to the bar for my shift drink.

The shift drink is a custom among restaurant staff, musicians, and a few favored regulars that some people think should be discontinued. (Not staff, musicians, or regulars, of course.) Cheap owners don't like the thought of giving a couple of free drinks to their hardworking serfs, and of course MADD and the police are against people having a few cold ones just prior to driving home; reasonably enough, I suppose.

29

I was sitting at the bar with the denizens of the Viper's Pit— Chip, Benny, Old Half-and-Half, and Bacardi Mike when my friend and fellow performer, Pat Garvey, joined me. He had finished performing at Murphy's Pub up the street, and had come down to Ireland's Own for a quick one and a yarn. I ordered us a couple of beers from Tommy Casey, the bartender, and we asked each other how our respective nights had been. Pat said Murphy's had been really busy with a good, friendly crowd, and that he had sold a "shitload" of cassettes. I told him about the nice night that I'd had, except for the two boyos in front.

"Look out! He's got a gun!" somebody yelled.

Chip and Bacardi Mike dived behind the bar, Benny and Old Half-and-Half hit the deck, and Rick Boyd, the other bartender, jumped behind Tommy Casey. The remaining stragglers flung themselves under tables, and Pat Garvey and I turned on our barstools to see what the hell was going on.

The two adversaries were now rolling on the floor amongst the spilled beer and overturned ashtrays. Their arms were extended above their heads, and one of the hands—I couldn't tell whose—held a snub-nosed .38 Smith & Wesson revolver. Another hand was clutching the gun hand at the wrist, and the two bodies were rolling over and over, cursing, and trying to knee each other in the groin in perverse mimicry of copulation.

Women were screaming; men were shouting, "Get down!" and the Viper's Pit denizens were peeking timidly from cover. Pat and I sat on our stools, drank our beers, and calmly surveyed the chaos. Each time the gun was pointed in our direction, we ducked out of the line of fire, bobbing and weaving with each roll of the copulants.

A woman shrieked, "Call the police! Call the police!"

"They are the fucking police!" somebody yelled from behind an overturned table.

Apparently, the two groups, unbeknownst to each other, were all cops—members of the city and county police departments, respectively. They had come to the pub for a little fun, when these two bozos, for reasons known only to them, acquired an unhealthy dislike for each other. And it had come to this.

Pat and I had ringside seats. We sipped our beers and gazed at the scene with detached fascination 'til uniformed city cops stormed in with guns drawn. They took it all in, separated the combatants, disarmed the lad with the gun, stood them both up, cuffed them, and marched them out to the waiting Black Maria.

Order was restored, and the last audience members departed. The staff and the denizens emerged cautiously from their foxholes and resumed their shift drinking. The incident, naturally, was the sole topic of conversation.

Rick Boyd said, "Everybody got out of the way when that clown pulled the gun, but Seamus and Pat sat where they were right through the whole thing. Didn't move. What the hell were you two thinking?" Before I could reply, Pat answered, "I was thinking that if I left my beer and took cover, it wouldn't be there when I came back."

CRTSO

Missile of September

Frank Emerson

One fall a few years back, I'm filling in for a pal in a joint in Atlanta. It's opening night of the college football season. The Notre Damers are playing the Michiganers. Big doings, I'm told. There are a few television sets in the place, including one near the dartboards. The game is on all of them. The place is chockablock with people. It's kind of noisy, but there are a fair number of folks paying attention to me, so it's bearable.

During the second set, I get a request for the "Notre Dame Fight Song." I say okay, and do it. People sing along and clap. A little while later, the Notre Damers score, and so I get the request again. I do it again. People sing along and applaud—same as before.

The third set comes along, and with it the same request. I kind of figure this is gilding the lily a bit, but the people seem to want it, so I sigh and start it again. I am surprised, but just about everybody participates in this third go-round. I say just about everybody, because there is evidently one Michiganer fan in the house. He is about to make his presence known in a not generally approved of manner.

The stage in this joint is a high one—maybe three feet. Tables start right at the edge and fan out and back toward the bar, which is maybe sixty feet from the stage. Dartboards and TVs are to the left of the bar. The stage lights are a bank of Fresnels which are hot and bright; it's kind of hard for performers to see more than a few feet in front of the stage. So anyway, I'm playing "Cheer, Cheer for Old Notre Dame" this third time around. All of a sudden, I catch sight of something—just a quick image—arcing under the lights, coming toward me. Reflexively, I step back.

There is a couple sitting in front of me, ringside. Somehow, the fellow sees the same thing I do, only he sees it better, I guess. I don't know why he is looking in that direction – which is to say toward the back of the room. Maybe he's eyeballing the game. Anyway, I'm glad he's in this position. Before you can say Jack Robinson, he stands up, stretches out his hand, and bats at something. At just about the same time, "Chunk"—a dart lands right between my feet. This is what the guy deflects. Someone has winged a dart at me from sixty feet away, for Christ's sake! The winger might not be a fan of the Michiganers, but it's a sure bet he doesn't care for all the hoopla and what not going for the Notre Damers.

I look at the dart, still vamping the song, trying to process what just takes place. I look at my cut-off man. He is ashen-faced. I thank him and tell him I am buying him and his date a drink. He says he'll accept and that he wants to buy me one back. I say I'll accept. I continue to vamp and announce that right about now, I'll be taking a break.

I unsling my guitar, pluck the dart from the floor, and start back toward the dartboards. My pal in front asks me what am I going to do. I tell him I want to return it to the fellow who threw it. He says, "You're going to return it to him?" "Yes I am. Right through his eye and into his brain." "Oh," he says, "then never mind."

I nab a waitress to ask her to send over the promised drinks and then make my way back to the dartboards. They are empty. No one is playing. This is curious because people are playing constantly all evening. I have the dart in my hand. Politely, I ask if anybody knows who was using darts with yellow flights. Well, everybody is John Gotti: nobody knows nothing. That is curious, too.

I must note here that there is a uniformed metropolitan police officer on duty, stationed inside the door. He is hired as a safeguard should something unacceptable transpire, such as somebody lobbing a missile at the musician. Just like the people at the dart boards, this guy, too, is Mickey the Dunce. No satisfaction from that quarter, either. I pocket the dart and go to the jacks – which is to say the men's room, where I concentrate on venting my bladder, if not my spleen.

That done, I am calmed down. When I come out of the facilities, I see that the owners—a father/daughter team—have just arrived.

Dressed to the nines, they have been to a wedding, where they have had a few pops, and are now feeling merry. I say hello, tell them the story and show them the dart. They do not so much as express one word apology or shock that such a thing goes on in their joint. Bupkis. Nothing. Looking at the dart, one of them finally says, "Oh, that's a house dart. It's one of ours." I said, "No, it *was* one of yours. Now it's one of mine." I put the dart in my breast pocket, turn and walk away.

After a minute or so of a little more calming, I go back on stage and play. The Notre Dame Fight Song does not get played again this night. Maybe it should be, just to see what happens, but it doesn't. I play a lot of other stuff, Irish and not, but with a certain wary intensity, which I feel is justified. I finish the night, pack up and get paid by check, I cash it there immediately—I am taking no chances. Then I leave town and that's that. This is the last time I ever play that joint. I never receive any commiseration from the owners. In fact, I never see or speak to them again. The dart? I still have it. It's on my office wall. It is mounted on a piece of varnished wood and has a little brass plaque below it. The plaque reads, "There's no business like show business."

Ain't that the truth?

∞

STRAY CHAT/ SEAMUS

DOR: Were you ever on stage and looked out into the crowd, realized they were drunk and out of control, and feared for your safety or someone else's?

SK: No. I've never experienced an audience that was so drunk that they were out of control, or a threat to me or anybody else. I've been with some seriously hammered crowds. Did a couple of conventions where all the conventioneers were footless drunk and all they wanted were loud, up-tempo songs like "Charlie on the MTA" and "Drunken Sailor." They wanted to slam their glasses on the table and yell as loudly as they could, and in a situation like that, you just go along with them. But I've never had anybody actually threatening towards me. Actually, uh...once I had a guy who was drunk one night up in Portland, Maine—really loud and obnoxious. So I zinged him, something like, "Somewhere tonight, a village is missing its idiot." Well, he took exception to this, jumped up on the stage, and attacked me. He tried to grab me round the throat, but I still had my guitar, and I was more worried about that, you know, so he missed, and instead of his hands going round my neck, his thumb went into my mouth. I backed up, and he pinned me against the wall by my cheek, with his thumb in my mouth. Tom O'Carroll started pulling him off me, and a bunch of guys came up out of the crowd, grabbed him, and threw him out. But to answer your question, no, I've never experienced a *whole* audience that was drunk or hostile.

C3⬥80

Dog Biscuits

Dennis O'Rourke

I'm onstage, working a packed room, and the room is humming. The audience is listening, responding. The music and the gargle are flowing. The bartenders, the waitresses are hustling. The magic is there. The club owner is content. He nods in my direction. By rights, he should be beaming, but some club owners, as a rule, will not beam. Their compliments to a performer delighting a crowd are doled out sparingly, often grudgingly. They are certain that anything more than a nominal acknowledgment will elicit requests or, in some cases, demands for more money. They are equally certain we are overpaid as it is. But we know when we've got a room moving, when it's our room, not theirs, and there is a generous satisfaction in that that renders the owner's tight purse strings mute for the moment.

So there I am, plying my trade with a will, joy in my heart, my voice soaring on whiskey wings, and all these good things happening around me. I've created the wave, and I'm riding high on it. Imagine that, if you will.

And then a fight breaks out.

I have on occasion asked a bartender or owner what he wants me to do if I'm onstage when fists are raised, faces are being pummeled, eyes are being gouged, boots are being vigorously applied to the balls of a prone, unfortunate soul, and samurai pool cues are slicing through the smoky air. All of this accompanied by the crash of upended tables, smashing glass, the wails of stricken, fleeing women, and the war roar of tequila testosterone. Do I have a part in the mayhem? (Remember a caped and pleading Mick Jaggar at Altamont? "C'mon, people. Stop fighting. Why are you fighting?") Surprisingly, I've had a few owners tell me to keep playing while they sorted it out. "The show must go on," "One or two monkeys don't stop the show," and so forth. But most advise me to cease warbling until order is restored.

What I will assuredly *not* do is leave the stage, toward which, for reasons unknown, the fight will inexorably gravitate. Visions of large bodies locked in full, furious grapple, falling atop my Guild, thus rendering it asunder, are bone chilling. Microphones and expensive speakers atop precarious stands are also at risk.

But what if one of the participants in the brawl is me?

I confess to an early low threshold of tolerance for hecklers and loudmouths and people just generally making fools of themselves. If I couldn't tease them out of the behavior, I'd skewer them with a quick zinger. More so in my younger days than now. Now, I tend to roll with it, let management take care of it, or better still, let the audiences give the guy the evil eye, or howl and hoot him down. It's safer. I've had my share of fights—and want no more, thank you. They can be costly.

Liam's Irish Tavern in Framingham, Massachusetts, thirty minutes west of Boston. A weeknight and a nice crowd. Halfway through my second set, a party of four comes in and takes a table just to the right of the stage, down front. Two couples, old and young. It occurs to me that the younger couple is married, and the older couple is one or the other's parents. The younger man is mid-thirties, middlin' height, and looks pudgy. Could be stocky, though. Can't tell. I know a few guys who look as though they might be pudgy pushovers in a brawl, but grab them by the arm and it's all redwood. This guy is wearing black-rimmed glasses over a fleshy, pale face. The wife is quite pretty. What is she doing with him? I think. Well, no explaining love.

But they're drinking pitchers of beer and munching on pretzels, and they seem to be enjoying yours truly. They send up a request on a napkin. I play it. Smiles and warm applause. I take a break. Horse around with Mark, the barman, and the waitress, Janine. Back up for set three, and somewhere early in, I bring out "Drunken Sailor," a clap-along, stomp your feet song. Some patrons pound the tables with fists or beer bottles. It does get them going. To my astonishment, a few bars into the tune, the pudgy guy (at this point I had placed him in that category) begins to howl and bark like a dog while clapping his hands. Good, honest-to-God barks, too. His wife and the parents exchange nervous smiles. A few in the audience are pointing and laughing, albeit good-naturedly. Nothing unusual for a patron with drink to give himself up to the juice and the joy of the moment. This is, after all, Irish music.

I play "Drunken Sailor" in E minor, and end it on the last beat with an E major. It says, "Boom, we're done." The audience is clapping enthusiastically, and sure enough, your man down front finishes with staccato barks and a long, drawn out howl. The audience is delighted, and so am I. Now I have an opportunity to mine a newly unearthed vein of comedy; for you see, when a member of the audience calls attention to himself by saying or doing something silly or whacky, he or she becomes fair game. A skewering is in order, and I'm to supply it. The audience expects it. Nothing harsh, mind, and nothing that could be hurtful. You just work with what they give you.

The laughter ebbs a bit, and I remain silent for a moment, eyeballing the canine pretender with feigned curiosity. He's now fidgeting in his chair, no expression on his face, staring to the right of me. I call through the microphone to the bartender. "Mark," says I. "Mark, no more pretzels down front here. We need a basket of dog biscuits, if you please. Some dog biscuits. Some Milkbones, on the double."

An easy shot, granted, but not a bad beginning. I know I can build on this. I bark and I coax the audience into joining me, which they do with glee. Then I howl. They howl. Then I look down at the table where sits the object of our collective teasing. He's as still and concentrated on me as a predator waiting to leap from the bushes. His face is stone. Silliness has been supplanted by seething rage. All of my alarm bells go off. I'm amazed by how quickly he's turned. Mother of God!

He's had a few beers certainly, but it's not likely he'll charge the stage, not with the wife and family there. But I do have to diffuse the situation. Pronto. (I've seen Seamus Kennedy bore in and really light someone up at times like this, and get away with it. How is a mystery to me. You'll have to see him and figure it out for yourself.) I give the table a smile and a "just kidding" wave and shake of the head. The other three seem to relax a bit, but stocky man (I had quickly transferred him to that category) is not going for it. He continues to glare. I move ahead with the set after admonishing the crowd that the bark and howl hour has passed. It's time, says I, for some rebel songs.

I sing. I try to avoid eye contact with my new foe. Just before the end of the set, in a move to placate him, I lean away from the microphone, look directly at the older couple, and ask if there's a song they'd like to hear. They both pipe up, "'Four Green Fields,' please." It's Tommy Makem's classic about the four provinces of Ireland: Ulster, Munster, Leinster, and Connaught. The old woman in the song is Mother Ireland. I heard Makem do it in concert with the Clancy Brothers back in the late sixties—in the Back Bay Theater I think it was. He brought the house down.

The older couple approves of my rendition. The young wife is examining the peeling paint on the ceiling, but my antagonist continues his eyeball assault. One more song, and I'm gone, up to the bar and into the cubbyhole of the waitress station. I call Mark over and tell him that the dog biscuits crack has earned me an enemy. He peers out at the table and says, "He doesn't look like much to me. You won't get any trouble from him."

"Maybe not," says I. "But having him out there glaring at me for another entire set is not going to be pleasant."

"You've got people glaring at you all the time, or haven't you noticed?"

"Ho-ho, heh-heh, Mark. I'll have another Guinness, please."

On my way to the stage, I notice two cops, civilian jackets over their uniforms, sitting in the back of the room. Just off duty. I know them well, and relief settles in my breast. They will step in immediately should something erupt. Now I can ignore the mad barker and concentrate on the music.

The house is almost empty. It's after midnight on a weeknight, and that's the witching hour for folks with straight jobs. But my prayer that my problem table has fled with the rest is unanswered. They're waiting for me. All smiles except for you-know-who. They've apparently decided to ignore him and take in my last set. So I oblige them, literally to the point where I'm singing anything they ask. Your man is sullen, but no longer fixated on me, and I'm actually having a good time. These three are listening, as are the few left in the house, including the two cops, my blood has been suitably warmed by Lord Ivey, and it appears I'm going to walk away from this without, thank Jaysus, a confrontation.

When I've finished, the three approach and tell me how much they've enjoyed the show. No mention is made of dog biscuits. Nor barks nor howls. They shake my hand and walk behind the stage, down the steps to the front door. I turn around, and to my chagrin, I find they've left someone behind. He's standing at the table, and he's ratcheted his sullen look back up to malevolence.

But I've been warmed by the music and the booze. And the cops are still there. I'm at peace. He's going to be easy to ignore. He'll realize his party awaits him downstairs, and he'll have to leave. I turn my back to him, and although I'm fairly certain he won't get physical, I put my guitar safely in its case before starting to break down the sound equipment.

His tirade begins with "You suck, you fucking asshole," and goes on from there. Nothing original, just the usual invective, and I give him a smile while wrapping up the mike cords. One of the cops is signaling for me to just continue ignoring him, which I do. This really gets him worked up, and his voice gets louder, more strident. He doesn't know the cops are behind him. But the tactic seems to be working. He's still spewing abuse, but he *is* moving towards the stairs. The problem is that now *I'm* beginning a slow burn. I do have several pints of Guinness in me, and the verbal abuse and taunts are getting harder to ignore, i.e. "You can't play a guitar worth a shit, and you sing like a fucking geek." There are still folks left in the bar, along with the staff, and they're watching it unfold. I know I'll be pissed at myself in the morning if I let this guy's crap go unanswered and he walks out the door, cocky. Oh sure, I'll be congratulated for my restraint by some, but there will be others who say, "Why didn't you put his lights out, Denny? I would have." And that will piss me off even more.

Another "Let it go" wave from the cops. The guy is at the stairs. He pauses a moment and then sneers, "You're a gutless m-f-er." My restraint crumbles. I take a few quick steps toward him, put my hands into his chest, and shove him against the wall. He comes back up with a punch, which I block with the side of my left hand. He's thrown the punch off-balance, so he pitches forward. I grab him in a headlock and start to squeeze. I realize immediately that this guy is all mush and flab. No stocky here. We're by the speaker stand now, struggling, and the Bose atop it begins to wobble. I see the cops get up and head for us. Mark and several patrons are on the way, as well. I look down at the guy, and his glasses are hanging off one ear.

Then I have one of those moments of epiphany. It suddenly becomes clear to me just how ridiculous this is. What the hell am I doing?

38

I could pound this guy senseless if I wanted to—if the cops would let me, which they would not. I'm thirty-four years old, I thought. Haven't I learned anything? This is just plain nuts. I even felt a stroke of sympathy for this poor soul. He had a helpless look on his reddening face. So I eased up on the headlock. Well, doesn't that give him room to maneuver, put both feet flat on the floor, and free his arm. He proceeds to swing up with his fist, and he catches me right in the left eye with a pretty good punch.

My moment of epiphany disappears in an instant, and I reengage my arm-lock around his neck with a will. It is my intention to separate head from torso. But the cops are there. Mark has arrived. We're pulled apart. The guy's glasses are still hanging from his face. He's limp and has to be held up. Suddenly the wife appears at the top of the stairs. She's aghast. She's at his side. One of the cops holding her hubby has let his jacket fall open, and his uniform is clearly visible. He says, "We saw the whole thing, Dennis. Do you want to press charges?"

The wife's jaw goes south. The barker's head is bowed. "Goddammit! The son of a bitch hit me, and now I'm gonna have a black eye!"

"So, do you want to press charges?"

The wife is silently pleading with me.

"No," I say. "No. The hell with it. Just get him out of here."

The cops release their grip, and then, I swear to God, the wife takes hold of her hubby's ear, pulls him out of the little circle, and hauls him, bent over like a repentant puppy, down the stairs. Bad dog. Everyone bursts into laughter.

I head to the waitress station, where Janine offers me ice for my eye and some wisecracks for my ego. Then I notice the throbbing on the side of my left hand where I had blocked his first punch. I now have a black eye, and the hand I use to chord the guitar hurts like hell. And for what?

In the morning, I wake up with both of these gifts *and* a hangover. I pick up the guitar and gingerly try to wrap my hand around the neck. The hand is still sore. I take it to a sports medicine guy. He says, "Bruised bone."

"Well, what can I do for it? Can I soak it in something?"

"You can soak it in whatever you like. You can soak your head, too, if you want. It's not gonna do any good. It's a bruise. It'll have to heal by itself, and that's gonna take two or three weeks."

That night, I'm back at Liam's. I can play, but it's a painful chore. Three more weeks of this? I whine to Mark. I whine to Janine. They're both grinning. My black eye has traces of sickly yellow. Mark says, "I'll get you a shot of Black Bushmills and some dog biscuits. You'll feel better."

PUBLICANS

Himself

Harry O'Donoghue

Victor R. Power doesn't suffer fools gladly. He is the sole proprietor, chief bottle-washer, cleaner-upper, cook, maintenance guy, mechanic, carpenter, sparkie, bartender, bouncer, and philosopher-in-residence of Kevin Barry's Irish Pub in Savannah, Georgia.

Savannah has well-established Irish connections and boasts one of the biggest St. Patrick's Day Parade parties in the country. St. Patrick's Day, like New Year's Eve, July 4, Oktoberfest, and a host of other yearly celebrations tends to bring out what I would call 'amateurs,' or part-time drinkers—respectful members of the community who don't regularly indulge in the art form known as 'boozing.' But once or twice a year, just to prove they still have it, they show up, hell-bent on having a good time, getting wasted on recreation chemicals, adult beverages, and whatever they can ingest, smoke, or otherwise get into their bodies.

Not all party animals fit into this category, no, no. We have the first-timers, God bless them. Somebody's young son or daughter, out and about, with no clue as to what the hell is going on. There should be a law—never mind, there is.

We have the good old boys in from the boonies, twelve to a pick'm-up truck, dressed from head to toe in the color of the day—that would be green—and drinking longneck beer by the caseload. The off-duty militia makes an appearance—America's finest, here to prove that they, too, on their off moments can be prizewinning arseholes. The usual smattering of other ethnic groups is present—black folk jammin' to rap and hip-hop with no regard for the sensitivities of St. Patrick himself; the Latino crowd, bound and determined to prove that you can be street-legal wearing only a few inches of material placed in strategic places on your body; the muscle-bound, the fatsos, the walking dead, the over-the-hill crowd trying to make people believe that they still have it, and not realizing they never had it; the curious; the tourists who thought this was a quaint Southern City (it is, but not at this time of year); and those of us obliged to cater, in one way or another, to this potpourri of humanity. God, the very thought of it makes me shudder.

And so, back to Victor R. Power.

Before Savannah became as popular as it is today, St. Patrick's Day was important because of its monetary effect on the town and the businesses therein. The few days around March 17 could float you through some of the year's off-times, so there was little choice but to deal with it. Tough to do when you are a man who marches solidly to the sound of his own drum, as Vic does.

In the days before the festivities began, things had to be prepared; a workable menu, doormen, entertainment schedule, extra staff, liquor orders, storage of more beer kegs, plastic cups, CO_2 gas, clean up material for accidents, and a multitude of small details—enough to drive a saint to drink, if you'll pardon the pun. You can imagine the scene on March 16, trying to get it all together—everybody running around like chickens with their heads chopped off, and into this frenzy waltzes TV people. A reporter and a cameraman from some obscure local news channel in North Carolina. Mr. Power himself, aided by a couple of small lifesavers with the magic V stamped on them, is relaxing in his inner sanctum two floors above, safely away from the conversation taking place at the bar below.

"Hello, Ah'm Melinda Wanbe, from Channel 37 WFCP, Windblown, North Carolina. We'd like to do a feature on yo quaint little place hare. Can we speak to Keevin?"

Bartender Tom (a real smartass): "I'm sorry. Kevin's dead."

"Ah'm so sorra to hea' that. When'd he da?"

"Oh, 'bout seventy years ago. Can anyone else help?"

"Weal, do ya'll have a manager could gimme some details, y'know, for ar newscast? Put y'all on the map?"

"We could use that. Most people don't know we're here," Tom says, eyeing the huge line forming outside, waiting for the place to open. "Let me check and see if Vic is available to talk to you."

"Vic, it's Tommy. We've got some TV people here want to talk to you, put you on the map. I told them you were hung over like a dog, but they still want to talk to you."

"Whaddya think?"

"I think you should get your sorry ass down here and say something to them."

"Fuck. Can Traci not do it? I'm busy."

"Traci is at a city meeting. C'mon down for a few minutes."

"You do it."

"Not being paid for that. I'll just tell them to piss off. You don't need the business."

"You're a prick, Tommy."

"Will there be anything else?"

Click.

"I'm sorry. Mr. Power is not available right now. If you could, call back later. His best time is between midnight and five a.m."

"Ah don't believe this. We're TV reporters. Never met people who didn't want to be on TV."

"Well, you just did now. Come on back and see us sometime."

I suppose anybody else would have done the interview, but Vic had done enough in his time, and in his defense, these things can be frustrating when the reporter has not done her research. So, as on many a St. Patrick's Days before, the bar fills up, the music starts, people drink responsibly (one hopes), and party until they fall down or are encouraged to go back to their lodgings, temporary or otherwise.

In the wee small hours of the aftermath, we sit, reflect, and marvel that it's over. Vic walks by.

"Only three hundred and sixty-four days till we get to do it again, lads. Can you hardly wait?"

On a related Paddy's Day story, some years ago, I was performing on the big day at Kevin Barry's. Frank Emerson and I were playing alternate sets, first-floor stage and ground-floor stage—up and down, up and down, like a fiddler's elbow. The upstairs bar tends to empty out first, so we would finish off by doing some songs as a duo before going downstairs for the last set.

Fatigue had set in, and I was not feeling my best, so I had been limiting my drinking. There was a sizeable audience in front of me, and they were somewhat animated after the day's partying. My colleague and friend Mr. Emerson approached the stage with a determined look on his face.

"Whenerwegonna do a duo?"

"Are you good to go?" say's I.

"Ready when you are. I'll get my guitar, and let's do it."

"Right, so."

It was almost midnight, and we had been going for twelve hours. There had been drink taken—for twelve hours. Onstage now, both of us with the usual earsplitting feedback, turn it up, turn it down, reset the

44

graphics, back off the monitor, take the master volume down a hair, too much on your guitar, add some bass to my mike—

"Oh, fuck it. Let's do one," he says.

"Whadd'll we do?"

"Anything, anything. Let's go."

A few pub standards, and we're getting adventurous. "Sing the 'Mary Ellen Carter,'" someone shouts. "Okay," we shout back.

Frank is in the middle of the third verse, getting into the song, eyes closed; I'm ready to join in on the chorus, "Rise again, rise again," but it doesn't come—nothing comes, and no sound from his guitar.

In the sheer joy of his performance, Frank had taken a step back, intending to come forward again and burst into the chorus. But there was a gap, a gap of about ten inches between the wall and the back edge of the stage, and into this gap went Frank's right foot. He fell backward, hit the wall, and ended up in an unflattering position—not quite down, not quite up, all to the enthusiastic roar of the assembled, who were beside themselves with joy at the unintentional choreography unfolding on stage. My left hand caught his shoulder before he fell completely off the stage. I pulled him upright, and like the trooper he is, he went straight into the chorus. He was a darling that night.

I decided it was time to order a large Bushmills for myself. We continued with a few more songs bolstered by a rejuvenated audience catching their seventh wind. Two songs later, don't I see from the corner of my eye Frank taking a step backwards again. I was more prepared this time and caught him before his foot got stuck.

"T'anks," says he.

"Fuck me," says I, and we never missed a beat.

The crowd could barely contain themselves at this point.

"Let's do 'Monteserrat,'" says I.

"What key?"

"I don't know. It's your song."

"That's right. Let's try A."

"Is that the key you normally do it in?"

"Mmm, t'ink so."

We charge ahead a few bars. Nope. Wrong key.

"Okay, let's do it in, aah, in—Look, you're on the bodhrán, anyway. I'll find the right key, and you jump in when you want."

"Fair enough."

The crowd is up dancing now. We're heroes. The whole first floor is moving to the rhythm of the music.

"Let's finish off with 'Brown-eyed Girl,'" says I.

"Wha'?" Frank says. The audience is shouting requests, howls, growls, catcalls, whistles, grunts, and guttural noises usually associated with medical emergencies. "Can't hear."

"'Brown-eyed Girl'!"

"Fuck it. I'll trust your judgment. Less have a drink."

"Grand. Slainte."

"'Hey, where did we go? Days when the rain came—'"

"Downstairs, everybody, for the last set. Don't forget your waitresses and bar staff. Give us fifteen minutes, and we'll finish off the night down there."

My own head was buzzing now. Vic came toward us. I thought he might be concerned about Frank hurting his ankle.

"Not so bad. I liked the dance routine. How do I get tickets for the next Hank and Frank Show?"

"Ha, ha, ya bollocks."

"Seriously," he says, "twenty minutes downstairs and we'll pull the plug. Enough is enough."

"Are you sure? The crowd is wound up. They'll want more than five or six songs."

"We've been at it all day. Fuck 'em. Let's get them out and have a few drinks ourselves."

"You're the boss. Let's go, Frank."

Six songs later, it's "Goodnight everybody, and safe home." The booing of the audience resonated through the building, but there would be no more on this St. Patrick's Day. It was a done deal; no amount of bribery, offers of free drinks, baring and touching of breasts (female, that is), kisses with tongue (pass—big pass), viewing of pierced body parts, tattoos, exotic undergarments, or stroking of egos would be enough to turn the stage lights back on. It was over.

"Well," says Victor R. Power, assessing the lay of the land over a fine Puerto Rican rum, "it wasn't so bad, after all. You two can come back and play next year, but no dancing—we lost the cabaret license."

We look around at the detritus of the day's revels. Another Paddy's Day gone.

"Anyway," Vic says, raising his glass. "Here's to ourselves."

I Break for Heavy Metal

Frank Emerson

A few years back, I was offered a job at a new joint. Now, Osama, as I'll call him for argument's sake, wasn't Irish. Not Irish-American, either. He did have considerable experience in the food and beverage industry. Ah, you know. You see these guys all the time. He wanted to cash in on what he figured was a sure thing—the Irish pub bit, or scene, or whatever he might call it in an offhand, not really getting the point, way. Many places are Irish in name, but that's where any resemblance to the real McCoy ends. I suppose that it is—maybe it always was—hip to have a place with an Irish moniker. I think "they" think it promotes drinking, i.e. dropping some shekels. How they arrived at the idea that the Irish could be associated with having a drink, I'll never know.

Anyway, Osama offers me a job at good money. He also asks if I'm willing to give him some advice. I'm flattered. I say yes, gladly, to both. I book a bunch of weeks over the year ahead and tell him I'm happy to help him out any way I can.

He gives me his story. "I made up this guy, Murphy, see, and he's the black sheep of a respectable Irish family in Ireland, see. He makes his living producing illicit alcohol and stealing horses. He gets caught. He escapes. He comes to America, where he changes his name to Mulligan, see, and he starts moonshining and stealing horses again. He makes a pile of dough and opens up a tavern on this very spot called Moonshine Mulligan's! What do you think of that idea? Great, huh?"

Well, the warning bells go off in my head, but I ignore them because Osama is paying good money, don't you know. I give a sort of a nod, and we proceed to the advice thing.

I tell him that it is all well and good and a mighty clever tale—I figured a little patronization wouldn't hurt— but I caution him that this homespun yarn isn't the entire recipe for success. Patience is the watchword. "Irish" pubs coming out of nowhere with no real tradition involved ain't quite the easy thing. Oh, sure, there will be an initial rush of business, but then the novelty of a new pub will wear off, and the clientele will thin until you can establish a solid identity. This is particularly true here because we are a college town, and college crowds are notoriously fickle.

47

Eventually, eventually, the regular patrons will come, and they will set the tone and the place will build. Patience. And consistency, as well. Irish ballad-type entertainment ain't heard on the top ten. You want an Irish place? You've got to say, "Here is who we are and what we offer. We're an Irish pub with Irish music, Irish food, and so on." You do not diversify. That works for some corporations, but you don't want to confuse your potential clientele. Period.

He agrees and assures me that this is what he wants. He names some of the performers with whom he has spoken. I know these names, and they're just fine. Everything appears copasetic. He seems resolute about creating a solid Irish pub. Sounds good. I don't go into the phony black sheep business and the cooked-up history being counter productive to what we're talking about. I'm thinking it is a minor thing that can be overcome. Besides, he had thought it up himself and was kind of giddy about it—proud that he was putting something over on the punters—his version of blarney, I guess. I hesitate only for a moment, but I figure, ah, so what. The guy is shelling out good dough. Just shut yer yap, do the job, and take the money.

Osama now asks me about the house music played over the sound system between the entertainer's sets. "What about it?" I ask. "What should it be?" he asks. I look at him squinty. Hhmmm. I remind him of consistency, and that, of course, it should be Irish or Celtic. Mix it up with ballads and tunes—traditional. He asks if I could get him some. I tell him I'd enjoy to. From my LP collection at home, I make him up a couple dozen tapes that would be more than enough to get him started and send them to him.

Okay. Now comes my opening night. I get there early to set up my gear, get the lay of the land, and so on. This is my first look at the place. Very nice. He has sunk some serious arragot into the joint. But something is amiss. I cop on pretty quickly.

Heavy metal music is playing over the house system.

This is not optimum. It clashes with the concept, the ambiance. It clashes with everything! I'm trying to sort out this new wrinkle, as I get ready to go on. I take the stage. It's a nice one, by the way, big, plenty of room, and there is a sound room of sorts—a little closet thing—upstage-left, with a tape deck. I go in. There's a heavy metal tape in the deck and the Irish tapes I made for the fellow are sitting off to the side, piled up on a table.

48

I push the stop button and remove the offending tape. I then go into my first set. After the set, I go back to the sound room, put in an Irish tape, and go to the Men's. The interval passes, and I come back into the music room for my second set. Irish music ain't playing. It's that other crap. I do the same thing I did before—take it out, do my set, put in an Irish tape, go to the bar in the other room. The scene repeats two more times. Heavy metal. I don't get it. Did this putz hear anything I said? I've got the next four nights to deal with this baloney. I figure I've got to send a message somehow, and I'm not talking Western Union.

Comes the next night, and I come to work. More poop on the tape deck. I prepare the same way as the night before—with one exception. When I take the poop tape out of the deck, I snap it in half and toss it aside. After the set, I put on an Irish tape. When I get up for my second go, there's another heavy metal thing playing. So I take that one out and break it. I do this each set over the succeeding nights. Four nights, four sets a night. Total for the week: sixteen spine-snapped heavy metal tapes in a heap. Remember, I let it go the first night.

A couple of things here are remarkable. First, none of the Irish tapes were broken—no retaliation, you see. Second, nobody said nothing about the fact that the other tapes kept getting busted. Go figure. I was waiting, just waiting.

Next gig is two months later: same story. This time, no mercy. The full five nights, four shows a night—twenty tapes destroyed. A few weeks pass. I work the club again. You got it. Repeat performance. I'm starting to dig this. I'm helping clear up air pollution.

About a week or so later, I get a call from Osama. No surprise here. He's depressed. He's declaring bankruptcy. I say, "Ah, that's hard luck," and I wait. Not a word about all those busted tapes. He's real sad, but seeing as how things are, he has to cancel my remaining two dates. "That's all right, Osama. I'll take the hit. Better luck down the road, eh? All the best now, bye."

Now, I'm figuring, with my two weeks canceled there are some forty-odd heavy metal tapes that still live and breathe because I didn't have a chance to get to them. Even now, they're probably inflicting themselves upon some innocent, unsuspecting customers in an other-wise charming bistro called something like Sake Yamamoto's, Kim Chi Charlie's, Adolf's Brauhaus, or some other joint Osama has opened up somewhere in the world.

As for the Irish tapes I'd provided, I never saw them again. Casualties of the Music Wars, I suppose.

GSBO

STRAY CHAT/FRANK

DOR: One of my favorite places to work and hang out in was Liam's Irish Tavern. Liam Haughey was quite a character. What's your take on the new breed of club owner? You've been in the business...?

FE: Well, thirty-three, thirty-four years—something like that. I remember Liam. Yeah, he was a character. I always thought he looked like Angela Lansbury's brother. He wanted to be called Bill Hoy, which was what he was called when he was coming up. Good guy. Gave a bunch of us a chance.

DOR: How have pub owners changed, if at all? Other than the fact that some of them have gotten old and died.

FE: Some of them have died, yeah. Some of them are dead, and some of them should be. (Laughs) I'm not sure that they've changed. There's always gonna be a certain type of fella who's a bastard. And I don't know if they've changed. They're the same people; some more successful, some less successful, some with attitudes—treating musicians as second-class citizens, music as an afterthought, and you can't help but be a little resentful of that, but if they're gonna pay you, you'll take their money or not work for them. Then again, some of them are just great and treat you like a mensch. As you know, I got pretty sick there a while back. I couldn't work for about a year. The hospital bills and everything were pretty horrendous. It really was touch and go. Well, three of these guys—owners, I'm talking about—held fundraisers for me. Lots of musicians donated time, talent, and money. You know this. You were one of them. So were Harry, Robbie, and Seamus, for that matter. It sure went a long way to ease the burden. The three guys were Danny O'Flaherty in New Orleans and Pat Garvey up there just outside Washington—who are musicians themselves—and my great pal here in Savannah, Vic Power, who can best and generously be described as a 'song stylist.' (Laughs) These owners are what I would call real gents. I could never thank them—or any of you—enough.

GSBO

There but for the Grace of God...

Seamus Kennedy

Jan Brady wanted to surprise her husband Don by bringing me out to do a house concert for his birthday at their humble lean-to in Hermosa Beach, California. My expenses would be covered and a PA system would be rented and set up pool-side, beneath the palm trees. She would see to it that Don was lured away on some pretext, giving the guests time to assemble. All I had to do was show up with my guitar and overnight bag.

The whole doings was planned to the smallest detail.

I was picked up at the airport and whisked to their house, where I did a sound-check and made sure that I wasn't going to be standing too near the pool while I was performing. As any entertainer can tell you, there's nothing like the thrill of holding a live microphone and an electric-acoustic guitar, and being pushed into a pool by a boisterous party-maker who knows bugger-all about conductivity.

Don's car came up the driveway.

The guests hid behind palms and bushes in the big back yard.

I stood in the shade of the fence and started singing. Jan had assured me that Don would think it was one of my recordings, which he constantly played around the house. She led him, unsuspecting, into the pool area, and I began singing "Happy Birthday" as the guests all leapt out from their hiding places, yelling, "Surprise!"

Don's face beamed with delight as he greeted friends and relations he hadn't seen in years, and he was genuinely pleased that he had been kept in the dark so successfully. He came over, gave me a big hug (It's a California thing—I'm still not used to it), and asked, "When the hell did you get here?"

"A little while ago. This thing was better planned than the D-Day landing."

"Well, great! Glad you're here. Let's have some fun."

I did a couple of sets of Don's favorite songs, and then caterers clad in black tie brought out the food. Smoked salmon, caviar, canapés, truffles, champagne, mimosas—and Seamus Kennedy singing Irish songs and telling jokes. Just like Saturday afternoons at my parents' house in Belfast—which only lacked the pool, the palm trees, the smoked

51

salmon, the caviar, the canapés, the truffles, the champagne, and the mimosas.

At about 7:30 in the evening, when the last guest had gone, Don, who really hadn't eaten much due to being the busy little birthday boy with his friends, asked if I felt like going out with them for a bite to eat.

"Sure," I said, never one to turn down the opportunity for good food, drink, and company. We drove into Los Angeles to a restaurant called Lawrey's, which is renowned for its prime rib. A valet-parking attendant took the car, and I was struck by the fact that nearly all the cars pulling up to the joint were Rolls Royces, Jaguars, Mercedes, BMWs, and the like. The parking-attendants wore tuxedoes while the owners of the vehicles were clad in T-shirts, shorts, and sandals—lots of tans, ponytails (male), and cell phones in evidence.

I thought, "Only in California."

After a couple of drinks, we ordered three prime rib dinners because prime rib is the *only* thing on the menu. Really. A huge side of cow is wheeled from table to table in a large, domed, stainless steel container. A server in chef's whites then slices off a slab of what your preference is—rare, medium, or well-done, and you can have as thick or thin a slice as you wish, while a server with another wheelie-steam table dishes out the veggies.

We had an excellent meal, and after a couple of post-prandial libations, they asked if I'd like to go to the local comedy club. As one who never turns down an opportunity to swipe new material for my own act, I agreed, and away we went.

When we took our seats a few rows back from the stage, I looked around to take in the scene. This is something all performers do when they go into a nightclub—check out the stage set-up, in case we ever get a gig there. I've even gone into strip-clubs with other entertainers, and while the most gorgeous, naked women are writhing sensuously around poles with enticing, come-hither looks, we're saying, "Check out those lights, man. Kliegs, good gels." "Yeah, how about that sound system? Look, Altec-Lansing Voice-of-the-Theater cabinets with 15" speakers and horns. We'd sound great through that, man."

The girls don't stand a chance.

Well, here we had a semi-circular elevated stage against a bare-brick wall, a bar encircling the stage with about nine or ten stools, good overhead lighting array with spots, floods, and follows, and a superb

52

sound system. Rows of four-top tables radiated out from the stage like spokes from a hub.

Nice.

As we settled in, I noticed two drunken sailors sitting at the bar, right in front of the stage, heckling a young comic who was doing his best to ignore them. They were talking loudly, weaving on their stools, waving their beer bottles aloft, and generally behaving like assholes. The comedian was so distracted that he gave up and left the stage.

The next comic was brought on, and he fared no better than the first, with the sailors haranguing him every time he tried to speak. He tried reasoning with them.

"C'mon guys, gimme a break. I'm trying to do my act here."

"What goddamn act? You don't got any act!" And they laughed and high-fived each other.

He tried zinging them, putting them down with insults. "If I had a village, you'd be my idiot," he said to one.

"Oh yeah," said the sailor, "and what would my buddy be?"

Stumped. No comeback.

Oh, God, I felt for this kid.

The next performer was introduced, and he swaggered to the microphone in the center of the stage. He wore a black leather motorcycle jacket over a white tee shirt, tight blue jeans, and motorcycle boots. He whipped a comb out of his hip pocket, and began to carefully comb his 50s-style pompadour. He lit a cigarette, took a couple of deep drags, exhaled, flicked the cigarette on the floor, and ground it out with the sole of his boot. Then he walked to the edge of the stage toward the sailors, where he extended his foot and kicked their beer bottles into their laps.

They started, "What the hell?"

He glared down at them and said in a broad New York accent, "If you fuck with me, I'll kick your fuckin' heads off! Just sit there and shut the fuck up!"

The stunned sailors looked all around the audience, hoping for some sympathy. Well, you'll find sympathy in the dictionary between "shit" and "syphilis," but not in a comedy club, so they just sat like a pair of scolded little boys as Andrew Dice Clay began his act.

After the show, I realized that I had yet to check into my hotel. Don and I dropped Jan off at the house and drove the short distance to the hotel, which was just a block from the ocean. I retrieved my guitar and overnight bag from the trunk of the car, and we walked into the small lobby. It was your standard Motel 6 sort of lobby, with a couple of cheap prints on the wall, three chairs around a coffee table littered with tourist brochures, and a Coke machine in the corner. In another corner was a table with a coffee maker and a container with sugar, artificial sweetener, and non-dairy creamer—all set for the "continental breakfast," which commenced at 6:00 a.m.

There was also a strong odor of alcohol—not the disinfectant kind, the drink-from-a-brown paper bag kind—which nailed us as soon as we walked in. Now, we'd been drinking, but this smell overpowered the booze on our own breath. It conquered our olfactory systems completely.

As we approached the front desk, we realized that the reek of cheap liquor was emanating from the night-clerk sitting behind it, blearily watching us through two of the finest, bloodshot eyes that it has been my privilege to witness. British mailbox red, they were, and beginning to glaze over as Don and I walked up. If they were *this* red from where we stood, imagine what they were like from his side. He could have hemorrhaged for a fortnight, and those eyes would not have cleared up.

"Good evening, gennulmen," he slurred.

Don said, "There's a reservation in the name of Kennedy for tonight."

"Lemme shee," said the clerk, and he began to thumb through a well-worn ledger, peering through one squinted eye until he came to the correct entry.

"Ah, here we are. Kennedy" and his breath would have gagged a hyena. Don and I tried to breathe only through our mouths, but that just made things worse. Because then we could *taste* it.

"Shign in, please."

He slid the guest register towards me; I lifted the ballpoint pen chained to it and signed my name, all the while averting my face from the toxic miasma he was exhaling.

Good God Almighty, what had this guy been drinking? Tuna Coladas made with ammonia?

He fumbled in his shirt pocket and took out a pair of reading-glasses, poking himself in the eye as he tried to put them on.

54

Bending over the guest register, until his face was about three inches from it, he squinted again and read aloud, "Sshheamush Kennedy. I knew a Sshheamush Kennedy once. He was an Irish singer."

"I'm an Irish singer," I replied.

"But thish Sshheamush Kennedy was an Irish singer back on the Easht coasht."

I said, "I'm from the East coast."

He continued, "He used to sing for me in my factory in Connecticut, at Christmas-time."

I did a double take. I shook my head and stared, because, slowly, through a morass of distant memories, recognition had begun to form.

"Ron? Ron Mooney?" I whispered.

"Yeah, I'm Ron Mooney," he replied, "Do I know you?"

"*I'm* the Seamus Kennedy who used to sing for your Christmas parties."

"Shon-of-a-bitsch. Fancy meeting you here after all thish time," he said. "What are you doin' all the way out here?"

"I'm here to do a show for my friend Don Brady, right here. Don, say hello to Ron Mooney; Ron—Don Brady."

They shook hands over the counter while my mind went back twelve years.

Ron Mooney had been a multi-millionaire with a large factory in Vermont. He had started with a machine shop turning out parts for small aircraft manufacturers. As he became more successful, the orders started to come in from larger manufacturers, like Boeing, Grumman, and Bell Helicopters, so he built a bigger plant.

Then came the huge government contracts for military vehicle parts, and Ron became extremely wealthy. He had a loyal and hard working staff that he rewarded with bonuses and a big Christmas bash every year at the finest hotel in town, and for four years in a row, I was part of their Christmas celebration. In all my dealings with him, he was very generous, indeed—a substantial paycheck, a good hotel, and an insistence that I partake in the largesse he provided for his regular employees before, during, and after my show.

He broke into my recollections.

"Goddamn! We had shome great hoolies, din't we?"

"We did, Ron." I agreed. "I had a ball doing them."

And his two red, rheumy eyes opened wide at the memory.

"What happened?" I asked. "What brings you out here to California?" I was hoping that he'd bought the hotel and was spending his retirement as an innkeeper who liked a little tipple now and then.

He focused his gaze on a spot on the wall over my shoulder and paused as he began to concentrate on remembering. His voice seemed to come from far away.

"I drank away the factory." He was not slurring now. "Got into the bottle and it all just went right down the toilet. The wife divorced me, and she got everything. Everything. The whole friggin' lot. I hadn't a pot to piss in, or a window to throw it out of, so here I am. This place gives me a roof over my head and some beer money, so I'm doin' okay." He shrugged. "I know, I know; I'm an alcoholic. You don't have to tell me. Fuck it; I'm a wino, okay? I've tried going to the meetings, but I just can't do it."

"What about your family?" I asked.

His lower lip drooped and harp-strings of spittle formed as he opened his mouth. The slurring started up again.

"Oh, they don't wanna know me. Goddamn ol' drunk. Afraid I'll embarrass 'em."

Don jumped in, "Ron, what's Seamus' room number?"

Ron, eyes practically shut, checked the ledger again before answering. "One-eighteen, right down th' hall. Here'sh th' key."

I took it, shook hands with Don, and did the California hug thing again. As he walked out the door, he told me he'd meet me for breakfast at 8:00 a.m. and then drive me to the airport.

I picked up my guitar and my bag, and turned to walk down the hall to my room. Ron had removed his spectacles and was sitting on a stool behind the desk with his head resting on his arms on the counter. He was starting to snore.

"Good night, Ron," I said quietly.

He lifted his head. "Wha'? Huh? Oh. G'night."

I recalled how this gentle, fun-loving man had been extremely kind to a young Irish entertainer starting out on a solo career. I had just broken up with my partner after eight years as the Beggarmen, and I was going it alone for the first time. I had many doubts about making it as a single, and I was debating whether to continue performing. Sure, I'd had a few reasonably well paying pub gigs, but nothing to convince me that this was where my future lay. Plus, I now had a wife and baby son to consider.

Well, Ron and some of his friends had seen the Beggarmen at the old Pumpernickel Pub in Vermont and had enjoyed themselves. He asked for one of our cards, so I gave it to him and promptly forgot about it. When he called me out of the blue sometime later to do his Christmas party, I explained that the Beggarmen were no longer together, and that I was a solo.

"No problem," he replied. "You can handle it. How does seven-fifty sound?"

At the time, I was making about four hundred bucks a week, so seven-fifty just before Christmas sounded angel-sweet to me. Nearly two weeks' wages for one night's work. Hosanna and hallelujah!

Well, the first party was a huge success, so Ron asked me back for the next three Christmases, with a raise each time. After each party, at the end of the night, when I had packed up my gear and the revelers had gone, he asked me to join him at the bar for a quiet couple of drinks. Just the two of us. He thanked me for a job well done, complimented me on my show, and handed me the paycheck. Each time, he also slipped me a fifty-dollar tip.

Thanks to Ron Mooney's confidence in me, and his generosity, my own confidence was boosted immeasurably, and I no longer had any doubts about my future occupation.

And I didn't have a clue about his drinking problem.

I took a fifty from my wallet and walked to the desk. Wrapping the bill around his glasses, I leaned over the counter and slipped them into his shirt pocket. Not much, but it'd buy him a couple of pints of amnesia.

I didn't sleep well.

Ron wasn't at the desk when I checked out in the morning.

⊂ॐ∞

Matthew

Frank Emerson

Matthew Mulcahy was an odd fellow for an Irishman. Oh, he drank, to be sure, but he disliked Irish whiskey. He claimed that it tasted like gasoline—petrol, to use the word he used. However, he more than made up for it with other choices. I know he enjoyed Guinness and Harp and certainly did his best to keep that corporation in business. He also enjoyed vodka. I think this was because of the potato connection. I believe he believed that vodka was native to Ireland and that by drinking it, he was only doing his bit for the home sod. One of his quirks was his insistence that his name, Matthew, be pronounced "Matchyou." This made everyone talking with him sound like they were from the north side of Dublin. It did wonders for his homesickness.

I forget where or when I first met him, but it's a safe bet that it was in a bar. Somewhere along the line, Matthew found himself the owner of a pub in Portland, Maine. He called the place Mul's Irish Pub, and to work there was to attend a constant party. We all enjoyed our bookings at Mul's and were always anxious to return. There were good crowds pretty much all the time. Everybody seemed to like the music and appreciated the performers' efforts. The girls were pretty, friendly, and cooperative. The staff, too, was capable, informed, and easy to work with.

Matthew was generally pretty happy, since the place was doing well. However, even on an off day, he was the picture of optimism, since he knew this was a temporary condition, and things were bound to be better tomorrow. He loved to have a good time and surrounded himself with like-minded people. He was also a firm believer in leading by example, so in many ways, was his own best customer.

After an evening of playing and singing and promises made and broken, any number of Matthew's friends would congregate around the bar for a nightcap. This would be after the place had closed and the casual customers had all headed home. This was probably the time of day that Matthew liked best. He was the center of attention. It is well known that late at night, when the liquor is going down, everyone becomes smarter, braver, funnier, and prettier. When you are the one supplying the booze, this goes double—and he often made it a double, for that matter. Matthew was in his element.

However, even the parties at Mul's, as fun as they were, eventually wound down. At such times, it was Matthew's belief that nothing would do but a big, fat, submarine sandwich. Not just any submarine sandwich, but one of a type invented by Tony O'Riordan, famous Dublin musician and gourmand. Tony's creation was a PLT—a pastrami, lettuce, and tomato—served on a big, thick, foot-long roll slathered up with butter. This gastronomic treat was on Matthew's mind one morning at about three o'clock as his party was breaking up.

A little less than a mile, and pretty much a straight shot from Mul's, was a waterfront place called the Sub Base. The entire menu consisted of submarine sandwiches, French fries, potato chips, and soft drinks. This was their daytime menu. It was also their nighttime menu. As long as anyone was hungry, they had the remedy. This made the Sub Base real popular with the after-the-bars-close crowd.

One night, Matthew swallowed enough booze that he didn't feel confident in his ability to successfully negotiate the road from Mul's to the Sub Base on foot. He concluded that it would be safer for him to drive. This might sound like an odd decision. So be it. But it was his decision.

Always a careful driver, Matthew was determined to take extra care that night. It was, after all, a straight road and barely a mile to the PLT. He popped a breath mint or two, got in his car, started the engine, and headed slowly toward the waterfront.

It couldn't have been two minutes later when Matthew looked to his left and saw a police officer alongside, motioning for him to pull over. Matthew was pretty sure he wasn't speeding, but he figured he should cooperate. He liked cops. They had a rough job to do. He contributed to their charities. Everything would be okay. Anyway, he had snarfed those breath mints, so he figured he was safe. He stepped on the brakes, put the car in park, and cranked down the window to see what was up.

"Good evening, Officer. Is there a problem?"

"That's what I was going to ask you, sir. May I see your license and registration, please?"

Matthew fished them out of his pocket and handed them over.

"Well, Mr. Mulcahy, do you have any idea why I pulled you over?"

"Uh, no, I don't, Officer. I don't think I was speeding. Was I?"

"No, you weren't speeding."

"I don't have any tail lights out, do I?"

"No, sir. You're lights are fine."

"Then, I don't know. Why did you pull me over?"

"Well, Mr. Mulcahy, we have a bit of a different situation here. You were not speeding. Your lights are working. Your license and registration are in order. But I'm afraid I'm still going to have to cite you."

"Why are you going to do that if everything is all right?"

"Well, sir, technically, you were off the road. By this I mean you were driving on the sidewalk."

"Oh, Jesus, Mary, and Joseph, Officer. I'm sorry. I just got off work, and I'm pretty tired. I was just going down to the Sub Base for a sandwich and coffee before I drive home. I'm real sorry about this."

"Sir, that's not all of it. Not only were you on the sidewalk, you were going about three miles per hour—max."

"Uh-oh"

"Yeah, 'uh-oh,' sir. I've got to tell you, this is the first traffic ticket I've ever issued, and I've been on the force for ten years now."

"Oh?"

"That's right. What I'm going to do is I'm going to drive you down to the station and introduce you around because the boys won't believe me."

"What do you mean?"

"Would you like to take a guess why this is my first ticket?"

Matthew shook his head no.

"It's because I'm not a traffic officer. I'm the beat cop. You remember when I motioned for you to pull over? I was walking alongside you. Now shove over. I'm driving you to the station."

Matthew never lived that night down—nor, as it turned out, did he want to. The story made the rounds all over Portland—how Matthew went to the stationhouse that night, stayed through the rest of the morning and absolutely charmed the whole precinct with his good nature. He was cited for "full time and attention," which is to say he was not giving adequate attention to the operation of his motor vehicle. I think the police were in error in this charge because it's obvious Matthew certainly was paying attention to what he was doing. How else could he have negotiated the sidewalk so neatly? But it's all in the past now, so I guess it's a moot point. Anyway, he was let off with a small fine and his promise to not give a repeat performance.

He became the darling of the precinct, and the cops became regulars at Mul's. So you see, it all worked out for the best. People still spent freely and drank plenty, but every one became more careful about drinking and driving. They reached the conclusion that a cab ride from Mul's to the Sub Base was a good insurance policy any way you look at it.

 os80

Bob Packer

Harry O'Donoghue

Bob didn't feel well. This voice thing was getting him down. It was a beautiful January morning in Florida, and he was puttering around the bar, adjusting pictures on the wall, moving, and re-arranging to make room for new ones he'd acquired. It had been almost eighteen years since he'd left Detroit and found his own little bit of paradise down on the Gulf of Mexico. Sure, he'd done well up there—worked for thirty years as an engineer for AMC and made a good living for his family. The job paid well, but the stress level was high. As a counter measure, he opened a little Irish 'joint' and reveled in the time he spent there, far away from the competitive atmosphere of the corporate world. The bar turned out to be quite a success, and for a while he was content being an engineer by day and a bar owner by night. Inevitably, as the bar grew more popular, it added to his already considerable stress level. The long Detroit winters weren't helping, either. It was clear to Bob that choices would have to be made.

"Been here too long, it's too cold, and there's too much stress," he'd say. "I'm outta here soon. Florida, sunny skies, warm breezes, laid-back lifestyle—yep, it do sound good to me."

He made a few trips down south to scout locations and decided to buy a small bar in St. Pete Beach, overlooking the gulf waters. It was a run-down, pre-fab job about the size of a doublewide trailer. Hell, it *was* a doublewide trailer when you got right down to it. He knew he could do a good job of fixing the place up, so he approached his wife Pat with the idea.

Pat was a strong woman of proud Irish stock, and though she applauded his decision to leave the Detroit life behind and relocate to Florida, she was more than a tad apprehensive. She knew a lot of the work would land on her shoulders—not the physical work, mind, but the promotional aspects of the business. She had a natural and immediate connection with people, so she would be the obvious choice to interact with customers. Bob was more reserved and had grown to dislike crowds, which was rather peculiar given the fact that he was planning to open another bar. His own people were Scottish.

"Why not combine Scotland and Ireland?" he'd said to Pat. "The place up north did well. We can create a Celtic atmosphere down here as well."

61

He even had the name picked out: the Harp and Thistle. He proudly announced, "What about that?"

Good as his word, he fixed the place up, made several trips to Ireland, bought a variety of odds and ends, photographs, posters, and assorted antiques, and hung them all over the place in what appeared no particular fashion. "Carefully planned disorder" was a phrase Bob liked. Very few knew that every picture or knick-knack hanging on the wall or from the ceiling was there because that was exactly where he thought it should be. See, Bob had a thing for neatness, didn't much care for the tardy look, no, not Bob. He insisted the bar be kept in a meticulous state of cleanliness, and he even landscaped the outside accordingly. One blade of grass blowing in the wrong direction was enough to upset him, so the small front lawn was clipped and trimmed to the 'nth' of an inch. The building itself was painted an eye pleasing green and cream.

The Harp, as it became known, had character, charm, and atmosphere to spare, and it thrived on Bob's insistence that it remain faithful to his original theme. He hired Irish musicians and offered his customers a taste of what it might feel like to be in Ireland or Scotland, sipping on a pint of Guinness. The venture was a huge success, and the Harp and Thistle became known all over the States as "that great little Irish bar on the Gulf Coast of Florida." Bob was pleased, and Pat was content playing the role of goodwill ambassador for the Harp. She had a penchant for wearing flamboyant hats and was called "the Hat Lady." Two of their daughters, Jennifer and Lori, worked at the bar, while the others, Colleen, Julie, and son Michael, visited and helped whenever they could. The enterprise was very much a family affair and yes indeedee, Bob was pleased.

Never what you would call a physical man—he didn't go to the gym, play golf, jog, or any of that stuff—Bob still considered himself healthy, for the most part. He had never had any major illness and had just turned seventy.

One day, he noticed that he couldn't project his voice—that he wasn't able to talk loudly. It seemed a little strange, but he assumed it was a cold or virus he'd picked up some place. It didn't clear up, though, and within months, his conversation was reduced to a whisper. It frustrated the hell out of him. Reluctantly, he went to see his doctor and had a thorough physical check-up. They couldn't find any reason why his voice was so weak, but there were other, more immediate, problems that showed up during the tests. There was a ninety-percent blockage in some major arteries, and surgery would be necessary. His cholesterol was dangerously high, and he had developed arthritis. He followed the doctor's advice and tried to prepare himself emotionally for the heart surgery.

"Bad news," he grumbled, "always bad news. That's why I stayed away from doctors for so long."

The surgery was a success; he recovered well, made some lifestyle changes, took a daily cartload of pills for the high cholesterol and arthritis, and within weeks felt better than he had in years. Only thing was, his original complaint, "the voice thing," he called it, which had been almost forgotten when all his other medical maladies were discovered, was still there. He hated to complain, but it was much worse. His conversation was barely audible. A specialist was consulted, extensive testing done, and the results, once again, were not good.

Pat sat in the doctor's office on a balmy May morning.

"Lou Gherig's disease," she said, repeating the doctor's words.

He looked at her solemnly. "There is no cure. I'm terribly sorry, but there's nothing we can do. There will be a little time before the end, but not a lot."

The words swirled inside her head. Across town, Bob dusted off the glass on a painting of Scottish hero William Wallace, and stood back to admire it. "Fits perfect right there," he said to his bartender.

"Lou Gherig's disease," Pat said again, as she fought back the tears.

***

Harry, Frank, and Carroll were standing outside Finnegan's liquor store in Savannah, the meeting point for their first ever concert tour as a trio. Normally solo artists, they had combined their talents and recorded a Christmas album fifteen months earlier. At the release party, they performed the album live, onstage, and the audience reaction was so enthusiastic that they decided to take the show on the road. Since then, a full year had passed, during which they struggled to re-arrange schedules to fit in as much rehearsal time as possible. For the tour, they decided to play some of their regular venues. It wasn't going to be a huge moneymaker—splitting three ways—but they wanted to test the waters and see if the show could be a hit. Their first performance was that night, November 27, at the Harp and Thistle in St. Pete Beach, Florida, 360 miles southwest of where they were standing.

"The last rehearsal yesterday went much better than expected," Carroll said, sliding a microphone stand into his van. Carroll was the musical director for the tour. Frank took care of publicity, and Harry organized the gigs.

"Not bad for three solo musicians getting together to do a concert tour—although Crosby, Stills, and Nash we're not," said Frank.

"We could call ourselves 'Cliff Climber and the Mountain Goats'. The audience might like that," Harry said.

All three laughed, but beneath the levity, they were concerned that the show might not be as tight as it should be.

"I think it'll be fine, plus the adrenaline will be pumping when we're on stage," reassured Carroll, slamming the back door of the van. "You know what they say, lads. It'll be all right on the night," said Harry. "But tell you what—it was a good day's work yesterday, and the show sounded great. Mind you, it was one hell of a long day."

"It's going to be a long one again today," muttered Frank as he stubbed a cigarette out with the toe of his shoe. He opened the door of his Chevy Blazer and put on his sunglasses. "Let's do this."

Carroll and Harry would ride together in Carroll's van, while Frank followed in the Blazer, and they would keep in contact by cell phone. To make the drive less tedious, Harry changed vehicles at every pit stop so nobody had to make the full trip alone. A little conversation can help eat up the miles. They rolled out of the parking lot at exactly eight-thirty in the morning.

Three hours later, Carroll pulled into a Shoney's in north central Florida. Frank parked next to the van, and he and Harry got out and stretched.

"Hope this is okay for lunch," said Carroll.

"Fine with me. I'm starving," Frank replied.

"Me, too," said Harry, "but remember to keep it slow after lunch, no speeding; this road is notorious. I got a few tickets around here over the years."

"Makes two of us," grinned Carroll.

"Three for three lads," said Frank, taking a pack of cigarettes from his pocket.

64

"Go on in. I'll follow youse in a minute."

"Thought you gave those things up," said Harry, finding an opportunity to ask the question he'd put off for days. Frank didn't bother to look up. He cupped his hands round the lighter, lit the cigarette, and took a big drag. "I did."

***

Bob's family had arranged for a hospital bed to be brought to the house. They placed it in the den, moved Bob from his bedroom, and hooked up the heart monitor machine and oxygen tanks. He had gone downhill fast in the couple of days since Thanksgiving and now spent most of the time sleeping. There had been several visitors over the holiday, and he conveyed his thoughts by way of a note pad. He seemed in high spirits; Thanksgiving was one of his favorite times of year, but he tired easily, and his writing was difficult to make out. His muscle control was almost gone. The hospice people had arrived, and they told Pat that it was down to a matter of hours.

Hospice people are generous, loving, and caring to a fault, and their purpose is to deal with the dying process. They understand how the body shuts down, and they remain so unobtrusive as to appear like shadows, seemingly emerging from nowhere to take a pulse or wet the lips of the sick person. The family was thankful to have them there.

The phrase "a matter of hours" struck Pat as ironic, or sad—pathetic, even—or something else; maybe it was a guilty feeling of relief. Bob had been suffering. She was so confused, she didn't really know. After almost fifty years together, all that was left was hours and minutes. She was trying to come to grips with that. It had always been Bob and Pat; he was the rock, he had always been the rock. Now he was being taken from her; it was simply ridiculous. Sure, there had been some time to prepare, but there's never really enough time, and now that it was finally happening, it came as no less a shock.

His breathing was shallow; his mouth was open, and his eyes half closed, showing only the whites. It was horrible. He was even being robbed of his dignity in these last few days. The hospice people said he could still hear and understand, and told the family to talk to him, to tell him it was okay to let go, that they loved him and were thankful for everything he'd done, that they would remember him always, but that his time here was over, and he should stop resisting.

"Let go, Bob, let go. We love you. It's okay, just let go."

***

The boys pulled into the Harp and Thistle parking lot just before three-thirty in the afternoon. They got out of the vehicles and walked around to loosen up after the long drive. Carroll leaned against his van, and Frank reached into his pocket.

"My back is killing me," complained Harry.

"It's just old age, Aitch—doesn't get any better," Frank said, lighting a cigarette.

"Let's get started with the load-in," Carroll said. "We'll get set up, do a sound check, and relax a bit before the gig."

Harry opened the back door of the van and grabbed one of the guitar cases. "Oh, listen, lads, we might have to go and see Bob. He's not doing so well. I spoke with Jennifer yesterday morning. She said he had a fairly good weekend and that she might bring him over in the car, or we can tip over to the house for a quick visit."

Harry had no way of knowing that Bob's condition had worsened drastically in the previous twenty-four hours.

"Jeez, Aitch, I didn't know it was that bad. He's never gonna— y'know—today?" Frank asked.

"Naw. Can't imagine. What are the chances of that happening?" replied Harry.

"Really," Carroll said, opening the sliding door of the van.

***

Jennifer walked into the bar. The boys were in the process of setting up the stage. She gave each a hug and asked about the trip down and how their families were doing—the usual, small chitchat.

"We'd like you to come to the house to see Bob," she said at last. It's begun."

"What's begun, Jen?" asked Harry.

"He's slipping fast. Mom would like you to come over right away."

"My God. Is it that bad?" asked Carroll.

"Yes. I'm afraid it is."

"I'll drive," said Frank.

During the few minutes it took to drive to Bob's house, the conversation was animated.

"I can't believe this is happening now, at this very moment, on the day, on the hour, almost at the minute of our arrival."

"We couldn't have planned it if we tried."

"I hate this kinda stuff. What do we say?"

"I haven't the foggiest. Let's see what happens."

***

The house had an eerie feel to it and an odor like a hospital room; difficult to describe, except to say, "That smell." Pat and Jennifer met them at the door, and greetings were exchanged in muted whispers. They were led into the den.

"Man," Harry whispered to Frank. "I hate this stuff. I don't know how to act."

"Gives me the creeps," Frank answered.

They entered the den and stood at the foot of Bob's bed.

"He can hear you, Harry, if you'd like to say something," Pat said.

Harry and Bob had become close in the last few years. They enjoyed lunches and early morning coffee together whenever Harry was in town. Bob, being much older, had well formed opinions about most things and wasn't the world's greatest listener. Still, it had developed into a warm, comfortable relationship. There were phone calls and an occasional letter when Harry was on the road or home in Savannah, but their friendship really blossomed when they hung out together in St. Pete Beach. Bob was an avid reader, and they would talk about and swap books they thought the other might enjoy. Bob had been in the Korean War and was an American patriot through and through. Harry respected and admired him for his unwavering beliefs, and Bob in turn admired Harry's professionalism, work ethic, and pride in being an Irishman abroad.

Harry stepped forward and held Bob's hand. He put together a few awkward sentences, never quite finding the right words to convey his feelings. He felt the tears coming, so he quietly moved back. Frank and Carroll walked to the side of the bed and said their good-byes. Bob lay motionless, except for an occasional, involuntary twitching of his mouth. When this happened, one of the hospice ladies dabbed a wet cloth on the dying man's lips.

The three men walked into the adjoining sitting room. Pat sat quietly on the couch.

"Pat, of course the show is off; we'll start loading our equipment and leave in the morning," Harry said.

"Oh, no. The show must go on tonight. That's what Bob wants."

"You're kidding me," Harry whispered, completely taken aback.

"The show starts at eight," said Pat, firmly.

***

Frank pulled up outside the Harp and motioned toward the waterfront bar across the street.

"Let's go over there—get away from all of this for a few minutes," he said.

They ordered three shots of Irish whiskey, drank them, and ordered the same again.

"Here's to Bob, boys."

"To Bob."

"Are we really going to do this show?" asked Frank.

"We have to. Pat was fairly insistent," answered Carroll.

"Hard to believe—weird, to say the least," said Harry.

They threw some money on the bar and walked across the street to finish setting up their equipment. It was just after five in the afternoon.

***

"A little more top end on my vocal, Carroll. I think Frank's is okay, and then you need to come up and check your mike level."

Harry was on stage; Carroll was sitting by the soundboard with his glasses on, adjusting levels, while Frank tuned his guitar.

"Hey, lads."

They turned to the figure at the door.

"Brendan. How's it goin'?" Frank said.

Brendan Nolan was born in Dublin, Frank's hometown. As a musician, he'd made quite a name for himself in Montreal, Canada before moving to St. Pete Beach in the early nineties.

"Been better," Brendan replied. "They want us over at Bob's house. He's dying."

"Already been," said Frank. "It was eerie."

"No, they want us to bring a guitar and sing. He's dying now."

"You're kidding," said Carroll, removing his glasses.

"Jesus," said Harry.

"Carroll, take your guitar," Frank called as he headed for the door. He reached out and shook Brendan's hand. "Nice to see you again, anyway—even under these circumstances."

"You driving, Frank?" asked Harry.

"No point in changing now. C'mon. Let's go."

***

The family was gathered around the bed. Pat stroked Bob's face, Jennifer had one of his hands clasped in hers, and Lori sobbed against his leg. His breathing was short, with much longer pauses in between. "Death is close at hand," Harry thought to himself, though he was surprised that particular line popped into his head. It was such a cliché.

The four men quietly stood by the foot of the bed. There was silence before Harry whispered to Carroll, who picked the opening notes to the old Scottish ballad, the "Bonny, Bonny Banks of Loch Lomond," and Harry started singing.

You'll take the high road,
And I'll take the low road,
And I'll be in Scotland before you.
For me and my true love will never meet again
On the bonny, bonny banks of Loch Lomond.

His eyes were closed tight, and when his voice faltered at the end of the first verse, Frank took over. Everyone joined in for the chorus, and the musicians took turns singing lead in the verses. They chose some of Bob's favorite songs, and while they sang "The Parting Glass," he took one last breath.

Oh, all the comrades that 'ere I've had
They're sorry for my going away
And all the sweethearts that 'ere I've had

Would wish me one more day to stay
But since it falls unto my lot
That I should rise and you should not
I'll gently rise, and I'll softly call
Goodnight and joy be with you all.

The hospice lady placed her hand on Bob's neck to feel for a pulse. Then she placed a stethoscope on his wrist. She looked at Pat and nodded.

Bob Packer was dead.

When the song was finished, the musicians walked quietly out of the room to allow the family some private time.

Pat followed.

"God, Pat. I'm so sorry."

"Oh, I know, Harry. What are we going to do?"

They hugged.

"Eight-o-clock, Harry. It's what Bob would have wanted."

"God, Pat, I dunno. I'm not sure we can do it."

"Please. The show needs to go on."

"We'll do the best we can, Pat, but it'll be tough."

"Thank you, all of you." She hugged each of the men as they left.

***

Back at the waterfront bar a few minutes later, the boys were having another whiskey in Bob's honor.

"Where's Brendan?" Harry inquired.

"Took off," said Frank. "Went back to his own place; said to say 'bye. Can't say as I blame him."

"I can't believe it," said Carroll. "How are we supposed to play after this?"

"Beats me," said Frank, "Making merry now? It's weird—spooky *and* weird—anyway, here's to Bob."

"Ho, ho, ho," said Harry grimly.

***

The Harp was packed at seven-forty-five in the evening. Carroll, Frank, and Harry were back at the waterfront bar for the third time, still trying to shake the day's events.

"If I have any more of this stuff the audience will have to make do with the recording. I won't be able to hit the notes on the bass."

"It'll be fine, Aitch, my boy," reassured Frank. "Although it seems strange that we're going through with this gig."

"We're well fortified, anyway. There'll be four on stage—John Jameson and us three. What do you think, Carroll?" Harry asked.

"Ready to roll, Aitch," Carroll replied, mimicking Frank, and downed the rest of his whiskey.

They put on their jackets, adjusted their ties, and walked out into the warm Florida night.

***

The boys had agreed not to mention Bob's passing until late in the show. They were hoping to create a festive holiday mood, and telling everyone that the owner had just died wouldn't help. Everyone knew anyway—bad news spreads fast. The odd thing was that it didn't have the effect one would expect. Everyone knew, everyone pretended not to know, and the night 'went like a charm,' as they say. Mind you, the performance was a bit edgy, but taking into account the long drive, the first visit with Bob, the first visit to the waterfront bar, the second visit with Bob, Bob's last musical requests, the second and third visits to the waterfront bar—and the fact that it was their first performance—they did well. The audience even gave them a standing ovation.

There was one surreal moment during the performance, and that was when Pat, Jennifer, and Lori walked into the bar. Bob's body had been taken to the crematorium, and Pat and the girls decided to spend the rest of the evening at the bar. Everybody expresses grief in their own way, peculiar though it may be, and the family wanted to be at the Harp. This was Bob's bar, his vision, his dream. In a way, at that moment, they were closer to him there than anywhere else. Nobody knew what to say when they arrived, but Frank broke the ice, congenial fellow that he is. He raised his glass high in the air and shouted, "Three cheers for Bob. Hip, hip, hip, hooray!"

The crowd roared with enthusiasm, and tears flowed freely.

Bob would have loved it. The show went on, and it was yet another memorable night at his Harp and Thistle.

***

It was mid-morning, and the three men stood beside Carrolls' van in the parking lot outside the Harp and Thistle. The sun was about as high as it could climb on a late November day in Florida, and there was a pleasant breeze blowing in off the Gulf. Most of the equipment had been loaded into the vehicles and the conversation focused on the previous twenty-four hours.

"Great night," said Harry.

"Agreed," Carroll replied. "The audience was into it—considering."

"Never mind the audience. I'm surprised *we* were into it, given the day's events," offered Frank.

"What a way to start a tour," Carroll said.

"No kidding," Harry said. "Let's hope the rest of it is a little less eventful."

"Now there's an understatement," said Frank. "If it's all like yesterday, the adrenaline rush alone will kill us."

Carroll went back into the bar and emerged a few minutes later with a smile on his face and a music stand in his hand.

"Idiot check," he said. "Always forget something."

"Well," said Harry. "Eight cities, eight nights. One down, seven to go."

Frank stubbed a cigarette out with the toe of his shoe and opened the door of the Blazer. He grinned at Harry and put on his sunglasses.

"Let's do this."

The Harp and Thistle Pub closed its doors for the last time on Sunday, September 29, 2002, just ten months after Bob's passing.

ᏆᏐ

English Sunday

Frank Emerson

One June afternoon some years back, I get a phone call from Traci O'Donoghue, Harry's wife. She is, at this time, the manager of Kevin Barry's, in Savannah. My pal, Victor Power, is the publican there, and it's my favorite place to play. After the usual pleasantries, Traci cuts to the chase.

"You know Vic's birthday is coming up, don't you?"

"Oh, well I know. The twentieth of next month. I'm booked with you guys then."

Now the reason for "well I know" is that Vic reminds me every year that he was born on the same date as the assassination attempt on Adolf Hitler in 1944. He further reminds me that he didn't have nothing to do with it, dammit, as he was only three years old at the time and wasn't allowed out of the yard. He is sincere about this.

"So, what's up, Trace?" I ask.

"Well, we've come up with an idea. One day, as close as we can manage to Vic's birthday, we're going to turn Kevin Barry's into an English pub. What do you think?"

What I think is *Yipes!* What I say is, "Jeez, Louise, Traci. How do you plan to do that?"

"A make-over," she says, "just like on *Oprah.*"

She tells me that she's been bouncing the idea around with some of Vic's friends locally, and she's been on the horn with others all over the country. Everybody thinks it's a great gag. Well, yeah—it'll be a great gag, sure enough, but I'm thinking there is one little element that makes the plot a little dicey.

If you take just the historical relationship between England and Ireland, you could argue that any Irish pub worth its salt would be the direct opposite of any English pub. Kevin Barry's is worth its salt and then some. It's a reflection of the man who owns it, and he is pro-Irish to the nines. At Kevin Barry's, you won't find plastic leprechauns or four-leaf clovers being passed off as shamrocks; no "bucket o'spuds" on the menu, no green beer. What you will find is straightforward Irish fare, with only minor changes to accommodate the American pallet. You'll find lager and ale and stout and Irish whiskey—none of it green. Lining the walls are period photos, newspaper clippings, and artwork that go to Irish literature and politics and the people involved. Vic even named the place after a young Irish patriot who was executed by the British in 1920. The music, of course, is Irish folk. He's worked hard to make it as real a deal as he could. He's proud of it, as he should be, and fiercely protective. So, when you plan the transformation of such a symbolic establishment—even as a harmless prank, and only for one day—you should sense a warning bell. With this particular place and owner, that bell should be clanging away like nobody's business. There is the possibility that instead of tickled—Vic will be ticked. And a ticked Vic ain't pleasant.

73

I consider this chilling thought and let it percolate for a while. Then it dawns on me what might tip the balance and make the gag work. Nobody likes a good joke better than Vic—the more so when the joke is on him. There's a kicker—and it drips with irony. Vic was born and brought up in Queens, New York, but his people on his father's side were from Waterford. His mother, wonderful woman that she was, was born in England. Vic insists that this was not her fault, and he loved her dearly. However, it's always been a sore spot with him that he is, in fact, part Sassenach. Turning his beloved Irish pub into an English tavern is really going to bust his chops. So, fasten your seatbelts. "English Sunday," here we come.

However, there is one other bit that could gum up the works. It's well known that Vic doesn't like anybody making a big fuss about his birthday. He's just not comfortable with it, okay? In fact, each year he lies low for a day or so until the whole mess blows over. I remind Traci of this, and ask how we're going to take care of it. She's way ahead of me. It's all set. Barbara and Eddie O'Brien, old friends of Vic's from the Virgin Islands, have volunteered to be the Judas goat. They've already invited Vic and his wife to join them for a little R & R at a resort down the coast. They'll pick the two of them up at the pub on Friday morning, the 19th, and bring them back on Sunday afternoon, the 21st. Vic figures this couldn't be better. How right he is.

I get into town on the Tuesday before the event to begin my week's work. The next three days are a little difficult. "Mum's" the word all right, but with all the winks and nods flying around, the place looks like the "twitch ward" at the state hospital. Luckily, though, Vic remains clueless. He goes through his yearly ritual of reminding me of his Hitler assassination connection. As usual, I shrug and commiserate, "Ah, whaddaya gonna do, Boss?"

He tells me, "By the way, Cheri and I are going to take a powder for a couple of days with the O'Briens. We'll be back Sunday afternoon. So please try to give me some business while I'm away, will you?" He's giving me the rib, see.

I tell him, "Boss, don't you worry about nothing. Everything's under control" But I'm thinking, *Oh, we'll give you the business, boyo.*

Friday comes around. Vic is happily looking forward to his getaway, but Barbara and Eddie are late arriving to get Vic out of town, and we've got our hands full trying to keep him away from the newspaper. You see, Traci has placed a big open invitation in the morning edition, asking one and all to show up Sunday afternoon and be in on the birthday hijinks. It's touch and go for a while until someone comes up with the perfect diversion. Vic is a hands-on owner, and when something breaks down in the pub, he's Johnny-on-the-Spot. Somebody mentions that one of the toilets—usually in the ladies' room—sometimes clogs up but good. Wouldn't this be the ideal time for this to happen? That sure would keep him occupied. Fate smiled upon us that morning with the Mother of all Clogs. As sweetly as possible, Traci informs Vic of the somewhat sticky problem, and Ba-da-bing!—we have our diversion. Off he goes, plunger in one hand, pipe snake in the other, cursing his luck and the world in general. Finally, the O'Briens show up, and Vic is out of the place like a shot. On his way out the door, he tosses me the plunger, and I finish unclogging the toilet. I'm not sure, but I think it's in my contract.

The Friday night show. Very nice crowd. Good business. Saturday, things run like clockwork. All day and into the night, the electricity builds. About midway through the evening, the out-of-towners start to roll in. There are folk from all over the place: Chicago, the Virgin Islands, New England. Of course, there's a big gang from New York. In between the "how-ya-doins" and the "good-to-see-yez," the caper is all anyone wants to talk about.

Some of these people have never seen the place, and they are duly impressed with what Vic has put together over the years. I hear one guy from New York say, "Holy crap! What a great jernt! Dis is gonna be great! You kiddin'? Fuhgeddaboudit!" He likes it.

The rest of the evening goes along real nice. The room is warm, friendly, and a little tipsy, which is nicer. Everyone's loose and in good humor. People are digging the music and conversation more than somewhat. By the three a.m. closing time, though, enough is enough. We've got to be back here tomorrow, noonish, to get the place ready, okay? Okay, they agree. Goodnights are said, and with go cups in hand, they teeter off to their hotel rooms.

Sunday. High noon-thirty. The walking wounded start shuffling in. They all call for a hair of the dog. Tommy, the bartender, knows a cue when he hears one. He turns to and starts pouring the cure-alls. The locals start to show. They throw in with us. Finally, everybody is more or less cured, and the signal is given to start the transformation. We attack like doughboys going over the top. Before you can say, 'presto-changeo', it's mission accomplished. We stand back and give the place the once over. Every Irish picture has been covered up with English travel posters or pages clipped from National Geographic or British Life. There are ads for Whitbread, Newcastle Brown Ale, and HP Sauce. All of the Irish portraits have been replaced with photos of the Royal Family—all looking like each other. There are so many Union Jacks hanging, you'd think Britannia still ruled the waves. The Irish menu? It's history. Gone are the Irish stew, the potato soup, and the soda bread. Now, featured items include tepid beer, tasteless mutton, and rubbery Yorkshire pudding topped with lumpy gravy.

The New Yorkers have solved the problem of the pub's name. They have printed up 100 menu covers, 1,000 books of matches, and a 4'X20' canvas banner to hang from the balcony. All of these bear the moniker "Trafalgar Square Pub" in bright red, Old English lettering. We figure that'll do it. He's gonna drop!

We're satisfied. Someone says we ought to have a drink on it. There are no objections. Tommy is a whirling dervish behind the bar. The cash register is ringing like sixty. It's music to his ears. Whatever Vic's reaction is to this whole magilla, the place is going to do a land office business—and it's all on Tommy's watch. He smiles to himself. Life is good.

It turns out we've been so efficient, the job is done in jig time. We've got at least another hour to kill before our man arrives. Like déjà vu all over again, someone suggests a drink. Tommy is up to the task. I'm thinking I should maybe do a few numbers to set the mood. I get on stage, but before I can say a word, I am pummeled with requests—most of them for songs. I announce that I'm going to try to do every song that's ever been written. If I don't know a request, I tell them, Harry, or Dennis, or Trish, or Tom, or Pat, or one of the other musicians will know it. We'll cover all the bases, no sweat. I start in, and everything is going great. Folks are singing and laughing. The place is chocker-block. People are spilling out into the street. We're having such a grand time that we almost don't care whether Vic shows up or not.

The phone at the bar rings. Tommy answers it. It's Vic's wife, Cheri, calling from her restaurant, the Shrimp Factory, just down the block. She's made an excuse to stop and is giving us the heads up. Vic is minutes away.

We watch the car as it comes up the street. It stops. Then starts again. Eddie tells us later that as they get closer, they can't even see the pub because of the crowd outside the door. Vic knows this just ain't normal for a Sunday afternoon. He's concerned.

"What the—? Wait a minute! Stop! Stop the car! What's going on?"

"I dunno," Eddie says. "Let's go see."

He pulls into the parking lot facing Kevin Barry's. Smack in front is that huge sign on the balcony: "Trafalgar Square Pub."

Vic sees it. "Oh," he says. Real soft.

This ain't an, "Oh, I get it," type of "Oh." This is a dumbstruck "Oh."

Cheri helps him from the car. Everybody is laughing and clapping. Vic is speechless. He is led across the street to the door of the bar. Louie, an old friend and employee, stands there as a greeter. He's decked out in the red costume of a yeoman warder from the Tower of London. Yeomen warders are popularly known as "Beefeaters." Louie is openly gay. Vic almost chokes up a lung at the joke. He's in tears as they bring him inside.

The place is packed to the gunwales. Just about everyone is dressed or draped in English colors: red, white, and blue—same as America— but what with all the "pip-pips" and "wot-wots" and "I say, old beans" being tossed out, it's pretty clear that today the colors are supposed to be English.

Vic shuffles into the music room. He's seeing everything at once. It's too much. He starts gulping air. Somebody hands him a drink. Down the hatch. Cheri hands him another one. He gives her a grateful look.

By now, I am on stage, guitar in hand, wearing a three-piece suit, bowtie, watch chain, and a bowler hat. I'm figuring this looks English. I'm trying to lead people in singing an English song, but since I don't know any, this is not my strong suit. I sing, "There'll Always Be an England." The crowd answers, "While there's a USA." I'm trying to think what to do next, when the crowd parts like the Red Sea. Four guys from New York come through the gap toward me. Artie Claudio, who is Irish by association, is their spokesman. He looks real serious.

"We've got an important telex here from England. We got to read it."

"Ah. You're just in time," I say, "Come on up, and fire away." I step back.

They climb up on stage. Artie comes forward to the microphone. He whacks it a couple of times.

"This thing working?" He glares out at the room. "Okay, then. Shuddup!" he instructs. "Here it is. Listen up! It says, '10 Downing Street, London. July 20. My dear Victah—Her Royal Highness, Queen Elizabeth and Prince Philip join me and the Queen Mum in wishing you a happy birthday. All is forgiven. We are glad you've seen the light. Welcome back to the fold. Much Love, Maggie Thatcher. PS, Have a toddy on me.'" He finishes off with three "hip-hip hoorays," a toast to Vic, and one to the pub. Then he raises his glass and roars "Arrgh!" into the mike. The crowd replies, "Arrgh!" Their duty done, the boys make for the bar.

Victor is watching all of this. His eyes look like somebody else is driving, and he's chuckling. I don't like the looks of this. He points to himself. I guess this means he wants to talk. I come back to the microphone.

"Ladies and gents, the man of the hour would like to say a few words. But first, we've got to do this." I start singing, "Happy Birthday to you," and the crowd joins in.

Now I'm really taking my life in my hands here because there are few things that Vic hates more than this song. I don't think he'll try any funny stuff, though. Too many witnesses.

We finish the song with lots of clapping and yelling. Vic gets back-slapped toward the stage. He is shooting laser beams at me with his eyes. I smile, a little uneasy, and reach out to shake his hand and help him up. He takes it in a grip that would crack walnuts. He pulls me toward him and tries to whisper in my ear, but the mike is in the way. So over the sound system come the first words he's spoken since he got here.

"You're dead! You hear me? Dead!"

The room explodes with applause and a lot of "Arrgh's!" This snaps him out of it, and he lets go of me. He motions for them to pipe down. He clears his throat.

"Holey Moley!" he says. "Pretty good joke. Pretty expensive joke, too! You got me! You got me good! But I want youse to remember—I know where all of youse live! You think I'm kiddin'? Hah! Seriously, all I really want to say is t'anks, and 'Up the Republic,' and God bless America!"

There's a big ovation when, in his own key, Vic starts singing "God Bless America." The crowd roars and takes up the song in their own keys as he steps back among them.

The night was endless—in a good way. There was lots of singing and playing by lots of musicians. If we didn't do every song that was ever written, we came close. There was a lot of laughter, a lot of catching up and there was even a little more drinking. It was like old home week for Victor, since he hadn't seen some of these people in years. Of course, he told every one of them, "You're dead." But I don't think he ever followed through.

So, let's say one fine day, you're in Kevin Barry's, and the evening is running down, and by chance, you bump into one of the old timers. You ask if he was there on "English Sunday." He asks, "You sure want to hear about it?"

You nod.

He says, "Buy me a drink first, and have one yourself."

You do this.

He takes a slug, shakes his head, and says, "Okay. Listen. Here's what really happened."

Then he launches into some crazy story. And it might be accurate. Then again, it might not. After all, time tends to blur things, particularly when they were blurry to begin with.

DIE FLEDERMAUS
UND DIE FELINES

Batman

Seamus Kennedy

I was booked to give a concert in Luzerne County Community College in Hazleton, PA in March 2001. It was the second time I'd done the gig, and a very pleasant one it was. LCCC is a delightful little rural campus on extremely picturesque grounds in North Central PA. It has a wonderful concert hall (actually a lecture hall with theater-style seating), excellent acoustics, and no restricted sight lines. There's a nice feel of intimacy with an audience of about 300 souls, enhanced by tastefully subdued lighting. The organizers of the concert wanted to have a Pre-Saint Patrick's Day show in the month of March, hence the presence of yours truly.

I arrived in Hazleton at about 4 p.m., and went to the hotel where the college folks had booked a room for me. The performance was to begin at 7:30, and since the venue was only fifteen minutes away, there was plenty of time for me to check in, shite, shave, shower, shampoo, shine my shoes, and shovel in some grub before show time. And to practice my alliteration.

I like to arrive at gigs at least an hour and a half early to set up my sound equipment, do a sound check, tune my guitar, arrange my CD sales table, and change into my work-clothes, or as some of my more cynical colleagues refer to them, the "clown suit."

Now, this particular gig also has a little wine and cheese and canapé reception beforehand, for the college VIPs and alumni attending the concert, to which the artiste is also invited. So at 6:30, when I had finished my setup and donned the motley, I wandered in to partake of their largesse and to schmooze. A little white wine (but no cheese! Milk products coat the vocal-cords with mucus and make the first four or five songs in a show more of an exercise in polite throat-clearing and gentle off-mike loogie-hawking than a musical interlude), some baby carrots, a few broccoli florets, and a couple of crackers for a balanced diet, and I dived into the glad handing.

"Hello! Good evening, glad you could come. Yes, I'm looking forward to the show. So nice to see you again. You have a request? Sure,

I'd be delighted to sing it for you. Yes, indeed, I have a new CD. It's on sale here tonight." Until at last it's time to go on stage.

The rest of the audience is already seated in the auditorium when the reception folks stroll in and take their seats. A lady from the organizing committee steps up to the microphone to make a few opening remarks and to introduce this evening's performer. That's my cue.

I start off with "Whiskey in the Jar," stopping the song to teach the audience the 1, 2, 3, 4; 1, 2; 1 clapping rhythm, and getting a few laughs with their initial ineptitude. I good naturedly single out some poor devil with no sense of rhythm at all, and have the audience teach him how it's done. It works! They're laughing, clapping, and really getting into the spirit of things. A few non-threatening jokes:

Murphy comes home from work and finds his wife crying her eyes out in the kitchen. "What's the matter? Why are you crying?" he asks. "I made dinner for you, and the dog ate it." "There, there," says Murphy, "don't cry. I'll get you another dog."

"Mrs. Murphy was half-Irish, half-Italian. She made mashed potatoes with her feet!"

I take off the guitar, set it on the guitar-stand, and pick up my bodhrán (pronounced 'bow-rawn.') Time to display my versatility and play a different instrument, if in my hands the bodhrán can be termed a musical instrument. I use it more as a prop for a comedy routine than an instrument, although I can back a reel or a jig adequately enough. A couple of paradiddles on the head of the wee drum with the beater, and I launch into a few bodhrán jokes:

"This is a traditional Irish drum. Away out in the west of Ireland, round Connemara, where they speak Gaelic, it's made with the skin of a goat, and they call it a 'bodhrán.' Down round County Kerry, it's made with the skin of a dog, and they call it a 'bow-wow-rawn!' Up in the north of Ireland, where I come from, we call it a 'boron,' and it's made with the skin of an Englishman!"

Great response! Boffo yuks! I'm on a roll! Then I sing "Here I Am Amongst You," while accompanying myself on the bodhrán, and the crowd claps along in time. The first scream startled the bejesus out of me. I jerked my head to the right, the direction from which the scream had come, to see what was happening. I'm singing all the while and another scream rang out, then another and another. I had no idea what was happening. Ladies were waving their hands over their heads, men were ducking, and that's when I saw it.

A bat!

A bat had gotten in from outside, via an air vent, and was swooping and diving all around the room, to the consternation of the fair sex and the amusement of the males. I stopped what I'd been singing and launched into the theme music from the old "Batman" television series. *Doo-doo doo-doo doo-doo doo-doo doo-doo doo-doo doo-doo doo-doo—Batman!*

Bat squeaks, ladies shrieks, men freak, bladders leak. What a sound. Men were laughing and trying to swat the poor thing as it flew wildly around the theater trying to find a way out. It flapped right in front of my face a couple of times, and twice it landed on a wall and began to crawl upwards like a miniature Count Dracula scaling the front of his castle to get to the unfortunate Jonathan Harker. Then someone would wave at it, and away it would go again.

With the incredible sang-froid of the born big-game hunter, I put down the bodhrán and picked up the lid of my bodhrán case, which for all the world looks just like the lid of an old-fashioned, circular, ladies' hatbox, and nothing at all like the devilishly clever bat-catching device I had just invented. If that little bugger flew down at me one more time I was going to crouch like Yogi Berra behind home plate (actually, I prefer Carlton Fisk. I'm a Red Sox fan), hold the bodhrán case lid out in front of me like an oversized catcher's mitt, and just watch the wee sucker slam into it like a Pedro Martinez fastball. Then, to the admiring applause of the men, and the grateful, adoring sighs of ladies now batting their eyelashes, I would manfully, yet tenderly, transport Die Stunned Fledermaus outside to his natural habitat and release him, none the worse for his experience.

He achieved another couple of frantic laps around the room. Some of the gents had removed their jackets and were swinging them at our furry, flying friend (boy, that alliteration practice is really paying dividends), but he easily avoided their awkward lunges and circled high toward the rear of the room.

This was it! Just like Moby Dick (Moby Bat?), I felt he was preparing for a run at me, his Ahab. I could sense it. My blood was up. Slowly, I turned, and step by step, I inched to the right of the stage. I had to position myself precisely; there would be no second chance.

The bat fluttered to the ceiling, slowed his wing-beats almost to a standstill (or should I say 'fly-still?') on a non-existent thermal, as though preparing to plummet, falcon-like, upon some unsuspecting prey far below. I crouched into my catcher's stance and eased the bodhrán case lid out in front of me. Just as the toreador knows his *momento de la verdad*—his moment of truth with the bull—I now knew that this was my momento de la verdad with the bat.

I could hear nothing but my pulse whooshing in my temples. Ladies were no longer squealing. Breathless, wheezing men were no longer laughing. The bat and I stared at each other, him with his little, blind, beady eyes, and me with my larger, but equally myopic, bespectacled ones. He flapped his wings once, twice, and then commenced his dive. A half-circle to add momentum, and he came right at me like a bat out of—no, wait! Forget that! I anchored my feet, crouched, and brought the lid up to receive the Pedro Martinez fastball; instead, at the last minute, I got a fluttering Tim Wakefield knuckleball! The bat hit the brakes, skipped once or twice like a flat stone skimming on a pond, and bounced up and over the poised case. Foiled!

He flew right by my head, around the room to where someone had opened an exit door, and took off into the night for a well-deserved feed of mosquitoes.

My valiant attempt to trap the interloper did not go unrewarded, however. I received a warm round of applause for my efforts from all assembled—the stouthearted men folk and their gentle consorts, the latter with much "Oohing" and "Aahing."

But to this day, I can't understand how the bat evaded the lid of my bodhrán case while flying at top speed. It's almost as if the little son of a bitch had radar or something.

ೞೞ

Catwoman

Dennis O'Rourke

I grew up in South Boston—the Irish enclave. The accents were Boston or Irish. City Point, Carson Beach, and Castle Island. Pober's on Broadway, where my mother took us every fall for our clothes for the coming winter. I remember a lot of corduroy. I went to the Hoar school, the Bigelow and

Saint Augustine's. My family moved to the suburbs when I was ten. I romanticized Southie over the years, so it was a kick to go back and work the Quiet Man Pub near Broadway Station.

A local artist had begun a large wall painting inside the pub depicting a scene from the movie of the same name. John Wayne and Victor McLaglen were about to come to blows over McLaglen's sister, played by Maureen O'Hara. The painting remained unfinished in the year or so that I worked there, and the owner, Taz Flynn, sometimes despaired that the artist would ever get around to finishing it.

Well, it was great to be back in Southie. A few times I went down there an hour or two early, to drive around the old neighborhood—the D Street projects—remembering all the good things, mostly how young I was. I liked the bar. Taz treated me well. He was a gentleman and one of the best club owners I ever worked for. I had good crowds and they seemed to like me. One night I found myself enamored of the charms of a very pretty young lady—slim, with reddish-blond hair and green eyes. She was accompanied by a not-quite-so-vivacious or attractive girlfriend who seemed content to hover in the background observing me. We've all seen a duo like this many times—the pretty and the plain; the chick and the mother hen; the one ruled by impulse, the other by caution. To reach the *pretty*, you had to mollify or impress the *plain*. On my third night, the mother hen was conspicuous by her absence, and I sat alone with the green-eyed beauty on my breaks. Either I had passed the test, or there had been a disagreement between them. In either case, here she was, clearly signaling her intentions. Sure enough, at night's end, I was invited back to her apartment for a drink.

I broke down the equipment in record time, loaded it up in my car, and followed her back to her house. It was the middle of winter, windless, but bitter cold. We arrived at her apartment about two in the morning. The street was dead quiet—not a soul stirring anywhere. This emboldened me to leave the equipment in the car, even though it was clearly visible through the station wagon windows. My blood was up, and I decided to chance it. Right then, hauling a bunch of equipment up the stairs was not my foremost concern. I figured that if she invited me to stay the night, after the frolic I was certain was in the offing, I could go down and bring the stuff in.

The house was a typical Southie three-decker, and naturally, she lived on the third floor. I followed her up to the landing. She opened the door and ushered me in to an oppressively hot apartment. She apologized, while telling me that she did not like to be cold. I took off my coat and sat down on the couch. A cat jumped into my lap. I like cats, but I'm allergic to them, most of them, anyway. I have no explanation why some bother me and some don't. With the ones that do, I get the whole smash—itchy, watery eyes, and sneezing. Since they don't come with warning labels addressed personally to me, I quietly shooshed him away. Then I noticed two more cats, one lying on a chair across from me and another sauntering around the room. There was cat hair clearly visible on the couch. Not good. It occurred to me that even if I was invited to stay the night, I probably could not. The deed had to be accomplished quickly, and I had to get out of there.

She joined me on the couch, and we sipped whiskey and chatted. My eyes were already beginning to itch slightly, so I made the move. She was willing from the get-go, and so I rolled on top of her. Articles of clothing were removed. I was beginning to sweat, it was so hot, but I slipped her jeans off and tried to concentrate on things peachy smooth and soft. I sneezed a couple of times, and then went on with the disrobing. I lifted my nose for a quick breath of air and found myself staring straight into the yellow eyes of one of the cats, now sitting on the armrest of the couch, watching us. This was only a little disconcerting. What bothered me most at that moment was that I was beginning to have trouble breathing. I could hear myself wheezing. I had asthma as a kid, and feared I was about to have an attack, the first one in years, but I was too far gone to stop now. Off with her blouse. In our rolling about on the couch, cat hair had contrived to cling to her bra. I sneezed again. She was concerned. I assured her that I was fine.

But my chest was heavy now, and even she could hear my wheezing. My eyes itched and watered. I had to give up. My heart sank, and I sat up, gasping.

"The cats," I said to her. "I'm sorry, but I'm allergic to your cats. I've got to go."

I put on my clothes. She sat there on the couch and watched me. The cats watched me. She walked me to the door. She hadn't put her jeans or blouse back on. Mother of God, she was sexy. The center of my universe was demanding an explanation. *Hey, where are we going? Are you out of your mind? Look what we're leaving behind.* I was in mental agony, and I was cursing my bad luck and all things feline, but

86

when I kissed her good night, I could swear I saw some amusement in her eyes. I wondered if this had happened before.

I went down the stairs and found the equipment still safe in the car. I drove home with the windows cracked, and soon my breathing returned to normal, and my eyes cleared up. Once home, I poured a double scotch that proved no help, and I went to bed at last, a profoundly disappointed fella.

I looked for her in vain the next few times I worked the Quiet Man. I asked Taz about her. He had a vague idea who she was, but couldn't tell me much. I hadn't paid any attention when I followed her home, so I could not have found that three-decker again if my life depended on it.

I think about Taz and the bar and Southie, sometimes. I remember that girl's face and figure, and those green eyes. Then I think about the painting on the wall of the bar, and I wonder if that at least had a successful finish to it.

CLUBS, PUBS, DIVES, LAIRS AND HAUNTS

Of Crows, Sci-Fi Rock, and the Bells of Hell
Robbie O'Connell

In the late nineteen-seventies, I was living in Ireland in an old country house that my parents had converted to a small hotel. Unchanged for hundreds of years, the house sat at the end of a long, tree-lined driveway, surrounded by rolling green pastures. The small town of Carrick-on Suir was over a mile away, and only the distant roaring of bullocks in the surrounding fields and the cackle of the crows nesting in the ancient beech trees splintered the silence. We were so accustomed to the crows that we were oblivious to the frenzied cacophony that accompanied every sunrise. Some of our guests, however, did not share our immunity. We arose one morning to find a very irate New Yorker anxiously pacing around. He had been awake for over three hours and in desperate need of a cup of coffee. "How the hell can you people sleep with those goddamn crows?" he demanded.

We were amused by the irony of someone from a noisy city being kept awake by a few birds, but with all the talk of crows, I could not get the old Scottish ballad "Twa Corbies" out of my head. In the song, a traveler overhears a conversation between two crows about where they will find their next meal:

As I was walking all alane
I heard twa corbies making a mane—
The tane unto the tither say,
"Where shall we gang and dine the day?"

In behint yon auld fail dyke,
I wot there lies a new slain knight—
And naebody kens that he lies there,
But his hawk, his hound, and his lady fair

I could not remember the other verse, but it was something about plucking out the eyes of the knight, which is considered haut-cuisine in the bird kingdom.

Around that time, my uncles, the Clancy Brothers, asked me to join their group, and soon I was doing concert tours in the States three or four times a year. Leaving the crows behind at nine in the morning, we would spend three hours negotiating the winding roads to Shannon airport. This was followed by seven hours on the plane and another hour waiting for the bags and clearing Immigration. By the time that we got a taxi and checked into our hotel in Manhattan, we had been traveling for twelve hours. It would still be afternoon in New York, so we would nap for an hour or two and then head off to some favorite haunt of my uncles, who had lived for years in Greenwich Village. They felt at ease back in their old neighborhood, but for me, this was still a foray into a strange, new world.

Manhattan's noisy streets at rush hour, the incessant horn blowing of taxis on a rainy day, the wailing sirens, and the endless flood of pedestrians was disorienting, but somehow intoxicating at the same time. Compared to Carrick, this was pure bedlam. I was puzzled by how our New York visitor could sleep through all this craziness and yet be kept awake by the cawing of a few crows.

The brash, in your face, attitude of New Yorkers was a genuine culture shock for me. The yelling of the waiters in the coffee shops and the pushy sales pitches of the store clerks—"Look, buddy, ya want it or not?"—made the tranquil Tipperary countryside seem like a distant planet.

The typical New York pub felt alien, too. In Ireland, you would never see little piles of money all over the counter, or sawdust on the floor. Here the jukebox blared away while numerous television sets competed against each other like a technological Tower of Babel. Worse still, it seemed nobody spoke normally—everybody shouted. And then there were the unmeasured shots. Holy shit! An Irish barman would be lynched by his employer for pouring an unmeasured shot. Still, American pubs had a vibrancy missing from Irish pubs, and I soon learned to enjoy that energy.

One of our favorite haunts was a pub on 13th Street called the Bells of Hell. Malachy McCourt had once owned it, and although no longer the proprietor, he and his brother Frank were still regulars. They were my uncles' longtime friends, and while they all happily chatted about their old exploits around a big table in the front bar, I would slip into the back room to hear the live music.

90

The regular band was a duo called Turner and Kirwan. They came from Wexford, and I had first met them a few years earlier, when we each played at Liam's Irish Tavern in Framingham, Massachusetts. Their music had changed totally and no longer had a discernable Irish connection. With only a synthesizer and a guitar, they played strange, original material that I immediately dubbed "Sci-fi rock." Pierce could make the most unusual sounds on the keyboards, and Larry's guitar playing was loud and wild, but their songs appealed to me. They were fresh and clever and culled from their own experiences. I loved hearing something so new and different, and I was not alone. They had a devoted following at the "Bells," and they always packed the house.

The audience was very artsy, and for the most part, dressed in black. It was like a throwback to beatnik days, except that the music was completely different. Everyone in the audience seemed a little spaced out, and I don't think it was just the beer. No doubt, some other beatnik customs survived. And like the faithful at an old-fashioned revival meeting, they would occasionally be taken over by the spirit of the music and jump up from their seats, singing and gyrating. I was too shy to join in and was content to sit in the back and watch the show, both onstage and off. I delighted in the contrast with the world I had left that morning and realized that the strangeness of it all would soon fade. It was like that jubilation we felt as kids when we charged out of the local cinema after the matinee and galloped our imaginary horses all the way home.

On the break one night, Larry introduced me to a friend of his called Fref. I chatted with him for a while, and found that despite his strange name, he was a regular guy. Only later did Larry tell me he was a world-famous clown from the Barnum and Bailey circus. You wouldn't find that in a Carrick pub, I thought, although there was no shortage of clowns of the non-famous kind.

Hearing all the new music and the strange synthesizer sounds was like stepping into the future for me. Was this where music was going? Would it be the next big trend? It was exciting to be part of this new, musical frontier. I imagine the patrons of the Cavern in Liverpool in the early sixties must have had similar feelings. Meanwhile, in the front bar, my uncles and their friends were telling stories, joking, laughing, and reliving their glory days. There is something for everyone in the Big Apple.

Late one night at the Bells, I ran into a couple I knew from my college days, who now lived nearby. It was great to see them, and they invited me back to their apartment for a nightcap. They had a massive aquarium in their living room, teeming with scores of multi-colored fish of every shape and size. When I asked what they fed the fish I received an enigmatic smile and was told that I was just in time for the feeding ceremony.

This ritual, performed with all the formality of some ancient sacrifice, consisted of carefully emptying plastic bags of small, live fish into the tank, where the voracious residents instantly set upon them. The high priest presided over the tank as a massive churning of water and feeding frenzy followed. The larger fish first circled their prey, then with a quick flash of fins, darted at the heads of the smaller fish and sucked out their eyes. This succulent appetizer preceded the main course, in which the eyeless victims were then devoured in large chunks. I was fighting back nausea when the elusive verse of "Twa Corbies" suddenly came to mind. I started singing:

Ye'll sit on his white hause bane,
And I'll pick out his bonnie blue eye—
Wi' ae lock o' his gowden hair,
We'll theek our nest when it grows bare.

My friends looked bewildered until I told them about the story of the Carrick crows and the "Twa Corbies." We chatted on for a while, but it had been a long day for me, and pleading an early flight the next morning, I bid them goodnight and started back to my hotel.

Out on the street, I was startled to find it was already daybreak. Walking by a vacant lot, I noticed a tattered homeless man stretched out on a pile of flattened cardboard. Was he dead or just sleeping? A handwritten sign beside him read, "Need money for beer." At least he's honest, I thought as I veered into the street to pass him. Dozens of pigeons pecked at the ground all around him. I had only gone a few steps when it hit me. Pigeons. Crows. Eyes! I stopped and spun around. I tiptoed warily back, scattering pigeons from the sidewalk. I was almost too scared to look. I garnered my courage and peeked. Yes, yes, it was all right. This fallen knight still had both eyes intact.

‹3❧

The Blarneystone
and How I Got to Work There

Frank Emerson

Somerville, Massachusetts lies between Medford and Cambridge, just across the Charles River from Boston. It is an "All-America City." At both ends of the town, there are signs that say so, just as big as life. I believe the moniker is an honor. I also believe the signs are there to let people know what they are getting into as they hit the city limits. I suppose "All-America City" means that this community symbolizes America—the good parts and the bad—but mostly good. I have not been there in years myself, but I remember it as not remarkable—overall, a pleasant burg. It is probably the same today. Maybe more so, which is fair enough.

Anyway, at the time I am knocking around Somerville, there is a hotel in Union Street by the name of the Hawthorne Arms. It has seen better days. In fact, I am of the opinion that the Hawthorne Arms has seen better days right from day one. It is by no means a flophouse, but there is little danger of it getting a star or two in the Michelin Guide. The Fanucci Brothers Construction Company owns it. I think that maybe they hold onto the hotel for spare parts.

Now, in the basement of the Hawthorne Arms is a pub called the Blarney Stone—an Irish place and a very popular watering hole. Local belief has it that the Blarney Stone floats the Hawthorne Arms.

The pub is a decent-sized room with low ceilings and no windows. The decorations are minimal, and the furniture is scarred–up, but sturdy, tables and chairs. There are eight or ten stools at the bar, but it is mostly a table-service type of place—and good table service at that. The drinks are generous and cheap, which is always welcome news. There is food—after a fashion. I find that as a rule, it is not wise to order a sandwich that has a personal history, so most patrons stick to the liquids. There is a good stage, a dependable sound system, and heavy-duty Kleig lights to show off the performer and help him work on his tan. Irish folk music is featured seven nights a week. The joint reeks with atmosphere, and it does more business than you would care to shake a stick at.

Along with casual customers, there are a slew of regulars familiar with the music and show their enthusiasm. There are no reserved seats, but some folks do receive preferential treatment. One of these is a gent named Tiny Biggs.

It is a given that the table smack dab in front of the stage is Tiny's territory. Should somebody be sitting at that table when Tiny strolls in, that somebody is well advised to pick up his stuff and shift to another location, pronto. Perhaps "stroll" is not the right verb. Tiny lumbers. He is pretty good at lumbering, too, considering that although he is well shy of six feet tall, he probably goes a good third of a ton in fighting trim. I am not talking "glandular case," here. He just has these appetites, you know. Also, it is well known that, figuratively and literally, Tiny is one of the largest turf accountants and loan arrangers in the metropolitan area. Of course, Tiny Biggs is not his real name. Personally, though, I never hear anyone call him anything but Tiny Biggs, unless it is "sir"—which is probably healthy for all concerned.

Tiny is about as Irish as the Fanucci Brothers—which is to say he is not. But he is absolutely ga-ga about Irish folk music. In the Blarney Stone, he is always very friendly, very quick to stand for a round, and he loves his beer. He always has a couple of beauties with him. Usually it is Wanda and Trixi; they hang all over Tiny. He does not seem to mind this. They might even be all married up together or some such—I am not sure—but it is none of my business, at any rate.

They always stay around for the whole evening, drinking buckets of beer and singing along to everything. The more Tiny drinks and sings, the more he sweats. The odd thing is that when he sweats, he starts to take off his clothes. I have seen this ruin a performer's concentration. Tiny never gets to the full Monty, mind you, but he gets close enough to make a person squirm, believe me. However, it never occurs to anyone to suggest to Tiny that he might want to cool it on this bit. The reason this never occurs to anyone is that a good deal of money changes hands among those who wager on when Tiny will start to disrobe and how far he will go with the routine. Groceries have been bought for a month and bar tabs paid in full on the strength of one of Tiny's collar buttons. It is an intriguing contest and provides a good deal of excitement for one and all. No one is more involved in speculating than the assistant manager, who is in the know and always seems to come out very well in the speculating department.

The assistant manager is named Carlos Sans. He is from Cuba and makes for an interesting fixture in the Blarney Stone. Carlos is an average-sized, average-looking guy who is very outgoing and generally seems very happy. This is fortunate, since Carlos is a veteran of the Bay of Pigs fiasco and is known to be a rough customer when agitated or around Castroites. Carlos loves to banter with the customers, but his accent makes Desi Arnaz seem like John Guilgud. Customers are sometimes not sure what the topic of conversation is or to what they are agreeing. There is a lot of nodding that goes on. As long as Carlos is smiling, you can pretty much figure that everything is jake.

All of these goings on contribute to the unique flavor of the Blarney Stone. People are nuts over the joint and want to be there, and more importantly, be seen there. This is especially true among the Irish musicians. The place is a legitimate and well-known showcase. Everyone wants to play there. It is what is known as a 'good gig'—with one little drawback.

The top dog in the place is Jerry Fleming. Do not get me wrong—he is a nice guy. He is also very efficient, genial, and very loyal to the Blarney Stone. He treats the Blarney Stone as if he owns it—which he does not. This is the main reason the Fanucci Brothers keep him on the payroll—he is very protective of the Fanucci Brothers' interests—particularly the Fanucci Brothers' money. There is no better example of how he protects the Fanucci Brothers' money than the wages he offers the musicians—not much. The thing is—Jerry is hip to the whole situation. Irish musicians are lined up and frothing at the mouth to get a crack at the Blarney Stone stage, so he is in the driver's seat. In a nutshell, he gives the musicians two choices: take it or leave it. Of course, he does this with a smile and means no ill will. That is just the way it is.

Since the room is a good one, and Jerry is known as a stand-up guy and well liked, most of us take it. Besides, even though it is short bread, the drinks are free, and you can always pick up a few bob by getting in on the Tiny Biggs action. Sometimes you have to go along to get along.

Now when I first approach Jerry with an eye toward performing at the Blarney Stone, he turns me down flat. I am momentarily flummoxed. Then I figure he is having me on and say to him, "Right." But he seems to mean it. Now I am really flummoxed. As I have a decent reputation on the music scene, I press him for a reason. Jerry hems and haws and shifts around a little, as he likes me well enough, and does not wish me to become wounded or indignant. I tell him I will not become either of these, or even irritated, but I would very much like to hear his story. Maybe there has been a misunderstanding and we can clear it up here and now. Jerry says, "Well, okay, then," and comes clean, roughly as follows.

It seems that one night, a while back, Jerry is on his way home from his shift at the pub when he is forced to make an emergency men's room stop. On a bet, he is off the beer and booze for a few days, and is not feeling himself. As a compromise, he drinks coffee by the urn. This keeps him alert and somewhat anxious. It also results in things such as emergency men's room stops.

On this particular night, he screeches to a halt at a pub called Red Biddie's. I happen to be appearing there at the time. He races through the front door and makes a beeline for the jacks. I recall the incident well, since from my vantage on stage, I see him flash by without as much as a "How do you do." I figure that is all right because from the looks of things, Jerry is a man on a mission. Anyway, at present, I am in the middle of performing a request from the audience, so I do not have time for any "How do you do," myself.

Now the particular request I am performing is out of the ordinary. In fact, when the request comes up to me, I do not think it is an honest-to-goodness request, but a rib. However, I turn the tables on the joker since I know the song. It is none other than "Oklahoma!"—from the musical. How I know this song, I haven't a clue. Some things in life just show up. So there I am, doing "Oklahoma!" and I am going great guns altogether. I have the audience wailing away and singing like there is no tomorrow. They are especially fond of the part where we spell out the word "Oklahoma," and they give out with great big "Whoops" and "Ya-hoos" at the end. They do this over and over again, and everyone is getting a big kick out of the whole production.

As this is going on, Jerry finishes his business and elbows his way through the crowd back toward the front door. Everyone is "Whooping" and "Ya-hooing" and carrying on. I manage to catch Jerry's eye and give him a nod. He gives me a wave as he heads out the door.

"There you have it," says Jerry. "That is my reason for not hiring you at the Blarney Stone."

I am at a loss, and I ask him to explain.

Jerry heaves a big sigh and says to me, "I know you now what—about a year?"

"I guess that is about right."

"Well," he continues, "in all that time that is the only time I see your act."

"But, Jerry," I say, "I was going great guns that night! The place was going great guns, as well!"

"Oh, yes," he says back to me, "but you only do show tunes. And show tunes will just not do for the Blarney Stone."

I tell him he has made a snap judgment and that he is in error. It is no use. Jerry is hearing none of it, for everyone knows that once he gets an idea in his noggin, it is stuck there. I do some fast thinking and go for his soft spot.

"What say I do a free night at the Blarney Stone as an audition and prove to you that I have the goods?"

Jerry nods and says, "Hmm."

I can see he's warming to the idea, as the price is right.

"Let us call it a free week and you have a deal," he says.

"A week? For free? Are you out of your noodle?" I ask.

Jerry smiles. "You know the two choices you have," he says.

Well, I know when I am licked, so I agree. It just happens that he has had a cancellation the next week, and I am open, so the deal is struck.

I do the week, and I go over very well. At the end of the last night, I am packing away my guitar, and Jerry sidles over to me. He is grinning from ear to ear. "Okay, he says, "I am convinced. Good job. Let's shake on it."

He reaches out his hand, and I reach out mine. He presses something into my palm. I look down, and what is it but folding money. Not much, but it is folding money.

"What is the story with this?" I ask.

"Oh, hell," he says. "I cannot hold you to doing a whole week for nothing. I just want to see if you would stick to your word. You are on the calendar from now on—booked steady. We will work out some dates. But I have got to tell you—there is a string attached. You must play "Oklahoma!" here at least twice a week. Those people at Red Biddie's were going crazy that night!"

Over the next few years, I have a regular gig at the Blarney Stone, and everything goes fine and dandy. Whenever I get around to taking requests, Jerry always sends up "Oklahoma!" It is never far along into the song but doesn't Tiny Biggs start sweating, the bets start to get put down, Carlos starts taking all action and in the middle of it, there is Jerry, large as life with the rest of the crowd, smiling, "Whooping," and "Ya-hooing" away to beat the band.

അൃൠ

Beer Springs

Seamus Kennedy

On the road, most musicians have a quiet bar to which they can repair to get away from the travails of the business. Usually, except for the shift drink, we prefer not to drink where we work. When I was performing at Dick O'Kane's Pub in Monterey, I used to frequent a joint on Lighthouse Avenue called Beer Springs. "Joint" is too classy a word in this case. It was a low dive—lower than a dachshund's bollocks. And dirty—Lord, was it dirty. I thought the windows were smoked glass, and they were—from decades of cigarette smoke that hadn't been washed off. Not your candy-ass, wussy, low-tar, filtered cigarettes, either. And that was just on the inside.

The owner was a cranky, anti-social old cuss who only opened when he felt like it, generally around 5:00 p.m., and then he'd close down again around eleven, when he went to bed. It was a one-room, narrow, old-style neighborhood joint with a twenty-foot-long bar running down the left side of the room and about a dozen or so barstools. No other furniture. No tables or chairs. A bare wood floor scarred with hundreds of cigarette burns, a pool table, and a cue-rack hanging on the left hand wall. This was definitely not a stylish, fern-bar, pickup, meat-market for yuppies.

I liked it mainly because a beer and a shot was a buck and a half, and the owner wouldn't talk to anyone outside of, "What'll you have?" The few other customers I saw in the place were mainly curmudgeonly old bastards like the owner, or young migrant laborers from Mexico and Central America who found the prices just right for their limited budgets. They'd play pool, smoke, and drink, while the old coots sat at the bar, nursed their beers and shots, and communicated (if at all) in monosyllabic grunts.

One evening, I had come in for a couple before heading over to O'Kane's for dinner and work, when a sign tacked on the wall caught my eye. It was a single 8" X 11" sheet of paper, crudely hand-lettered in Magic Marker which read: *No More Ecuadorians Will Be Served 'Til I Find Out Who Shit In The Wastebasket.*

Now that's what I call a bar.

∞

The Soap Creek Saloon
Robbie O'Connell

What do you do when you are middle of a tour and you have a couple of nights off, but not enough time to make it worthwhile going home and coming back? You look for a "filler gig." That's what we call a show you would not normally want to do, but which beats sitting in your hotel room staring at a television. More often than not, you get a bad sound system and a tough crowd. You would be much better off watching reruns of Seinfeld for the umpteenth time. Once in a while, though, it turns out to be something totally unexpected.

During one US tour with the Clancy Brothers, we had a few free nights in New York City, and our agent found us a good-paying filler gig. We agreed to do it and thought no more about it. Then the contract and directions arrived at our hotel. Our destination was a bar called the Soap Creek Saloon in a remote, unheard-of corner of New Jersey. We joked about the name and wondered if we should wear cowboy hats for the occasion. Other than the address, we had no information about the place, and our expectations were not high.

We crossed the mighty Hudson and headed into the sunset as all good cowboys should. We drove for a few hours, making several wrong turns, but we finally reached the town we were looking for, if you could call it that. We were in the middle of what appeared to be a sprawling industrial estate. It felt like a scene from Kafka's nightmarish novel "Amerika." The directions were useless. We could not find any street with the name we were looking for, or even one that sounded remotely like it. We even broke the golden rule of the male driver, stopping several times to ask for directions, but no one seemed to have heard of the Soap Creek Saloon. This was not a good sign.

We checked our watches, wondering if we would make it by show time. It was already 8:00 p.m. Crossing an old railway line, we arrived in a dilapidated area that looked like it had barely survived Armageddon. Suddenly, there it was. A run-down, neighborhood tavern with a broken Budweiser sign in its last death throes, weakly emitting its final neon flickers. To our great surprise, however, the parking lot was full of cars and pick-up trucks, and as we unloaded the instruments, we could hear the jukebox blaring the Clancy Brothers Greatest Hits above the babble of the raucous crowd inside. At least we had a full house.

The owner, a brawny Irishman named Jack, was waiting at the door. "Thank God ye made it, boys," he shouted. "I was starting to think ye wouldn't show. But it's all right; ye're only fifteen minutes late."

Our request for a dressing room or a place to tune up met with a look of incomprehension, but after some consultation, we were shown to a narrow liquor closet about the size of a horsebox. Trying to unpack and tune the instruments amid the cases of booze and kegs of beer was like an old Marx Brothers' routine. An impatient Jack stuck his head in and asked if we had our sweaters, the white Aran fisherman sweaters that were the Clancy Brothers' trademark. Tom pulled his sweater from his bag and held it aloft. We asked about a sound check.

"Ah, don't worry about that," he said. "As long as you have the sweaters, it'll be fine."

We insisted we had to do a sound check, but he assured us that all we had to do was get up on the stage, wearing the sweaters, and everything would be "grand." By now, the impatient, beer-swilling crowd was giving us the slow handclap.

"To hell with it; let's go," Tom Clancy said, pulling on his sweater like a soldier girding his loins for battle. He was always the most anxious to get on stage. Standing next to him in the wings of a theatre while we were being introduced was precarious. With the stance of a boxer about to enter the ring, elbows pulled back, and barrel chest puffed out with enthusiasm, he reminded me of a greyhound ready to spring from the trap. Before the introduction was even finished, he would catapult onto the stage. I was always terrified that an unintended jab from his sharp elbow would pulverize my guitar.

The stage was tiny but we found a few microphones on rusty stands and took a minute to adjust them and make sure they were switched on. Meanwhile, the audience roared, whooped, and hollered. I never saw such a pumped-up crowd. Bobby and I banged out the introductory chords to "Brennan on the Moor," our usual opening song. The second we opened our mouths to sing, the whole place instantly burst into song with us. It was like a massive, drunken karaoke convention. Not only did they sing on every chorus, but they sang *every* line of *every* verse, as well. And it wasn't just the first song. It was every song, all night long. We were bewildered at first, but we soon began to enjoy it, and as they matched us song for song, we matched them beer for beer. What else could we do?

By the end of the show, it was hard to tell the performers from the audience. It was one big, merry sing-along. Tom invited people up on stage to have their pictures taken and kept them there to finish the show with us. Jack, the owner, flashed a satisfied smile in all directions. When it was over, we had to refuse dozens of offers of drinks and undying friendship. Several of the guys insisted on carrying our instruments to the car and seeing us off. A big gang of them gathered outside the door and whooped and hollered again as we pulled out of the parking lot.

We drove in silence for a while, trying to fathom what had just happened, until at last, in a voice that only a former Shakespearean actor could muster, Tom proclaimed, "So *that* was the Soap Creek Saloon."

ᏨᏌᏅᎤ

Cash the Check

Dennis O'Rourke

There was a joint in western Massachusetts that had a dicey reputation. I'd heard stories that the owner was a bit of a wacko and that there had even been a shotgun blast through the bar window one night. I avoided it. But Leo and I were hard pressed for work one week, and when an agent called with a weekend gig there, we grabbed it. We drove out and rented a hotel room. We played. On both nights, the place was nearly empty. Not even the owner showed. The few kids there couldn't wait for us to take a break, and then they were up at the jukebox. "Billie Jean" played over and over. We were in a gloom on-stage.

When we got back to the hotel on Saturday night, I sat on the bed and looked at the check. I thought about how empty that room had been on a weekend. "Leo," says I. "I think it might behoove us to dig in here, stay an extra day, and get down to this bank first thing Monday morning." He grew concerned. "Den, that's another forty bucks out of our pay."

"I know, but I got a bad feeling about this."

We spent Sunday rehearsing in the room, watching TV, treated ourselves to a nice dinner, and turned in early. We were at the bank the next morning as the manager turned the key. I marched up to a teller's window and placed the check and my license in front of her. She picked it up, and her face betrayed recognition.

"Have you ever been to this place?" I asked.

"Not lately," she said.

She punched in some numbers, and her face grew a slight smile. She began to count out the money. When she was done, I looked her square in the eye and said, "We got here just in time, didn't we?"

Her eyebrow went up like a jump rope and stopped. She inclined her head in my direction, smiled, and returned to her work. We left the bank with the cash.

CREW

Matt Talbot's

Seamus Kennedy

The Beggarmen were now three. Yes, Tom O'Carroll and I had taken a new partner, one Patsy Whelan, instrumentalist extraordinaire, from Bal-lyfermot, Dublin. Not that Tom was "ordinaire"—far from it. But Patsy's skills on fiddle, guitar, and mandolin gave us a depth we had not previously enjoyed. Now we could play reels, jigs, hornpipes, and other fiddle pieces, Irish and American, as well as our pretty extensive repertoire of songs, and it freed Tom from carrying the entire instrumental load of the Beggarmen. He no longer had to take off the guitar and put on the banjo, lay down the banjo, and take up the mandolin, set the mandolin down to play a slow air on the whistle, stick the whistle in his pocket, and take up the guitar again. He and Patsy could cut the instrument swapping by fifty percent. I, on the other hand, played guitar only, sang, and told jokes to drunks while the two boyos did all the work.

And Patsy could fiddle. "The Mason's Apron," "Ragtime Annie," "The Four-poster Bed," and the showstopper, the "Orange Blossom Special"; he really tore into the music with Tom's sparkling five-string banjo picking right behind him. And for once, we found ourselves actually practicing and rehearsing. Imagine.

Well, we'd been playing pubs around the Boston area for several years—the Black Rose, the Village Coach House, the Blarney Stone (both the one in Dorchester and the sister ship in Somerville), with the occasional foray into the hinterlands of Framingham, to Liam's Irish Tavern, and even to the boondocks of Lowell, Lawrence, Springfield, and believe it or not, New Hampshire. With the addition of Patsy, gigs were plentiful, and things were looking good.

The O'Malley brothers opened a new pub in South Boston. It was called Matt Talbot's.

Matt Talbot was a wretched drunkard in Dublin around the turn of the twentieth century. Here, in more politically correct times, he'd be called an alcoholic. But back then, he was a rummy, a drunk, a wino, a dipsomaniac, a slave to the bottle, and a martyr to the drink, who was constantly getting soused, langers, mouldy, shit-faced, pie-eyed, stupid, steaming, vomiting, falling-down drunk. And abusive, to boot. Eventually, he became elevated to the status of derelict.

In school, we were told horror stories of Matt Talbot's drinking, and how it had reduced him to subhuman behavior, wallowing in all sorts of filth and degradation with other unspeakables, the lowest of the low. Nothing you wouldn't hear today at an ordinary AA meeting. But, since this was back in the days before AA, Al-Anon, Al-Ateen, self-help, or twelve-step programs, poor old Matt had to do it all himself. He stopped drinking, became very religious, and started going back to the Church and the sacraments. A daily communicant, he began to fast (Not that there was a pick of meat on him. There was more beef on a butcher's apron.), and to do penance for his years of intoxication. Any money he could get went to the poor and less fortunate.

And he began to mortify his flesh.

He became a flagellant and compounded this religious discipline by wrapping chains around his body á la Jacob Marley. These things, on top of the malnutrition and the ravages of the demon rum, soon took their toll. Matt up and died, and they found his body decomposing in a squalid, Dublin tenement. At first, it seemed the chains had eaten into his dead flesh, but it was later surmised that in life he had wrapped them so tightly that his living tissue had grown *around* the chains in much the same way that the branches of a bush will push through a fence or ivy will curl through a trellis.

Naturally enough, people began to think of him as a saint.

The Church used him as an example of how God can turn around even the most degenerate of souls if they want it badly enough and are willing to make the necessary physical and spiritual sacrifices. People began to pray to Matt to intercede with God on behalf of loved ones who were on the slippery slope of the odd tipple. He was nominated for beatification, the first step to becoming a saint.

The O'Malley Brothers decided to honor Matt Talbot by naming a pub after him. And the Beggarmen were hired to play there.

It was a small, pleasant place with young Irish and Irish American clientele that liked its Clancy Brothers, Dubliners, and Christy Moore. The Guinness poured very nicely, thank you, and all in all, it was a fine place to perform. Friday nights in any bar can be crowded and hectic, with space at a premium, so folks tend to flock tightly together. It's a frotteurs' paradise, not that I would know.

Well, this particular Friday night, the place was hopping, full of kids having a good time. They were into the music, singing along with the songs they knew and clapping along with the up-tempo ones they didn't. Tom, Patsy, and I were cooking. We were hot. We flew through a set of reels, and the crowd started stomping. Then we played a few jigs. Some folks got up from their chairs then and began to perform that peculiar form of Terpsichore that resembles nothing more than a marionette getting its strings cut one by one. They hop up and down in place and call it an Irish jig. You see it a lot on St. Patrick's Day, and it's as much like a real Irish jig as my arse is like a Steinway piano.

I must mention one important detail. Although Matt Talbot's was a fine place to play, it had no stage. So we were on the floor—mike stands, amplifiers, instruments, and all. Be that as it may, and I'm not sure that it ever was, the crowd began to stand up in front of us and form a circle in order to do some class of a square dance or a céilí set. We fiddled, picked, and strummed furiously as the dancers started to bounce up and down, hands flailing wildly. I thought, "That's not Irish—that's Scottish dancing."

Two very attractive young lassies in their early twenties broke into the middle of the circle and began the dance move known as "advance and retire." That's when you take a couple of steps up to your partner, face him or her for a couple of beats, and then take a couple of steps backwards, away from said partner. The music kept going, and they went round the circle, advancing and retiring with everyone in the group.

Then they started to remove their garments.

Now, I don't know the céilí or square dancing term for this, but it certainly isn't "advance and retire," or "allemande left," or "promenade right." The crowd started clapping louder, hooting and hollering and shouting all manner of encouragement, which caused the young ecdysiasts to shed more garments along with their inhibitions. As they gyrated in the middle of the circle, flinging blouses, socks, jeans, and caution to the wind, the crowd closed ranks and because we were floor level, we, the musicians, the most important part of this entire show— all musicians will tell you that—couldn't see a damn thing.

Was Matt Talbot watching in horror from on high?

A bra flew up in the air, and then another—and still we couldn't see the girls. Patsy was standing on tiptoe, fiddling to beat the band and screaming into his mike, "Sit down! For Jaysus' sake, sit down! We can't see!"

A pair of panties soared ceiling-wards. Tom, ever polite, ever the gentleman, still picking the five-string, was yelling, "Ah, c'mon now, give the band a chance! Please! Fair's fair. Please!"

The other pair of panties followed.

I shouted at a wall of backs, without missing a chord or a beat, trying to buck-leap to see over their heads, "Sit down, fuck yez! Sit down, you assholes! Let us see! Bastards!" Still we kept playing. And still, the crowd kept dancing, clapping, and shouting. God, it was hot in there.

Then the ladies started to reverse the procedure. As their clothes were tossed to them in the center of the ring, they started putting them back on, and within a few minutes, they were once more fully clad. The Beggarmen finished the set. The audience cheered, gave the girls a big round of applause, and dispersed back to their tables for a well-deserved, cool, refreshing beverage. A couple of folks came up to us and said, "You guys are great. That's the best dance music we've ever heard."

Tom, Patsy, and I went to the bar for a few pints, to commiserate and bemoan our wretched luck. We started wondering what we could have done, short of building a stage in three seconds, like Wile E. Coyote, to enhance our view of the proceedings.

I said, "Did it occur to you two that if we had stopped playing, the crowd would've broken up, and we'd have seen everything?"

Tom and Patsy each took a sip of his pint, leaving a pencil-thin Guinness mustache, looked at each other, looked back at me, shook their heads, and in unison said, "No."

⊂ॐ∾

Canaries, Crubeens and Come-All-Yes
Robbie O'Connell

I was wandering around at a folk music festival recently when I heard the unmistakable, strident wail of a bombarde, the ancient Breton pipe that sounds like an oboe on steroids. The piercing sound took me back instantly to a little pub in County Kilkenny, Ireland and a marvelous summer's night we had in the late 1970s.

Power's pub was one of the last of a dying breed of authentic Irish pubs that served as the center of the universe for those who were fortunate enough to live nearby. It was a pub, grocery, hardware store, living room, and community center, all rolled into one. The ersatz Irish pubs found now in every major city on the planet may strive to recreate the atmosphere of such an establishment, but they can never hope to match the real thing. Besides, I have never seen one that had a brown canary or crubeens, but more about that later.

The pub, hardly more than two hundred square feet, was one of a handful of small buildings that comprised the village of Tullahought. Divided by a partition with a swing door, one side was a compact shop with a six-foot-long wooden counter, which also doubled as the bar; the other side was the pub area, where we would sit and talk, sing come-all-ye's, and play music. The shelves behind the counter contained a vast assortment of domestic, recreational, and agricultural necessities that belied the apparent limitations of the space. Whatever was not in view would, upon request, magically appear from beneath the counter. Unusual requests would initiate a lengthy expedition into the mysteriously dark back room that either culminated in success or an apologetic, "I know we used to have that, but I don't know what became of it." Then, as if the passing of time would shake it loose from its hiding place while another pint was poured, "I'll look again in a minute."

On one shelf, next to the Kellogg's cornflakes and Daz detergent, just above the Castrol GTX Motor Oil and the replacement bicycle tube, was a stack of Hohner harmonicas. My request once for a closer look at one resulted in a fruitless search through eight or nine empty boxes. It appeared they had all been loaned out in the frenzy of one of many great sessions and never returned; a hidden blessing for the unknowing buyer of a used harmonica.

Canaries are usually green or yellow, but the bird perched in the cage in Power's pub was a tobacco brown. He owed the incomparable hue of his plumage to years of cigarette and pipe smoke, which hung from the ceiling every night like the mist rising from an upside-down pond at dawn. The walls and ceiling also had a chestnut-colored sheen, like the patina on an old portrait of someone's long dead ancestor.

His cage hung from the ceiling near the back door of the tiny pub. A red Sacred Heart lamp hung above the fireplace, its scarlet glow illuminating not only the cage, but also the mantelpiece with the pictures of Pope John XXIII, JFK, and Eamon DeValera, the ubiquitous Holy Trinity of 1960s Ireland.

I often wondered about the prevalence of Sacred Heart lamps in Irish homes and pubs. I recently discovered that, back in the thirties and forties, they had been used to entice the wary residents of rural Ireland, not known for embracing change of any kind, to subscribe to the newfangled service of electricity. The Catholic Church, like an "Irish Taliban" in those days, ruled every aspect of Irish life and no doubt promoted the adoption of this holy device. If you got "the electric in," you could bask in the sacred and perpetual red glow of the holy lamp. Occasions of sin would find it hard to flourish in such a godly light. Seemingly, this was irresistible to the devout people of rural Ireland.

In a country where class distinction was sometimes akin to the caste system of India, Power's pub was a great leveler. Farm laborers, judges, musicians, accountants, poets, tinkers—everyone who walked through the door fell under the spell of Margaret's old-fashioned hospitality and maternal concern. Social standing meant nothing. Margaret and her brother Jim, both unmarried, were the proprietors and staff. Margaret loved a good music session or a singsong. As soon as the greetings were dispensed with and the pint was on the counter, the first question was always, "Will ye sing a few songs tonight?" After a couple of pints and a bit of catching up on the local gossip, we would bring in the instruments and settle into the corner beneath the canary cage. Many a night, when Margaret knew instinctively that the session would go on into the wee hours, she would slip away for a few minutes to boil up a big pot of "crubeens." Known in polite circles as pig's trotters, crubeens needed to be boiled for about four hours. They were greasy, hairy, and revolting to look at, but they were a godsend after seven or eight pints of Guinness.

We'd sing and play, talk and drink, oblivious to the passage of time until Margaret decided it was time for us to go. Officially, closing time was 11:00 p.m. in winter and 11:30 p.m. in summer. In reality, it depended on the whereabouts of Sergeant Hurley, a spectral figure from the Waterford city Garda Siochana station. Not since Cromwell ravaged the area in the mid-1600s had any man been as reviled as Hurley, and as deservedly so. He terrorized every licensed pub within a thirty-mile radius of the city. Like the Viking raiders of old, this killjoy struck suddenly and decisively and then just as quickly disappeared, leaving behind the carnage of unfinished pints and the smoldering remains of abandoned cigarettes.

Legally, pub patrons had twenty minutes after closing time to finish their drinks and vacate the premises. Hurley would lurk in convenient dark shadows outside the pub and bide his time until twenty-one minutes had passed. Then, like a hawk menacing a mouse, he would swoop. The "found-ons," as the drinkers were called, were summoned to appear in court, and usually received a small fine—no great penalty. The consequences for the publican, on the other hand, were far more severe. A hefty fine and an endorsement on the license were the usual punishment. A third endorsement meant the permanent loss of the publican's license, an economic catastrophe for the owner and a social disaster for the drinker.

Margaret had already received one endorsement and lived in terror of another, so reports of Hurley's activities and appearances were the number one topic of conversation. Certain patrons would swear that they had it on excellent authority that Hurley was sick or gone on holiday. Others claimed to have received a phone message that he had been seen only twenty minutes before in a far-flung region of the county.

That would ease fears a little, but there was still the threat of a raid by the local gardai from Carrick. Generally, they were more civil and gave a five-minute warning for the house to be cleared. If the evacuation were prompt, the publican would only receive a stern warning. However, the later the hour, the less civil they would be, and if caught "in flagrante" pouring pints, the owner would most likely receive a summons to appear before the circuit court judge.

One night, I took a couple of Breton musicians—Yves, a bagpiper, and Gwenael, a bombarde player—to Power's for a session. They were part of the official delegation from Tregunc in France, who were visiting my town, Carrick-on-Suir, for a town-twinning ceremony. Anyone who has ever heard bagpipes up close knows they were not designed to be played indoors. However, the bombarde, as its name suggests, is even louder. It makes the bagpipes seem like a whisper.

When I introduced my friends to Margaret as French musicians, she insisted they bring their instruments in for a few tunes. In vain, I tried to explain to her that they were incredibly loud, but she insisted that would not be a problem. Within a few minutes, the walls were vibrating and the stunned customers were ordering more pints to buttress the assault on their ears.

After a while, it did not seem so bad. Maybe we all went a little deaf after the first onslaught, or maybe the sound seemed more manageable with the extra pints and the increased heart rate. A mighty session ensued, with songs and conversation providing occasional aural relief.

The men's room or "the jacks," as it was commonly known in country pubs, usually consisted of a whitewashed wall in the back yard with a narrow channel at the bottom, which the plentiful flow of rain kept hygienic. When I rose to go out to the yard, I noticed that the birdcage appeared vacant. That was odd. Had the canary managed to escape? Upon closer inspection, I discovered the poor bird stretched flat on his back in the bottom of the cage, his two feeble legs sticking up like twigs. He was stone dead. The bombarde must have been like a nuclear explosion beneath his cage. My first impulse was to try to revive him, but he was beyond help. Having spent his life in the glow of the sacred heart lamp, there could be no doubt that he had gone to a better place. I decided that discretion was called for and the next morning would be time enough for his sad fate to be discovered.

The session continued uninterrupted and now and then, a tantalizing whiff of boiled bacon drifted out from the bubbling pot of crubeens in the kitchen. It must have been well after midnight when the door opened and in strolled a uniformed garda. He silently glared at the occupants. I felt panic rise in my chest. Margaret had not noticed him yet. Like a stage garda with his thumbs tucked into his tunic to intimidate, he marched in like a soldier on parade. Slowly and deliberately, he advanced through the crowded room, a wave of panic spreading before him. Suddenly, there was a mass exodus for the back and front door. Pints were abandoned in the rush to escape. Margaret and Jim frantically picked up glasses and bottles and shoved them under the counter. In less than a minute, we were all outside in the street.

From the squad car parked across the street, another garda proceeded to the premises. Some of the more affluent scurried to their cars, while the car-less and more intoxicated, now on safe ground, stayed to observe the raid. The more experienced among us, pints hidden beneath our coats, whispered the good news. "It's only the Carrick guards, not Hurley. She'll probably get off with a warning."

After a few minutes, both policemen reappeared and ordered everyone to clear off home unless they wanted to be arrested. We began to disperse, but took our time and watched as the police car headed back to Carrick. As soon as the car lights disappeared over the hill, the regulars turned and headed back towards the pub. We had to make sure that Margaret was all right. We huddled outside the door for a few minutes until she opened it a crack. She appeared shaken.

"Are they gone yet?" she asked.

"What did you get?" someone enquired.

"They left me off with a warning," she answered. Congratulations were uttered all round, and several people sat on the benches outside the door.

Those with drinks removed them from beneath their coats while those without looked on enviously. Someone actually had the gall to ask, "Any chance of a large bottle, Margaret, just to calm the nerves?"

"In the name of God, do ye think I'm mad?" came the reply.

"But they're gone now; you can just slip it out the door," he pleaded.

The door was emphatically shut. We were all silent as we pondered the meaning of this abrupt retreat. A few minutes passed in silent anticipation. It was like waiting for the election of a pope. Would it be white smoke or black? Some of the locals took the delay as a positive sign while those of us from further a field were ready to admit defeat.

Then the door opened a crack again, and a steaming dish of crubeens was thrust out to eager hands.

"No use wasting these," Margaret announced. "At least this is legal."

Within five minutes, the music was playing again, and the bottles and pints began to slip out through the partially open door. Even if the guards came back now, they could do nothing. The door would be shut. There was no law against eating crubeens out in the public street.

I decided it was be a good time to break the sad news about the canary, even though it didn't seem all that important in the wake of the raid. A few people laughed, and one sensitive soul muttered, "Ah the poor little fucker." It was decided that this feast of crubeens and pints would serve as his wake, and we continued to eat, drink, and talk in his honor until the first red streaks of dawn appeared in the lightening sky.

Pubs like Powers, once found all over rural Ireland, disappeared quickly in the "television" age. As Ireland dragged itself into the twentieth century, turf fires were replaced by central heating; the soft murmur of real conversation gave way to the brash jangle of commercials, and the red glow of the Sacred Heart lamp gave way to the flickering television screen endlessly repeating football matches and cop shows. The modern, impersonal lounge bar with its neon lights, red Naugahyde booths, and Formica-topped tables had arrived. No more could you hear the shy rendition of a local song, or a sad, slow air played on a battered tin whistle. No canaries, no crubeens, and no come-all-ye's.

CREO

Clean Cabbage in the Bucket

Frank Emerson

This one particular Saturday night, I am sitting at the bar of a joint called The Bucket. I do not wish to tell you what city I am in, for reasons that will become clear sooner than later. It is my first visit to this watering hole, and I am drinking a cocktail by my lonesome. Now generally, I do not go in for this sort of caper, as I believe that when a person drinks cocktails by his lonesome, he is in bad company. However, I have a good reason; I am in a very low state. I am lower down than Billy Barty's bellybutton, lower than the East River when the tide is out, which is to say, I am not in the happy-go-luckiest of moods. Since this condition is often known to be more contagious than the mumps, I figure it best not to be around too many people. This is only common courtesy.

It turns out that the saloon is just what the doctor ordered. Although the place is not new, but it seems The Bucket has not yet grasped the concept of paying customers.

Saturday night in the pub business is usually considered the big night of the week, and yet I am alone at the bar, except for one citizen at the far end. It looks like he has been here for some time now. There is an empty glass and a crumpled pack of smokes in front of him. He is slumped over the bar, his head turned sideways on crossed arms and cutting Z's like there is no tomorrow. He has worked up a nice drool puddle and seems to be very much at home in his surroundings. With several "ah-hems" and "excuse me's," I manage to coax the bartender away from his book to take my order. Now, I own up to the fact that ordinarily, I, too, find the on-going saga of Archie and Jughead to be mighty riveting stuff, but there is a time and place for everything, and at this time, I wish to purchase a cocktail in this place.

Well, I finally get my drink. I light a cigarette and take a gander around the room. It is not a bad-sized place. There are forty or so tables scattered around and about, but it looks like thirty-five of them are dead empty. The in-use tables are strictly boyfriend-girlfriend situations, all cozy, nuzzley, and such.

In a far corner, on a well-lit, triangle-shaped stage, there is a fellow on a stool, playing guitar and giving out with Irish ditties into a microphone. As I listen to him, I think he is not half-bad.

I am of two minds. Though I am definitely marked down as being very much in favor of cozy nuzzling between boyfriends and girlfriends, I am also in the business of giving out with Irish ditties myself. Consequently, I am feeling sorry for this fellow who warbles his lungs out on tunes while the lovey-dovey couples at the tables do not give two hoots about his tunes, his lungs, or any other part of him. They are in the midst of "Of course, I will respect you in the morning," so I have to admit it stands to reason that Irish tunes about war and famine and English bad guys and such probably do not rank high in their plans for the evening's hi-jinks. Even though I think they are being plumb rude to him, it does not seem to bother the guy on stage. He just goes from ditty to ditty to ditty as easy as one, two, three. The fellow has spunk; I give him that, but being as how this is really none of my never-mind, I put the whole scene on the back burner and swivel around to the bar. I start to ponder my own circumstances, and how, on a Saturday night, I happen to be on my lonesome drinking cocktails in The Bucket.

At present, I find myself at liberty. This is not to say that I am free to go bowling or take in the ballet, which, incidentally, I do not do even on a bet. "At liberty" is a hip, music way of saying, "At present I do not have any gig whatever." For that matter, "gig" is a hip music way of saying, "Employment playing music in order to earn some cabbage." In the real world, this is what is known as a "paying job." What is more, I do not have any gig whatever for the next whole month. This means there is no cabbage coming in—which is what puts me in this low state. How I come to be at liberty is because a fire breaks out in this flea-bag of a joint on Porter Street, where I am performing for the past week, and am booked for the month ahead.

This information comes my way only about five hours ago, when I get a phone call from the owner of the joint. At first, I am stunned. To get a phone call from an owner is out of the ordinary, but I figure maybe he has a special song request and wishes to give me time to learn it. I am way off the mark. He does not have a request, but instead, proceeds to bellyache about his cabbage situation. I think nothing of this at first, since owners are always bellyaching about their cabbage situations. As he whines away, I figure he is going to ask me not to cash my paycheck, which I am due to get at the end of my twist tonight, for a few days. After you have been around this game a while, you find that this is not an uncommon request from an owner. Sometimes he robs Peter, temporarily, to pay Paul. The next week, it is the other way around. Usually it works out okay, so I am not alarmed. However, in this case, I am way off the mark yet again. Twice in the same phone call. A new record.

It seems that because of one thing or another—such as the ponies and the doggies and professional baseball teams, all of which he has made unofficial investments in, but none of which function as he bets they will function—this owner finds himself to be very low in the scratch department. This gets my attention, because I know that, dollars to doughnuts, his state of affairs has a lot to do with my state of affairs. I get the chilly sweats. This is starting not to sound too good. What makes things worse, he tells me, is that he has borrowed some of the invested scratch from certain unlicensed parties, who now want it back, along with the vigorish, the interest, due them.

He tells me he's cogitating on this kettle of fish night and day. As he has no desire to do any sleeping with any fishes, he determines there is nothing he can do but resort to the old curve ball to remedy the situation. What he does is he contracts with some independent businessmen, who specialize in such matters, to see to it that a blaze breaks out and burns his joint to the ground. He is banking on the insurance pay-off to satisfy the parties who stake him in his investments and to put him back in the black.

I am shocked, thinking that these are nothing but false pretenses, and I do not approve of false pretenses, except when nothing else will turn the trick. Further, I am thinking that this just might constitute fraud—the practice of which insurance companies and old John Law generally frown upon. I also think maybe I should drop a dime on this moke. But I come to my senses. It is common knowledge that some John Laws, as well as some insurance big shots, often accompany this particular owner when he pays his visits to the doggies, ponies, and baseballers. So maybe this whole set-up is a legitimate compromise. So why don't I just keep my dime in my pocket and my trap shut, which is exactly what I end up doing. Even now I would not speak of this except that the statute of limitations has run out. At any rate, he lets me know that the fire is to be both grease and electrical in nature, just to be on the safe side, and is to take place after business hours tonight.

After he gives me the skinny on this lark, he suggests that I might want to swing by his place and remove my sound equipment before the main event. In addition, I can have the night off. He gets a little catch in his throat as he tells me that he figures that this is the least he can do under the circumstances. Then he explains the circumstances. Not only will I be out of work for the next month, but since the independent businessmen he has contracted with require 'up-front, good faith' money, he is tapped flatter than a pancake and unable to pay me for the work I did for him all this past week. He says that he feels very bad about the situation, but business is business.

Now I do not know anything about business being business. I am just a simple ditty-warbler, and this puts me in a tough spot. However, my hands are tied, so I am as polite as you please as I tell him that I feel very bad about the situation, as well. I also agree that yes, this is the least he can do—the very least. There is nothing left but to thank him for the information and offer him my sincere condolences on the scheduled misfortune. I tell him I will be by directly to pick up my stuff, which is what I do after hanging up.

I drive to the place, stow my gear in the trunk, give the joint a "sayonara," and set off in the direction of downtown. I feel like somebody kicked me in the stomach. What I need now is a cocktail, for I am of a mind to wallow. When you want to wallow, there is nothing that will do but a cocktail, and the bigger, the better. This is all I think about as I drive around. For no particular reason, I make a left turn at the next stoplight. Three storefronts down, I see a flickering neon sign. I pull level with it and read, "The Bucket—Cocktails." I'm thinking this hits the nail on the head. A cocktail served in a bucket should do me just fine. Of course, I know this is not what the sign means, but there is poetry about it, so I pull into one of the many blank parking spots, secure the car, and in I go. This is how I come to be on my lonesome in The Bucket of a Saturday night.

So here I am, having a good wallow and percolating on this and that—like what am I going to do in the way of cabbage for the next month. I further percolate how George M. Cohan said "Life's a very funny proposition after all." He is dead now, but he is also dead right, particularly when it comes to the professional music dodge.

I am stewing away when I hear the fellow on stage start winding up his show. He makes his thank-yous and goodnights to the audience—which is me. I give him a round of sympathy applause, which appears to startle him. From his reaction, I gather he does not hear the sound of clapping in some time. He squints in my direction. It seems he knows me, for he gives out as follows:

"Jeez! Frank! Hello! Hang on a second. I'll be with you in a minute."

This phrase doesn't really make sense but I know what he means, so I hang on. He packs away his junk, picks up his stage cocktail, comes over to the bar, and plants himself on the stool next to me.

"Well, well, well, Frank," he says. "It has been a while. How are tricks with you?"

Now that he is up close, I recognize him as a fellow traveler on the circuit who goes by the name of Obie something-or-other, and whom I know from a few years back. The reason I don't place him when I first come in is because he now has a forehead that stretches way, way, back on his noggin, and he sports a big walrus soup-strainer on his top lip. He's also up a good two weight divisions from the welters to the light heavies since I last set eyes on him. Considering this, I cannot be blamed for not pinning him right off the bat, since he looks a bit different these days.

As we shake hands I say, "Yes, indeed, Obie, it has been a while at that, hasn't it? But to answer your question: tricks are not so very good with me right now."Before I can give him the lowdown on my goings on, the front door, which is right behind me, opens, and two knuckle-draggers in overcoats step in and station themselves on either side of the entrance. They give the joint a real slow once-over and then nod to each other. Knuckle-dragger #1 continues to eyeball the room, while knuckle-dragger #2 turns back, re-opens the door, and holds it. Who steps in carrying a briefcase but a sawed-off little guy wearing a Homburg hat—a dead ringer for Al Pacino in Godfather III, only without the kindly puss. He walks slowly past me, goes behind the bar, and approaches the first cash register. He rings it open and commences to stuff the till with cabbage that he takes out of the briefcase. He does the same thing with the second register.

I am thinking this is odd. He has things all mixed up. He is depositing, instead of withdrawing. I am about to point out this error, when Obie gives me a gentle shot in the right kidney and waggles his head from side to side. I take this to mean I should keep my yap buttoned, which I do.

The guy in the Homburg finishes stuffing cabbage in the tills, snaps his now empty briefcase shut, and nods to the bartender, who nods right back at him. He then turns, gives Obie and me a real slow up and down once-over, and makes a little snort sound. Then he nods to the two knuckle-draggers, and the three of them go back out the door—the knuckle-draggers leading the way. The whole show takes maybe two minutes, even if you count all the nodding and the little snort.

"Hmm," I say to Obie after the door shuts and I take a slug of my cocktail, "that was really something to see." I start to light a cigarette, but Obie puts his hand on my arm.

"You're wrong about that, Frank. You do not see nothing. Nothing! Do you follow?"

I am pretty sure I do follow, and I tell Obie as much.

"Yes, but are you sure you really follow?" Obie leans into me. "Listen to me," he says. "The sawed-off little guy in the Homburg? That is nobody else but Mr. N. He owns this establishment. On the street, it is even money that the 'N' stands for 'No witnesses.' Now do you get it?" He sits back.

Dawn breaks on old Marblehead as I finally get it. In spades. But curiosity still has the better of me.

"But, Obie," I ask him after a bit, "this 'nothing' which I do not see, and which Mr. N does not do—does it happen often?"

"Like clockwork. Each and every night," he answers.

Then he takes a slug of his own cocktail, shakes his head, lets out a big, long sigh, and slowly looks around the room. He has a sad half-smile on his kisser. He turns back to me, and I see that his peepers are all dewed up.

"I will tell you one thing, though," he says, "I truly wish this was not my last night. I am going to miss this old rat hole, for this is, without a doubt, my best gig ever, but I have another engagement, and I am duty-bound by the professional warbler's code to honor it."

Of course, I know all about the code, but I am surprised about what he says about this gig and this rat hole. I do a long pan around the room. Three of the couples at the tables are in such a state of heat that they are near spontaneous combustion. The citizen draped over the other end of the bar is now stretched out on the floor, his head on the bar rail, still cutting Z's pretty good. The bartender seems to be snoozing as well—although he is propped up on his elbows.

"Excuse me, Obie," I say. "Please do not take offense, but you must be giving me the rib. This is really your best gig ever?"

"Without a doubt," he says as he pulls a hanky from his hip pocket and gives his schnozz a little toot.

I am starting to feel worse for Obie than I do for myself. I give him a pat on the back.

"Obie, Obie, Obie," I tell him, "I am very sorry for your troubles; you must be having some real bow-wows for gigs. Look, I am not flush by any means, but if it will help, I can stand you a sawbuck or two on a temporary basis."

Obie snuffles and gives a chuckle. "Why that is a very kind offer, but no, thank you. It's not necessary as I do very nicely right now." He does a quick scan right and left. "Here, take a peep at this."

With that, he wrestles from his front pocket a wad of cabbage that would choke a yak.

He leans into me again and whispers, "They pay cash money and plenty of it. And there is no paperwork, if you catch my drift." He throws me a wink.

"Well, well," I say, as Obie stretches and sticks the wad back in his pocket. "I catch your drift very well indeed. That makes this gig a horse of a different color. Does it not?"

"Yeah," he says. "Green."

I certainly cannot disagree with this logic, and I further understand why Obie is so crazy about this old rat hole. Now that I study it more carefully, the place does have a certain scruffy attractiveness about it.

"Obie," I ask, "how do you get booked in this charming room?"

"Oh, Marty handles that," he says as he points toward the snoozing bartender. "I take it you are interested. I'll tell you what—let me go sound him out on the subject."

Obie sidles over to Marty, the bartender, who turns out not to be snoozing, but just resting his eyes. They nosh for a minute or two then Obie comes down the bar and plunks back on his stool.

"By any chance, you are not available next week, are you?" he asks.

"As a matter of fact, I am. It so happens I am at liberty at the moment," I tell him.

Things are starting to look up, but I really catch a break when Obie continues.

"Well, it is as good as done, then. You do Monday through Saturday, nine-ish until whenever it is safe. You get your cabbage before the start of the night on Saturday. I won't tell you how much cabbage; I want it to be a surprise."

I raise my hand to object, but Obie waves it aside and jumps right back in. "I know, I know," he says, "none of us like surprises, but I will make book that you will like this one, believe you me.

118

What is more, since we go way back, I don't even want a finder's fee this time. Deal?"

"Deal," I agree. And we shake on it.

"All right, then," Obie goes on. "Now that we are finished with that, maybe you can help out with a problem that just came up. Marty here is in a bit of a bind. You see," he explains, "there is this John Denver-type group what is supposed to start right away, but there was an unfortunate mix-up, and they cannot shake loose from their present gig until next month. Do you know of anyone who can finish out the rest of the month after you?"

I cannot believe my good luck.

"Look no further," I say. "I can do the whole, entire month! You see, the way it is I am booked over at that flea-bag on Porter Street, but—"

"Oh," says Obie, as he all of a sudden smacks himself in the forehead. "Of course! The fire! Sheesh, I forgot all about that. Tell me: does that take place already?"

While I do not understand how Obie evidently knows about the fire before I do, I figure it is just one of those things.

"No, that's slated for later tonight," I tell him.

"Uh-huh," he nods. "Well then it is as good as settled." He slaps the bar. "Hey, Marty!" he yells. "I got you covered." Obie gives me another wink. "I talked Frank into doing the whole, entire month for you. Don't forget, now; you owe me a favor for this. Right?"

Without opening his eyes, Marty nods a couple of times, which I take to mean "right." I am thinking there's a whole lot of nodding goes on in here. It is a curious habit, but probably of no matter.

Two days later, I arrive to begin my month's residence in The Bucket. I set up my gear and promptly at the crack of nine-ish, I give Marty a nod—just to show I cop to the lingo—and wail into the first set.

Well, the whole month goes down pretty much the same as the night I bump into Obie. The number of customers falls between a few and some. Marty moves on to Betty and Veronica and rests his eyes a good deal. And every night, Mr. N and his knuckle-draggers arrive to stuff cabbage. For myself, I am able to practice some new material without the fear of being interrupted by things such as applause. In return, I receive a nice, thick, green wad of generous denominations at the end of each week. It is a gratifying experience for one and all.

My stay eventually ends. I thank Marty, wish him luck, and give him my card. I let him know I am interested in playing The Bucket again, some time down the road. We exchange nods, as comrades in arms do, and I leave.

Two weeks go by, and I am holding forth with Irish ditties at my next gig. I am keeping the customers, building an audience, and the house is raking it in. Naturally, I do all the old, familiar crowd-pleasers about war and death and whiskey and the like. In addition, the new material I was able to work on while playing in The Bucket throws a ripple into the act. Customers are thrilled to hear new ripples now and again, so the show is going down a bomb, which means "very good" in Irish music talk. Mind you, the cabbage is nowhere what I get in The Bucket, but it is good enough, so I am content.

That Sunday afternoon, my phone rings, and I answer it.

"Frank? Marty."

"Marty? Marty-from-The -Bucket Marty?"

There is silence on the other end of the line.

"Marty, are you nodding?"

"Oh, yeah, sorry. Yeah, it's me."

I ask him what's up, and he commences to tell me that things at The Bucket are not doing so hot these days.

"Well," I say, "that's not what I hear. I hear that the Bucket is full to the brim."

Marty admits what I hear is true, and that that is why things are not doing so hot. Then he lays the whole story on me.

For the past two weeks, the John Denver-type group has been playing and carrying on about high mountains, roads in the country, and going away on jet planes. At first, everything is hunky-dory. The place is a crypt. Slowly though, customers start sticking around and listening. Then more come in, and more follow them. Marty falls behind in his reading, and his eyes are very tired, which depresses him. It turns out that this John Denver-type group is not too shabby. As a matter of fact, they play pretty good. At this time, you see, John Denver and his music are more popular with the public than American cheese.

Well, push comes to shove, and just last night, the customers arrive like a plague of locusts. They pour into The Bucket. They all have funny little eyeglasses, look sincere and say things like "Cool" and "Far-out." They are all daffy about this John Denver-type group, and they know all the lyrics, which they sing out just as free as I don't know what.

There are so many customers, in fact, that when Mr. N shows up, he has to have the knuckle-draggers run interference for him. Even with this assist, he is just able to squeeze into his own joint. To make matters worse, the customers are dropping so much of their own green, he is only able to stuff a few leaves of cabbage from his briefcase into the cash registers. This upsets him. The reason why this upsets him is if there is anything Mr. N loves more than anything else, it is stuffing cabbage from his briefcase into cash register tills. Marty explains that Mr. N loves this so much because he believes it cleans his cabbage, which, for some reason, he thinks is all dirty. Personally, I cannot make heads or tails of it, but I don't waste time thinking about it. It is business, after all.

Eventually, Mr. N is able to get Marty's attention. He asks Marty to please kindly tell him what in Heaven's name goes on here—only he does not use those words. Marty nods toward the John Denver-type group.

"It is them," he explains. "The kids go bananas for them. I think they are what they call a 'draw.' They are a hit."

"A hit!" says Mr. N. "Who said anything about a hit? There's not going to be no hit. But since you mention 'draw,' I will draw you a picture of what is going to happen and what you are going to do. You will pay the band a month's worth of cabbage and give them the gate at the end of the night—tonight. Understand?"

Marty understands.

"By the way," he continues, "do you still have that Irish guy's phone number? The one who just finished here a few weeks ago?"

"You mean Frank?" Marty says. "Yeah, I think so, why?"

"I want you should call him and see if we can get him back."

"Okay," says Marty, "but what if he is all booked up?"

"Then get somebody else," Mr. N snaps back, his eyes all snakey–ish. Then he stops, takes a deep breath, and puts his eyes back to normal. "Look, Marty," he says. He puts his hand on Marty's shoulder, real palsy-walsy, and explains, "It doesn't matter. Just get any guy who plays Irish music. Okay?" Then he love taps Marty on the cheek two times. "Okay?" he asks again.

"Sure, okay," says Marty. "No problem. But you know, up until now I do not know you are such a big fan of guys who play Irish music."

"Oh, my, yes," says Mr. N. "I am a huge fan. They don't draw flies. So you see, guys who play Irish music come in very handy if you wish to do some cabbage cleaning.

Marty explains all of this to me and asks if I can come back to The Bucket, starting tomorrow. I tell him that although I am very flattered that they think to ask me, I am currently not available. But I tell him I'll be glad to nose around to see if I can dig up someone who is. Marty thanks me, says he owes me, and hangs up.

I start nosing, but I cannot sniff out any guys who play Irish music who are at liberty, and if they are at liberty, they do not wish to associate with either knuckle-draggers in general or Mr. N in particular, since, this Mr. N, I am told, is less than savory in the reputation department. Personally, I think this is a bum rap. Although he is no Little Mary Sunshine, Mr. N never says "Boo" to me; in fact, he hardly ever even gives me a nod.

It turns out I don't have to worry about the problem, for I hear through the grapevine that a day or two later, fortune falls in Marty's lap. Who pokes his mug into the Bucket but Gargles McGarrigle. I know Gargles, and he is none too savory in the reputation department himself. This, however, is because he is a notorious mooch, and a song thief to boot. He is as lacking of talent as he is full of ugly—which is to say, boatloads. Not only does he have a face like a doorknocker, a couple of years before, Gargles receives a review, which reads, "Last night at the Corkonian Pub, Gargles McGarrigle played Irish music. Irish music lost."

How this toothache of a man exists as long as he has in the music racket, is anybody's guess. It may not be proof that there is no God, but there is certainly no justice.

From all of this, you might think Gargles is tailor-made for The Bucket, and you would be right. Gargles auditions one night and the joint empties quicker than 23-Skiddoo. Even Marty is tempted to take a powder, but he does not. What he does is he hires Gargles on the spot as the permanent house band. It is a marriage made in heaven. Customers avoid the place as if it is a TB ward, Mr. N is tickled pink with his new discovery, and Gargles is rolling in cabbage.

The operation continues just as smooth as you please for some time until finally, disaster strikes. Irish music catches on with the public— even that which Gargles flings at them. No matter what obscenity he commits on the music, the crowd does not seem to care. They flock to hear it. The Bucket overflows with customers, and Gargles succeeds in croaking himself right out of a very good gig.

Of course, all of this happens years ago. Things are different these days. I still knock around the pubs, doing as well as can be expected, I suppose. Obie gets out of the performing end of the business a while back, makes a deal with Satan, becomes an agent, and doesn't return phone calls from guys who play Irish music. I don't know what happens with Gargles. I only know one day he disappears completely from the circuit—which is about the only good thing he ever does for the music scene. Rumor has it he enrolls in a law school he reads about on a book of matches, but that might not be true. My travels nowadays do not take me anywhere near The Bucket, but I hear it is still at the old stand, Marty still behind the bar. I hope by now he has the whole Archie, Jughead, Betty and Veronica mystery figured out. But I wonder what he thinks of the Reggie situation, and who does what with who.

I am told that The Bucket now features Flemish music, whatever that might be. Personally, I do not know from Flemish music even if it slaps me in the mush. In what is a stroke of marketing genius, the joint is now called the Flem Bucket. That moniker alone should keep customers at bay and ensure that Mr. N has plenty of clean cabbage for years to come.

TRAVELING, OR ON THE ROAD AGAIN...VAL-DER-REE, VAL-DER-AH!

The Behemoth

Dennis O'Rourke

It was a station wagon; a Pontiac Catalina Safari—a '74, I think. It was big, and it was heavy. It was the second wagon I'd owned. Neither was a car of choice. My sound system was Shure columns, five feet high, and it dictated my mode of transport. Some kid had broadsided the first—a little Ford wagon—totaled it, and I had to buy the first thing I could find, hence, the Behemoth. This was the late seventies. It was a gas-guzzler. I had it for a couple of years and through a few adventures.

The first one was, well, not really an adventure—more like an exercise in buffoonery—but thanks be to God, it occurred before everyone was armed with video cameras. If someone had caught this on tape, I would have dug a hole in the earth and pulled the grass over me. I don't feel too much of a fool *telling* the story, but I certainly wouldn't want to see it on tape.

I'd finished a night at Liam's, hung around while the staff cleaned up, and had a few pints with them. I jumped into the Behemoth and headed for home, forty minutes away. The urge to relieve myself was upon me almost immediately, and by the time I hit Rte 128, a three-lane highway, I was squirming. There was nothing for it but to pull over and make a run for the trees. There was an overpass ahead, and I stopped on the other side of it, jumped out, and shot up the hill that sloped down from the bridge. When I got behind some bushes, I set about my business. Waves of relief. It was a mighty torrent, and I knew it was going to take a while. Mindful of that, I turned around to eyeball the car, praying a state trooper had not taken an interest in it. The sight that greeted me was far worse. Horrified, I saw the Behemoth moving slowly along the embankment, and the reason was immediately clear. In my rush to get out of the car, I had not taken it out of gear, nor had I closed the door.

I was not even close to finishing the business at hand and had difficulty closing the dam. In a panic, I turned around, and at a brisk trot, I headed down the hill, holding the mickey sideways, aiming away from

125

me. The car was now moving toward an embankment that fell away to a ditch. The torrent ceased just as I reached the door. I threw myself headfirst into the front seat and pushed down on the brake with my hand. I reached up and put the car into park. I backed out, zipped up, and looked around to see if anyone had witnessed my loping down the hill, mickey in hand. Seeing no one, I got in and sped off.

The following night, after hours, I told the story to the staff at Liam's. I acted it out, and they loved it. Even the man himself, who was never an overly humorous guy, got a kick out of it, and that made the whole ridiculous episode worthwhile.

***

There was a blizzard on its way. I had heard the reports the night before, and they were only more ominous the next morning. I was scheduled to work in Mul's up in Portland, Maine, and since it was only a hundred and twenty miles, most of it Interstate, I decided to leave early and beat the storm. I was certain I'd be all right. Those folks were well practiced, and they knew how to handle a snowstorm; they had snow-removal down to an art. Besides, local weather forecasters back then were an art form of their own when it came to a little uproar in Nature—mild hysteria. They caused milk, bread, batteries, flashlights, and toilet paper to fly off grocery shelves. Their neatest trick however, was being able to explain away that hysteria days later when the threatened apocalypse had failed to materialize.

I loaded up the Behemoth and started out at noon, under light flurries. Soon they gave way to a thicker, heavier snow that accumulated quickly. Visibility grew poor, traffic snarled, and I was forced to slow down. Before I reached the New Hampshire line, it was stop and go, and the quarter-mile of road I could see ahead of me was filled with brake lights. In four hours, I had made a mere sixty miles. Cars were beginning to slide. I tightened my grip on the wheel and hunched forward. By God, I was going to make this gig.

When I reached the tollbooths at the Maine turnpike, the speed limit had been lowered to thirty-five. Night had fallen. My headlights illuminated the road for only a few feet, and in their feeble beams, all I could see was the wild, gypsy dance of snow. It was five o'clock, and I grew more anxious. I decided to chance going a little faster. I squinted through the windshield, trying to home-in on the rear lights of the cars ahead of me. When I got to them, I passed and speeded up, looking for the next set. I was doing fifty when the back of a slow-moving semi appeared like a giant wall in front of me. I braked and swerved right, but the left front end of the Behemoth hit the truck's rear end with a crunch. In seconds, I was off the road and down in a ditch. I sat there, shaken and furious. The truck's lights had been off. He was gone, undoubtedly unaware of what had just happened.

I got out and examined the damage, and it was considerable. The fender was all torn to hell, but the headlamp was still in place and still shone. I was looking at a costly repair job. Well, that was more reason to continue. No show, no dough. But now I was stuck in an enormous snowdrift. I jockeyed the car back and forth, stomping on the accelerator, and whipping the shift from "drive" to "reverse." The engine howled, and the car rocked, but all I managed to do was simulate a carnival ride for kiddies. I wasn't going anywhere. I cursed the truck and its driver a thousand times.

I stood by the Behemoth and watched in frustration as cars and trucks moved slowly past me. Then I began to curse myself—all the usual, useless self-deprecations. If I had taken my time, I would likely still be out there with them—moving at a crawl, but moving.

I was stranded perhaps an hour when a truck pulled over. He got out and commiserated with me, but there was nothing he could do. However, his standing rig and the flashing hazards of my car caught the attention and curiosity of the driver of a pick-up. He assessed the situation and promptly produced a towrope. In a few minutes, I was back out on the road. The Behemoth was wounded, but moving.

I finally made it into downtown Portland and the pub by eight-thirty. I parked in front and ran up the steps, relief flooding my heart. Matthew, the owner, and several of his staff, who had been watching the storm through the windows, met me at the door. Matthew was aghast.

"Jaysus, Dennis. For fuck's sake, what are you doing here? We're just about to close up. The whole town is shutting down. This is gonna big a big one."

He took me to the bar and poured me two fingers of cognac. I sat there, miserable and exhausted. Then I realized I hadn't had anything to eat in over eight hours. I headed into the deserted kitchen, opened a fridge, and found a lump of turkey roll. I made a sandwich and wolfed it down, even as I noted a funny taste.

Matthew had arranged for his entertainers to room at an old hotel a few blocks away. I got back in the Behemoth and slowly made my way there. I parked, got my guitar and suitcase, and went inside. I checked in and went to the room—a tiny, drab, musty-smelling affair about four stories up. The wind howled. I turned on the TV and sat on the bed, disgusted with myself. The local weather forecasters announced a possible two feet before it was all over. I was in the middle of a daydream about having been born with good sense when the first cramp doubled me over. What the hell was that? Had to be nerves. I began to think a hot shower would serve me well when the next cramp arrived, forcing me to lie on the bed. In the next hour, they came in waves. I grew nauseous. I went to the bathroom and hung my head over the porcelain telephone, but all that came up was a giant, foul burp redolent of the spoiled turkey roll I had eaten.

For the next twenty-four hours, I lay in the fetal position, utterly incapacitated by food poisoning, while the storm raged over Portland. At eleven o'clock the next night, I felt well enough to sit up and turn on the TV. Johnny Carson made me laugh a few times, and I knew the worst had passed. The phone rang in the morning. It was a girlfriend of mine. She came over, and together we dug the Behemoth out from the snow. (Well, she did most of the work. I was shattered.) My heart sank when I saw the damage in the eye-searing glare of the sun on the snow. We walked to a breakfast diner, and I managed some dry toast and black tea. Around us, the locals cheerfully discussed the storm and some of the car accidents it had caused. One old Yankee proclaimed, "Now, what kinds of fool do you suppose would have been driving around in that mess? Big fools, a-yuh."

My companion looked at me with a little smile.

I said, "A big fool is right. The big fool in the Behemoth. A-yuh."

***

I was coming back from a gig in Connecticut. It was three in the morning, and I had just hit the Massachusetts Turnpike at Sturbridge. There was an all-night Howard Johnson's there, and I pulled in to get a cup of coffee and an English muffin. It was early March, and it was

128

chilly, a light mist in the air. I was inside for perhaps thirty minutes. When I stepped out into the parking lot, I took note of the fact that it had turned quite cold in that short period. The air was clear and still. Well, I thought, this *is* New England.

I was out on the Turnpike in a jiffy and settled in with the fifty-five mile an hour limit. I wasn't in any hurry. The gig had been good, and I had a wad of cash in my pocket. All was right with the world, and I was headed to Boston down a road that was surprisingly free of traffic. Now, that started me to wonder. This was a heavy route for tractor-trailers, no matter the time. I couldn't see any taillights ahead. I was mulling this over when I began to notice the odd car or two on the other side of the Turnpike, headed west. They were stopped, pulled to the side of the road, and their hazard lights were flashing. I had time for one, "Uh-oh," and then I lost control of the car. It spun around once and then again as I flailed at the wheel in a panic, trying to steer out of it. "Don't touch the brakes, Denny," I shouted. I began to importune the Lord for intervention. The car had become a pinwheel, a dreidle, a fifty-five-mile-an-hour spinning top. The road was an ice-rink. My sound equipment careened from side to side in the back, the crashing sounds increasing my panic.

Then the car suddenly stopped whirling, straightened out, and headed in a direct line down the middle of the road. Backwards. At fifty-five. The Behemoth had become the Boston Bobsled.

I held onto the wheel with one hand and turned my head—so sharply, it hurt—to see where I was going. A few seconds later, I realized I was drifting to the side of the road, and just ahead was an overpass bridge abutment. It seemed likely I was going to plow into it, rear-end first. I ignored my own shouted warning and began to tap lightly on the brake. It made the car shimmy slightly from side to side, but kept it on the road until I had gone under the bridge. At last, I hit the gravel on the edge and was able to bring the car to a stop.

I spent a few minutes convincing my heart to stay where it was. It wanted to leave me there and run home. When I was sufficiently calm, I got out and cautiously stepped onto the empty highway. There was a paper-thin sheen of ice covering the road, and I skidded and skated around on it for a few minutes. The temperature had dropped so quickly, the mist had turned to ice.

I got back in the car and waited. A quarter of an hour later, a salt-truck rolled slowly past me. I turned the car around and fell in behind it. A mile down the road, one of those trucks sat facing backwards, apparently having suffered my earlier fate. I saw a few of those on my trek home. It was necessary at times to stop and let the trucks go by. I went at a crawl, but made it home safely, albeit three hours later than I had planned.

I hauled my guitar and equipment into my apartment. My hands were curled, as if still holding onto the wheel. I had the tightest anus in New England that night. I shakily poured a double Bushmill's, pried my jaws apart, and poured it in. I rolled myself a giant jazz-cigarette. An hour later, at six in the morning, I tottered down the stairs and made my way out to the parking lot. I patted the Behemoth on the hood and said, "Let's not do anything like that again, okay?" Then I went to bed.

C33&D

STRAY CHAT/FRANK

DOR: Let's talk about accommodations. We're conducting this interview in the entertainers' room at the Kevin Barry Pub in Savannah. It's a 150-year-old cotton warehouse. Now, while this building has its charm, you wouldn't call this the lap of luxury.

FE: No, this is sensory deprivation. You can miss nuclear winter easily. You have no idea. It's a good thing there's such a thing as clocks because you wouldn't know what time it is.

DOR: There are no windows.

FE: There are no windows—that's right. I have to tell you about what happened to me in here once. I'd been playing the room for a few days, not sleeping very well. I felt a little under the weather. Anyway, I finished the night. Came up here around two-thirty or three and took a shower. Even though I'd had a couple of drinks, I wasn't real tired, so I turned on the television and lay down on the couch. When I came to— Fox News was on. I look at my watch and it's just after seven o'clock. Well, I guess some circuits were crossed in my brain because I thought I'd slept all day, and that it was seven *p.m.* I jumped up, took another shower, and dressed in my stage clothes. I was hungry, but I figured I should make my daily seven p.m. call to my wife—which I did. She sounded a bit confused, and asked if I was okay. I told her, "Yeah, of course—just a little tired is all." She said she was glad, but wanted to know why I was calling her at seven o'clock in the morning.

DOR: And what did you say?

FE: Hell, what could I say? Oops—my error. I gave her a short version of what happened and told her I'd talk to her about it later—twelve hours later. She was a pretty good sport about it. Even thanked me for getting her up for work since she'd overslept.

DOR: Ah, the silver lining...

FE: Yeah.

DOR: Can you recall the best accommodations a club has ever given you?

FE: Yeah, actually, I can. There's a place in north Georgia called the Chateau Élan. I don't play there anymore. It's not a particularly endearing job. However, the accommodations are such that I was afraid to touch anything. It was just too nice for the likes of me. I was afraid something would break, and I would have to buy it. It's just—real nice accommodations.

DOR: And they were? A hotel, or—?

FE: Hotel. There was a golf course—a couple of golf courses—there, and they would put you up in the—in the hotel; we called that the Big House, or in one of these golf villas, which were pretty much your own townhouse. But it was beautiful. Like I say, I was afraid to touch anything or use anything.

DOR: I've had some experiences where I've been afraid to touch something, not because it was so elegant or wonderful—because of...

FE: Because of cooties? Because of cooties?

DOR: Disease, or—

FE: Cooties! Cooties! Don't want the cooties to get you!

DOR: (Laughing) How many of *those* situations have you been in? Turned around and said, "Well, I'll just get my own hotel."

FE: Yeah, well, a couple. A couple where I just said, "I'm not going to do this job," and turned around and drove three hundred miles back home. Said, "This is not gonna work out the way that it should." And I could sense—this was not gonna be a good feeling, even if I went onstage that night. I said, "I'm not gonna feel good about this, so I'll bite the bullet."

DOR: Because the accommodations were that bad, you would just—

FE: Horrible. Horrible. It was a basement, a windowless basement, and I had to share a bathroom with a guy down the hall I didn't know. And cement block walls, no TV—no nothing, you know. Old furniture. I said, "Hang on. I don't need this. I could have done *this* by myself."

DOR: What town was this? You don't have to mention the club.

FE: Washington. And I felt real bad about it. But I said, "This is just—This is not going to be a pleasant experience for either party."

DOR: How did the club owner react to that? Did he offer—?

FE: No, there was no offer made. I think the whole idea was that I was kind of doing them a favor. Not "kind of"—I *was* doing them a favor. I came down on my fee, and— Well, "Work with us. Work with us." Okay. And alarm bells should have gone off at that phrase. They just didn't come through on their end of the deal. And I said, "This is not going to work." The owners were out of town, and they couldn't get in touch with—well, with any of them. One guy was on holiday for three weeks in Europe, and another guy just did not return the calls, and the other fella just—I guess there was no answer. And I said, "This doesn't bode well for me." And I said, "I'll see you later. No hard feelings." Shook hands with the manager. I had worked with him before, and I said, "I'll see you down the road sometime."

൫൭

STRAY CHAT/SEAMUS

DOR: You were once accidentally locked in an Irish pub.

SK: (Laughs) No, it wasn't accidentally. It was deliberately. It was during a snowstorm in Boston, I was working in the Black Rose, and I had been drinking, *and* I couldn't drive home. Everybody else was within walking distance or short driving distance, so they could make it home. The owner just decided he'd better lock me in the pub for the night, and I agreed with that. Rather than have me drive or walking and hurting myself, he locked me in the pub, and I thought, "Oh, this is great. This is going to be like a kid in a candy store. Oh, look at all this drink around here." I thought it was going to be like Aladdin's cave—jewels dripping everywhere. I could help myself. There's single malt scotch, Bushmill's Black Label, there was Guinness, there was Harp, and there was Bass, oh, my God. By the time I went back and pulled myself a pint, I realized I didn't want to get drunk after all, so I pulled the pint, lay down on a bench, and went to sleep 'til the staff came in the following morning.

FLAT-TOP, ROUND-BACK BOXES

Tony's Guitar

Frank Emerson

Tony O'Riordan is a great pal from Dublin. He's tall, maybe six-feet-two, or so. Big culchie hands. A nose, as he used to say, like Murray the Cop from *The Odd Couple* television program. A great smile. An infectious laugh. He's a very talented performer and a multi-instrumentalist. On stage, he doesn't so much hold his instrument, as much as he appears to surround it. We performed together for five or six years as Ourselves Alone.

One night, I think it was in '77, we're working in a nice place in White Oak, Maryland, outside DC, called the Irish Inn. The joint is crowded. We're having a good night. We manage to play through the dinner hours without putting anyone off their feed, and now it's about ten or eleven o'clock, and it's going well.

A citizen comes up to the stage and asks if we'd let his cousin sing a number. Never ones to buy a pig in a poke, we ask whom the cousin is. Point him out. The guy says, "Not him. Her. That's her over there—with the black hair." He points. "She was first runner-up for Miss Hawaii last year," he says. We look and then double take. I say, "I think that would be all right." Tony nods, real slow like. We get the girl's name, make the introduction, and both of us extend a hand to help her on to the stage. She gives her hand to me. It's nice. Wow. That's what everybody says—just like that, "Wow." Eat your heart out, O'Riordan, I'm thinking. She says she won't be needing our help—she'd like to play guitar herself, if we didn't mind, and could she borrow one of ours, please? Tony's guitar is off him as if he'd greased the strap. He hands it to her. She smiles, drops my hand, and takes the instrument.

We offer her a bar stool to make her more comfortable. She cuddles onto it real nice. She waits as we adjust the microphone height. (I think maybe we took longer to do this than was really necessary). It's all set now. We exit the stage. She smiles and kind of hunches the guitar underneath her McGuffies. She starts to play and sing. What she sang— who remembers? Bum notes? Who cares? She was superb. She finishes her tune. Lots of applause. Before I can say thanks and let's put your hands together for— Tony starts shouting, "More! More!" and the audience takes up the chant. It's a friggin' pep rally. She complies and follows that one up with a third. Finally, she's had her fill. She says thanks and begs off to even greater applause, especially from us.

We remount the stage. Tony is very quiet. She returns his guitar and goes back to her table. I re-sling my guitar and glance at Tony to get the okay to start the next number. Tony is standing stock-still, holding his guitar, and staring at it, pretty much at the spot where the girl had parked her pontoons. I ask if he's okay. He looks at me. Then at his guitar. He does this again. The crowd is mum. They are watching us. Tony is oblivious to them. He looks at me one more time. He's real serious. His microphone is live. His eyes well up a bit, and he says, "You know what?"

"What?" say I.

"I'm never going to wash this guitar again. Ever!"

And I know for a fact he never did.

CƷ♥Ɔ

The Martin

Seamus Kennedy

She was beautiful. Full-figured with wonderful proportions, well rounded in top, and slightly larger and more rounded in the bottom.

My first Martin D-28 guitar. Ever since coming to the United States in 1971, I had wanted a Martin. Top-of-the-line, elite, the best in the world in acoustic guitars. Everybody who was anybody in the folk/country music field played a Martin. The Kingston Trio, Johnny Cash, Doc Watson, Liam Clancy, Bob Dylan, Joan Baez—they all played Martins. Strong of tone, sweet sounding, resonant—sturdy and delicate at the same time. And I wanted one badly.

I'd been happy with my black Hagstrom with its nice bass thump and my Yamaha FG-180 and its light bass, but twangy, middle range. Very serviceable instruments indeed for a young, aspiring Irish folk singer fresh on the American/Irish pub scene, but they weren't Martins! They did not have the cachet of that superior objet d'art. Other, established, Martin-playing folkies would not take me seriously with a Hagstrom or a Yamaha. I had to have a Martin.

My partner, Tom O'Carroll, and I were a duo called the Beggarmen. We had become reasonably well established playing in Irish pubs and restaurants around the Boston area, with the occasional foray to the wild northlands of Lowell, MA and the hinterlands of Springfield in western MA.

We were making $400 a week between us in those heady days in the early '70s; working five nights a week in places named the Limerick Pub, the Keg, the Blarney Stone (Somerville and Dorchester Divisions), Liam's Irish Tavern, the Shed, the Lamplighter, the Castle Arms, and Brock's. I played rhythm guitar and did most of the talking and singing, while Tom played all the real music on banjo, mandolin, guitar, and penny whistle. He also sang harmony on just about everything. If I do say so myself, for a couple of guys who hadn't really made up their minds that this was to be their life's work, we were pretty good—tight, musically.

But I didn't have a Martin!

So, I saved $20 a week until I had the requisite $750 for a 1974 Martin D-28. Brand new from the big music store at the corner of Newbury Street and Mass Ave in Boston that had agreed to hold it for me and not sell it to any usurper who came in with the purchase price in hand. It said so, right there on the price ticket—"Reserved for Seamus Kennedy. Deposit Paid."

I had been going into the store, twice a week, for the 38 weeks it took me to save the necessary cash. I would stand and admire it, then take it down and strum it gently, lovingly, and then carefully replace it on its padded hook high on the wall, away from the grasp of marauding musical jackals.

The big day came. I was like a kid at Christmas! I couldn't wait to rush down to the store, lay down the balance of my money, and take my treasured beauty home. At nine a.m., I was standing outside the store with all the eagerness of a wino waiting for the pub to open when it dawned on me—the music store didn't open until eleven a.m. Shite! I'd forgotten that many music stores open later in the morning because (a) most musicians don't get up until eleven or twelve, and (b) most music store employees are musicians themselves.

So I paced and I waited, and when I finally gained entrance, I rushed inside to make sure that my darlin' was still there, paid off the balance, and watched as the store clerk, beaming, took her down from the hook and handed her to me. I placed her in the royal blue, plush-lined, hard-shell case,

136

just as proudly and carefully as Mary placed the swaddled Baby Jesus in the manger. I closed the lid, making sure all the latches were secure, and swept out triumphantly into the Boston morning air.

Later that afternoon, Tom and I were scheduled to perform for a group of senior citizens at the Blarney Stone Pub in Davis Square, Somerville. Jerry Fleming, the manager of the club, and a very good-hearted fella (for a manager), was bringing a group of elderly folk from a nearby nursing home and laying on a luncheon for them, with Tom and I as the featured entertainers. This would be my first opportunity to let the new Martin strut her stuff in public.

We got there an hour or so before the folks were due. I showed Tom my pride and joy. He expressed suitable admiration for her appearance, but sat there in perfect awe after he had played a few licks on her medium gauge Martin Marquis strings.

Then we set up our PA system—two Kustom Kasino speakers that looked like padded caskets, with a four-input, high impedance Kustom Kasino amplifier. Tom and I each had a microphone stand with two mikes. The top mike on each stand was for our vocals and, clipped on about halfway down, another mike for our instruments.

My baby was going to say its first words.

We switched the amp on and did the standard "One-two, one-two, testing!" sound check in the vocal mikes. Then I strummed a G chord into the instrument mike. Oh, the resonance! Oh, the clarity of tone! Deep bass, clear middle register, bright treble. This is indeed the finest acoustic guitar in the world. And it's mine.

The old folks came in, about twenty-five of them, and Jerry and the staff showed them to their tables. A nice buffet lunch was set out, and they dutifully went through the line, filled their plates, and returned to their seats. The waitresses brought their drinks, and they got stuck in with gusto.

Tom and I started up. A couple of nice rousing songs to get the show off to a lively start—"Whiskey in the Jar" and "The Wild Colonial Boy." The D-28 was singing like a bird! Then I told a few jokes, and Tom did a song. We announced that we were going to play a couple of reels and jigs on the banjo—"The Devil's Dream," "Cripple Creek," "Merrily Kiss the Quaker," and "Donnybrook Fair." Tom's left hand moved deftly up and down the neck of his Ode five-string, fingering the melody while his right hand masterfully picked the notes. The Martin played a perfect background rhythm all by herself.

Two ladies, moved by a spirit of Hibernian dance, decided to favor their assembled cohorts with a jig, and to many calls of approval and encouragement, they rose from their table, came onto the floor in front of the stage, and proceeded to dance with as much enthusiasm as their elderly legs could muster in 6/8 time.

Now, in Irish céilí dancing (similar to American square dancing) there is a move known as "the céilí swing," in which partners swing each other round in a tight circle while retaining a firm grip on each other's elbow and waist. These two ladies had obviously been damn fine dancers in their halcyon days, but time and gravity had taken their toll, and their once graceful swinging skills had eroded to the point where centrifugal force took over. As they whirled with gay abandon, Partner A could no longer control Partner B, who spun from her grasp, and was catapulted, like a comet escaping the sun's gravitational pull, right towards me.

She barreled into my mike stand. The top mike caught me smack on the mouth, the lower mike smashed into the body of my beautiful D-28, caving in the lower bout beneath the bridge. I heard the "Crunch!" as the wood splintered and cracks spider-webbed across the varnish. Silence. Everybody stared. The lady ended up on the stage, at my feet, sprawled on her back, groaning.

Tom and I leaned over at the same time and said, "Are you all right?" Then we gently lifted her up and walked her back to her table, where she sat down to compose herself, catch her breath, and regain her dignity. She got a big round of applause from her friends and a promise from her partner never to do THAT again.

When we got back onstage, Tom glanced down at my guitar then looked at me with sympathy. I stared at my pride and joy, my D-28, the Martin, now battered and mutilated, and looked back at Tom disconsolately.

He whispered, "Let's finish the set."

And I said, "Okay."

ෆ๛

The Ovation

Frank Emerson

For many years, I played a twelve-string guitar. I did this for a couple of reasons. First, it was not that commonplace in Irish pubs. It also brought a unique sound to the jigs and reels, and a different ripple and color to the songs. My weapon of choice was a Guild. I suppose I've had three or four of them. Finally, I decided to make a change on the advice of Danny O'Flaherty.

O'Flaherty is an old pal and a fine multi-instrumentalist from Connemara. He now operates a successful pub in New Orleans. I work about six weeks a year for him. Danny plays an Ovation twelve-string, and he thought I would be better served by this make for a number of reasons. The guitar has an on-board volume control and EQ. These things are handy. The sound readily cuts through pub noise. This is handy, too. Finally, it was designed to be tuned in concert pitch. This was news to me. You see, generally, twelve-strings have to be tuned lower than other guitars because the pressure exerted by all those strings on the bridge can cause it to lift right off the face of the instrument. (That happened to me one night during a show many years ago. Since I could barely play the damned thing at the time, it hardly made a difference, although it was disconcerting.) What you do is you put the capo on the second fret and then tune up in concert pitch. That eases the pressure and you can feel somewhat secure. It is not particularly efficient, however, as twelve-strings have a notorious reputation for not retaining their intonation, especially after you do something like actually playing a song.

You don't have to worry about this with the Ovation. That sounded good to me. My only objection was the fact that the guitar has a round back. I always figured that strapping one on to play would be something like humping a camel. This was probably an unfair estimation on my part since I'd never tried playing one, nor had I humped a camel. (Still haven't done the latter.) I tried out Danny's guitar one night at his invitation, and was pleasantly surprised. I figured I should look into the Ovation.

On my drive back home from New Orleans, I stopped into The Guitar Center near Oak Ridge, Tennessee. They have walls of guitars—a great selection. (Some people call them axes. I don't.) I asked a clerk, who looked to be about thirteen, to let me have a gander at some twelve-string Ovations and others, so I could compare. He asked me what I had been using. When I told him Guild, he said, "Nice make, but they're not very forgiving, are they?" That pretty much summed things up nicely, so I figured this fellow would give me the straight dope. I tried out a Martin, Gibson, and a few Ovations. He pulled an Ovation out that was bottom of the line: No fancy mother-of-pearl inlays, no gold tuning pegs, just a straightforward journeyman guitar. The fellow says, "Here, try this. I think it has a great sound. And it's easily the best deal in the store." I tried it. He was right. I liked it and liked the price. So it was love at first sight. And boy, what a difference it made in the clubs. Life was so much easier. I felt like I'd just come in to the 21st century.

So anyway, a few months go by, and I'm really enjoying this instrument. I'm performing at Kevin Barry's Pub in Savannah, and it's Pearl Harbor Day, the 59th anniversary. A Friday. I've prepared a tribute set. It goes over well, and the audience is right with me all night long. I play late. We're all digging it. I finish up after two a.m. I beg off and sit down with a couple of folks for a brief chat. I say, come on into the barroom and meet a couple of pals of mine who are Army Rangers. We go in, and I make the introductions. I guess about fifteen minutes pass, and I excuse myself to put the guitar away, promising a quick return to have a brief nightcap before the place locks down.

I go back to the stage. Blessed as I am with keen observational skills, I notice that the guitar is not where I left it. Nor is it anywhere else in the room, which is now devoid of customers. I figure someone is being a wisenheimer, playing a joke. I go back to the Rangers and accuse them of as much. Blank looks. They don't know what I'm talking about. I figure, "Uh-oh." So we scour the building, we check the street, and we come up empty.

I'm getting more and more steamed. My language is getting bluish. I'm figuring some guys—at least two—came in when the room was empty and saw that guitar. One kept an eye on us in the bar, while the other thief grabbed the instrument and scarpered through the side door, which was out of our sight. That they fixed only on stealing the guitar was evident because there was a tip jar full of money unmolested on the stage. They just unplugged the guitar and bolted.

You know how sometimes you get so unreasonably furious and frustrated that only a blind and illogical act will do? And that at best it will only garner a pyrrhic victory? Well, that's pretty much how I felt. I wanted to get my hands on the gobshites, beat them half to death with the guitar, and then shove the broken pieces so far up their individual rectums that when they walked, their arses would play "Off to Dublin." Then I would have ended up having to buy a new guitar anyway.

140

Well, the thieves were never caught, and the guitar never turned up. I rained curses on the beastids that night; a good, healthy rant. And although they didn't know it, they had a bunch of Rangers interested in them, as well. Not a particularly healthy state in which to find one's self.

The next day, I had to find a new guitar for the gig that evening. I try a couple of music stores. Got an offer from one to give me the loan of a $3500 Taylor twelve-string. That's nice, and it's real pretty, but it makes me nervous just looking at it. I figure that if something costs $3500, you should be able to move into it. I also figure, if I bump it, I've bought it. I said, No, thank you. Finally, at Annie's Guitar's (Annie Allman—yes, the same family), I find a new Ovation she just got in but it's a six-string. It seems there aren't any twelve-string Ovations in town. The six-string will have to do. It does sound good, and it has nice action. I tell her the tale, and she cuts me a very fair deal.

The only thing is—it's what they used to call Chinese red. Now, I have a Chinese red Chevy Blazer, but it would not be my color of choice for a guitar—or a car, for that matter, but I didn't have the luxury of choice in either case. Anyway, the guitar sounded good, and in the end, that's what matters most. Tom O'Carroll heard it that night and testified as much.

"It sounds fine, Frank," says he. "But you still might want to get rid of it."

"Why do you say that?"

"Well, it looks like a big tie tack."

He can be an awful wise guy sometimes.

THE EYES OF TEXAS—
THE GLARE OF THE BOVINE

Texas

Harry O'Donoghue

I met Randy in a club in Philadelphia. He was a trucker from Texas and had a warm and personable demeanor. He said he enjoyed our act, and we had a few drinks after the performance. This was back in the eighties, when I was still playing with Terra Nova. As he left, he waved a copy of our touring schedule and said, "Never know where I'll show up. Maybe down south somewhere."

Sure enough, he walked into Kevin Barry's about ten months later. It was then I learned that he was not only a driver, but that he and his brothers owned and operated a sizeable haulage business from their Houston-based HQ. All very interesting stuff to me; you see, I had long been fascinated by the huge eighteen-wheelers and had hoped someday to get a gawk inside the cab of one. I wanted to see if they really had a telly and a bed that could accommodate two for nocturnal or afternoon delights, and a small fridge and a drinks cabinet, and a built-in sound system, and an air/heat unit—and everything trimmed in gaudy, crimson, Italianesque, stain-resistant cloth. Okay. So maybe I let my sordid little mind meander. C'mon, the possibilities are endless—but as a wee man once said, "Not tonight, Josephine." I wasn't invited to have a look-see, despite my attempts to steer the conversation in that direction. Instead, we were invited to the family home if ever we happened to be in Houston. Not much chance of that, I thought.

A few months later, a phone call led to an unexpected three-week contract in a small pub called Keaneally's in—where else? Houston, Texas! Now, my recollection of the details is a little sketchy, but I believe it was summertime, because our Volkswagen bus had no air conditioning, and I remember it being a particularly arduous journey from Georgia to Texas. It was bloody hot! The owner, John Flowers, and his wife were lovely people, and they invited us to stay in the carriage house overlooking the pool. All very nice, indeed. The pub was a lackluster affair, and not particularly interesting. However, we did meet some delightful folks during our stay, and Texas' hospitality surpassed its reputation.

One night, the bold Randy showed up with his family, and they seemed to enjoy our stage antics. We were invited to a barbecue at their place the following Sunday.

"Y'all ain't never been-a Texas if y'ain't been t'Texas brrrbqueue. Y'all cumin Sunday. Hell, we'll cumin pick you guys up. Won't be no problem, none tall. Noon okay?"

I replied, "Well, Ahmm jes' figgerin' that'll be plum fine with us there, Randy. We mostly always rise jes' afore the crack-a-noon any-house, so we'll get ar lazee butts up'n out the scratcher a few minutes arlier'n Sunday. Yessiree, got you a deal thar."

Actually, I said, "Thanks very much. We'll be sure to be ready."

The drive to the cookout took less than an hour, and I was some-what disappointed at how—well, ordinary their place was. They lived in a decent-sized house in a medium-sized sub-division, in the 'burbs as it were; pretty houses in pretty rows in a pretty part of town, all with manicured, pretty gardens—not what I expected from a family of truckers. All the family members were in attendance—children running around, brothers, sisters, in-laws, outlaws, and the usual smattering of aunts, uncles, friends, and a couple of neighbors. The beverage of choice was Lone Star beer, the unofficial national brew in the Republic of Texas. My partner Trish and I gladly accepted this Texas hospitality, can after can after can. The food was brought in from a pit behind the house, and it was sumptuous and plentiful—all in all a pleasant social Sunday afternoon. When the eatin' was done, one of the children asked if I would play for them.

"Sure," says I, in my best Texas drawl.

Children are the same all over the world—so full of love, joy, and acceptance—and these kids eagerly sang and laughed along with the strangers and their funny accents. Photographs were taken for posterity. Here I was at a barbecue in Houston, Texas—a long way from my home on the banks of the Boyne.

A little while later, Randy came in from the back yard.

"Hey, guys—got a little surprise for you out back. C'mon see."

"A-ha," I thought. "My long-awaited look into the world of the long-distance trucker—my chance to check out the cab of one of these monsters."

We went outside, and what did we see? Two horses, fully saddled. Horses!

144

"Horses," says I.

"Whaddya think?" says Randy.

"Horses?" say I again.

"Magic. I'm on," says Trish. "What about you, Puppy?" (Her nickname for me.)

"Gimme a break, Babby. (My nickname for her.)

"Y'all ain't been-a Texas less you had a real, old-fashioned cowboy horse ride. Give it a try."

Trish was up in the saddle in a flash, looking comfy and content. She had chosen the smaller of the two animals. The other beast was big; I have no idea how many hands, because—well, I just have no idea, but big is the word that comes to mind. It was a *big* animal.

"He's a big'un, Paddy. You afraid?" says Randy's brother. God, I hate when people do that.

"No," says I, gritting my teeth as I grabbed the saddle horn and hoisted myself up. "I've done this before."

And so I had. When I was about seventeen, a bunch of us would go to the local riding stables in Beltichburn on the Termonfeckin road, three miles outside of Drogheda. No experience was necessary. You simply got on, held on, and hoped for the best. Most of the animals stabled there fell into the 'nag' category and were safe enough until they made the turn for home. Then all bets were off. Maybe they smelled the hay or knew it was naptime—I don't know, but they would run 'hell-for-leather' 'til they got back to the paddock. There was no controlling any of them. They were possessed, and if you fell off, not only did you risk the chance of serious injury, but you had to walk the rest of the way back. The humility of it! I remember those walks vividly.

So, here I am mounted on a big gray horse in the backyard of someone's house in Houston, Texas, thinking, "God help me."

Trish click-clicked her mount, and off they trotted toward the field at the far end of the property. I followed suit and click-clicked, but all my guy did was shoot a disinterested nod in my direction and proceed to munch the grass.

"Giv'im a little stirrup; couple-a-kicks should git'im movin'," came a voice from behind.

So I obliged. Bad move, bad move. Stupid! The reaction was immediate, we were "off to the races."

Just how long is it supposed to take a horse to get to a full gallop, anyhow? Seemed like we got from zero to sixty in a couple of seconds. I had a fistful of hair and reins and was holding on for dear life. He made for the field, changed his mind suddenly, turned back toward the house, and made a beeline for the driveway. Only trouble was there were vehicles in the driveway—two full-size pick-up trucks and a small Toyota. How we squeezed between the two trucks is something I'll never know. My eyes were closed tight, and I was having words with God. When I opened them, we were galloping full clip through the front gardens of neighboring houses. Onlookers were shouting words of encouragement and advice.

"Pull hard on the reins, son."

"Show him who's boss, boy."

"Don't let him get the better of you."

My own verbal reaction was more precise. "Fuck this!"

It's a frightening thing to have absolutely no control of a situation that seems to be getting worse by the second, but I was holding fast; if I was going down, I'd take hair, skin, and leather with me. We made tracks through I'm not sure how many front lawns, when he turned sharply and nearly lost me. My arse was in the air, my left foot came out of the stirrup, and I couldn't get it back in. I let go of the reins and lost what little control I had. I shouted every obscenity I knew and grabbed his mane with both hands. I was very afraid and very pissed off—and my delicate region was taking a hell of a pounding.

By now, the neighbors could see the effect a galloping horsey was having on their well-tended lawns and flowers, and it wasn't a pretty sight. Their shouts of support turned to angry threats on our return lap, but there was nothing I could do except close my eyes tight for the re- peat truck maneuver in the driveway. Safely back at home base, he put the brakes on (something I was ill prepared for), and came to a sudden stop. That would be—a dead stop.

I didn't!

My other foot came out of the stirrup and, in what seemed like slow mo- tion, I glided along his neck and landed on my bum right in front of him.

I swear that animal winked at me before he sauntered off to eat some more grass. I swallowed hard and laughed along with the amused Texans, but in truth, I was shaken and shaking. I had regained my com- posure when Trish trotted up.

"Not gonna try it, H?"

She had missed the whole show.

"Naw, not today. Maybe another time."

Guffaws and stifled laughter filled the air. I made toward the house.

"Never again, Randy."

"Well, Harry. Least you can stand up proud 'n say you been to the great state of Texas. Yee-ha!"

જ૪ગ

The Stampede

Robbie O'Connell

In the fall of 1996, I got a call from Liam Clancy asking if I would come to Ireland to perform with him at the post-premiere party of Neil Jordan's film, "Michael Collins." A grand nephew of the film's hero, also named Michael Collins, was one of the city councilors in Waterford City, so this was a special premiere. The plan was to have Liam Neeson, the star of the film, make an appearance prior to the screening of the movie, and at 10:30 p.m., we would all repair to the Granville hotel, where Liam Clancy, Martin Murray, and I would perform for an hour.

The concept of time in Ireland does not conform to any known scientific laws. It was midnight before the crowd assembled at the hotel, and a little after one a.m. when we finally got started. We found that the audience was more interested in talking about the film than listening to us, so we finished our set and headed back to the bar. Ironically, some of the same people who talked all through the concert now wanted to hear more music. A classic Irish session was soon underway, and when I left for bed around six in the morning, it was still going strong.

I awoke at two the following afternoon, feeling as fragile as an empty egg. After I figured out that I was still alive, I cautiously made my way to the shower, where a half-hour under a cascade of steaming water revived me enough to go in search of breakfast. I cautiously made my way to the hotel dining room, where Liam joined me a little later. His condition appeared even worse than mine, so we picked at our food and didn't say much.

There are certain kinds of hangovers that make you philosophical. Your everyday perspective has shifted, and everything seems infused with deep meaning. Even the most mundane things appear profound. You suddenly realize how wondrous the mechanics of a flush toilet are, or you watch, mesmerized, as a seagull hovers overhead then dives down to snatch a discarded orange peel. Phrases of songs you never knew start playing in your head. Lines of poetry you have not thought of for years suddenly surface. This alternative perspective of reality is a gift not to be wasted, and we were not the boys to let an opportunity like this pass us by.

It was November, the sky was clear, and the thermometer was hovering around the freezing point. We decided it was a perfect day to take the long way home. In Ireland, that means driving on the back roads and stopping at small country pubs along the way. It's a rural adventure that is best indulged on crisp winter days when the sky is blue, the muddy roads are frozen, and every country pub has a big fire blazing. These frosty days are also perfect for connecting with the old world—visiting graveyards and ruined castles or searching for Sheila na Gigs. An hour or two of tramping through frozen fields and climbing over brambly ditches can make a hot whiskey taste like the nectar of the gods.

I realized that our back-roads itinerary would take us close to the Knockeen Dolmen. I persuaded Liam that he had to see this archeological wonder. It's a three thousand-year-old burial mound comprised of giant standing stones of granite, capped with a monstrous twenty-ton boulder. This may not be the average person's idea of a good time, but in Waterford, my hometown, we revere our ancestors, particularly when a hot whisky is involved.

But the Knockeen Dolmen is not easy to find. It lies hidden on farmland, surrounded by a maze of narrow, winding roads—roads from which careless travelers may never return. We were on the third wrong turn when we noticed several dogs wandering around. That's not an unusual sight in rural Ireland, where dogs have their own social network, independent of their masters. You will often pass dogs on the road as they hurry to business meetings or stagger home from the pub, but there seemed to be more dogs than usual wandering around. Liam was no dog lover, and I could sense his anxiety level rising. At last, I spotted a familiar old iron gate and announced triumphantly, "This is it!"

"Okay. Where *is* this thing?" Liam asked, with all the enthusiasm of a flat pint.

148

"We just have to climb over this gate, cross the field, hop over the wall, and it's right there," I replied.

"You must be joking," said Liam, looking wide-eyed at me. "Do you expect me to climb over that gate in *this* condition?"

It took a while, but with the aid of several snide remarks about his manhood and assurances that there were no dogs in the vicinity, I managed to coax him into the field. We still had to walk about two hundred yards to the far wall, where the dolmen awaited. The field was sloped—the higher ground on our right and the lower part rolling down for a quarter of a mile to our left. The grass was tall and spongy under foot, so with heads down, carefully scanning the terrain for cowpats and soggy spots, we advanced from tuft to tuft.

"This is great," I said, with forced exuberance. "Plenty of fresh air to clear the head."

"Where the hell is it?" Liam asked, impatiently.

"Just inside that ditch," I said, pointing to the wall about fifty yards ahead.

Suddenly, we heard a long note from a horn or bugle, immediately followed by a deep rumbling sound. We looked up the hill. A huge herd of frightened bullocks was stampeding directly towards us. It was exactly like a scene from an old cowboy movie, minus the clouds of dust. We looked wildly around. Not a rock or tree was in sight—nothing but the open field.

"Jesus Christ!" I screamed. "Run!"

We were running like hares when we spotted a telegraph pole fifty feet ahead. It didn't look like much protection, but it was all there was and our only hope. We made a dash for it. With hearts pounding, we lined up behind the pole, trying to make ourselves as thin as possible. Terrified cattle thundered by on either side of us. Hundreds of hooves battered the ground, just inches away, like the roar of a massive waterfall. The smell of hot, hairy animals filled our nostrils. Specks of mud dotted our clothes. We stood there, panic-stricken, limbs trembling, adrenaline racing through our veins. It was Armageddon, for certain, at least for us. Then, just as suddenly as it had begun, it was all over.

The silence that followed seemed unnatural. We were so shaken we just stood there, waiting for the panic to subside. We could not believe we had survived. We stared at the cattle, now milling uneasily at the lower end of the field. If that telephone pole had not been there, we would have been trampled to death for sure.

"Let's get the hell out of here," said Liam.

"But we're almost there," I pleaded. "Just take a quick look over the wall." We had almost paid a dear price in this effort, and I was not about to give up now. Reluctantly, he followed me as far as the wall.

"Is that it?" Liam asked, with little more than a glance at the ivy-covered heap of stones.

I nodded.

"Right, then," he said. "Let's go."

There was no arguing with him. He'd had enough.

Still keeping a wary eye on the cattle now huddled in the lower corner of the field, we crossed back the way we had come. As we were getting into the car, the bugle sounded again, and we realized what had had happened. There was a foxhunt in full pursuit somewhere nearby. Though we couldn't see them, we could hear the muffled shouts of the riders and the faint barking of the hounds. That explained the unusual number of dogs we had seen earlier and the spooked, charging cattle.

"Where are we, anyway?" asked Liam. "What's the nearest village?"

"Dunhill is about three miles," I replied.

"Great!" says he. "Harney's is just the place."

The whole surreal episode was still very much with us, and we were both in need of a little something to settle the nerves. A short drive brought us to Dunhill and Harney's pub. A fire was blazing in a big stone fireplace, and, feeling a bit more relaxed and secure, we sat up at the bar. It was mid-afternoon, and there were only two other customers. One was reading a paper while the other stared into space. Jim Harney, the proprietor, appeared behind the bar. He was delighted to see Liam.

"I can't believe it," he said. "We were only talking about you last night. Paddy Barron is staying here, and he was asking about you." He went on to explain how Paddy, an old friend of Liam's, was home from the States for a short holiday, but had gone to Dublin that morning and was not expected back for several hours.

"He'll be really disappointed to miss you," Jim said, setting two creamy pints of Guinness on the counter. We both put twenty-pound notes on the bar, but Jim insisted that the drinks were on the house. We chatted with the other customers, one of whom we learned was a psychiatric nurse unwinding from a hard week's work.

150

I have often noticed that the search for mutual acquaintances seems to be of primary importance among strangers in Irish pubs. Maybe it's that old suspicion of the outsider that still lingers in the countryside, but after a few minutes, we established that we had some friends in common and settled into conversation.

Two more pints appeared, and our twenty-pound notes remained untouched on the counter. We related the story of the stampede, which was already assuming mythic proportions for us, but the locals were unimpressed. It didn't sound like such a big deal to them, but reliving the ordeal, we realized just how narrow our escape had been and how lucky we were. It gave us that heightened awareness of being alive and seemed like a cause for celebration. Liam spotted a dusty old bottle of Midleton Special Old Malt whiskey on the top shelf. Never having seen that particular brand before, we thought a little taste would be appropriate to the occasion. We insisted Jim take the money this time. He quickly poured out two very generous glasses, but to our embarrassment, dismissed our efforts to pay.

"No, no," he said, shaking his head. "Sure that wouldn't even cover it."

This was getting awkward now. We wanted to stay, but we couldn't just sit there drinking and not paying. Liam had an idea.

"Well," he said, "If you won't take the money, we'll have to sing for our supper."

I went out to the car and brought in Liam's concertina and my guitar. We relocated to the other end of the room, where yellow flames were dancing in fireplace. The few people who had been sitting at the bar moved with us. Liam picked up his concertina and played a couple of O'Carolan tunes.

Turlough O'Carolan was the last of the great Irish harpers who traveled the countryside in the early eighteenth century, visiting the big houses and entertaining the Gaelic aristocracy. These bards were held in high esteem and both revered and feared. If they considered themselves well treated, they would write songs of praise for their patrons, but they were equally quick to defame those who did not meet their expectations.

Our miraculous pint glasses never seemed to be empty, and we sat there in the firelight singing shut-eye songs and playing sweet old tunes. At one point, someone was moved to quote a couplet from Tennyson's "Ulysses." Liam instantly sprang into action.

"It little profits that an idle king,
By this still hearth among these barren crags—"

151

To the surprise of all, he recited the whole poem, all seventy lines, from start to finish. It was a masterful performance. His voice was full of emotion, particularly when he reached the final lines:

"Tho' much is taken, much abides; and though
We are not now that strength which in old days
Moved earth and heaven, that which we are, we are;
One equal temper of heroic hearts,
Made weak by time and fate, but strong in will
To strive, to seek, to find, and not to yield."

I saw huge tears flowing down the cheeks of the psychiatric nurse. She looked stunned. Evidently, she was not accustomed to this kind of fine madness. I sang a song of my own, which had been inspired by the nearby village on Dunmore East:

"I was walking the road to Dunmore,
One evening as often I'd done.
And my heart was as heavy as stone,
I was thinking of times that are gone
When we walked arm in arm on the shore
And we watched the waves roll on the sea
Never thinking that there'd come a time
They'd be rolling between you and me"

Although I had often performed that song, it was as if I was truly hearing it for the first time. Every song and tune that afternoon felt timeless and perfect. It was like stepping back in history, I thought. Surely, it must have been just like this for the old bards. We were in the zone now. Not even the arrival of several boisterous customers coming in for an after-work drink could break the spell.

A little later, Jim's wife, Mary, appeared. "Come on now," she said, "Your dinner is on the table. Just leave the instruments there, and we'll take care of them."

She marched us upstairs and sat us down before a table laden with steaks, potatoes, and vegetables. There was food enough for a dozen hungry men who had worked the fields from dawn to dusk. Bottles of wine were opened, glasses were filled, and with appetites sharpened by pints of Guinness and Special Old Malt whiskey, we attacked the feast manfully.

The dinner was nearly finished when the door opened and Paddy Barron stepped in. Hugs, handshakes, and good-natured insults were exchanged. Another bottle of wine was opened, and then the stories began.

"Remember the time we..."

It was fascinating stuff. I heard stories of poets, musicians, and "great nights" in Greenwich Village, tales of wild and crazy characters, most no longer living. After an hour or two (I'd lost track of the time by then), we headed back down to the small bar on the other side of the pub for a session. The instruments were waiting for us. Even if we had *wanted* to leave at that point, it would have been rude to do so after all the hospitality we had received. So we extracted a promise from Jim that he would let us pay for our drinks from here on out, then we picked up our instruments and settled in beside the fire. Within minutes, the room was packed with regulars, and it soon turned into a mighty session. Several local singers eagerly joined in, and we carried on singing and playing way past the official closing time.

At about two o'clock in the morning, ten hours after we stopped in for *one* drink, we finally took our leave. After a lengthy string of farewells, we stepped outside. The sky was riddled with stars, and frost was settling on the roadway. The world seemed strange, different, like it does when you leave a dark movie theatre and step out into daylight. It took us a couple of moments to get our bearings and locate Liam's car.

Anxious to avoid police cars on our homeward journey, we discussed the pro and cons of the different routes we could take. Liam handed me his car keys.

"You have an American license," he said. "You better drive."

If there was logic to this, I failed to see it, but it had been such an extraordinary day that I did not argue. We drove carefully and slowly, kept to the deserted back roads, and eventually made it home safely.

A TRIO OF TALES IN WHICH SEAMUS JOURNEYS TO ALASKA

Crabs I

Seamus Kennedy

I want to make it clear from the outset that this story is NOT about the scourge of traveling entertainers everywhere, that irritating critter lurking unseen only to show up suddenly and make our lives miserable.

I am referring, of course, to the dreaded sourpuss. The person who sits right in front at a show and absolutely does not want to be entertained. He or she is usually there as part of a larger group who are celebrating some occasion and are out for a good time, while the crabby one is bound and determined NOT to enjoy him/herself. This manifests itself in many ways, such as refusing to laugh at jokes while everyone else is splitting their sides roaring, or in audience participation bits like the "Unicorn" or the "Moonshiner." The rest of the group is frantically gesticulating, but the crab will sit with arms tightly folded across the chest, tight-lipped, with a grim look bordering on a snarl welded to the visage. Usually the others will try to get the uptight one to relax. "C'mon! Lighten up! Let's have a good time," they will laughingly exhort with claps to the back, which only serves to reinforce the dour one's demeanor.

This is where I come in.

The guy is a perfect target for me. I direct my attention on him, establish eye contact, and regard him as my very own pagan baby to be converted and saved from the ignorance of his ways by my missionary music and humor. And the rest of his group—the choir to whom I am already preaching—eat it up.

Now, two things can happen at this juncture: my ministrations and the efforts of the group to make the "heathen" see the error of his ways, will have the desired effect, the person will crack a sheepish-looking smile, and looking somewhat abashed, will slowly thaw and join in the merrymaking. Saved! Hallelujah! Or, as happened in Ireland's Own one memorable Saturday night, the aggrieved one will stand up, yell "Fuck you! Fuck all of you," and storm out.

On this particular night, his companions said, "Ahhh, let him go. He's no fun, anyway. He's just being a jerk," to which I replied that I was sorry, that I didn't mean to drive him away, to which they in turn responded, "Don't mind him. His mother died yesterday."

No, this is not *that* kind of crab story.

For the past twelve years, each January has seen me going to Alaska to perform for a couple of weeks. Alaska in January is great for entertainers because folks need relief from the grip of winter, so they turn out in droves. Most shows are ticketed events with many performances selling out ahead of time. Thank God for SAD (seasonally affected disorders) and cabin fever.

My friend Pat Beattie is my self-appointed agent/ booker there, and he does a great job filling in two weeks (now three) with lucrative and extremely enjoyable gigs. The second year I was scheduled to go up to the Great Land, he suggested I bring my wife Dona and our two sons, Damian and Matthew, along. I did so, and they got to see sights many folk don't get to see, such as moose walking in the streets of Anchorage or coming into people's yards to forage for food. Or the Northern Lights. One of the gigs Pat booked was in Nome, way up North, not that far from the Arctic Circle, with the former Soviet Union a hop, skip, and a jump to the West, just across the frozen Bering Sea. Dona came with me, while Pat and his wife Cathy looked after our boys, along with their own brood of four.

The concert was held in the Nome Mini-Convention Center, which also serves as the headquarters for the Iditarod Dogsled Race. The audience was wonderful and warm, and I'm glad they were, because it was thirty degrees below zero outside. We also got to meet the only two Irishmen in Nome, Kevin McCaffrey from Co. Cavan and his buddy Richard O'Brien from Wicklow. They're both honest-to-God gold miners—an occupation they didn't pick up in Cavan or Wicklow, I can assure you.

Kevin is a big bear of a man, with a full beard and a zest for life, who looks every inch the typical Alaskan sourdough—albeit with a Cavan accent, "don'cha know?" He is also a wizard on the ould harmonica, so I called him up on stage with me during the show, and we did a set of reels and jigs, which the audience loved. He has since become a firm friend, and I look forward to seeing him in Nome each year.

Richard is somewhat less ebullient and a bit more cerebral, but a lovely man and great craic nonetheless. When the show was over, the boyos invited Dona and me to the Arctic Native Brotherhood Club for a few jars, an invitation we eagerly accepted. When we had quaffed a couple, my wife mentioned that we had been in Alaska for a week and had not yet eaten king crab, that succulent Alaskan delicacy renowned the world over. Kevin and Richard explained that most of the king crab caught in Alaskan waters was for sale to the lower forty-eight states or for export, and not usually eaten by the locals except in high-falutin' restaurants. However, they said, if we wanted Alaskan king crab, then by God, Alaskan king crab we would have! Kevin abruptly jumped up and left the ANBC, pulling his parka on as he rushed out.

Dona and I continued our conversation with Richard and a couple of the locals and learned some fascinating facts about Nome in winter. For example, there is not much in the way of trees that far north—a few scrub pines in the permafrost, maybe, so for the Christmas holidays, Scotch pines, Douglas firs, and other Yuletide greenery are barged in from the lower forty-eight. When Christmas is over, the trees are not dumped on the sidewalk to be collected and ignominiously incinerated. Oh, no. They are lovingly hauled onto the ice of the Bering Sea, which is essentially a gigantic back yard for the buildings and houses on the western side of Front Street. Holes are augured into the ice, and the trees are placed upright therein; then, when the ice has once again filled in the holes, there is a little park of pine trees out on the vast expanse of the white and frozen Bering Sea. A sign is erected which reads "Bering National Forest," and plywood cutout silhouettes of bears, reindeer, and moose are strategically placed among the trees. No hunting permitted.

When the spring thaw, or "breakup," occurs, the trees are swept out to sea in a perfect example of ecological recycling. Incidentally, in Nome, as in other Alaskan communities, there is a pool as to when the breakup will take place. Large sums of money are wagered (legally—it's like a lottery) on the exact month, week, day, hour, minute, and second that the ice breaks, and the winner, obviously, is the person who guesses most accurately.

At the beginning of March, the famous Iditarod Dogsled Race is run from Anchorage to Nome to commemorate the celebrated serum run, when diphtheria serum was brought to Nome to quell an outbreak of the disease by a relay of brave and dedicated mushers. Well, the Iditarod in Alaska is like the Superbowl in the lower forty-eight, with all sorts of attendant attractions and events, the most unlikely of which is the Bering Sea Open Golf Tournament. Yes, indeed, golf fans, there is a golf tournament held on that barren, icy, seascape each March. Astroturf mats with holes, flags, and tees are brought onto the ice to make an eighteen-hole golf course. Naturally, it's the same nine holes going out and coming back.

Colored balls are used—imagine trying to find a mishit white ball out there—and the golfers in their Carhartts winter golf finery play the course. If you over club slightly, you don't find yourself playing out of the rough, you find yourself playing out of Russia.

The door burst open, a gale blew in, snowflakes fluttered in the doorway and died as Kevin, carrying a big cardboard box, made a dramatic reappearance. He set the box on the floor and turned to Dona and me.

"You haven't had king crab legs since you came to Alaska, eh? Well, by God, you will tonight."

He opened the box and lifted out the biggest crab I had ever seen. The shell was about fifteen inches across, while the eight legs were easily two and a half feet long and four inches in diameter. And it was still alive and kicking, its wee black eyes glittering on their stalks.

"Richard, grab the other one," he said.

Richard reached into the box and lifted out another crab, which to my eye was identical to the first, but it might have been handsomer.

"Right," says Kevin, "which one do ye want?"

"Oh, no," says Dona, "we couldn't eat your crabs."

"Not at all!" roars the bould Kevin. "Richard and I were out ice-fishing yesterday, don'cha know, and we're allowed to keep these for ourselves. Isn't that right, Richard?"

"'Tis," says Richard, anticipating the title of Frank McCourt's sequel to *Angela's Ashes* by a good nine years or so.

"Which one do ye want?" insists Kevin.

"Oh, no," says Dona again. "I can't. Seamus, you pick it."

"Oh, God," says I, not wanting to condemn an innocent king crab to death. "I don't know."

"All right," says Kevin, "here's what we'll do. We'll set the pair o' them on the floor here, and we'll race them the length of the room, don'cha know, and we'll eat the loser. Richard, set your lad down here beside mine, and we'll let them go."

"Grand, so," says Richard.

By this time, a group of natives and locals had gathered to witness this epic race by two evenly matched contestants; favorites were chosen, and wagers were made and accepted. The brace of racers were placed against one wall and given a nudge with the toe of a boot. They're off! They began to scuttle sideways (I nearly said "crablike") down the room, their claws clacking on the hardwood floor. The crowd began to cheer for their favorites:

"C'mon, the homely one!"

"Let's go, gorgeous!"

"Okay, okay, time to give it the gas!" as one and then the other took the lead, until finally there was a winner. The homely crab just nipped the handsome one at the post by an eyestalk.

"Right y' are," declares Kevin, and he lifted the victor back into his cardboard box.

"Richard, we'll take this runner-up back to the house, and Seamus and Dona can have their Alaskan king crab."

"Fair enough," said Richard, ever the talkative one.

I felt guilty. It was as though I had been at a gladiatorial spectacle in the Coliseum and had turned thumbs-down on a truly valiant combatant who merely had the misfortune to slip and fall before his opponent. In fact I was sure I'd heard the two crabs communicate telepathically with me before the race: "Caesar, morituri te salutant!"

Dona felt guilty *and* horrified, as though she had been present at a terrible accident, and was powerless to whisper the Act of Contrition into the ear of a dying victim.

Now, Richard and Kevin had a house that they had been renovating not far from the Native Brotherhood Club, to which we then repaired. Whipped by the Arctic wind, Dona and I carried a couple of six-packs from the club as we followed the lads through the snow to their humble abode.

Once inside, we stamped our feet to knock off the snow, and gazed around as Richard placed the crab in a large ice-chest. It was a scene of chaotic construction. Bare studs, Tyvek, batts of insulation, exposed electrical wire, bare bulbs, sheetrock, boxes of nails, sawhorses, sawdust and power tools, and cold. Lord, it was cold!

The two boys camped in another room while they were rebuilding the house, and this roughed-in, unfinished mess was to be our banquet hall.

Richard fired up a big kerosene heater, which almost immediately projected heat throughout. We began to thaw, and Kevin lit a propane gas stove, upon which he placed a five-gallon cauldron of water.

"Sit yourselves down," he invited. He and Richard placed a plank between two sawhorses, and upon this makeshift love seat, Dona and I sat. We cracked open a can of beer each while we waited for the water to come to the boil, and Kevin pulled out the ould mouth-organ, the "oral Wurlitzer," and began to play a few come-all-ye's. We sang and had another beer, and finally the water was bubbling furiously.

"Here we go now," said Kevin, and like a warden going to bring the condemned man from his cell to the death chamber, he got up and walked over to get the crab. I half expected Richard to walk behind him reading verses from the Bible. He lifted the crab and plunged it head-first into the boiling water.

"It's quicker when you put 'em in headfirst. That way, they don't suffer," explained Richard. It made sense. If someone were to plunge me headfirst into a cauldron of boiling water, I'd try to die as quickly as I could, too. Kevin, meanwhile, had melted a pound of butter on the stove and poured it into four coffee mugs. After about ten minutes, Chef Kevin announced, "He's done. Let's get him outta there."

He turned off the propane, and using a rag, he reached in, grabbed a leg, and lifted the crab out. It had turned bright red. He snapped off all the legs and gave two big ones to Dona and me. Each leg was about twenty-six inches long in two segments.

We all sat down, popped open a beer each, and began to crack the crab legs. The soft meat fell easily from the shell; we dipped each delicious morsel in the melted butter and decadently crammed it into our mouths. There was no chewing at all. It was sweet and tender and contrasted beautifully with the warm, salty lipidity of the butter, and the hoppy bite of the beer. The crab liquor and butter ran down our chins, and we didn't bother to wipe it off. It may have been thirty below outside, but in here, it was womb-warm with good companionship and the best of food and drink and music. I didn't feel guilty anymore.

Neither did Dona.

ଔୡ

Crabs II

Seamus Kennedy

Kodiak Island is called the Emerald Isle of the Aleutian Chain, which extends way out into the Gulf of Alaska and the Northern Pacific, like a long pinky finger sticking out from a closed fist. It is the largest of sixteen islands, with the city of Kodiak and five native villages providing the bulk of the human population. The animal population is comprised of sea lions, sea otters, elk, mountain goats, and deer, among others.

But the most famous of all is the Alaskan brown bear, *Ursus horribilis*, the great grizzly, which can weigh in at 1400 pounds or so. Or as Alaskans are proud to boast, "The largest land carnivore in the world." Just as in Ireland, heavy cloud often covers this island, so that it doesn't suffer from extreme heat or cold, and from the air, the lush vegetation appears as verdant as that of the Old Sod. We may have forty shades of green in Ireland, but I'd say there's probably thirty-seven or thirty-eight in Kodiak.

Commercial fishing is the primary industry on Kodiak, with canning, packing, and other related businesses providing jobs. In fact, Kodiak is one of the largest fisheries in the US. During the summer months, it is also a mecca for sport-fisher persons, hunt-persons, and outdoors persons. (Damned political correctness!) There are three main cultural influences on Kodiak, both in the city and in the native villages. The first is the Aleut (Alutiiq in their native tongue), the second is the Russians, who, under Alexander Baranov, established fur-trading settlements in the late 18th and 19th centuries, and the third is the American influence. This occurred when the United States purchased Alaska from Russia in 1867—a deal known at the time as Seward's Folly, for the secretary of state who persuaded the US government that it was a helluva bargain.

Not only did America continue trading seal and otter furs, a major whaling and commercial fishing industry began, as well, and of course lumber, gold, and other valuable minerals were discovered on the mainland. The village of Old Harbor grew up near one of the first Russian settlements, Three Saints Bay, and in the summer, one can see an old, Russian Orthodox Church with the "onion dome," and a graveyard complete with Russian crosses, which feature a smaller crossbar near the top.

The local arts council booked me to give a concert there in January a few years ago. The gig was set up by a friend called Emil Christianson, an Old Harbor native, who had seen me perform in Anchorage and thought I would be just what folk in his village needed in the dreary days of winter. So, with my small PA system, my overnight case, and my trusty guitar, I flew from Anchorage to Kodiak. From there I caught a small plane to Old Harbor, a thirty-minute trip, flying in light clouds through a gap in the mountains to land at the airstrip on the outskirts of the village. I was met at the plane by Emil, who brought my gear and me into town. He had booked me a room in the local hunting-lodge, which in the summer would be filled with visitors, but which was empty right now. Except for me, of course.

It was warm and comfortable, and the solitude was relaxing. The show that night was to take place at 7:00 p.m. in the community center, a multi-purpose building right in the middle of the village. It was there that the villagers came to town meetings, political rallies, commercial-fishing seminars, income-tax advice classes—and Bingo.

Emil took me to the community center at 6:00 p.m. and helped me bring the gear into the little hall then he left on other business. I had just started to set up my equipment—mounting the speakers on their tripod stands and connecting them to the amp-mixer, when the locals began to filter in.

"What's going on here?" they asked.

"I'm doing a concert of Irish music tonight," I replied.

"Oh, yeah? Who are you?"

"My name's Seamus Kennedy. I'm an Irish entertainer, and I've been booked to do a show for you folks this evening."

"But what about Bingo?" they chorused plaintively.

"Well, I've been hired to do an Irish show. I don't know about Bingo. Maybe you can have your Bingo right after me."

"Who the hell hired you?"

"Emil."

"Where is he?"

"I don't know, but I've got a contract here—"

The bingo-caller came over and heard what was transpiring, and said, "Yeah, Emil mentioned something about this. We gotta have this concert tonight."

"Bullshit. We always play Bingo. Why the hell do we gotta listen to Irish music, anyway?"

"Because Emil hired him, that's why. Son-of-a-bitch."

"Yeah, yeah," they grumbled.

By this time there were seventy-five disgruntled Old Harbor natives in the community center, and I had the privilege of re-gruntling them for two

162

hours. Well, I finished setting up, took my place in front of the microphone, and started on one of the toughest audiences I've ever had to work.

First song—"Whiskey in the Jar." My audience kick-starter. Get them clapping along, laughing at the ones who can't clap in time. Up-tempo, bouncy, opening number. Nothing. Stone faces—seventy-five of them—glaring at me eating into their Bingo time. "The Black Velvet Band." Sing along on the chorus; act out the chorus. Silly stuff.

Nada. Zip.

A couple of jokes.

"Murphy and the wife come home from vacation, and their house has been broken into, and everything's been stolen. Murphy calls the police, and the only available cop in the area is a K-9 policeman. He pulls up in front of Murphy's house and gets out of the car with his dog. Murphy looks out the window and sees them walking up the driveway and breaks down crying. His wife says, "What's the matter? Why are you crying?" Murphy says, "We come back from vacation, our house has been broken into, every stick of furniture we own has been stolen, and they send over a blind cop!"

Silence.

"A little girl watching her mommy making breakfast in the kitchen notices a few gray hairs peeking out through her mom's lovely thatch of red hair and asks her, 'Mommy, where do gray hairs come from?' Well, her mom's kind of irritated, and says, 'When little girls are naughty and bad and make their mommies angry and sad—that's where gray hairs come from.' The little girl sits down and says, 'Oh.' A few minutes later, she says, 'Mommy?' 'What is it, dear?' says the Mom. 'You must really have pissed off Grandma.'"

Not just silence, but the kind of silence where you hear crickets chirping, like in the old Daffy Duck cartoon.

Flop-sweat. Dying with my boots on.

Ohhh-kayyy! Another forty-five minutes of this hell to go. I keep hammering away, a song here, a joke there, like dripping water trying to erode their façade of disinterest. Façade, my ass. Fifteen minutes to go 'til the end of the set. Then, out of the blue, a laugh. Not a belly laugh or even a guffaw—just slightly more than a chuckle—but a laugh nonetheless.

In desperation, but trying not to show it, I try another joke. It works! Another laugh! And another. I've got them! With fifteen minutes left in the first half, I've won them over. Another audience participation bit and they're all clapping along.

I change moods by introducing a wrist-slashing Irish ballad, and they're all ears. They listen attentively and applaud effusively when it ends. Yes! I've done it.

"Thank you very much, ladies and gentlemen. Thank you. I'm going to take a little break right here, and I'll be back for the second half of the show in about fifteen minutes." I stepped away from the microphone to bask in the warmth of their applause and adulation, only to hear, "Second half! No, no! What about our Bingo?"

Right on cue, Emil came back and rescued me from what could have been an ugly scene. He pulled me aside and said, "Seamus, I'm really sorry, but I didn't promote this like I should have. I've been out of town, and didn't have a chance to let the folks know what was happening tonight. They were expecting Bingo, not Irish music. So, here's what I'll do—I'll give you the check for the full amount, and you don't have to play the second half of the show. Is that fair?"

"Fair enough," says I.

He turns to the crowd and yells, "Seamus Kennedy has kindly agreed not to do the second half of his show, so you can play Bingo! How about that?" A huge cheer goes up, and I get a bigger round of applause for not performing than for performing.

I pocketed the check and performed the fastest breakdown of equipment I've ever done, and got the gear out of there and back to the lodge, where I changed into my street clothes. It was just after eight o'clock. There were at least six hours left before I could even contemplate going to sleep. A bar was called for, a few drinks, some music, a little relaxation.

Did I mention that Old Harbor is a dry town?

Because of a high alcoholism rate, there are no bars or liquor sales in the village. In the town of Kodiak, yes, but in Old Harbor, no. So, after wandering the streets like a derelict for half an hour, trying to find someplace to get a drink, I trudged back to the community center. And I played Bingo.

Now, I'm not the world's greatest Bingoista, I'll be the first to admit, so I bought one card for a dollar, and sat down with my little colored stamp between two elderly natives, a husband and wife, who were playing approximately ninety-six boards each. They were feverishly marking their cards, which were spread out in front of them, while I sat with my one little board, unable to figure out what to do. Out of pity, the old guy started marking my card as well as his own.

He nudged me in the ribs and whispered, "Shout 'Bingo'!"

I did, the checker came over to look at my card, and sure enough, I'd won three hundred dollars. Now, I may be Irish, but I'm not dumb, and I figured that people who'd been deprived of an hour of Bingo would not take kindly to the cause of said deprivation winning three hundred of their spondulicks. Accordingly, I rose and announced that I would like to purchase the next card for everybody in the place, which earned me another thunderous ovation, as though I had just finished singing again.

Hey, it cost me seventy-five bucks, but I still came out two and a quarter ahead.

The next day, I was supposed to fly back to Anchorage. Due to fog, which occurs frequently on Kodiak, all flights in and out of Old Harbor were canceled, and I was forced to stay over in the lodge. There isn't a lot to do in Old Harbor in the winter, unlike the summer, when there's plenty to do. I couldn't do the tourist thing, because all the tourist things were closed for the season. I walked around the village and visited the cemetery and the Russian Orthodox Church, and took lots of close-up photographs of bald eagles, which are regarded as pests by the locals.

To someone from the lower forty-eight, where the bald eagle is an endangered species, this magnificent bird is a majestic sight, whether in flight, perching on a tree limb, or soaring down and skimming the wave-tops to rise up with a salmon thrashing in its talons. But to the natives and locals on Kodiak, they are a pain in the ass. They are as common as starlings or street pigeons, and eagle-poop on a windshield is a lot bigger than pigeon or starling poop.

And God forbid you should let a puppy or kitten or even a full-grown Chihuahua out of the house to do its business unattended. Eagle chow! And much like street pigeons, they are unafraid of humans. I walked through flocks of them on the ground in Old Harbor, and they just parted casually to let me through. I'm glad they never saw Alfred Hitchcock's *The Birds*.

So, for two foggy days, I walked with the eagles, ate in a diner, and slept in the lodge at night—and not a drop to drink. On the third day, I checked the radio report again—still fogged in, no flights out. I was contemplating trying to catch a couple of eagles and training them to carry me out, when a knock came at the door. I opened it, and the knock was still there, attached to the hand of a local fisherman called Jerry Christianson.

"Hey, Seamus, you're probably bored stiff here, listening to the fog reports, eh?"

I allowed as how I was, and he said, "You wanna come out in my boat crab-fishing with me?"

I played it real cool and said, "Ohboyohboyohboy! Would I! Huh, really! Can I please, pleeeease!"

Jerry took that as a "Yes."

Down to the dock we went, where he kitted me out in foul weather gear, and we boarded his boat for a trip out on the briny deep. There was just the two of us, and Jerry had brought along a box of four dozen dead ducks. Well, actually, they were duck carcasses with the breasts and legs removed. I asked why there were no breasts and legs, and he said, "We eat them; the rest we use to bait the crab pots."

"What kind of crabs?" I asked.

"King crabs," he replied.

He went on to tell me that he had forty-odd crab pots marked by buoys in the waters around Old Harbor, and we were going to winch them up, one at a time, and take out the crabs. Sounded good to me! Jerry started the motor on the boat and guided her out into the bay.

There was a brisk breeze blowing, and it was nippy, but not freezing as we headed out towards the crab-grounds. In my head, I was singing Ewan McColl's great song, "The Shoals of Herring," about the herring fishermen who risk life and limb in fair and foul weather in the North Sea.

"With our nets and gear we're faring,
On the wild and wasteful ocean;
It's out there on the deep
That we harvest and reap our bread,
As we hunt the bonny shoals of herring."

We arrived at the buoy marker for the first crab-pot, and Jerry hooked a chain from the winch on the boat to the connectors on the pot. Then he hit the start button on the electric motor, and the winch began

166

to reel in the crab-pot. It broke the surface, and we manhandled it on board, a four-foot square steel cage covered with heavy-duty wire mesh with a hinged lid. On one side was an opening through which the crabs could enter, but not exit.

And there, inside, was a king crab! The carapace was 15" across, and the legs were two feet long. I was as excited as a kid on Christmas Day! Jerry showed me the procedure for extracting the crab from the pot. Raise the lid, grasp the crab with both hands on either side of its shell, lift it out of the cage, and set it in a large holding-pen on the deck of the boat. Toss a duck carcass into the crab-pot, close the lid, wrestle the cage onto the gunwale of the boat, and push it overboard. It will sink to the bottom, to be marked by the floating buoy on the surface. Disconnect the winch, motor over to the next crab-pot, and repeat.

"Oh, it was a fine and a pleasant day,
Out of Yarmouth harbor I was faring,
As a cabin boy on a sailing lugger,
For to hunt the bonny shoals of herring."

The first one wasn't too bad. Get into a rhythm, and it gets easier, although the crab pots were heavy and cumbersome, and I banged the bejeebers out of my shins a few times, which caused a spate of naughty words and colorful Irish phrases.

"Jesus H. Murphy and all the saints! You rotten rat's miscarriage of a bastardin' big tea-strainer!" being among the least profane.

"You're up on deck, you're a fisherman,
You can swear and show a manly bearing,
Take your turn on watch with the other fellows
While you're hunting for the shoals of herring"

It didn't seem to faze Jerry at all. I think he may have heard similar expressions in his time. But we worked steadily for about four and a half hours, hauling and lifting, sweating in our slickers. I didn't wear gloves, and my hands began to show the wear and tear of the rough metal of the crab pots, the coarse crab shells, and the cold salt water. Cuts, scrapes, and abrasions decorated my sissy, namby-pamby, guitar-playing hands, which were feeling the effects of actual manual labor.

"Oh, the work was hard, and the hours were long,
And the treatment, sure it took some bearing,
There was little kindness and the kicks were many,
As we hunted for the shoals of herring."

Finally, the last king crab was put in the pen, the last crab-pot baited and lowered, and it was time to head back to the village. Jerry started the boat, swung her head 'round, and steered for home. I thrust my hands deep into the pockets of my slicker to try to bring them back to life with what little warmth there was. They were numb, cold, and starting to smart from the salt water in the cuts and scratches. I took them out, blew hard on them, and tucked them into my armpits.

"Sweating or cold,
growing up, growing old, and dying,
As we hunt the bonny shoals of herring."

We were still a couple of miles away when Jerry said, "Well, Seamus, a good workman is worth his pay."
"Oh, no, Jerry," said I. "You don't have to pay me. I enjoyed this day immensely. I was glad to have something to do."
But he insisted, "No. I believe in paying my crew."
And with that, he opened the boat's medicine cabinet and took out a bottle of Jack Daniels.

ೞ

Honey

Seamus Kennedy

"There are strange things done in the midnight sun by the men who moil for gold.
The Arctic trails have their secret tales that would make your blood run cold;
The Northern lights have seen queer sights, but the queerest they ever did see
Was the night on the marge of Lake LeBarge I cremated Sam McGee."

Robert W. Service, "The Cremation of Sam McGee"

Well, I'm merely a Cheechako visitor, not a sourdough pioneer miner, but I can attest to the fact that there are strange things done and queer sights to be seen.

January 2002. I have a gig booked in the pioneering town of Nome on the shores of the frozen Bering Sea. My flight from Anchorage is at 6:00 a.m., and because of new security measures, I have to be at Ted Stevens Airport at 4:00 a.m. Now, most musicians I know are nocturnal and are usually just getting home at 4:00 a.m. In fact, if truth be told, we sleep hanging upside down in dark closets with our elbows tucked into our armpits until it's time to wake and flutter from our lairs for a feed of insects before heading off to the next gig.

So, completely sleep-deprived from the previous night's work in sub-zero temperatures, I am dropped off at the airport by my friend Pat Beattie, who is a civilian, and a normal person, and completely unused to the hellacious hours kept by the fine folks in the entertainment community.

I check my guitar and case containing my clothes, shaving gear, and CDs to sell, and I try to find the bar. Whoops! It's four in the morning; the bar won't open until eleven a.m. Well, heck, poop, and tarnation! So I find a newspaper rack and purchase, for the paltry amount of fifty cents, the latest edition of Alaska's finest weekly—the *Nome Nugget* (motto: *Illegitimus Non Carborandum*—honest to God), with a big ad for my appearance that evening. Good! I'm still booked to appear.

The Alaska Airlines Boeing 737 has been modified for cargo and passengers. The passenger compartment is composed of the tail section of the aircraft, in which there are seven rows of seats, three abreast, from row twenty to row thirteen. At the front of the passenger section there is a huge bulkhead, behind which is the cargo bay, and in front of this lies the cockpit, which in these politically correct times of female pilots and such is now referred to as the "flight deck," although "box office" might work, too.

We don't board through a jet way; instead, we go outside the building and walk around the wing to the rear of the plane, where we mount the stairs to find a pair of stewardesses (modern translation: flight attendants), bundled up in parkas and huddling together for warmth, to welcome us aboard. There are fifteen other hardy souls on board for our flight of an hour and a half up to damn near the Arctic Circle.

Seasoned traveler that I am, I immediately inflate my little U-shaped pillow, which I place around my neck like a Budweiser Clydesdale's collar, lean back, and even before takeoff, I'm sound asleep. I miss breakfast, because the airhostesses (sorry—flight attendants) don't want to wake me. Bless them.

When I do wake, we're on the ground in Nome, so we walk down the stairs again into the chill morning air, twenty below zero, and across to the small, one-room terminal building. There's not enough room to swing a cat, just bounce it up and down. My contact for the gig is an old acquaintance, one of the only two native Irishmen in Nome, Cavanman Kevin McCaffrey. We shake hands and exchange manly Irish hugs, you know the kind of thing—real quick, no lingering contact, and no looking into the other guy's eyes.

We collect my luggage and go out to his pickup truck. Our breath condensation is freezing and forms ice on our beards and whiskers, so that we resemble an extreme version of the "Got Milk?" ads. The bed of Kevin's truck, like every other pickup truck in Alaska in winter, is filled with snow. The suitcase is flung into the snow-filled bed, which is a fine shock absorber, while my guitar comes into the cab with us. And off we go to my hotel.

On the way, Kevin informs me that tonight's show is in a place called the Fort Davis Roadhouse, and not the mini-convention center where it has been held in years past. The mini-convention center is a converted bowling alley with one of the best hardwood floors I've ever seen at a venue, because they left the alleys in place when they changed the joint. The stage is where the pinsetters used to be. I really liked that venue.

He also informs me that I'm doing a kids' show for the local elementary school at 2:00 p.m. It is now 8:30 a.m., and I'd like to get a few hours' sleep before the school gig, so Kevin drops me off at the hotel, and promises to come back and get me at 1:30.

I wake from a sound sleep to the buzzing of my alarm at 1:00 p.m., jump into the shower, and primp for the kids. My eyes look like pissholes in the snow, and my mouth feels like the inside of a Sumo wrestler's diaper. I have a hangover without the benefit of any alcohol consumption. Aaahh! Exhaustion and sleep deprivation—nature's natural intoxicants!

I hear the honk of a truck-horn, and Kevin's outside waiting to take me to the elementary school, where I'm to perform for the little dar-

170

lin's. In the school gymnasium, there's a small PA system set up. Powered mixer and a couple of Peavey speakers, with a mic stand and a microphone. I can plug my guitar right into the board. Great! No set up.

The show for the kids goes really well. They participate in the activity songs; they laugh when I get the teachers and the principal doing weird noises and actions, and the adults have a good time watching the children enjoy themselves.

Kevin and I head over to Fat Freddie's, across the road from the Glue Pot Café for lunch. (Isn't that a great name for a dining establishment?) Reindeer sausage, eggs, and home fries with a pint mug of coffee. Then time for a walk over to the folks at the *Nome Nugget*. The publisher is a lovely woman called Nancy McGuire, and we've been friends since the first time I came to Nome back in the early nineties. She plugs my shows in the paper, has one of her reporters interview me afterwards, comes to the performances, and gives me coffee and doughnuts every time I step into the paper's tiny offices.

We shoot the breeze and do some catching up, when whoops! It's time for another nap before the evening performance. I hit the hay at 4:30 p.m., and Kevin says he'll come and get me at 6:30 to set the gear up for the 8:00 show.

Another nap, another shower, and I'm waiting for Kevin at the door when he pulls up in the pickup. We drive a couple of miles south along the coast, out of town, and come to the Fort Davis Road House. It's a restaurant/bar with a very nice menu of fresh seafood and steaks, soups, and salads. Inside, there's a pair of Shure Vocalmaster half-column speakers and a Peavey-powered mixer with all the appropriate cables and connections.

Kevin and I find suitable locations to place the speakers. We don't want them too low or too near a table, in case the customer at that spot wants to keep his hearing. So we stick them up in two corners, angled in towards the center of the room. I pick a central location, designate it the stage, and we do a sound check to make sure all is well. "One, two; one, two." Have you ever heard a sound check where the performer counts higher than two? Neither have I.

I plug in the old guitar, and to make sure it's functioning, I quickly run through Mozart's "Rondo Alla Turca," followed by Beethoven's "9th Symphony." Well, okay. I strum three chords, listen for tone and volume, say, "That's just fine," and unplug it.

Nap time! Just kidding.

There is, however, time for a bite to eat before show time. A couple of venison burgers and a salad for Kevin and me, and before I know it, it's time to don the motley. It's a full house of people who have heard me before, and still they came back. They all have dinner and several drinks, which make the owner of the establishment very happy, and the show goes smoothly. On top of that, I sell quite a few CDs, which makes me feel loved and appreciated. This is really the only reason I perform. I was never loved and appreciated as a small child, so now I seek love and appreciation (and affection, as well) from total strangers in bars. Well, it's a great line for picking up chicks.

After the show, when the audience has gone home, it's "winding-down" time for the artist (me), the promoter (Kevin), and the owner (Walter). Kevin's wife, Barbara, and Walter's wife, Teri, are also present for a few après-show cocktails. We're enjoying our drinks when Walter says, "I'd better go and let Honey in." He gets up from his barstool and goes to the front door, admitting a flurry of snowflakes. Stepping outside into the chill night, he calls, "Honey! Here, Honey!"

I'm sitting with my back to the door. Kevin and I continue to converse with the ladies at the bar. Walter rejoins us, and I hear the sound of clicking and scraping of nails on the hardwood floor of the bar behind me. Kevin says, "There's Honey. Good girl, Honey."

I turn around to see a huge animal with matted, brown, curly hair, its short tail facing me and its head bent over, eating something from the floor, and I think, "My God! That's the biggest Irish wolfhound I've ever seen! It's easily four and a half feet high at the shoulders." I look at Kevin and ask, "Is that an Irish wolfhound, or a Scottish deerhound? I've never seen a dog that big."

I turn back to look again, and it lifted its head.

That's when I saw the antlers. And the hooves. I did a double take, and the others all laughed.

It was a reindeer. A real one, walking around the bar like the family pet she was, eating Tootsie Rolls and begging for treats. She came over, snuffled around at my pockets, and nuzzled my legs. Someone gave me a handful of Tootsie Rolls to give her; I petted her, slapped her flanks, and ran my fingers through the curly pelt. A damn reindeer!

Kevin McCaffrey, with his fine white beard, plays Santa at Christmas for the kids, and Honey plays one of his reindeer, courtesy of

172

Walter and Teri and family. She also has a starring role in the local Nativity pageant, and is quite the local celebrity. Had I been drinking heavily that night and seen a reindeer in the bar, I believe I would have sworn off drink forever.

The following morning at seven o'clock, Kevin drops me off at Nome Airport. It's a little warmer now, just fifteen below, and after I check my luggage, Kevin hands me a package.

"Here's a little something to help you remember your trip," says he.

"You shouldn't have," I say. "I really enjoyed myself again this year, so thank you very much, indeed. Should I open it now?"

"No," says he. "It'll keep 'til later."

We said our goodbyes with another handshake and another manly hug, you know, and I boarded the 737.

When we had reached cruising altitude, and the seatbelt sign had been turned off, I stood up, opened the overhead bin, and took down Kevin's package. Sitting down, I began to unwrap it. I couldn't believe it.

It was three pounds of reindeer sausage.

DOG AND PONY SHOW

Charles Beauregard Finnegan

Harry O'Donoghue

"**A**bby, same again, please."

"Sure thing, big guy. Three Heineken's, coming up."

They were the only ones sitting at the Hyatt Regency bar, which overlooks the Savannah River. The "big guy" was Vic Power, owner of Kevin Barry's Irish Pub, located one block west of the hotel. To his left was Trish Rogers, one-half of the folk group Terra Nova, while her partner, Harry O'Donoghue, sat to his right. Vic liked to use the nickname "Handsome Harry," and Harry in turn called Trish "The Babby." Her nickname at least had a story to it.

The previous month they had been performing in San Diego and on a night off, they decided to hit the town. The first place they entered was a run-of-the-mill bar/restaurant with, of all things, an Irish bartender—a sharp-witted Belfast man. Trish did not have her passport on her, and although she was in her mid-twenties, she looked younger. No ID meant no alcoholic beverage; no alcoholic beverage meant no point in being there, so she was anxious to leave.

"You have a quick one, Har, and let's get outta here."

Harry ordered a drink from the bartender, who replied, "One colder-than-hell beer on its way, and maybe something for the babby there?"

She was not impressed, but Harry found it so amusing that he declared, "Babby. Perfect, just perfect."

"Fuck you, too," she muttered.

Vic dreamed up Harry's "handsome" tag. He delighted in meeting new people, flashing a mischievous grin, and declaring, "Vic Power, they call me 'the big guy,' and this is Handsome Harry O'Donoghue from Ireland. You can see why they call him that, the good-looking bastard, but me—not a tall man, not a muscular man, not a fat man—you'd wonder why they say "big guy." Dunno myself, but that's me—'the big guy.'"

So there they sat, on a balmy Saturday afternoon in May, "The big guy," "the babby," and "Handsome Harry."

"Here she comes. Look at her. She's beautiful. Look at her skin and the way her hair falls on her shoulder."

"No kiddin', big guy; she's a beaut," Harry answered.

"Ah, t'anks, my beauteous Abby. You look lovely today. Have I told you that?"

"Yes, about a dozen times, and if it's not you, it's Harry. Stop it; it's making me blush."

"You might as well be talking to the wall as talk to these two eejits, pet," Trish said in disgust.

Abby smiled, placed the beer on the counter, turned, and walked to the other end of the bar.

"Ah would you look at the legs on her, Handsome."

"Yeah, and the way her skirt moves on her."

"Would yiz, for fuck sake, give it a rest? Yizzer like a pair of dogs in heat." Trish slugged her Heineken and slammed the bottle on the bar. "I'm gone. I'll see yiz later at the pub. Good luck."

"Testy, isn't she?" said Vic.

"Ah, but she'll get over it, always does," replied Harry.

"Now, listen, Handsome; what are you doin' Tuesday?"

"I've a date."

"No. In the daytime?"

"Nothin' much."

"Gonna pick up the new dog. Can we use your station wagon?"

"What new dog?"

"Bought a dog, a beagle—no, a-a-bloodhound, or maybe it's a basset—you know, one of the ones with the long ears and mournful faces; look like they just come from a funeral."

"Why?"

"Why not? Plus it'll be company for me upstairs at the pub."

"You think?"

"Sure. It'll be great. What about Tuesday?"

"No problem. Me 'n' the Babby'll be there. She knows about dogs. Let's go early. I don't want to be late for the date."

"Okay, so. Let's have the one and done. Abby, when you get a chance—?"

"Jeez, here she comes. Look at the curves of those hips and the top two buttons of her shirt undone."

"Come on now, you two. I can hear you. Stop it. It's embarrassing."

"Ah, now, Abby."

***

"Hello."

"Rose, is Vic there?"

It was Tuesday, eleven a.m., and Harry was on the phone to Kevin Barry's Pub. Rose was the cook and lifeblood of the kitchen. She had been working with Vic since he opened the place on Halloween, nineteen-eighty, and pulled double-duty answering phones, receiving orders, and fending off salesmen when Vic was incapacitated or simply didn't want to see anybody.

"I saw him a little while ago; he's doing the bank."

"Tell him we're on our way, be there in fifteen minutes. Babby, let's go."

"Hold your horses; lemme just get me purse. Grand, we're all set."

Exactly fifteen minutes later, Harry was standing in Vic's office.

"The Babby's gone to get a book. She'll be right back. You ready?"

"Just have to finish last night's receipts and stop by the bank; it's on the way."

"How far is this place we're going?"

"What place?"

"To pick up the dog."

"Charles Beauregard Finnegan, you mean?"

"The dog has a name? Where in the name of God did you get that mouthful? Charles Beau—whatever Finnegan?"

"Beau-regard, Charles Beauregard. Has a nice ring to it, don't you think?"

"Whatever floats your boat. Anyway, how far?" Harry was getting impatient.

"Dunno. It's out the country. You hungry?"

"I had breakfast an hour ago. Did you not eat yet?"

"No, but I'm fine. Gimme ten minutes to finish the paperwork, and we'll drop it by the bank on the way."

It was almost an hour later when Vic opened the back door of the Ford station wagon and slid in.

"All they have to do is count the fuckin' money, and they have machines that'll do that, mother—"

"Now, enough, Mr. Power. There's a lady present," Harry intervened.

177

"Where?" Vic looked in every direction.

"Here, you pratt, and if you give me any guff, I'll take the jaw off you," Trish replied from the passenger seat.

"We're off. Head for I-16," Vic ordered from the back seat.

***

"I think it's this exit, Handsome. Slow down."

"Do you know how to get to this place? Have you a phone number or something?" Harry's impatience was growing with each passing minute.

"Not to worry. It's all under control. Exit here and go right a few miles." Vic sat back and closed his eyes.

"Okay, big guy, it's been more than a few miles now. We've been on this road for forty-five minutes. Are you watching?" Harry glanced at his watch.

"Maybe it was the next exit—hmmm," Vic mused.

"Ah for fu—"

Harry was cut short.

"Turn here, right here."

Harry jerked the wheel to the right, and the station wagon veered onto a small dirt road.

"No. the other way—left."

"You said right, turn right, for Christ sake."

"No, I meant turn right here. Turn left right here."

"In the name of all that's holy," said Trish from the passenger seat, "I'm trying to read me book. Stop jerking the car all over the road."

"Blame Marco Polo in the back seat there," Harry replied as he pulled the vehicle over and made a u-turn. "Is this the right way?"

"Yeah, said Vic, with confidence. "It's a little way down this road. The woman told me to look for a small grocery store, just like that one up ahead." He rolled down the window and pointed to the store. "Anyone hungry? Pull over."

"What?" said Harry. "I thought you said you weren't hungry."

"That was ages ago. You hungry, Trishie?"

"I'd eat all right," she said, closing her book.

Reluctantly, Harry parked the wagon outside the small country store.

178

"You stay here, Handsome, and keep the horses running for the get-away. Me 'n the babby'll get the stuff."

"You're a funny man, Mr. Parr. Coulda been a comedian," Harry replied sarcastically.

Ten minutes later, the two came out of the store and climbed into the car.

"What did you buy? Everything they had?"

"Easy now, boyo," Vic replied proudly. "Look what we have here."

He pulled three cans of Coke from a brown paper bag, followed by a sliced loaf of bread, three plastic knife and fork packs, and the prize of prizes—three cans of sardines.

"Sardines. Good Lord. Haven't had them in ages. Used to eat them all the time growin' up."

"Me, too" said Trish. "And the big guy here says it was the same for him growin' up in New York."

"Let's make some sammys," Vic said. "And, look, they're the nice ones, packed in olive oil."

All three sat in the station wagon, eating sardine sandwiches and reflecting on days gone by, days when the sardine sandwich was a normal part of one's diet.

"Okay," said Harry, wiping his mouth. "Which way, now?"

"Down this road to the second dirt road, left about a mile, then right; the lady said I can't miss it." Vic sat back contentedly.

The directions proved accurate, and within ten minutes, they pulled up in front of an old, rambling farmhouse with a high wire fence around it, presumably to keep the animals in.

"I'll just hop out and pick up Charlie," Vic said.

"Should we come with you?" Trish asked, but Vic was already out of the car and running toward the house. He knocked twice before disappearing around the side of the house, and within minutes, he reappeared, carrying what looked to be a full-grown beagle hound in his arms.

"Is that him?" asked Harry, and not bothering to wait for an answer continued, "I was kind of expecting something smaller, like a pup, maybe. That thing looks like it's full-grown. What are you doin' carrying it? Does it not walk?"

"You're the one who's in a hurry. He looked a little disorientated, so I picked him up. Open the back door."

"Ah, he's lovely," said Trish. "He's not that old, either. Slip him in there, and I'll sit in the back with him."

Vic slid into the passenger seat. "Let's go."

"That's it?" asked Harry.

"That's it, boyo. Home."

Harry turned the station wagon and pulled away from the farmhouse, but they hadn't gone a quarter of a mile when the dog started howling.

"Oh, lemme open the window for him. He just needs air," Trish assured the boys. Charles eagerly poked his head out the open window and stopped howling.

"Look at that," said Vic. "Ears flapping in the wind. He's happy as a pig in shite." All three laughed at the line. Liam Reilly, piano player and songwriter with the Irish pop group Bagatelle had recently told Harry something that had happened when he was driving to Dublin from Cork a couple of months back. Apparently, Liam was listening to the *Larry Gogan Show* on Radio Eireann during the call-in quiz segment of the program. An old farmer was on the line trying to answer as many questions as he could in sixty seconds. He wasn't doing very well, and the seconds were slipping by. Larry then asked, "Complete the following phrase: As happy as—?"

"A pig in shite," came the answer, quick as a flash, on live radio, as well.

Mr. Gogan was flustered and stammered, "No, Larry. Actually, 'happy as Larry' was what we were looking for." Another priceless moment in Irish radio. The story had traveled far and wide since. Harry glanced back. "There's a lot of him hanging out the window. Watch him, Babby. Trish was already reading her book and simply nodded.

"Right here, Handsome. This is the turn."

Harry turned the wheel to the left.

"No, the other way, remember? You need to reverse directions going back." Vic was pointing to the right.

"Oh, for—" Harry hit the brakes and jerked the wheel to the right. The wagon responded by skidding along the dirt, and her back end sailed around to the right. He straightened her up, hit the gas, and she lurched forward.

"Nice goin', McQueen," said Trish from the back seat.

Harry looked in the rearview mirror, ready to respond, but something was wrong.

180

"Where's Charles?"

"Huh?" said Trish.

"The dog, where's the dog?"

Trish looked out the back window. "Jesus, he fell out; he's on the road back there."

Vic turned to look. "You let the dog fall out? How the hell did ya do that?"

"I didn't let him fall out. He fell out him-fuckin-self. Turn round. I hope the poor divil's not hurt." Trish was beside herself.

Harry turned the vehicle around, and all three were astounded to see the animal sitting in the middle of the dirt road, looking unconcerned.

"Would ya look at that," said Vic. "He's one of us."

Harry pulled up alongside the dog. Trish opened the door, and Charles hopped right in, none the worse for his adventure.

"Maybe you might close the window a little, Babby."

"Drive or you'll not make your date—alive, that is."

***

The next time Harry saw Charles Beauregard Finnegan was one month after the pick-up/ fall-out day. It was Sunday evening, and he was walking into Kevin Barry's for the evening's performance. Vic was leaving, and Charles, wearing a red bandana with a piece of rope tied to it, was with him. Vic held the other end of the rope.

"Going for walkies, are we? And Charles looking so sharp 'n' all," Harry observed.

"The girls love it, and they think I'm so cute," said Vic with a grin on his face as he set off along River Street. By the time they returned, Harry and Trish, as Terra Nova, were onstage.

Vic thought it might be nice for Charles to catch part of the show, so he removed the rope, and the dog sauntered over beside the stage and sat down. Trish was in the middle of a song, and Charles looked up at her with adoring eyes. The audience thought it was so quaint. When she finished the song, she leaned down and patted the animal on the head. He looked content to be part of the act. Harry took lead vocals on the next number, but as soon as he sang, the dog started howling. Harry stopped singing. Charles stopped howling. Harry started singing again.

The animal started howling again. Vic was doubled over in the archway, laughing hysterically. So was the audience. Charles was a hit!

For the next three weeks, Charles became part of the Terra Nova show, and everybody loved him. Photos were taken with him, and he was petted and *coochie-cooed* and fussed over. The whole scenario could have gone on forever were it not for the night Charles overindulged on Kibbles 'n' Bits. In the middle of a "duet" with Harry, he gurgled, shook his head slowly, gurgled again, and let fly. Not a pretty sight, especially while folk were enjoying dinner. That was Charlie's swan song.

***

"Hey, big guy. How's t'ings?"

"Not so bad, Handsome, and yourself?"

"Grand. Listen, I haven't seen Charles Beauregard in a few weeks. Not since the night. What's he up to?"

"He's gone."

"Where?"

"Sent him to a place out in the country—Canine Psychiatric Care Center, or somethin'."

"You're kiddin', right?"

"No, it's a home for bewildered dogs. They take good care of them. He was nuts, anyway."

"Tell you what—he'll be missed round here."

"Yeah, especially by you, but that's just 'cause he made the act better."

The Unicorn

Dennis O'Rourke

College bars are a double-edged sword. Beautiful young women on the one hand. Loud, beer-swilling, young men on the other. Let's talk about the former.

Durty Nelly's in Gainesville, Florida. Go Gators! It's a Saturday night. It's hot and crowded. And it's cleavage night. The girls are all sporting low cuts. Boobs everywhere. The guys don't know where to look, so they drink more and get louder. I sit on a stool, singing, drinking scotch, and calmly awaiting the arrival of the first female supplicant with a song request.

They do this in a couple of different ways. The first is to come to the foot of the stage and wait for my signal to approach. When I've given that, they shyly step up to make their request, sometimes looking nervously back out at the audience to see who's watching them. Then there are the girls who ignore territorial boundaries and rules of behavior, and boldly march right up onstage without permission. (These women always marry well.) Once there, however, both groups make their request in a similar manner. They get close in on me, fold their hands in front of them, and bend slightly, or rest their hands on their knees and lean into me. Either way, the blouse or the halter-top falls away and a twofold paradise is revealed.

A young lady chooses the shy approach. She's slim, raven-haired, and wrapped tightly in a black, spaghetti-strap, mini-dress. She bends down, and I gaze into her eyes while my peripherals romp in her exposed pasture. She asks if I will play "The Unicorn," and if it would be all right if she and her friends came up and did it with me. I always try to make it a 'women only' thing anyway, so I readily agree to her proposal.

Most entertainers like to bring people onto the stage to do "The Unicorn," Shel Silverstein's ode to that mysterious creature of myth. We make a set piece out of it. It can be a great deal of fun. We pick folks out in the audience who might know the mime that accompanies the lyrics. We'll order them onstage. If they demur, we'll encourage the crowd to force them up with applause.

At Nelly's tonight, the five girls charge the stage when I invite them. (I've had as many as a dozen up there. There's nothing or no one as happy, carefree, and uninhibited as a college girl after a few beers.) Now I get my supplicant and her four friends to form a line in front of me, facing the audience. Instead of cleavage, I'm entranced by a row of undulating, young female bums. The sight is so breathtaking that I resolve to sing some of the verses twice.

Everyone in the audience is standing, some of them on chairs. I sit behind the line of girls, singing lazily, stretching the song out to its limit.

Tight jeans, shorts, and skirts. Long, tanned, bare arms waving in the air.

I pick up the tempo on the last chorus, and I sing it again and again, faster each time, so that my troupe is flapping and flailing their arms wildly at the end. The guys in the audience are howling. The song ends, and the girls jump around hugging each other like excited children. Then they line up to hug and kiss me before they leave the stage. Warm, young faces, tender lips on my cheek. Breathless thank yous in my ear.

The last to greet me is the raven-haired beauty. She kisses me and thanks me for allowing them to do the song. She turns to leave. She stops and turns back. She leans down to me again. Peripheral cleavage. There is a puzzled expression on her face. In an earnest, innocent voice, she whispers a question in my ear.

"When *did* the unicorns become extinct?"

THE FOREIGN ELEMENT

Full Moon Over Managua

Robbie O'Connell

There's a full moon over Managua, and the wind is in the trees,
The stars are shining clear tonight; there's music on the breeze.
The palm tree silhouettes against the sky look like a painted scene
As I wonder to myself who really is the enemy.

All nine of us were enjoying a post-concert nightcap in the hotel bar in Quito, Ecuador. We seemed to be the only customers in the long, narrow bar, probably because it was too expensive for the native clientele. The token air conditioner did little to relieve the clinging humidity, so we made an effort to cool off with local beer, not very effective, but a good excuse. Our group consisted of six Green Grass Cloggers, three of whom were also old-time musicians, along with fiddler Susie Gott. They all hailed from North Carolina. The Irish legation consisted of our fearless leader—banjo player and singer Mick Moloney—and me.

We were discussing our departure for Nicaragua the following morning when Moloney was paged. This was unusual so late at night, and as he went to take the call, we wondered if something was wrong. The tour, organized by the National Council for the Traditional Arts, had begun three weeks earlier, and we still had two weeks to go. As musical ambassadors of the USA, we sometimes did two or three performances a day, but we also got to hang out with local folk musicians and dancers almost everywhere we went. Sometimes, after a show, local musicians would take us to a pena, a sort of folk nightclub featuring regional performers—the kind of places we would never have found on our own, and the music was always excellent.

Most of our concerts were free, and the admission fee for the others was so low we were assured of a good-sized audience just about everywhere. So far, the tour had gone smoothly, and we were enjoying every moment of it.

Our first stop had been Uruguay, an eighteen-hour flight from the USA. The capital city, Montevideo, felt so European that we could have been in Spain. Statues of heroes on horseback proudly ruled every square. The first night we sauntered out of our hotel around nine p.m. looking for nightlife, but it seemed like the whole city had gone to bed. However, by eleven p.m., as we were returning, it suddenly turned into happy hour. The streets echoed with the shouts and whistles of jubilant teenagers cruising the streets. The bars and restaurants instantly filled up and stayed that way for the next five hours. "Someone should have told us," we complained as we traipsed back to our hotel, too tired now to party.

Our first concert in Montevideo was a great success. The theme of our show was the Appalachian tradition and its antecedents. We played a mixture of old-time Appalachian songs and dances interspersed with Irish and Scottish songs and tunes. We were concerned that people would not understand our songs, so we had the lyrics translated and printed in the programs. People from Ireland, the Appalachian Mountains, and South America all shared a common background of economic hardship and political repression, so our audiences had no trouble identifying with our songs, which echoed these themes.

The following day, we set off confidently into the hinterland for another show in Paysandu, a small provincial town that seemed like it was still in the 1930s. There weren't many cars, but the ones we saw were antique American models from the era of the black and white gangster movies, and we were amazed by the genius of the local mechanics who kept them running.

A few days later, we flew north to Bolivia. The airport in La Paz is more than 13,000 feet above sea level, and as you step off the plane, you feel light-headed and disoriented. Although musicians often aspire to a similar state of intoxication, this time it was accompanied by a slight nausea, which took all the fun out of it. We were housed in the Sheraton Hotel in La Paz. This was a five-star hotel, far superior to any Sheraton I had ever seen. For about $20 per day, we lived like royalty. Meals and drinks were so cheap it seemed sacrilegious not to take advantage of it. We were warned that drinking alcohol was the worst thing we could do for altitude sickness, so we adjourned to the bar and discussed it over a few beers. We all agreed that they were wrong.

Living in such style quickly lost its luster when we stepped out into the streets and markets of La Paz. The poverty all through South America was shocking, the contrast between affluence and subsistence was distressing. There seemed to be no middleclass, just disgustingly rich and disturbingly poor. It was easy to see why there were so many coup d'etats and why folk heroes like Che Guevara were so popular. As we drove through the streets, young males continually gave us the finger. The local version, thumb extended between the index and middle fingers, was new to us, but there was no mistaking the intent of the gesture. As Americans, we were seen as symbols of foreign imperialism, and comparing the dismal conditions that the natives lived in to the decadent opulence enjoyed by visitors to their country, it was hard to blame them.

One morning we set off for a boat trip on Lake Titicaca. We followed winding roads out of La Paz into the Altiplano, seeing nothing but an occasional llama and a few bowler-hatted Alymara women. Even though we were 14,000 feet above sea level, snow-capped peaks stretched into the clouds ahead of us. A small motorboat was waiting to take us to Suriqui Island, about an hour's journey out into the lake. On the shore, there were several traditional boats made from the papyrus reeds that grew in abundance nearby.

In the 1970s, Swedish explorer Thor Heyerdahl had built papyrus boats like these, but much larger, for the famous RA expedition. He sailed across the Atlantic from Egypt to South America to prove that the ancient Egyptians could have made the journey. The first expedition failed when the papyrus craft became waterlogged after a few days. Research soon proved that the molecular structure of the papyrus plants in Egypt had changed over the past 3000 years, but the papyrus in Lake Titicaca was identical to that used by the ancient Egyptians. So Heyerdahl traveled to Bolivia and brought the papyrus and local boat builders back to Egypt for another attempt. The success of the RA 2 expedition made worldwide headlines and the boatmen on the lake are extremely proud of that.

When our boat reached the island, swarms of begging children surrounded us. It was difficult to give change to some, but not others. We felt guilty and privileged when confronted by such overt poverty, but mostly we felt a sense of helplessness.

Suriqui was home to a celebrity. Paulino Estaban had built papyrus boats for Thor Heyerdahl and sailed the Atlantic with him. When I asked what it was like crossing the Atlantic Ocean, he mimed cowering in terror of the massive waves, and swore he would never venture out of Bolivia again. Now he owned a ramshackle gift shop where he sold models of the RA boats to tourists. Being a big fan of both Heyerdahl and model boats, I bought several models in different sizes. Paulino was eager to have his photograph taken with us, and proudly posed with his wife and two llamas, symbols of his wealth and importance.

Apart from a few puffy white clouds, the sky was a deep blue as we sailed back to shore. The snow-capped Andes jutted through the clouds into the heavens and created a sense of being on top of the world. I'm not sure whether it was the altitude or the bottle of brandy we shared on the boat, or both, but I'll never forget the feeling of elation and lucidity on that lake. Back on the mainland, we were treated to a dinner of fried lake trout, which had been caught since we left, and I have never since tasted fish that good anywhere.

Once again, we journeyed to some of the provincial cities. Cochabamba was best known as the cocaine capital of Bolivia, and as foreigners, we were eyed with suspicion and made to feel unwelcome. I had my camera confiscated by the local police in the city park, but after much pleading and explaining in a mix of English and the few words of Spanish I knew, I managed to get it back. Back at the hotel, I discovered that they had confiscated the film. I was later informed that a simple bribe of a dollar would have solved the problem instantly. Not being a seasoned traveler, that solution had never occurred to me.

Our next concert was in Santa Cruz, in the lowlands. It was in a nineteenth-century opera house fronted by a vast tree-lined square. We arrived in the afternoon for a sound check only to discover that a massive right-wing political rally was underway in the square. My first thought was that we had stumbled upon a film set, but our driver assured me that it was real.

It was a complete throwback to Nazi Germany. Flags bearing swastikas hung all around the park. Flatbed trucks, rigged with massive loudspeakers, blocked the entrance to the theater. The guttural ranting of the politicians was like footage from a documentary of the Third Reich. Thousands of agitated voices roared their approval or disapproval. It was a scary scene, almost surreal. We elbowed our way through the throng and made it to the stage door. Relieved to get safely inside, we discovered that the event outside was a commemoration of a massacre that had taken place in the theater years before when a score of political figures in the audience had been gunned down in the middle of a show. This was not good news. One of our gigs in La Paz had been postponed because of an assassination attempt against the US ambassador. The police in Cochabamba had been less than friendly, and now we had a Nazi rally and massacre commemoration to deal with. I think it safe to say we were a little uptight that night. However, the concert went on without incident and, with great relief, we all celebrated our survival back in the hotel that night.

A few days later, we were in a hotel in Guayaquil in Ecuador, arguing over iguanas. A couple of the cloggers had gone out exploring early in the morning and came back filled with excitement about the iguanas they had seen in the park a few blocks away. I went rushing off to see them, but not a single iguana could I spot. I was sure I had been set up and a great laugh was being had at my expense. When I got back to the hotel, I accused them of lying to me. They explained that the iguanas' natural camouflage made them difficult to see at first, but if you sat still and looked at the trees, you would see them. I was even more suspicious now of a practical joke, but they persuaded me to try again. So, back at the park, I sat on a bench and stared at the trees. Suddenly, I saw one. Then, I saw another and another. It was like a Gestalt puzzle. Once your eyes and brain adjusted, you saw them everywhere, like miniature dinosaurs sitting in the trees. It was a thrilling sight, and I was grateful that I had not missed it.

After Guayaquil, we moved north to Quito, whose only claim to fame seemed to be its gold jewelry and Panama hats. It appeared that the best hats were made here, and not in Panama, so we did our tourist duty and stocked up. Twenty years later, I still have one that I use when I'm fishing.

The proximity to the equator and the high altitude made sunburn a real danger here, but we did not know that at first. Mick got the worst sunburn I have ever seen after only a half-hour at the hotel pool. Irish skin is ill equipped for these equatorial regions, and he was lucky that he did not have to be hospitalized.

Now we were waiting in the bar for Moloney to return from his phone call and hoping that our plans to fly to Managua next day were not in jeopardy. Relations between the governments of the USA and Nicaragua had been tense for some time because of US backing for the Contra war, which in 1985, appeared to be escalating. When Mick returned, he told us that the plans had all changed. He had just received word from the US embassy in Quito that the Reagan administration had imposed a trade embargo against

Nicaragua, and the government would not allow us to go to Managua. We were sorely disappointed at this development. We had been looking forward to visiting this little David, so troublesome to the US Goliath, and wanted to see for ourselves what was going on. Now we were in limbo. Our next scheduled country on the tour was the Dominican Republic, but they were not expecting us for another ten days. What was going to happen to us? Where would we go next?

Next morning, at breakfast, Mick surprised us all. He had just received another call to say that our visit to Nicaragua was still on. The word from the embassy was that the Sandanista government had concluded that as cultural ambassadors, we posed no threat to their regime. So, after hastily packing bags, we were carted off to the airport.

Flying through the Andes in a propeller plane is not the most relaxing way to travel. The aircraft was like an antique bus with wings and as noisy as a hundred lawnmowers. Peering through the scratched windows, the mountain peaks looked close enough to stretch your arm out and touch them. I had to banish stories of plane crashes and cannibalism from my mind.

The other unnerving aspect of the flight was the body odor, which literally took our breath away. The majority of the passengers were rural South Americans, many of them women sporting the bowler hats that had become so familiar to us in Bolivia. They were dressed in many multicolored layers of wool. You expected to see live chickens in cages beneath their seats. It appeared that personal hygiene was not highly regarded in this region. Unlike the Irish farmer who took a bath once a year, whether he needed it or not, these people obviously suffered from hydrophobia. I had experienced some smelly feet on Aer Lingus flights over the years, but that seemed like eau de cologne in comparison to the odor that assaulted our nostrils now. In an attempt to escape the near lethal pong of our fellow passengers, we wandered up and down the aisle, like pearl divers, holding our breath as long as possible, desperately trying to keep from gagging. We were eventually forced back to our seats by our impending and very welcome approach to the Managua airport. Through the windows, we saw dozens of anti-aircraft guns lined up along each runway. Welcome to Nicaragua!

The customs officers were rude. They tore our clothes out of the bags and flung them around the table. They seemed angry with us gringos for visiting their troubled country and were determined to find something wrong. They made no effort to repack our bags, and tried to rush us on before we had any time to do it ourselves. Carrying an American passport was not the way to endear you to these people, but finally, after many questions, arguments, examinations, and delays, we were in our minibus, en route to the Intercontinental Hotel.

The streets of Managua were deserted, apart from a few eighteen-year-old soldiers in battle fatigues, with machine guns slung over their shoulders. I had played concerts in Belfast during "the Troubles," but despite the unease and threat of car bombs, the streets were still bustling with shoppers, and life seemed relatively normal. These empty, silent streets reminded me of Thurles in County Tipperary, when a Munster Hurling final was underway, and I wondered if everyone had not slipped away to a big soccer match.

The Intercontinental hotel was home to dozens of foreign reporters there to cover the Contra war—a hundred miles or so to the north. The lobby was filled with press, coming and going, day and night. Maybe this was because of the newly imposed embargo, but it felt like everyone was waiting for something dramatic to happen. Tragedy is always news, and the reporters were gathered like hungry animals waiting for someone to fill the trough. They were affable and cynical at the same time, as we chatted, and everyone we spoke to seemed to think that US policy in the region was misguided, even those from the conservative press.

After we settled in, we were taken to the US embassy for a "briefing." This consisted of a warning to stay away from areas of combat and to beware of interacting with the local people or buying drugs. In keeping with official US policy in the region, they informed us that we were the good guys and these Sandinistas were no good communists. I asked if it wasn't un-American for our government to try to overthrow the freely elected Sandinista government. After all, weren't they the legitimate representatives of the people, and hadn't they replaced a brutal dictatorship? Shouldn't America be supporting democracy, not undermining it? In answer, they cited irregularities at the polling booths as the justification for US interference. I found this answer unacceptable at the time, but hilarious fifteen years later, during the Florida recount in the 2000 presidential election. Ah, well, what do I know? I'm just a humble musician.

Our first concert was in the local arts and culture center, which was unlike any such center I had seen before. It was a derelict building, the ruins of the Grand Hotel that had been destroyed in an earthquake in 1972. All that remained was the ground floor, which had been roofed and made structurally safe. Multicolored, ornate batiks hung from the ceilings, strange Indian paintings covered the walls, but my favorites were the carved wooden figures that looked as if they had melted and assumed rounded and twisted shapes. A glimpse of further treasures ahead appeared now and then through jagged gaping holes in the stone walls. Outdoors, there was a huge stage in what was formerly the pool area, while the auditorium, which held about a thousand seats, was under cover, in the now-defunct ballroom. The whole place was like a colorful garden that had bloomed on a pile of rubble and, as all good art is meant to do, it created a sense of awe.

Our first show began at dusk. A massive yellow moon rose slowly before us like a huge spotlight. It was so big you could see individual craters on its surface. As soon as we began to play, darting shadows flickered through the arc of the stage lights. Bats! Dozens appeared in front of us, beside us, behind us, everywhere. They seemed particularly agitated by the sound of the banjo. I guess if the joke "Welcome to Hell, here's your banjo," is true, at least I won't have to worry about bats when I get there. We quickly developed an expertise in avant-garde choreography as we bobbed and dipped while we played our instruments and bats dive-bombed us. Maybe the little critters were irritated by the music, but the audience was enthusiastic and friendly. To our relief, there were no shouts of "Yankees, go home!" We performed for two nights to sold-out houses, and by the second night, we even grew accustomed to the bats and only ducked our heads occasionally.

During the day, we went to visit the local sights, including a live volcano in Masaya, not far from the city. A wooden viewing platform on the crest of the crater enabled us to see right down to where the lava bubbled, smoked, and belched spirals of thick, grey smoke. I watched, fascinated, as hundreds of bright green parrots wheeled through the smoke plumes to their nests, which clung to the walls of the crater, attracted, no doubt, by the free central heating. The vivid flashes of green wings amid the grey smoke of the crater were an unexpected and memorable sight.

Nearby, in Masaya, we found an open-air market where we could shop for souvenirs. Wandering through colorful stalls filled with local produce and crafts, we were astounded to hear a voice call, "Hey, Moloney! How are they all in Limerick?" A stranger rushed over to shake Mick's hand and explain that he was an ex-patriot, Chilean dissident who had lived for two years in Limerick, Ireland, Mick's hometown. He had fled to a reconciliation center there when his life had been threatened by the Pinoche regime. Still unable to return safely to Chile, he had settled in Nicaragua, where he felt more at home. He had recognized Mick from a photograph in the newspaper promoting the concert, and they had a great chat about mutual acquaintances. It is said that the world gets smaller everyday, and here was proof, indeed.

Some people take photographs as mementos of their travels, but although I usually bring a camera, I find that writing a song about the experience can be a powerful way to preserve memories. Songs and smells are like a time machine, taking you back to a particular place or time. I jotted down some thoughts and ideas as we traveled, and when I got home, I wrote a song to try to capture the feelings of our Nicaraguan sojourn. I subsequently recorded it on a CD called *Never Learned to Dance.*

Several years later, at a folk festival in Pennsylvania, I ran into Trish Miller, one of the clog dancers from that tour. She told me that one night, not long before, while she and her husband John were driving home from a gig in up-state New York, she was astounded to hear "Full Moon over Managua" on the radio. She hadn't been aware that I had written the song, and she said she cried as all the memories of the South American tour came flooding back.

In the Casa Grande garden, we sat at evening time
Politely making small talk while the waiters poured more wine.
And it seemed like some old movie that I saw so long ago
'Til I looked out through the chain-link fence at the city down below.

CHORUS:

There's a full moon over Managua, and the wind is in the trees,
The stars are shining clear tonight, there's music on the breeze.
The palm tree silhouettes against the sky look like a painted scene
As I wonder to myself who really is the enemy.

194

And up in the northern mountains, not so many miles away,
Silent eyes watch through the night waiting for the break of day
And the smell of burning wheat fields still lingers in the sky,
With the silence sometimes broken by the crack of rifle fire.

I saw a woman rocking on her porch, her eyes as hard as steel,
A machine gun cradled in her arms where a baby might have been.
She said that though she hadn't much, at least it was her own,
And she'd rather die than go back to the way it was before.

I never will forget the night, at the ruins of the Grand Hotel,
The cloggers danced their hearts out, and we gave the music hell.
And the bats flew like mosquitoes as the moon rose overhead,
And we knew that we would never all have such a night again.

ଔଞ୍ଚ

Détente or Not Détente—That Is the Question, or I Dé-tente, Don't Ask Me

Frank Emerson

This story could not have taken place just anywhere. It had to have taken place in a pub that has 'a listening room'—a room where the music is not an afterthought. Rather, it is the focal point. When you perform in one of these places, it is nearly like a concert. It just so happens that Kevin Barry's Pub is the premier place for listening rooms. Therefore, that is where the tale unfolded. And it is all true. I only made up some of it—honest.

It came to pass that this particular Wednesday in 2003 was just an average mid-week performance night. I was doing okay. Business was nothing to alert the media about, but it was respectable enough.

As far as I was concerned, the audience was doing okay, as well. What they lacked in numbers, they made up for by being with me right from the get-go. I was pretty confident that the night would turn out just fine. I read somewhere that the ideal audience is reasonably intelligent, aware, and just a little bit drunk. This little group of people fit that description to a "T." I couldn't help but be enthused. They were laughing, crying, singing along, and clapping. Not only that, but they were doing it in all the right places—which was icing on the cake.

That was the way things stood when, all of a sudden—BLAM! The doors to the room flew open, smacked against the wall, and in came about a baker's dozen or so guys. They didn't appear to have dates—unless they were dating each other. They were very neat and looked to be wearing designer suits. I was a little curious, but not concerned. Maybe they were just part of a convention of extremely well dressed men about town. I suppose anything is possible in this day and age.

They gave me individual glowers as they trooped into the room and headed toward the far end. That was fine by me. I didn't care how pretty they were; if they were surly, I surely didn't want them right in front of me.

As I mulled on this, my attention was taken back to the door. Three other fellows were jabbering away to the hostess and gesturing toward the gathering of fashion, which had now shoved some tables together, sat down, and started snapping their fingers at the waitress.

Remember, while I was taking all of this in, I was still singing and playing. I more or less went on automatic pilot with the slam of the door. I finally arrived at the end of the tune. The audience gave me what could only be termed 'sympathy applause,' since they too noticed the commotion and undoubtedly felt sorry for me. That was all right with me. Hell, I'll take any applause any time.

I have to tell you about the three jokers who had cornered the hostess. They sidled into the room, giving the place the once over. They made their way to seats on the wall across from the baker's dozen. It looked as if they were riding herd on them. The thing is—they were diametrically opposite each other, sartorially speaking. Whereas the group looked like they'd stepped out of GQ, these fellows looked like they were wearing somebody else's suits—somebody much larger than they. In fact, it looked like there was actually room for somebody else to be in there with them. The whole set-up was boggling.

Meanwhile, the waitress noticed the snapping of the fingers. A word about this practice: waitresses just love it when customers do that. It's so much more direct than taking the time to say, "Excuse me" or "Pardon me." Consequently, she seemed real glad to have these beauties in her section—if you catch my drift.

196

They started ordering in a loud, rumbling, almost grumbling manner, "Beer! Here! Guinness! Here! Beer! Here!" and so forth around the table. I had already started into another number, and these chowder heads were throwing my concentration off. They were regular pains in the neck, or lower.

As a rule of thumb, I try not to interrupt the flow of a performance by even acknowledging such antics. There is a tactic that I have found works pretty well in times like these. It is a radical gambit perfected years ago by Benny Goodman, which he used on transgressing band members. It was referred to as "the ray." It was a look from Benny's eyes that was said could dry the Brylcream in Gene Krupa's hair. I have refined it for use on rude punters in the audience. I call it "the Death Ray." I figured this would take care of things. I wound myself up, inhaled, exhaled, inhaled again, and let 'em have it, full force. I have to tell you. Death Ray? Fiddlesticks! It didn't even slow them up. These guys were formidable. They had me stymied.

I decided to vamp a while to give me time to decide what to do. I shrugged to the audience. They shrugged back. We did this back and forth for a while until I went back into the song, having come up with no reasonable course of action. As I sang, I looked toward the three guys in the bad suits.

By now, they each had a glass of beer on the table. As I watched, I noticed something odd. Every once in a while, one would make what looked like a little spitting motion into his cuff, take a sip of beer, touch his ear, and nod to the others. I was suspicious of this, but concluded it was none of my business—just a custom of whatever region of Hell from whence they came.

I was in the middle of percolating on this when one of the three got up and came toward me. He was carrying a full pint of Guinness. I hoped this would be a friendly encounter, but truthfully, I didn't know what to expect. Sure enough, he put the pint on the stage next to me, straightened up, and made an "okey-dokey" sign with his thumb and forefinger. Then he pointed to the chowder heads, nodded to me, and went back to his table.

You have to understand—I like Guinness as much as the next fellow does. In fact, I believe it is just as good for you as Sir Arthur says it is. Furthermore, I believe that all that bellyaching about cirrhosis and unlawful prescription of alcohol by those buzz-kills at the Food and

Drug Administration is nothing but a load of hooey. However, the stuff does tend to make me bilious. I've found that burping into the microphone tends to put people off—even if you are real sincere and use the burp skillfully.

All that accepted, I decided it was best not to appear ungracious. I looked out, smiled, and nodded to the fellows in the way of expressing thanks. Soon after, I finished the tune, and it was time for a break. I took off my guitar, turned on the break music, picked up the Guinness, and carried it with me to the bar. There, I ditched the stuff and ordered a whiskey. Then I went hunting for the hostess to see if she could give me the low-down on what had been going on.

The hostess on duty that particular evening was Joyce. I like her a lot. I like her husband, too. Not only is she good looking, she knows her "p's and q's" in certain situations. For twelve years, she was on the job with the police department. She left as a sergeant. I know I can count on her. Joyce is actually something of a legend in the pub world. One time, a little while ago, a few young yahoos in the bar were having a hard time holding their liquor. They were feeling their wild oats—as well as a number of the female customers and a waitress or two. They were cut off and asked to leave. They balked. The call went out for Joyce. She immediately copped on to who was the leader of the pack, walked up to him, and took him by the hand. With a deft little bit of "twisto-changeo," she had the young man on his tippy-toes making "Ai-yi-yi" sounds like Desi Arnaz as she led him right out the door. His buddies wanted no part of this and so followed their leader out the door like so many ducklings. Joyce was definitely someone to have on your side.

I saw her by the front door and headed over there. I said hello and asked her what was up with the fellows in question.

"Oh, they'll be okay," she said. "They're just foreign is all. They'll get used to things and settle in after a bit."

"Fair enough," I said, "but what about the pretty boys?"

Joyce looked at me as if to say "you yutz," but she was nice enough not to do so. Instead, she explained, "That's who I'm talking about. They're from the consulate of the Republic of Georgia. You know. Like Russia?"

Oh, I knew "like Russia" all right. The Soviet Republic of Georgia—where Stalin was born. "Well," I asked, "what about the three guys in the lousy suits?"

She looked left and right over her shoulder and leaned into me. "US State Department. Escorts."

Thinking back, I figured out what they were doing when they spit into their cuffs and tapped their ears. Walkie-talkies. Why, they were probably talking to Colin Powell or somebody like that. Still and all, though, the picture was about as ironic as anything I'd ever seen. The Reds were dressed like *Queer Eye for the Straight Guy*, while our boys looked like they were wearing Khrushchev's hand-me-downs. I couldn't let it go. I had to ask one more question.

"Joyce, look. Why do you think they're wearing those sacks?"

Joyce furrowed her brow and squinted in their direction. "Well, let's see. State Department escorting foreign dignitaries. Either they're all on the Atkins diet and haven't had time to make alterations, or they are all packing heat. What do you think?"

"Oh, I think number two," I said.

Joyce nodded and smiled. "Me, too. Don't worry about a thing. Everything will be fine." She went off to solve another problem while I was left to wonder how this whole scene would work out

I started thinking about the former Soviet Republic of Georgia and Eduard Shevardnadze, the guy who was in power. He was a bum, but he was our bum—at least for the time being. If I could just sing something in Russian, I'd have them eating out of my hand. This could be a big foreign relations coup. I might even get a medal. I tell you, visions of sugarplums danced in my head.

I wracked my brain for the rest of the break looking for anything I could do in that Bolshoi lingo. I thought I'd have something by the time I got back on stage, but nyet.

As I was putting on my guitar, I had one of those epiphanies. I remembered an old tune that the Weavers used to play. I was sure it would do the trick. I announced to the audience that we had some visitors from the former Soviet Republic of Georgia, and that I would like to do a tune especially for them. I started a fast vamp in the key of C and then slammed into "Tzena! Tzena!" going lickety-split. I was getting absolutely no reaction from the Russians. Hell, I'd have thought they could have at least appreciated the effort. Lousy Commies.

Just then, I had another epiphany; I wasn't singing in Russian. I was singing in Yiddish. Now I really did feel like a yutz. Oy. I wallowed in this for a while as I sang through the song as quickly as possible.

I finished with a "Hey!" the way the Weavers did, and I think that explosion brought on my third epiphany. I announced that "Tzena! Tzena!" had just been a warm-up number and that now I would play the real song from the Republic of Georgia. They looked at me in what I took to be hope-filled expressions. I nodded, smiled, swallowed, and did a slow run in the key of C and slid into "Georgia on My Mind."

Well, holy moly! You'd think I'd just launched Sputnik. They started singing, clapping, and shouting things like, "Da! Da!" and "Tovarich! Irishki!" Now I'm not certain about this next thing. Remember, I was singing at the time, they were going a little mashugga, and their language at the best of times sounded a little like stomach rumbles. But I think I head one of them gurgle out, "Hoagy Carmichaelski! Da! Da!"

I finished the song. They erupted. Didn't we all become just the best of friends? From that point on, I could do no wrong. Of course, I had to play "Georgia on My Mind" about eight more times, but it's a good tune, and I like it, so it was jake with me. On top of that, every time I did play it, a fresh pint of Guinness would show up on stage. I figured what the hell—perestroika. Then I'd go ahead and drink it. The burps would come along, but that seemed to be okay. I think they thought I was trying to speak their language, so they liked the idea that at least I was giving it a shot.

All in all, the evening progressed very nicely. The place reeked with international brotherhood. Between the Georgians and their State Department keepers, it was smiles all around. Finally, it came time to call it a night and for everyone to toddle off. The boys had run up a pretty hefty tab. The headman had a look at it, tacked on a big tip for the waitress, and through one of the State Department guys, explained that the whole thing should be forwarded to the Georgian Consulate. A check would be forthcoming within the week.

Normally, this arrangement would have been fine and dandy. This time, however, turned out to be not so normal. It came to pass that three days after this evening, before the bill could be processed, the Republic of Georgia under went a velvet revolution. There was a bloodless coup d'etat. Eduard Shevardnadze and all of his people were out on their former Soviet bottoms. All records, pacts, and IOU's were rendered null and void—including the bill from Kevin Barry's.

I heard later that Vic Power, who owns the joint, made good on the waitress' tip. As far as payment for the drinks was concerned, he was out of luck.

If you were to look at the whole thing from a fair perspective, you could construe it as a lesson learned. But what would be the point in that? I think I can speak for all concerned when I say that it will be a hot day in Minsk before any of us trusts any more Russkies—former Soviet, Menshevik, or just plain old Bolshevik. And one more thing. It's a good thing that 'Hoagy Carmichaelski' ain't that guy's real name—at least, I don't think it is.

WAXING PHILOSOPHICAL AND GETTING REALLY LIKE DEEP, YOU KNOW?

Fortune Favors the Innocent

Robbie O'Connell

I first arrived in New York in the early '70s on a summer break from university in Dublin. Thousands of Irish college students invaded American cities every year in search of summer jobs. Ireland was in recession, and for many of us, the money we could save here was the only hope we had of staying in college for another year. Within a few days, I got a job behind the counter at a Howard Johnson's in Times Square. This was serious culture shock for me. It was not just the disorientation from the noise and aggression of Manhattan or the unfamiliarity of the crazed multi-ethnic work environment. It was also the ice cream.

In Ireland, we had two flavors of ice cream—vanilla and ripple, although, occasionally, if the planets were in correct alignment, you might encounter banana. Ho Jo's boasted twenty-eight flavors, some of which I could barely pronounce, never mind recognize. I had no clue what pistachio or butter pecan was, and it didn't help that my fellow counter slave, from Thailand, seemed to call every flavor "balalla."

The restaurant slang for putting in orders was another ordeal. If you didn't know that "Adam and Eve on a raft" was two poached eggs on toast, or that "whiskey down" was rye toast, you were at a serious disadvantage. Most terms bewildered me, but if I tried to order in layman's language, the cooks completely ignored me and my customer would complain about how long his order was taking. And for this I was earning the princely sum of thirty-five dollars a week. I was certain to be fired, so after two weeks, I quit.

As a teenager, I'd played folk music in pubs and clubs around Ireland and England, but I had no idea there might be opportunities to perform in America. I was unaware of the fledgling Irish pub scene until much later, so I set out to find a "regular" job. By chance, I ran into a guy I knew slightly from college who told me about an available job as a doorman at a co-op apartment building on the Upper East Side. He claimed it was a piece of cake. The only things I would need were a pair of black shoes and a white shirt and tie. They would supply the rest of the uniform. All I had to do was open doors and push elevator buttons. The clincher was the pay—over one hundred dollars a week. I went for the interview, determined not to let this opportunity slip away.

Mr. Pedersen was the super—a serious looking individual with a Marine-style crew cut and an attitude to match. He asked a few questions in a bored monotone and seemed satisfied with my answers. He sent me into another room to try on some of the uniforms, with the admonition, "If you find one that fits, you've got the job." I eagerly found a jacket that fit me fairly well, but the pants were another story. It seemed as if midgets had previously manned the job. After several futile attempts to find a reasonable fit, I was ready to give up. There were no pants there for someone six feet tall. The job was mine to lose, and I had no other prospects. So I took up the search again, this time being less exacting in my measurement requirements. At the time, I wore a size 34"x34". The closest I could come to that was a 42" waist and a 28" leg. If I were auditioning for a clown position with Barnum and Bailey, this would have been perfect, but I badly needed this job, so I got creative. I found that by bunching up the waistline and letting it slide several inches below my navel, the pant legs only looked a couple of inches short. Once I buttoned up the jacket, the unmade bed look in the middle was hidden from view, although with the fly about halfway down my thighs, I must have looked like a stallion in a suit.

I summoned my courage and walked out to be inspected. He looked me up and down, walked around behind me, and came full circle. He had a sour look of disapproval, and hope was fading fast, when he burst out laughing, shaking his head, and sputtering. I finally made out that he was saying, "You can start on Monday." The job turned out to be tedious, but my sartorial improvisation provided a running joke for the rest of the summer.

When I arrived back in New York the following summer, I wandered around for a couple of weeks, but I could not find work of any kind. The recession had hit America, too, and even menial jobs were scarce. My cousin Michael O'Brien told me of an Irish pub that was looking for a singer. I jumped at the chance. Michael had been successfully playing Irish music in the northeast for several years, and on his recommendation, I got a gig at the Limerick Pub in Lowell, Massachusetts. Not only did they offer me a weekly wage that was more than three times what I had made the previous year, but I only had to work four nights a week and I got a rent-free apartment as well. After the previous summer's Ho Jo and clown suit debacle, this was extraordinary good fortune.

Lowell, in the early '70s, was a depressed city. The stench of pessimism drifted like diesel fumes around the abandoned red brick mills and deserted streets. One pub even sold mugs of beer for a nickel, a sure sign of desperation. But I was upbeat. I had a good job and a place to live. My apartment was in a shabby house on a rundown side street, but though it was not fancy, I was thrilled with it. What a novelty to have a place of my own! The only downside was that I didn't know anyone my own age, but when you're young and play music, it doesn't take long to make friends.

One night, I got into conversation with a regular patron of the bar—a pony-tailed guitar player from Tennessee. Let's call him Steve. He was a few years older than I was—a college dropout who made his living driving a taxi. We discovered we shared an interest in folk and old time music. He had a wonderful record collection of old time, bluegrass, gospel, and Appalachian music as well as recordings by Dave Van Ronk, Arlo Gutherie, and Doc Watson. These LPs provided the soundtrack for my summer. He also had friends who were bluegrass musicians, and he took me to some of their sessions. It was music I would never have heard back in Ireland, and I had a ball.

Steve had an old, beat-up car, and he willingly became my chauffeur for the next month. We made forays down to Cape Cod, out to western Massachusetts, and up to New Hampshire. I was stunned by how beautiful the countryside was. It was particularly amazing that even the towns were full of trees. In Ireland, our vision of the USA was that of a vast concrete jungle. This undoubtedly came from the endless succession of urban crime dramas on television. I was not the first Irish person to be surprised at just how rural, vast, and beautiful America is. When you tell someone in Ireland that you drove eighteen hours to a destination, he looks at you in disbelief. Even an hour's drive is a long journey over there.

That summer, I met a bunch of Steve's hippy friends, mostly college kids, and got a little taste of what was left of '60s counter-culture. One night after my gig, in the company of these holdovers, with "Johnny Walker-wisdom running high," as Leonard Cohen put it, the conversation came around to the various techniques of growing pot.

One claimed that, back in the spring, he had planted a few dozen plants in the woods out in Sturbridge. Then the inevitable realization fought its way to the surface of his brain.

"Man, those plants out there ought to be ready for harvest just about now!"

It was well after midnight when we set out for Sturbridge, about fifty miles away. Once there, we spent hours driving up and down little dirt roads, stopping and scrambling out of the car when our weed farmer thought he recognized the field in which he'd sown the crop. Several times, we thought we'd found it, but with only the headlights of the car for illumination, we didn't have much of a chance. If anyone had seen our bunch of hairy drunks driving into fields in the middle of the night, pulling up weeds and trying to smoke them, they would have given us a wide berth.

Daylight and sobriety arrived simultaneously, and we reluctantly gave up the search. We made our way to a grove of pine trees on the bank of a clear lake that reflected the streaks of color in the morning sky. It was incredibly beautiful, but we were too tired to enjoy it. I felt like one of the heroes in the old cowboy movies that I had watched growing up as we unrolled our sleeping bags on the spongy pine needles and went to sleep. A few hours later, I awoke with a pounding head and dozens of mosquito bites all over my face and neck. I was more than ready to beat a retreat to my comfortable apartment, but nothing would do our hemp farmer but to give it one last try. Amazingly, in a matter of minutes, he found the right field, gleefully uprooted the plants, and tossed them into the trunk of the car. I was nervous that the cops might stop us, but Steve was careful to observe the speed limit all the way home. To this day, the hippies of Lowell sing his praises.

I thought I was doing well at the pub, and my confidence was growing with each performance. I got on fine with the owner Jack Durkin, although the manager Hank and I never hit it off. I had played there for about a month, regularly dodging requests for "Danny Boy" and "When Irish Eyes Are Smiling." It was not the kind of Irish music I wanted to play, so I suppose it was inevitable I would run into trouble. One night, a drunken patron came up on stage in the middle of a song and shoved an unknown quantity of dollar bills through the sound hole of my guitar. He then proceeded to sit at the front table and demand I play all his favorite songs that he had just paid for. I didn't know even one of them.

The drunk sought out Hank and complained bitterly. The following day, I was told I had better look for another gig.

This was disaster. I still had another six weeks before I was due back at college in Dublin, and I had to save enough money to stay there until the following summer. I had no place to stay and no idea where to look for a gig. But fortune favors the innocent, and the following week I found one at Liam's Irish Tavern in Framingham, about thirty miles away.

The tavern was empty the afternoon I arrived. I sat at the bar and waited for someone to show up. Eventually, a barman appeared, and I asked for a beer. He looked me up and down and asked to see my ID. I just laughed and said, "I'm the band." He stared at me in disbelief for a few moments before he poured the beer.

I did not know it at the time, but Liam's was to become a big part of my life in the not-too-distant future. It was an easier room to work than the Limerick pub. The stage was well positioned, and the audience was inclined to listen. They also gave me a modern apartment nearby, rent free, so I had no complaints.

Food was served on the ground floor, and the bar and entertainment were on the second floor. The restaurant attracted a big dinner crowd, most of who would venture upstairs afterwards for the music. These middle-aged folks were a much better audience for my kind of music than the college crowd that took the pub over some years later. I had some great nights there and learned very quickly how to hold an audience, even if it meant learning songs I didn't really want to sing.

It was a very friendly pub, and between sets, I would sit at the tables and chat with the audience. One night, during a break, I sat down to talk to a very attractive girl who seemed to know the words to all the songs. Her name was Roxanne, and it turned out that she also played guitar and sang. We fell in love, and two years later we were married and singing together at Liam's. Now, thirty-two years and four kids later, I wonder what path my life might have taken if that jerk back in Lowell had not stuck those dollar bills into my guitar.

ೱ

STRAY CHAT/HARRY

DOR: In the book, you chose to tell some of your stories in the form of dialogue. How did you come up with that idea, and where do you think you got that wonderful ear, the flair that you have for it?

HOD: What I hear in the Irish character is great "speak," as they call it—the Irish "speak." It's wonderful to me. It's very rich. Tom O'Carroll and I have spent a long time talking about this; talking about the different accents and the different ways people use— I find it very, very engaging. It was not a conscious decision to sit down and use dialogue. It was just what I was used to hearing. I think one of my stories has the old gent from Kerry with his, "Do ooh have—?" He's got, "Do ooh have the 'Hills of Kerry'?" And he'd ask me this all the time. I love that, you know? And I love Cork people, who have a tendency to go into the falsetto when you ask them a question. It's so melodic.

"Aru from Cork, aru?" And up they go into the sky with the falsetto—"Aru, aru?" It's so melodic. And the Northern Ireland accent is a little bit sharper. I always can tell a Belfast man by his. He'll say, "Where are you from?" I'll say, "Drogheda." He'll say, "Oh, Droggeda." I love the accents, and I love the use of the language, the way they speak, the way they use it—you know. "Mrs. Murphy. She died last week." "What did she die of?" "She died of a Tuesday." I love the richness in that. My brother, I don't know if he made it up or not, but I use it onstage. "I called me mother today." And she says, "Oh, I can't delay long on the phone. I have to go the graveyard." "Oh, God," I says. "Who's dead?" And she says, "They're *all* dead." (Laughing) I love that. And sometimes, you know, when you write it, I hope people will understand with several of my stories the flow of language is different. Occasionally, when I write something, Traci will say, "That's wrong. It doesn't read right." And I'll have to read it to her. I'll have to speak it to her—where the punctuation goes, to make it understood. Because when you read it, it doesn't make any sense, but when you actually say it... The punctuation makes it work. There is a richness to it that I love very, very much.

CRED

The Boss

Dennis O'Rourke

The Boss. His name was Dennis O'Rourke. My father's father. Huge, gnarled hands he had, with long fingers, and a thick mane of white hair combed straight back from a high and noble forehead. He was six foot, three inches. He was Ireland to me. I had only two dreams when I was a kid—to go to sea and to live for a time in the land of his birth.

He was a musician, a concertina player from Skibboreen. I never heard him play it, and I wonder how must that little instrument have looked in those mighty hands? And when and why did he put it down?

Perhaps it was this. There was the bitter truth about him that when the whiskey siren sang in his young man's ear, my grandfather gave himself up to her—was awash in her. The booze would prompt his eternal banishment by my granny when their family was still young. My father and his older brother filled his place as the man of the house, and then Uncle Joe, when my father went to New Guinea in World War II.

He would come to the housing project on 150 D Street in Southie where we lived in the fifties. He would come to baby-sit the three of us—me and sisters Elizabeth and Kathy—when my father and mother were invited out to a party, or on those special and rare evenings when they would go to a nightclub, perhaps a show at Blinstrub's. That would have required some scrimping and saving, but they managed it occasionally.

We'd have long been put to bed though we were none of us within a hare's leap of sleeping. But there would be no children underfoot at these times, looking for this, wanting that. Not while my mother indulged herself in the very great pleasure of dressing up, and certainly not while my father complained about having to wear a tie. "Ted Williams doesn't wear ties," he would grumble. "Why do I have to?"

Finally, when they had made good their escape in a heady rush and whirl of perfume and Old Spice, my grandfather would look in on my sisters first in the one room, while I lay abed in the privileged sanctum of the only son's room, waiting impatiently for his massive frame to fill my door and blot out the light from the kitchen.

The booze would get him locked out of our little apartment sometimes. My father would learn from his brother that the Boss was on a binge, and Da would mutter that he was in no mood to listen to foolish talk. So when we heard the slow, solid rap of one of Grandpa's mitts on the door, my father would silence us all with a fierce shush and an angry swipe through the air of his own not inconsiderable paw.

The big hand would fall upon the door again, a little harder, the way you'd think, if he wanted to, he could have easily broken it down. All of us sitting in silence. Then, as if he were ashamed he'd banged so hard, he would softly call out my father's name and then my mother's, and I would whisper, "Da, why can't he—?" But Da would turn a look on me that would fry milk, and I'd button up. One last time, Grandpa would call out, "Frank? Betty?" his voice echoing in the concrete and steel hall. Then another silence. In my mind's eye, I could see him turn around, a little unsteady with the drink, his big frame stooped. In my mind's eye, I could see him take hold of the metal banister and move slowly down the steps one flight, into the shadows of the stairwell, out into the night, and the hot heart inside me breaking with the sadness of it all.

Ah, Grandpa. Grandpa.

On the night of my First Communion—seven years old I was—I lay awake in my bed, suffused in my newly bestowed holiness, caught up in the radiance of religion. The murmur of my parents' voices from the kitchen, talking over the day's events, nudged me away and out of my fervent dream of being devoured by lions in the Coliseum, and the certainty of immediate sainthood in heaven, where baseball could be played all day. I heard my father mention Grandpa, and I was suddenly upright in the bed, listening keenly. Grandpa had been told in which church the ceremony was to take place—Saint Peter's and Saint Paul's on Broadway. But shortly before all the scrubbed and starched angels were to march down the aisle, there wasn't a sign of him. Drinking or no, my father knew the Boss would not miss this, his then only grandson's most holy Catholic rite of passage.

Now I crept to the foot of the bed, close to the door, to put my ear on my father relating how he suddenly had a thought leap up at him and give him an idea where Grandpa might be. He spoke of slipping out a side door and taking off at the gallop for several blocks through the warm, spring sunshine, 'til he arrived at Saint Peter's, a Lithuanian church. He went slowly down the main aisle, blinking in the dark, down past the rows of pews that were empty save for a handful of old women muttering prayers fiercely, as if they were certain that without these supplications the whole of the wicked world would perish. And there, right up front in the first pew, "As tall as a redwood, even sitting down," Da said, was Grandpa. Sitting alone, waiting to watch me make my First Communion. Sitting alone, in the wrong church.

He wasn't drinking. The two Saint Peter's had confused him. He got up, followed my father out, and made it to our church with precious few moments to spare. By then, there was just room enough for my father to squeeze into the pew with Ma and the sisters. So when I spotted Grandpa waving to me, it was passing him at the back of the church. He was smiling. The procession began at a crawl, and then stopped, although little feet continued to shift in place. I turned around to him again, and saw his granite face wet with tears. I had no idea then how close he had come to missing it all.

When my parents' conversation turned and continued to other things, I lay back in bed. My dreams of lions and sainthood and base-ball had vanished, and I went to sleep with the picture of him sitting tall and white-haired, alone in the dark of the wrong church.

And so, on the nights he watched over us, he would take leave of Kathy and Elizabeth and come into my room, and secured within two giant mitts, I was lifted high. The low growl of his laughter, and some-times the whiskey breath. The fabled gentleness of the giant. No one could hurt me while he was there, while he held me in his arms.

And how solemn he was, demonstrating the execution of the sign of the cross. High drama. Again and again, 'til I had it right.

At last, before he left the room, before I slept, he would sing a song or two, a ballad in a rich brogue. It was so long ago, and I was so young, that I can't remember the sound of his voice, and I can't re-member a one of the songs for sure. Only that they were Irish.

Well, the booze killed him in the end. I was nine or ten, and wasn't told, I don't know why, 'til a week after he was in the ground.

Yes, I wanted to see the country where he'd been born, where he'd been young, and I finally got to Ireland on my twenty-fifth birthday, after two years in the Merchant Marine, sailing oil tankers. So you see, I'd realized both my childhood dreams the morning I stepped onto Irish soil in Shannon. I met some wonderful people and had some great ad-ventures in the time I lived there. I achieved dual citizenship, as well. I believe that would have made him proud.

The booze, the booze laid him low. He died in an unheated room somewhere in the Back Bay. Alone. Dead three days before anyone thought to look in on him. All alone.

There is a verse in *Carrickfergus* that sometimes brings him to mind when I sing it:

I'm seldom drunk,
'Though I'm never sober,
A handsome rover

From town to town.
Ah, but I'm sick now,
My days are numbered
Come all ye young men,
And I'll lay me down.

Ah, Grandpa. Grandpa.

ᏨᎠᎣ

The Point Is...

Harry O'Donoghue

"I'm sick of this. It's bloody well ridiculous. I know it, you know it, and she knows it. I'm over this parenting deal. I gotta go."

Parting words to my loving wife on the front steps of our house before leaving for work earlier today. The reason for such harsh words? Well, without getting into the nitty-gritty of raising twins (one boy, one girl, for the curious minded), this latest salvo came about because my little girl got "sick" at school, and I had to go take her home. To me, it was the "crying wolf" syndrome. I knew it; it's happened before, but I wasn't able to stand firm, so I drove to the school and picked her up. She went straight to bed, and my day went straight to hell. My wife says, "God doesn't like ugly." She may have a point.

Before I continue, I know you're probably thinking, "Not much of a reason to be so nasty," and you would be right, but by the time you read this, my daughter and I will have hugged, kissed, and made up. I will have apologized. "Dad was really tired, sweetheart." And we'll have moved on.

So let's.

As the wife says, "God doesn't—" and He didn't today.

I headed down to Kevin Barry's to make sure there was a mic stand and suitable cables for the musician who was scheduled to perform tonight. The traffic was heavy, and I caught every red light along the way, and then had to circle the parking lot upward of twenty times (slight exaggeration) before finding a spot. There is a point to all this—read on.

212

So I was more irritated when I got back to the house in the early afternoon. I fell asleep while sitting down to "relax for a minute, breath deeply and regain your composure, Aitch, old son."

I slept for over an hour, and when I awoke, I was groggy and felt like crap. It took a while to get back to full steam.

I was in a foul mood leaving for the gig. On the way, I phoned a friend, Liam Reilly, back in Ireland, and though the connection was lousy, we chatted. He asked where I was headed, and I answered, "GSU to perform for the Centre for Irish Studies." I instinctively turned around to look at my guitar on the back seat, only it wasn't there. I ended the phone conversation abruptly (sorry Liam) and called home.

"Hey, sweetie; yeah, it's me. I forgot my guitar. It's in the den. I can't believe this; I'm doing a ueey and heading back to town. This is unfuckinbelievable for fucksake. I'll—huh—Okay, good; yeah—meet you at—where? Oh, the ramp getting on to I-16. Great, t'anks."

I think after many years with me she's heard enough expletives to last a lifetime, so she cuts me off the first chance she gets. There is a point; I'm getting to it, hold on. We met at the interstate entrance on 37th Street, and I chucked the guitar onto the back seat of my car. "T'anks, dear; you're a lifesaver—again."

"Be careful driving. You have plenty of time. Don't rush."

But I did rush. I'm lucky I wasn't caught speeding on the interstate, and when I got to Statesboro I ran a few amber lights—one of them may have been more red than amber, come to think of it, and I cut a guy off while he was trying to change lanes. He gave me the finger, and I deserved it, but I *was* in a hurry.

I made the gig with minutes to spare, walked onstage, nodded to the audience, and switched the power on. Nothing. "Shit." (Whispered)

Upon inspection, it turned out the staff had unplugged my equipment to use the vacuum cleaner. No biggie, just another irritation. I replugged and began with, "Good evening, and welcome to the Irish Pub Nights here at—" and I was off! When my first song was finished, I said, "T'anks," and looked around the room. The house lights were on, and I could see all the faces. One of them was unfriendly. Blow me down with a feather if it wasn't the man I cut off—the same one who shot me a bird. Unfuckinbelievable—again! Must have been Murphy's Law, or something like that. What could I do? I gave him a curt "sorry" and started to sing.

Now here's the point.

There is something about music that's—well, simply stated—magic. It can transform you, move you, and take you to a different place, and not just the listener, but the performer, too. No matter what the day has been like, no matter how foul my mood, no matter that there's somebody pissed off at me sitting up front, when I take the stage and start singing, it all goes away. I find myself in a place where nobody can touch me. I'm among old friends—my songs. They ask nothing of me; I just mouth the words, and like old troubadours, they perform. These are songs I know well; they've been tried and tested, and they know how to work the audience. "Black is the Colour," "Ride On," "The Old Dun Cow," "Take Her in Your Arms," "The Boys from the County Armagh," and many more. By the time I'm on my third or fourth number, all of the day's troubles, mishaps, and irritations are far away. I'm in a cocoon, if you will—a comfort zone I've come to know and love well. Why, even earlier tonight, a lady came to the stage and asked would I sing the song I wrote for my daughter. I gladly obliged, and as I sang, I fell in love with that same little girl I had been so horrible to only a few hours before. Made me want to cry right there on the stage.

My point is that music is a magnificent gift. It's part of the language of the Muses, presided over by nine goddesses, daughters to Zeus and Mnemosyne. Calliope—epic poetry. Cilo—history. Erato—lyric poetry. Euterpe—music. Melpomene—tragedy. Polyhymnia—religious music. Terpischore—dance. Thalia—comedy. Urania—astronomy.

Right now, you might be thinking, "And still the wonder grew, that one small head could carry all he knew"—or not!

I have a reference book, a big reference book, right here beside me, and I referred to it for the names of the lovely young goddesses. But, back now to the point. A song can make you laugh or make you cry, make you think of a time gone by, make you think of a loved one far away, or close by. Music can soothe and enchant, and we who perform are as moved by it as you who listen. A simple point, really!

৻৶৳

STRAY CHAT/ROBBIE

DOR: Do you think there's another folk revival in the air, the way it was in the early sixties?

214

ROC: No. I don't think there will ever be that kind of folk revival again, because people re-discovered folk music when it had almost disappeared. I think there will always be an audience for folk music. It continues on a sub-level. It has its ups and downs, depending on a few people that get popular—if, you know, one or two folkie-people get big record contracts and do well for a while. Everybody says, "Oh, there's a folk revival." But you know, around this area, in New England, the folk clubs here, mostly in Unitarian church halls and stuff—they've been going for the last thirty years, most of them. Some fade away, and new ones pop up. I think people reach a point where they want to hear songs that have substance to them and something they can relate to, and you know, there's a lot of humor in folk music. There's very little humor in popular music, you know; it's all broken-hearted stuff. People get to a certain stage that they—they are drawn to folk music; if they haven't grown up with it, you know, they kind of find their way, and it's usually through one performer that they like. And you got guys today, like Bill Staines, that travel all over the country. He has an audience everywhere he goes. He'll never be a big, big name, but he's highly respected, and he has his own circuit. He does whatever he wants to do. There's lots of singers like that. I'm kind of in that category myself. I can go—pick and choose what I want to do.

०३४०

You're Not Irish

Robbie O'Connell

A song is like a virus. If it gets into your system, it can stay in your head for weeks before it runs its course. If you are lucky, it will be a song you like and can enjoy. On the other hand, you can just as easily be haunted by some horrible song playing over and over in your head until you are ready to scream. A certain Barry Manilow song comes to mind, but I dare not name it or even think about it, or it will instantly add itself to my cerebral play list and torment me for God only knows how long.

Songs, like certain foods, also have a limited shelf life. You can love a song for years, but then, just like milk eventually turns sour, you hear it once too often, and you go off it. Oddly enough, this usually happens with the best songs. Because they are good songs to begin with, they are played more often, and then suddenly one day your ears reach the saturation point, and you never want to hear it again.

"Danny Boy," is undoubtedly the world's best-known and best-loved Irish song. Its melody is an adaptation of a traditional Irish tune, known as the "Derry Air," or sometimes the "Londonderry Air." There are several theories about where and when it originated, but many musicologists now believe that it is a variant of a tune written by Rory Dall O'Cathain (Blind Rory Keane), a legendary Irish harper who died in 1712. The original Gaelic words have been lost, but in 1913, when Fred Weatherly, an English songwriter, added new lyrics, it quickly became one of the most popular songs of all time.

However, for me it hit "saturation point" when I was about fourteen. Admittedly, mine was an unusual case. Growing up in a small hotel in Ireland, where wedding receptions were a major part of the business, I heard hundreds of wedding singers mutilate the song every weekend. Every time they reached for the high note at the end, I pictured a pole-vaulter hovering over the twenty-foot bar, striving to defy gravity for as long as possible before dropping to the ground like a deflated balloon. Then the audience, like an enthusiastic home crowd at the Olympic Games, would roar their appreciation for the valiant effort.

Sad songs, in general, are a two-edged sword for a performer. It is ironic that the better a sad song is received, the more difficult it is to follow. It is hard to climb out of the emotional trough and bring the audience back to a lighter mood. Another problem is that people hearing sad, emotional songs for the first time may be greatly moved, but those who have heard the song many times before may develop an urgent need to go to the toilet. This kind of ambivalence puts those of us who sing for a living in an awkward position. It is challenging to sing a song, knowing that some of the audience is cringing while others are enjoying it.

I recorded a song called "Kilkelly," which falls into this category. People either love it or hate it. It is similar to "Danny Boy" in that it is very sad, but unlike "Danny Boy," the lyrics of "Kilkelly" are grounded in historical reality. Peter Jones, the song's composer, came across a bunch of old letters that had survived in his family across several generations, probably sitting in some dusty old attic all that time. The letters were written to his great-grandfather who had immigrated to America from the village of Kilkelly, in County Mayo, in the west of Ireland. They span a number of years, from shortly after the potato famine to almost the turn of the century, and chronicle the family throughout that period. It is a genuine slice of history, and the sense of the loss and separation felt by these Irish emigrants is palpable. Although the story is sad, it is not cloying or sentimental, and it captures the reality of those tragic times in a way that few songs ever have.

The potato famine of 1845-1847 resulted in the deaths of over a million Irish men, women, and children. It also started a massive wave of emigration from Ireland. Subsequent failures of the potato crop over the next few decades made sure that exodus continued. Between 1845 and the turn of the century, an estimated five million people left Ireland, most journeying to America. Many Irish-Americans have told me that their forbearers who had left Ireland never wanted to speak about it. It is hard to blame them when all they had to remember was hunger and hardship.

The vaudeville-era songwriters were aware of this and wrote many sentimental songs that idealized the old country. While these songs were hugely popular with the Irish Diaspora and in Ireland, some of the native Irish found them hard to stomach. Songs like "Toora-Loora-Loora" created a sentimental, idyllic past that to many people, folksingers in particular, come across as inauthentic and kitsch.

Over a singing career spanning thirty years, the response I received to Kilkelly has far exceeded that of any other song in my repertoire. I sang it on a television series called *Bringing It All Back Home,* and I have received scores of letters and emails from all over the world about it. The story is almost always the same. People hear the song and are moved by it. They call the radio or television station to find out who sang it, and then contact me to tell me how much it meant to them. Several people, who heard it while driving, have told me that they became so emotional they had to pull off the road.

Other people hate the song. Often before a show, someone will beg me not to sing it because it is too sad and will make them cry. Then there are those who have probably heard it once too often or who are made uncomfortable by the subject matter. It must be particularly difficult for those who have recently lost a loved one or are having family difficulties. Songs can evoke powerful memories, both good and bad. They can be either a great comfort or an unwelcome reminder.

I was unaware of such subtleties when I first came to the USA as a college student and found work singing in Irish pubs. Everywhere I traveled, I was inundated with requests for "Danny Boy." Actually, it was more of a demand than a request.

"Sing 'Danny Boy'!"

"I'm sorry, I don't know it."

"What do you mean you don't know it? Of course you know it."

"No, I'm afraid I simply do not know the song."

"You're not Irish. You can't be Irish. You don't know 'Danny Boy'?"

And so it went, night after night. They almost attacked me when I gave my standard response. At one point, with an eye to my safety, I actually tried to learn it, but I quickly discovered that I did not have the range to sing it properly. The last thing the world needed was another bad rendition of "Danny Boy," so I decided instead to write a song about not singing it. In truth, it would be fairer to say that the song wrote itself.

When first I came to the USA, with my guitar in hand,
I was told that I could get a job singing songs from Ireland.
So I headed up to Boston; I was sure it would be all right.
But the very first night I got on the stage, I was in for a big surprise.

CHORUS

They said, "You're not Irish, you can't be Irish; you don't know 'Danny Boy"'
Or 'Toora-Loora-Loora' or even 'Irish Eyes.'
You've got a hell of a nerve to say you came from Ireland,
So cut out all the nonsense and sing 'McNamara's Band.'"

To tell the truth, I got quite a shock, and I didn't know what to say,
So I sang a song in Gaelic I thought that might win the day.
But they looked at me suspiciously, and I didn't know what was wrong;
Then all of a sudden, they started to shout, "Now sing a real Irish song."

218

The next day, I was on my way, for Chicago I was bound
I was ready to give it another try and not let it get me down.
From the stage, they looked quite friendly, but I'd hardly sung one word
When a voice called out from the back of the room, and what do
you think I heard?

Now I've traveled all round the country, but it's always been the same
From LA to Philadelphia, and from Washington to Maine.
But sometimes now I wonder if it's a secret society
And it doesn't matter wherever I go, they'll be waiting there for me.

Saying, "You're not Irish, you can't be Irish; you don't know
'Danny Boy'"
Or 'Toora-Loora-Loora' or even 'Irish Eyes.'
You've got a hell of a nerve to say you came from Ireland,
So cut out all the nonsense and sing 'McNamara's Band.'"

The first night I performed "You're Not Irish" in a noisy pub in Boston, I was a little apprehensive about how the audience might react. I thought they might get mad at me for desecrating their favorite songs. But luckily, some people immediately picked up on the vaudeville rhythm of the tune and started clapping along. Others just heard the familiar words, like Toora-loora-loora, that seemed to blend in with the beer and the general buzz in the place. However, a handful of people caught the satire in the song and smiled knowingly. I was delighted to see it working on all the different levels, and I thought that at last I had the antidote to the "Danny Boy" request. Alas, I was sorely mistaken.

These days I usually finish my concerts with "You're not Irish." But I'm afraid it has turned into a self-fulfilling prophecy. Invariably, as I leave the stage, some wit will call out for "Danny Boy" as an encore, and the audience cracks up. So the "Danny Boy" fans had the last laugh, after all.

Note—An interesting online history of Danny Boy is available at: http://www.standingstones.com/dannyboy.html
The Kilkelly letters are viewable online at:
http://towns.mayo-ireland.ie/WebX?14@213.hmHiaKGX5pD.5@.ee880b5.

☙❧

Musing on the Music

Frank Emerson

Roy Blount Jr. said, "If you were a member of Jesse James' gang, for example, and people asked you what you were, you wouldn't say, 'Well, I'm a desperado.' You'd say, 'I work in banks.' It took me a long time to say, 'I'm a writer.' It's really embarrassing."

I've kind of felt that way at various times over the years about being a folk performer/entertainer—musician, if you will. It comes and goes. It certainly comes when I've had a bad night. But not always. Lately, the embarrassment pops up less often, which is good, I suppose, since I've invested most of my adult life in the business. I mean this is what I do, for better or worse. I like to think that I've gotten better at it through time. But sometimes I still ask myself, "To what purpose?" I read somewhere that Spencer Tracy, as good an actor as he was, used to think that play-acting was a rather silly way for a grown man to make a living. Ditto here, sometimes.

I figure anybody worth his salt would like to think he does something worthwhile. If it doesn't make a difference in things, it should at least make a positive contribution. Now, before I got into this game, I did a number of other things to make a living, including, but not limited to, the armed forces, teaching, coaching, digging graves, and being a teamster. The problem was that although all of these can be seen as making a difference or contributing, I just wasn't a particularly great shakes at any of them. Well, maybe I wasn't so bad at the grave-digging gig, but it was kind of creepy.

So I decided to try to get paid for what I had been doing for free and give this here racket a shot. To my surprise, I kept getting jobs and being paid for them. It wasn't too long before I found myself actually making a living. What's more, I was enjoying it a great deal. Both factors made me feel lucky and guilty.

The fact is I feel very comfortable on stage after the first song or two. Before that, I'm a wreck. The vibrato is in my knees. The stomach is gurgling away, and I'm certain I don't know any material. (It's kind of the same way I feel before a fight—until I am hit once. If that doesn't land me on "Queer Street," I can usually put up a good showing.) Anyway, once that first figurative punch is thrown, i.e. the first song is sung, I do okay. To be honest, I feel pretty safe and secure behind that wall of light.

All of this only contributes—it seems to me—to the childishness of the thing. I mean, you're standing there in front of a bunch of people in a bar, saying, in effect, "Look at me. Listen to me. You should be paying attention to me. Cut the chatter. There'll be time for that during the break, I promise. Right now, give me your attention." Then you proceed to hold forth.

I don't know whether folks realize this or not, but there is a real love/hate relationship between a performer and the audience. You see this when you ask a performer how the night's job went down. I'll bet he'll answer with something like, "I murdered 'em," or "I killed 'em." Oh, it's a control thing, to be sure. But really, isn't that just a little bit immature? And you get paid for it, to boot.

Well, this whole business ain't the cure for cancer. At least, that's the way I always used to feel, and I guess sometimes still do. Some years back, I was talking with Tom O'Carroll about this whole thing. He pointed out that one reason clichés are, in fact, clichés is because they ring true in most cases. Case in point: "Laughter is the best medicine." There are studies that indicate there just may be something to this. Robin Williams made a movie about a doctor a few years ago to illustrate it. I don't know whether it's a stress thing or some sort of chemical reaction in the body that laughter relieves or touches off, but it appears that humor—laughter—can help heal. I said, "Fair enough, but what about when we do a sad song?"

"Release of grief is healthy. Everybody knows that," he answered, looking at me as if I were a bit slow. He also mentioned that some of the songs and tunes we play, and even some of the things we say as performers make people think. "And what's wrong with that? Unless they think too much and figure you're full of baloney."

I suppose there's nothing wrong with any of it. The only time it's wrong is when you do it lousy.

Now, I don't want to overstate the importance of this thing of ours. It doesn't provide the answer to any eternal question. It's not the cure for cancer or even the common cold. What it does do, I hope, is provide some comfort or release, or a spark to fire off some synapse for many folks who work hard every day doing whatever it is they do: contributing. Maybe the escapes we offer will help them do their jobs better, with a lighter heart. And maybe one of them has it in him to provide the cure for cancer or the answer to an eternal question. I suppose we do perform a service of sorts. We entertain. And I guess in the scheme of things, that ain't so bad. In the meantime, though, I'll always feel a little guilty—if only because I enjoy it so much.

HOLLISTON HIGH SCHOOL AUDITORIUM
SUNDAY, SEPTEMBER 22, 1974
2:00 P.M.

Pubs" in Dorchester and Somerville, the "WARREN TAVERN" in Charlestown, and the "IRISH PUB" in Harwichport, as well as singing pubs and clubs in Ireland and England.

EMERSON AND REED

THE BEGGARMAN
They are a fine trio of Irish Musicians who met in New York. They formed the "Beggarman" and were an immediate success at such places as Matt Kane's "BIT O'IRELAND" in Washington, D. C., "THE SHIELING" in New York and Chicago's "EMERALD ISLE PUB." They have played concerts and engagements at most of New England's well-known folk clubs and Irish clubs. This trio is unique in that they play many and various instruments.

ROBBIE AND ROXANNE
ROBBIE and ROXANNE are a fine duo, singing the best in contemporary folk songs. They provide a delightful contrast in any musical program.

TONY O'RIORDAN
TONY O'RIORDAN is as good as his name. The fact is O'Riordan translated from the Gaelic means "The King's Bard," and he lives up to it with a liberal dose of Dublin humour. Since his American debut at the "LAMPLIGHTER" in New Hampshire, he has had a phenomenal success. He has appeared at such popular clubs as "LIAM's IRISH TAVERN" in Framingham, the "BLARNEY STONE

Concert Poster

Tony O'Riordan & Frank Emerson, The Dubliner, Washington, DC, Jan 1981

The Beggarmen: Tom O'Carroll & Seamus Kennedy, 1975

Dennis O'Rourke in the living room, 1968

Robbie & Roxanne O' Connell with Tony O'Riordan, 1973

Frank Emerson & Elizabeth Emmett, Weathervane Theater, Littleton, NH, summer of 1972

Harry O'Donoghue singing for the children, Houston, TX 1984

Dennis onstage at Liam's Irish Tavern, 1980

Seamus Kennedy   Patsy Whelan   Tom O'Connell

THE BEGGARMEN

1974

228

Frank at C&O Canal, Washington DC, September 1984

Dennis: Album cover out take, 1981

Tom Clancy, Odetta & Robbie at the Newport Folk Festival, mid-eighties
(Photo by Fionan O'Connell)

Harry with Vic Power, meeting Danny Doyle at the Savannah airport, 1987

Dennis with Leo Egan and friend, 1982

Seamus Kennedy, 1996 (Photo by Leo Matkins)

Jimmy Keane, Mick Moloney & Robbie O'Connell, 1986

To Seamus Kennedy
With best wishes,
Ronald Reagan

President Ronald Reagan, Pat Troy & Seamus at Ireland's Own, Paddy's Day, 1988

A merry patron performs "The Unicorn" with Dennis at the Eaglebrook Saloon, Paddy's Day, 1996

Harry O'Donoghue at the 1998 Savannah Irish Festival

Dan Rainey, Frank Emerson, Arlene Kinder, Neil Foley, Ray Kinder,
Frances Emerson at Matt Kane's, Washington, DC, 1983

The Clancy Brothers & Robbie O'Connell

Promo shot, 1989
(Photo by Jim Freher)

Promo shot, 2005

Dennis on the fantail of the cruise ship HORIZON, 2004

Seamus, the Jumping Kilt, 1999

REQUESTS, OR
"YOU ASKED FOR IT, SPARKY."

The Sparrow and Other Tales of Requests

Harry O'Donoghue

It's probably one of the stupidest things I say on stage—and I say it every night. Don't ask why. It must be some sort of subliminal preconditioning, or something. Still, there it is, every time I take the stage, "If you have any requests, send them up." Now, being that I perform in clubs, pubs, and the like, taking requests is expected. The audience likes that sort of thing, but encouraging them—well, that's another matter altogether. I really need to learn to leave it alone and wait for folks to send 'em up in their own good time. But no, I have to egg them on.

"So, do you take requests?" said the sparrow-faced gentleman in a club in Tampa, Florida. This was right after I had blurted my "Any requests?" line. I nodded yes, and thought, "He really does have bird-like features—and stupid, too."

He was waving a crumpled dollar bill.

"Big spender 'n all," I thought.

"Can you play 'I'll Take You Home Again, Kathleen'? My mother used to sing it to me."

"Before or after she hit you in the face with a skillet pot?" (C'mon, you know I didn't say that—well, not aloud.)

"It's not a song I normally sing, but I have the words somewhere. Yeah, I'll do it for you."

"Thanks," says he, as he ceremoniously dropped the G. Washington into the tip jar. I rummaged about for the words, found a key I thought might suit, and away I went.

Now, I'm aware that I'm no John McCormick, Caruso, or such, but I gave it my best shot in the only voice given me, which is more 'folksy' than 'big tenor-ish.' I thought my rendering wasn't half-bad. My requestee thought differently.

I saw him coming—the Sparrow—pinched lips, beady eyes, solemn face. All that was missing was the movie music—*daa, da, dum, daa, da dum, daa, da, dum.*

"Uh-oh," I thought.

244

In the instant before he reached me, an old rhyme from my child-hood in Drogheda jumped into my head:

"If I had the wings of a sparrow
And the dirty black ass of a crow,
I'd fly to the top of the Tholsel
And shit on the people below."

Dunno why I thought of that, but there it was, and there he was, right in my face.

"That was the *worst* version of that song I've ever heard. It was horrible. You murdered the song. Call yourself a singer? You jerk."

At the same time as he was loosing this less-than-subtle critique on me, his hand was in the tip jar, extracting his dollar bill. He balled the note in his fist (Is there not a law against defacing government property?) and rammed it into his shirt pocket.

"Asshole," says he, as he marched away.

I must confess to having been momentarily dumbfounded, but I recovered quickly and called after him, "If you'd like to hear another one, let me know."

***

"Hey, buddy, great job. Do the Dublin song 'bout the train, would ya?"

"Don't think I know that one."

"Sure you do; you did it the other night when I was here."

"Hmm, I can't think which song it could be."

"It's the one about the railroad in Dublin."

"Let me think on it, and if it comes to me, I'll do it."

"C'mon man, it goes *dee dee dee dee da da—*"

"Ah, look, this isn't a good time for you to be singing into me ear. What will the crowd think?"

"Dee dee dee dee dee da da da and the railroad ties."

"My God, you're right. I know it well. Sit down, and I'll do it."

Another happy customer.

The song is called "Dublin in the Rare Old Times." He was so close.

"Can you sing 'Danny Boy,'" said the sixty-something, bleached blond with the beehive hairdo.

"Look at the state of the place, sweetie. It's half-ten on Paddy's day. The crowd won't sit still for a song that slow."

"Pleeeese, pleeese, I love the song. It'll make me cry if you sing it."

"It certainly will when you hear my rendition, love, but I'm not sure it's a wise move."

"Oh, will you do it for me? Will you? I'll get the audience to be quiet."

"Jesus. In for a penny—here we go."

Nobody listened—nobody.

Five minutes later, she's back at the foot of the stage.

"I thought you said you'd sing 'Danny Boy.'"

"I did."

"No, you didn't."

"Bloody well did, but you were talking down there."

"I would have heard it."

"I think not. Anyway, I just finished it, and it's no repeat Thursday. So there you go."

"So, you're not going to do it?"

"Ah, for God's sake, sweetheart, go'wan and have a drink. I'll do it later for you."

"You will?"

"Certainly."

"Promise?"

"Promise." Yeah, right. Keep taking the tablets.

***

Charleston, South Carolina, in the not-too-distant past.

Five young men at the table directly in front of the stage. "Where's the local band?"

"Off this week. I'm sitting in for them."

"Can you do some Zeppelin?"

"Did some in the first set."

"How about 'Rocky Top'?"

"Don't know it."

"You don't know it?"

"Let me rephrase. I don't perform it."

"What about 'Sweet Home Alabama'?"

"What? This is an Irish place, lads. Gimme a break."

"Well, do 'Sweet Caroline,' or 'The Wall.'"

"Pink Floyd's 'Wall'?"

"Yeah, that one."

"You guys have got to be kidding."

"C'mon, man. How about 'I'm a Believer'?"

"By the Monkees, right?"

"Yeah, that one."

"Would ya ever cop on? Where did you hear these songs—not from the local band?"

"Yeah, man. They sing 'em."

"Fuck me."

"Whoa! Okay! You're all right, dude. Can we get you a drink? And don't worry about the songs; we don't really like 'em, anyway. Sing us something Irish."

***

An elderly couple were sitting in the back of the room at the Harp and Thistle in St. Pete Beach, and during my first intermission, the gentleman beckoned me to come join them. He was, as it turned out, a Kerryman and had been away from Ireland for many years, but had lost nothing of the broad West Kerry brogue of his childhood. She was from the same area in the south of Ireland, and seemed quiet and supportive as she leaned into his shoulder.

"Now, buachaleen, tell me—do uo (pronounced like "you," but without the 'y,' as in ooooh) have 'The Hills of Kerry'? Do ou, now? Do ou have it?"

"I do," says I, noting the richness of his speech. I was intrigued; instead of asking if I *knew* the song, he asked if I *had* the song.

"Well now, Garsun. If ou do indeed have it, will ou do for us, now will ou?"

"I will," says I.

"Ladies and gentlemen, I'd like to dedicate the first song to the 'young' couple in the corner, all the way from County Kerry in the southwest of Ireland. Give them a nice hand."

The rest of the audience applauded and looked toward the corner table. He acknowledged with a slight nod.

"Oh, the palm trees wave on high
All along that fertile shore
Adieu, you Hills of Kerry
I ne'er will see no more
Oh, why did leave my home
And why did I sail away
And leave the small birds singing
Around you sweet Tralee?"

I glanced over at them. The old man smiled and winked at me as "herself" nuzzled a little closer into his shoulder.

***

As my performance progresses into the later hours on any given night, requests are shouted to me instead of being written down. It's then that I use my escape line: "Ladies and gentlemen, the request line is now closed."

ಞ

STRAY CHAT/FRANK

DOR: You and Tony went through a brief period where you refused to do the "shite"—that being songs like "The Unicorn" and "Seven Old Ladies Stuck in the Lavatory." What was behind that decision, and how did it go down with club owners and audiences?

FE: Hmm. That's interesting. What was behind the decision was just an attempt to— Not that we were castigating anybody who did this stuff, because *we* did it, certainly—uh, but just to try to move away from it. That was what was behind it—just a decision to move away from that type of material. As far as the customers went, it didn't go down with the people who requested those things; it didn't go down well at all with them.

DOR: Because they felt a song like "The Unicorn" was representative of Irish music?

FE: I think representative of *pub* music. I don't think they would say, well, "This is real Irish stuff." Maybe they did. Maybe I'm wrong in that, but they just wanted— Because it was *their* song. They wanted to hear it. Somebody's favorite song is "Love is a Many-Splendored Thing." Somebody else's favorite song is "The Unicorn." Listen, it's apples to oranges. Did it go down well with club owners? As long as the cash register kept ringing, they didn't care what we did. If it looked like it was affecting the business adversely, then they had an objection. But if it didn't, they had no objection, so.

DOR: How do you spend your free time when you're out on a road trip that might be a couple or three weeks? We have a great deal of time to fill or kill, as the case may be, between the time we get up and the time we have to go to work—sometimes getting up at ten or eleven in the morning and not having to be onstage for another ten hours.

FE: (Laughs)

DOR: Well, for example, I work out on the road.

FE: I do, too, a little bit, though most of my workouts are done at home. I feel more comfortable there, and I work out daily. When I'm on the road, I might work out, but I'll do a lot of reading and some writing and practicing—just going through old material that I haven't done in a while to try to resurrect it and make it sound fresh.

DOR: So, you *do* rehearse on the road.

FE: Oh, yeah.

DOR: Material. How do you pick new material? Especially the newer songs that come out—how do you pick and choose? Well, I'm gonna do this one, but I'm not gonna do that one.

FE: Well, most of the newer songs that come out I don't do. The "newer" songs for me are older songs. And it's just— If it strikes my fancy.

DOR: By older songs, you mean some that might be forty or fifty years old?

FE: Or more, yeah. And that holds true for both Irish and American tunes.

DOR: You chose to record a song that was a favorite of mine back in the late sixties. I'd like to know your reasoning behind not just resurrecting it for the stage, but recording it—Peter Sarstedt's "Where Do You Go to, My Lovely?"

FE: "Where Do You Go to, My Lovely?" Write that down. We both said the title in unison. (Laughs) Yeah, I had just— Well, doesn't everyone have that memory of Paris? (Laughs) I don't know. I just think it was a real neat song and did not get its due. It was real popular, not necessarily with a cult following, but people who've heard that song say, "Oh, yeah, I loved that song back in the sixties." And so I said, "Well, it was good then, it's gonna be good now." It just conjures up this feeling. And the poor people of Paris, they're, uh— Ah, to hell with the damned French. (Laughs) Maybe you'd better strike that.

∞

"Requests—I've Had a Few, But Then Again, Too Few to Mention."

Frank Emerson

With apologies to Paul Anka, that malapropism is more or less partially to the point of this here ramble. You see there? I can equivocate with the best of them.

Contrary to the title, though, I get requests all the time. Some of them are even for songs. I welcome these. (The others tend toward the suggestion that I perform a physiologically impossible feat. These I don't welcome.) I love to get legitimate song requests. A request can be a tool to gauge the audience and help you tailor your show. The fact that a request is submitted lets you know that at least that citizen wants to hear you play, wants to be entertained. You can establish some nice rapport. Theoretically, I guess, the more requests—the more rapport. Certainly, there are exceptions. I am sure you know whom I mean— those dateless charmers who have an uncontrollable urge to shout, "Freebird" at random moments, usually while I am trying to introduce a song. They are kind of hard to ignore, so I just tell them that I generally try not to play any "fowl" music. Whew—boy, I apologize. Even I have to groan at that one as I write it.

Most of the time, though, people are sincere about wanting this or that song. Rather than shout it out, they are kind enough to take the time to jot down on a napkin what they figure is the title of the song. Then, they will catch the eye of a waitress and slip her a buck to bring

250

it up to me. Requesters are generally willing to leave it up to my judgment as to where I place it in the set. Now, I say, "What they figure is the title" because sometimes they are *juuust* a little off the mark. I don't mean to make fun of these folks. They are considerate and all, but over the years these written gaffs have handed me some good laughs. I've tried to hang onto all of them. I don't know, maybe they listened too fast, or weren't quite paying full time and attention the first time they heard the song. Maybe the singer, and I include myself, wasn't enunciating up to snuff when they heard it. I mean, jeez, any number of things could contribute to title mutilation. All of the following are examples of actual written requests I have received. They are in bold type and use the original spelling. I've also included the real titles in quotes and a couple of thoughts on each—all in the spirit of good fun.

Where Has All the Green Grass Gone?—I guess this fellow was trying to get two for one. Or maybe he was a member of NORML and meant it as a lament. "Where Have All the Flowers Gone?" and "The Green, Green Grass of Home."

"The Black Velvet Band" is requested a lot. I have received it in the form of **The Black Velvet Man** and **The Yellow Hat Band**. The one that threw me for a loop, and seems to be a mix-up between a song, a movie, and a book was, "Please play **Black Velvet,** or any other song about a horse."

Boola-Boola Father Murphy. Although this request might be described as the Rebellion of 1798 comes to Yale, what they wanted was the PJ McCall song "Boulavogue."

Shaun O'Fauty and **How about an Italian Song**; also, **Mozzarella's Band**. From the same table at different times in the evening. They meant "The Rising of the Moon," another song about 1798, in which Sean O'Farrell is mentioned. The second one needs no explanation. Creedence Clearwater came to Wexford when I received **Dark Moon Rising**.

Pete St. John's "Ringsend Rose" (Ringsend being a section in Dublin) gave rise to **Rings and Row** and **Rings and Rose**. Pete's anthem to Dublin, "The Rare Ould Times" was heard as **The Railroad Tyes** and **The Railroad Boy**.

"The West's Asleep" became **The Wrist's Awake** and "Molly Malone" became **Dublin's Fist City**. God only knows what they could have been thinking.

251

The odd mating of Phil Coulter's "The Town I Loved So Well" and Melanie Safka's "Look What They've Done to My Song" begat **Look What They've Done to My Town, Terry.**

"The Marine Corps Hymn" was requested as **USM Core Song**—probably by some squid, since they don't know no better.

Scottish tunes have not been exempt. I've received **The Friar of Scotland** for "The Flower of Scotland," about Mel Gibson—sorry—I mean William Wallace. **Scot and the Brave** would refer to "Scotland the Brave." An entirely overlooked minority came to the fore in the request for **The Star o' Rabbi Burns**.

"The Galway Shawl" was requested, I suppose, by some Vikings with an axe to grind as **The Norway Shawl**. Employing the rarely used Buckwheat phonetic spelling, the same song came up to me as **The Gaw Way Shaw**.

The Peter, Paul, and Mary classic "Stewball" became **Slow Baugh was a Rare Horse**. Maybe the requester was stewed when he first heard the song, which really wouldn't be that rare.

I think a couple of Teamsters made the requests when "The Rose of Tralee" became **The Rose of Trolley** and "Annie Laurie" became **Annie Lorry**.

"Rosin the Bow"—a traditional song about an Irish fiddler who is quite secure in his life and how he will conduct himself after death. One time, somebody figured it must be French-Canadian. Written in a neat hand on a Canadian dollar bill was a request for **Rosin Le Beaux**.

The great song from Donegal called "O'Donnell Abu" (O'Donnell For Ever) got mixed up, somehow, to become **O Donald, O Blue**. Song about a blue tick hound named Donald, I guess.

The song popularly known as "Whiskey in the Jar" has a lilt for a refrain that starts out "Whack Fol the Dario." To someone's ear, this became **"Black Balls for Daddio"**—which is how it came up to me and which probably makes more sense in the world of romance.

I've received **The Maid of the Sweet Brown Owl** for "The Maid of the Sweet Brown Knowe" (knowe = hill), **The White Rover** for "The Wild Rover," and **Where is the Rose?** for "Red is the Rose."

A silly song such as "Seven Drunken Nights" became variously: **Seven Drunken Old Lads**, **Seven Drunken Knites**, and **Seven Drunken Knights in the Streets of London**—gaining nobility, spelling, and location along the way.

252

Some folks from South Boston, Massachusetts should have been ashamed of themselves when they requested "Southie is My Home Town" as **Sulky**. Likewise, I guess they got their consonants mixed up when "The Ballad of Charlie on the MTA" became simply **MCA**.

The Vatican Drag put a whole new spin on Tom Lehrer's "The Vatican Rag."

Banjo Patterson's well-known Australian tune "Waltzing Matilda" was not immune. I've had requests for **Dancing Matilda**, **Waltz Sing Mathilda**, **Waltzing Ma-bloodly-tilda,** and one demand for **Anything Australian except "Waltzing Matilda."**

I got one, one night, for "Kevin Barry." Great song, except that it was written **Kinvin Berry**. Jeepers, "Kevin" doesn't sound anything like "Kinvin." I don't even think there's a word "Kinvin."

I received one for **a song about Dairy**. I guess they meant "Derry," but they were spelling it with a Southern accent. Something from the "Isle of Skye" (off the Scottish coast) became **"something from the Aisle of Sky."**

Gerry Rafferty wrote a funny song about a series of mishaps that befall a hod carrier on a building site. It is known by a couple of titles: "Why Paddy's Not at Work," "The Sick Note," "Dear Boss," and probably others. The fellow who asked me to play it one night couldn't remember any of them. Instead, he lurched up to me and said, "Hey, man, can you play **The Roof Dude's Excuse**?"

Stan Rogers' "Barrett's Privateers" became **Harrigan's Pirates** in a case of mistaken identity. In what might be considered a political statement, Tommy Makem's "The Four Green Fields" lost an entire province when the request came up for **Three Green Fields**. I wonder which one they meant to exclude.

People have sent up drawings—that must have taken a while to complete—to serve as requests. A man and a woman working at looms was their way of asking for "The Work of the Weavers." A bunch of fellows, armed to the teeth, piled into an automobile flying along a dusty road, a tri-color waving above, was meant to indicate "Johnson's Motor Car." A somewhat gruesome drawing of a poor fellow hanging from a gallows, a halo above his head, a shamrock within the halo, and the initials KB on his chest, meant for me to sing "Kevin Barry."

Once, when I was working with Tony O'Riordan, we were handed a folded sheet of paper before we started the evening. On it, under the heading *Requests*, were typed out four complete sets and the following:

In the interest of making your act more concise, we have decided to prepare this for you to perform of an evening. This is provided to you as a service, free of charge, to enable you to do less thinking during your musical celebrations. As we all know, thinking causes cancer—an ill we would wish on no man or poodle. Fear not! This isn't the last you've heard from us.

It was signed with love and affection by four or five people who shall remain nameless. But then:

PS, boys! If you've ever wondered why some of the establishments you frequent have hired you, remember the saying, "Hire the handi-capped. They're fun to watch."

How about them apples? But I guess the request I remember most was from a pretty girl who'd been kind of giving me the eye all evening. I couldn't help but notice, and I was flattered. I saw her writing on a napkin. She finished, stood up, and walked toward me. Just in front of the stage, she stopped and held up the napkin for me to see. On it was written, in a very nice hand, "Please play 'The Mountains of Mourne' sometime tonight. Love, A Fan." She sashayed back to her seat. Now this is a very good request, indeed. However, at that exact time, I was singing that exact song!

CELEBS—OR RUBBING SHOULDERS WITH THE "A" LIST

Happy Trails

Seamus Kennedy

There are two kinds of people in the world—those who think Gene Autry was the best singing cowboy, and those who think Roy Rogers deserves that distinction. I am a proud member of the Roy camp. As a kid, my friends and I would troop down to the local fleapit cinema on Saturday afternoons to catch the latest installment of a Roy or Gene serial. Heated arguments would ensue as to which of the two was the best; there was always a bit of horseplay—no pun intended— and wrestling on the ground, just like our movie heroes, whose white hats never came off during the fights. But it was not enough to be a Roy supporter; you also had to be a Gene detractor. And vice-versa.

"Roy's much better than Gene! Gene's an old fella! Roy's younger and faster on the draw and can fight better. And Trigger's better looking and smarter than Champion. Champion should be pulling a coal-cart! He's just a big, stupid dray horse!"

Not even Gene's wonder horse was spared.

But really, now, that magnificent, golden palomino was a much more handsome and intelligent steed than Mr. Autry's big, brown, bag o' bones.

In the early '60s, when the Roy Rogers television show came to UTV in Belfast, my fellow Roy fans and I were ecstatic. Thirty minutes of our hero, once a week when we came home from school, with Pat Brady and Nellybelle, and Dale and Buttermilk, riding the range and fighting the varmints. We were equally happy that Gene's show was not shown on the telly in Ireland. I don't know why this was. Perhaps the TV programmers hated Gene, too.

But for us, the show always ended too soon, with Roy and Dale aboard Trigger and Buttermilk singing their closing theme song—a song I still sing on stage to this day:

Happy trails to you, until we meet again.
Happy trails to you, keep smiling until then;
Happy trails to you, until we meet again.

Who cares about the clouds when we're together?
Just sing a song and bring the sunny weather.

Happy trails to you, until we meet again.
Happy trails to you, keep smiling until then;
Happy trails to you, until we meet again.

***

In May 1997, I had just finished a gig at Fort Irwin, in the Mojave Desert in California. Fort Irwin is where army cavalry units practice desert warfare. I'd performed there for the soldiers a couple of times before, and incredible as it may seem, they wanted me back. Some members of the 11th Armored Cavalry Regiment—the famed Black Horse Regiment—had seen me perform in Ireland's Own in Alexandria, VA in '94; they had seen my interaction from the stage with members of other outfits like the Old Guard and heard me do my humorous tribute to the US Armed Services. So they asked if I'd like to come out to the Mojave and perform for them after their desert maneuvers. Never having seen scorpions and coyotes and rattlesnakes and cacti close-up, I, of course, said, "Yes."

The 11th Armored Cav, and the 60th Guards Motorized Rifle Division are based at Fort Irwin, and they take on all comers from installations all over the country in simulated battles and war games. They play the bad guys, with the fictitious Eastern European-sounding moniker—Krasnovians. Of course, they know the terrain and the conditions much better than their opponents, and despite the fact that they have outdated tanks, weapons, and equipment, they really kick ass.

Other units come in full of urine and acetic acid, determined to whup some Krasnovian derriere with superior, high-tech, modern weaponry. But those 11th Armored Cav Krasnovians, with their tactical advantage and desert know-how, usually send the other guys home with their tails between their legs like whipped curs—beaten like rented mules. So great is their domination of their opponents, that in twenty-odd years of such maneuvers, the Krasnovians have only been beaten once.

I did my show for both victors and vanquished, who seemed to get on remarkably well together after the hostilities, at a function in the

NCO club. There was lots of revelry and merrymaking, if you catch my drift; and, boy, can those Krasnovians party! Indeed, I held my own end up so well that I received a certificate from the CO making me an honorary Krasnovian—an accolade I will cherish always—and I promise never to do anything to bring dishonor on the proud state of "Krasnovia."

It so happens that Fort Irwin is just down the road apiece from Barstow, which is not too far from Victorville, the home of the Roy Rogers Museum. I had always wanted to visit the museum, mainly because I'd heard stories that Trigger and Buttermilk and Nellybelle had been stuffed and mounted and placed on exhibit. Nellybelle—a stuffed Jeep—that, I *had* to see! So at 10:00 a.m. on the morning after the Fort Irwin victory celebration, I found myself pulling my rented car into the parking lot of what looked like an old Western fort in the movies. From Fort Irwin to Fort Apache in one hour. The museum had just opened, and to my surprise, there were only five other people waiting to get in—two British couples from Manchester and London, and one Scotsman from Glasgow. So this Irishman joined them, and conversing as we entered, we discovered that we were all Roy Rogers fans. Between us, we had seen all of his movies and television shows. The Scot owned most of Roy's recordings, from his days with the Sons of the Pioneers in the 1930s right up to the present day. Plus, he knew all of the songs. Now that's a fan!

Folks, I am here to tell you that it's true. Trigger *is* stuffed and mounted, as is Trigger Jr., and Buttermilk, and Bullet, the German shepherd. Really. Honest to God. Nellybelle is not. Come on, now, how could anyone stuff a Jeep?

Pat Brady is, though.

Just kidding! He's not. Had you going there, for a minute, didn't I?

The rest of the exhibits consist mostly of glass display cases with lots of Roy and Dale's memorabilia—their western outfits with the fringes, the hand-tooled cowboy boots, the hats, and the gun belts. I was especially taken with Roy's fancy-tooled gun belt with the full bullet loops, twin holsters, and matching six-shooters. The rig weighs close to forty-five pounds, and I remembered Roy running and vaulting onto Trigger's back wearing this hardware in his movies and TV series. I said to my new companions, "My goodness, that man must have been fit! His legs could probably kick-start a Boeing 747!"

258

The walls were festooned with mounted animal-head trophies from hunting expeditions, alongside rifles and shotguns of all descriptions, and Indian regalia—headdresses and beaded arrow quivers presented by various tribal leaders. Some of the cases contain lobby cards, posters, and movie stills, along with scripts and publicity shots from his long career. There were copies of the many recordings made by Roy and Dale, with sheet music and lyric pages. We learned that Dale had written their famous theme song and the children's gospel song "Jesus Loves Me."

Then our little group came upon a case that really grabbed our attention.

Roy and Dale had toured Great Britain and Ireland with a show in the early '50s; and here, right before us, were some of the many photographs taken of them in Belfast, London, Manchester, Dublin, and Glasgow. We all stood around the exhibit "oohing" and "aahing," and pointing out things we recognized to each other. They had appeared at the Hippodrome Theatre in Belfast—long since altered to a multiplex movie theater. The gent from Scotland was reminiscing about the old Empire Theatre, where they were appearing in 1951, when from behind us we heard a lady's gentle voice.

"Oh, yes, Roy and I really enjoyed our trip over there."

We turned around and were astonished to see Dale Evans standing there. A smiling, plump, grandmotherly figure in a blue gingham dress, looking much younger than her eighty years, she introduced herself and shook hands with all of us. We introduced ourselves and told her where we were from, whereupon she told us that she and Roy had a house just a couple of miles away in Apple Valley. When she asked if we would like a guided tour of the exhibits, we could scarcely contain ourselves. Would we? We were like school-kids. "Oh, yes, please, Miss! Please, please!"

For an hour, she escorted us around the museum and described each of the items, and she delighted us with a few trivial tidbits on movie making: "It's so boring; you just sit around all day until you're called to shoot a few minutes of a scene, and then you sit around some more. Did you know Roy did all his own riding and most of his own stunts?"

We asked if Roy ever came into the museum himself, and she answered, "Usually he's here every day for an hour or so, but he's not feeling well today. In fact, I'd better go check on him now."

And with that she graciously excused herself and left to see to Roy.

We thanked her profusely and watched her walk out. We began to babble incoherently, recounting everything that had just happened, unable to believe our good fortune. A private tour conducted by a real-life movie star, the queen of the West herself. Dale Evans, the lovely bride of the king of the cowboys, allowing six complete strangers into her world with Roy for the most fascinating hour we'd ever spent. Wow!

I'm so glad she didn't marry Gene.

Happy trails, Roy and Dale.

ଓଃ৪ଠ

STRAY CHAT/FRANK

DOR: You appeared briefly in the film *Love Story*.

FE: (Laughs)

DOR: Could you tell us about it, and how has your movie career been going lately?

FE: (Still laughing) Well, there's been some gaps in my movie career, lately. I was also in a film called *The Fume of the Poppies* with John Garfield's kid. Got twenty dollars for that one. And *Love Story* was just a casting call, and the casting director—I assume it was the casting director—said, "Okay. You. You. You. You." It was just the first forty people in line. "Sit in the stands." So, we sat in the stands. It was in Cambridge, Massachusetts, and all the hockey games were filmed at once. And we were the same—the same crowd in every hockey game. And—

DOR: There were hockey games in the movie?

FE: Yeah, there were hockey games.

DOR: Is that where Ryan and what's-her-name met?

FE: Yeah, I guess so, I guess so. What's her name? (Laughs)

DOR: Ali Magraw!

FE: Ali Magraw, yeah.

DOR: So, you were in the background, behind Ryan O'Neal and Ali Magraw.

FE: I was part of it, I was part of it. Although a friend of mine actually sat right behind Ali Magraw, and you can see him in the movie, but you couldn't see me. But we got twenty bucks and food. So it was okay.

DOR: And your movie career lately?

FE: They've, uh— They've stopped calling.

ଓଃ৪ଠ

Cool Balls and Large Ants

Dennis O'Rourke

I bumped into a couple of movie stars along the way.

The first was Gary Merrill. He was living in Portland, Maine, and I was there to play a new place called Mul's Irish Pub. Matthew Mulcahy opened it in the late seventies. He told me he'd been passing through town and had occasion to look up someone's name in the phone book. He was struck by the plethora of Irish surnames. A green light bulb went on in his head; he got the financing and opened up in a converted warehouse on Congress Street. The place was an immediate success. It was a huge, one-room affair with a thirty foot high ceiling—not the best acoustics.

Matthew was from Limerick, a great and generous character, and one of the best club owners I've ever worked for. On the phone, he said with a laugh, "Give 'em a few of the come-all-ye's, Dennis, the 'Wild Colonial Boy' and the rest. Ah, sure I don't have to tell you. You know what to do." I liked him right away.

The first night I worked was a Wednesday, and the place was roaring. There were a few tables and chairs; most of the mob was standing. They responded to the clap-alongs by dancing, and the floor shook under their feet. The bar itself was small and located in the front of the club, a good distance from the stage. The stage itself was high, and I had an unobstructed view of everyone and everything. Halfway through the night, I noticed a fella at the bar with his back to me, who raised his arm and clenched his fist at every rebel song. This was a pleasing sight, as most of the audience was oblivious to the material I was doing—drinking songs or rebel songs—it mattered not, so long as the tune was up-tempo. Introductions only made them impatient, and the novelty, the thrill of a new watering hole in Portland, had them yammering away like demented magpies. It was as though they were meeting each other for the first time at a giant cocktail party. When the night was done, I was sitting with Miriam, my wife at the time, and Matthew, having a jar. I inquired about the patriotic gent at the bar.

"Ah," says Matthew. "That's Gary, Gary Merrill—the movie actor. Do you know him?"

Well, I certainly did. He'd been in any number of films and TV shows. *All About Eve* had been his most famous movie. He had met Bette Davis on the set, and they had been married for a time.

The next day, we walked over to the pub for lunch. It was busy. The man himself was seated at the bar proclaiming in a stentorian, baritone voice what a great sandwich he had just devoured. His conversation with Matthew continued, even as Matthew went about his work up and down the bar. It was as if they were the only two people there. When he had a moment, Matthew waved us over, and we were introduced. Gary, as he insisted we call him, was generous in his praise of the effort I had put forth the previous night. I, in turn, mentioned his own work, and he waved a hand dismissively. At the time, he was making the rounds of schools reading Carl Sandburg. In the course of the conversation, he revealed that he had purchased an old lighthouse. He was on his way there now, and would we like to join him? We followed his little sports car out to the seashore. He drove, or should I say zipped, along at a good clip—the top down. It was a warm, hazy day in mid-summer. I was tickled. Gary Merrill, the movie star. Miriam had never heard of him, but she indulged me.

The stately lighthouse came into view. We parked our cars, and he unlocked the door, explaining that work had ceased for the moment, until he could put together a little more cash. Up we went. He pointed out where the bedrooms would be, the kitchen, and so forth. When the tour was over, he asked if we'd like to take a walk on the beach. Of course, along the way, I peppered him with questions about Hollywood—did he know this actor, and what was that actor like? I knew I was blathering like an idiot, but he was kind and patient. He'd moved from Hollywood to get away from what he called "the reactionary thinking of the place." I wonder what he'd say about it now.

We got back into our cars and he led us to his house. He told us we were welcome anytime; the door was always open, whether he was there or not. He showed us how to supplement the heat, should it be cold, by turning on the gas stove, and where the baggie of green was hidden. He bade us a sincere farewell and told us he'd see us at the pub.

He was there that night and every night during my run. During a break, Miriam and I were seated amongst some Irish-born ladies who raised an eyebrow when I pointed Gary out at the bar. It seems he had quite the reputation as a character, and not everything he did was approved of by the ladies. He joined us. The ladies questioned him about my abilities, and he was forthcoming on my talent.

"Sure," says one of them. "Then why can't you get him on the *Mike Douglas Show*?"

He threw his arms in the air and in a loud voice said, "I'd love to, but I can't get *myself* on the damn show." The ladies sank back into their chairs. Gary's exuberance apparently was a bit intimidating.

On my last night, after hours, we were again seated with Matthew. I mentioned the ladies' apprehension when it came to Gary Merrill. He laughed and told us a few stories about him. The one I remember is this: He was in the pub one afternoon for lunch, and the pub was filled with courthouse employees, lawyers, and judges. As usual, Gary was having a conversation with Matthew as if they were the only ones there. On that particular day, he was wearing a kilt.

"I had a full house," Matthew said. "The courthouse crowd, you know—having lunch and talking quietly. I'm down at the end of the bar, and Gary is bellowing away about this and that. Finally he yells out, 'Matthew, do you know why I wear a kilt?' 'No, Gary,' says I. 'Why do you wear a kilt?' The whole bloody room goes quiet. 'I wear it,' he says, 'because it keeps my balls cool out on the golf course.' Everyone starts calling for their check."

I saw him a few more times, and he was as kind and generous. He died in 1990.

***

Younger people know James Whitmore as "Brooks" from the movie *The Shawshank Redemption*. They might even remember his years as spokesman for the plant food, Miracle-Gro. This was the stuff to use if you wanted big, healthy plants. But in my mind, James Whitmore will always stand out as one of the stars of one of the best science fiction movies of the fifties—*Them*. It was predicated on the harmful, potentially disastrous effects of radiation left after atomic bomb tests in the American southwest. It opens in the desert, not far from Los Angeles. People are being found dead, murdered in the most horrible way, terrified looks on their faces and all the salt sucked out of their bodies. Turns out that atomic bomb testing has mutated the ants. They're as big as a three-story building. They get into the storm drains under Los Angeles. Two kids go missing. Whitmore is the courageous cop that saves them, and in the process is killed by one of the giant ants.

I was in some town in the mid-west, somewhere in Missouri, I think, attending a convention for the National Association of Campus Activities. It was a talent convention in a hotel. Entertainers paid a fee and set up individual booths in a big hall. The college kids would roam around with their advisors and book talent for their schools. I was less than optimistic about my chances. The acts around me had huge photos, fancy graphics, and videos to snare the kids. Also, I had been unpleasantly surprised at a meeting I had attended the first day. The moderator, addressing the newcomers to NACA, nonchalantly announced that we were unlikely to get any work the first time around. My hand shot up in the air. I allowed as to how, in all the material I had received from NACA—a foot-high pile of it—there was no mention anywhere of first-timers coming up empty. Between the fee, hotel, and travel, I had spent some dough. The moderator coughed and stammered out words of encouragement. I was to look at this as "doing groundwork," "learning the ropes," "Quack, quack, quack."

I was in a blue funk, seated in my booth, and that didn't help me with the kids, certainly. I decided to have lunch in the lobby of the old hotel. My eyes strayed around the room and settled on a solitary figure seated at a table across the floor. The profile was familiar. I put on my specs and recognized James Whitmore. Now, I had been living in Nashville for ten years and knew you did not approach stars. You let them be. It was an unspoken rule. But I was so bored and depressed, I decided I was going to introduce myself, to say hello. Besides, my encounter with Gary Merrill had been rewarding.

I strode over. He had settled back in his chair, had his pipe in one hand and a tobacco pouch in the other. I came to a halt at the other side of the table, stuck my hand out over the plates and announced, "James Whitmore. My name is Dennis O'Rourke." I startled him. He looked at my outstretched hand and then at the pipe and pouch. He reluctantly, slowly put down the pipe and extended his hand cautiously. I opened with what I was sure would be an icebreaker and lead to the invitation to join him.

"The last time I saw you, you were being devoured by a giant ant in a storm drain under Los Angeles."

The effect was immediate and couldn't have elicited a more opposite emotion in him than what I had attended. I swear his face imploded, growing cloudy and dark. His eyes narrowed, and he clenched his jaw. He scowled and sat back in his chair.

"Yeah," he said. He looked away from me as he growled. "The goddamned things are everywhere. I see them in my cellar and in my backyard. I can't get rid of them."

My blunder was immediately apparent. *Them* was not the work he wanted to be reminded of. I'd pissed him off mightily. My dream of a pleasant chat vanished. I had to say something nice, a follow-up that would get me off the hook, and then I had to get out of there. I don't know where it came from but I shot it out.

"Well," I said. "Have you considered the possibility that they might be getting into the Miracle-Gro?"

He raised an eyebrow, fixed me with a look, and then to my relief, he smiled. A reprieve. Now to get the hell out of there.

"I didn't mean to disturb you," I said. "I've seen a lot of your work, the one man shows, Will Rogers and Harry Truman, especially. I saw you sitting here and thought I'd say hello and thanks."

He nodded, and I rightly resisted the urge to shake his hand again. I turned around and retreated to my table. I watched him get his pipe going, stand and leave. I took comfort in the certainty that he would forget me two minutes after he left the restaurant. But I'll go on remembering him. I'll see him struggling in vain to escape the clutches of that giant ant. I'll rent the movie. Hell, I'll buy it; it's that good.

And the NACA convention was a bust, just like I knew it would be.

അ

My Rocky Mountain High

Seamus Kennedy

Like just about all folkies, I had a few John Denver songs in my song-bag, and in the early '70s they went over well with audiences. Great for singing along. Well, one night in the early '80s, I was performing at the Dubliner in Washington, DC. John Denver and Raoul Julia were in the audience. JD was in town lobbying NASA to go up in the space shuttle, and RJ was in town promoting a movie. They were friends, and they met in the Dubliner for a few drinks.

I sang a parody of "Country Roads" called "Concrete Roads," about the New Jersey Turnpike, and they were both tickled; in fact, John Denver came and stood in front of the stage and wagged his finger at me in mock admonishment, laughing. On my break, Raoul Julia asked me to get John up to sing a few songs. I said, "Oh, God, I couldn't do that. The man has the night off. He's not working. It's not right."

Raoul Julia just said, "He *loves* to perform. Go on, just ask him."

So I started the next set, sang a song or two, and said," Ladies and gentlemen, you've all noticed a very special performer in the audience, and I'd like to ask John Denver if he'd be kind enough to come up here and favor us with a couple of songs."

No sooner had I said it than he was up on stage beside me. "I'd be glad to do a few songs. May I borrow your guitar?"

I gave him my old Martin D-28, and he said," Now I'd like to do 'Country Roads' *my* way!"

He did about ten minutes explaining how he came to write the song with Bill and Taffy right there in Washington, DC, after a gig at the Cellar Door. Then he sang it, and everyone in the place sang along. He sang a couple more, and then said, "I'd like to ask Seamus to come here and sing one with me."

I got up and said, "Do you know any Irish songs?"

He said, "Nope."

I said, "Then let's do one of yours."

He said, "After what you did to Country Roads, I don't think so!"

He asked if I knew 'Home on the Range.'

I said, "Sure."

So we launched into it; I sang lead, and John Denver played guitar and sang a sweet tenor harmony beside me into one mike. When we'd finished, he got down to tumultuous applause.

I said, "John, I have a couple of albums for sale here. $6 each. Want to buy a couple?"

Surprised, he shook his head and politely declined.

"Come on, you cheap prick, " I said. "I've bought twelve of yours!"

Well, he doubled over with laughter, and I thought he was going to bust a gut. He straightened up, went to the bar, and bought two pints of

Guinness; he brought one over to the stage and handed it to me. We saluted each other with our pints, and he went back to join Raoul Julia.

I finished my set.

ೞ෬

The "Great Communicator" and Me
Seamus Kennedy

March 17, 1988.

I have a very long day ahead of me in Ireland's Own, and I'm not looking forward to it in the least. To say I don't feel like performing today is an understatement. I want to go back to bed and wake up tomorrow when it's all over.

Yes, it's the annual Irish Tet Offensive—St. Patrick's Day.

I've been booked to play from one in the afternoon until one the next morning in a marathon that is not so much an exhibition of musical ability as it is a test of stamina and endurance, and I begin to imagine every possible way for the day to become a nightmare.

Starting at ten a.m., there will be a line of people around the block paying $5 a head to gain admittance to an overcrowded pub from which the tables and chairs have been removed to squeeze in the maximum number of revelers and accommodate the standing-room only crowd. Pictures have been taken off the walls to thwart light-fingered souvenir-hunters. Speed, efficiency, and lawsuit avoidance are the watchwords of the day, so all drinks will be served in plastic cups. No breakage, no washing—just toss 'em. Blender drinks such as daiquiris, margaritas, or pina coladas are *verboten*—far too time consuming. The only mixed drinks will be whiskey with water or soda, gin and tonic, or screwdrivers, which can be served in seconds. There are a few "beer-stations," comprised of a keg of Guinness and a keg of beer, scattered throughout the premises, which are manned and womanned by servers who pull pints of each from the taps as fast as they can, adding a dash of green food coloring for those poor, misguided souls who think a green beer is particularly Irish on St. Patrick's Day.

The limited menu will be corned beef and cabbage with boiled potatoes and carrots, and lamb or beef stew, all of which have been prepared in advance in huge boiling vats resembling witches' cauldrons. I'm not privy to the chef's secret ingredients, but I believe I heard him muttering something about "eye of newt, wool of bat, wart of toad, and tail of rat."

These choice delicacies are served on Styrofoam plates and bowls, with a white plastic knife, fork, and spoon wrapped in a green paper napkin; absolutely nothing that can be used as a weapon in the event of a brawl, unless, of course, you happen to be G. Gordon Liddy.

The overall effect of this fine dining experience is that of a Depression-era soup kitchen, without the pleasant ambiance.

The entertainment begins at ten a.m. I am the day's headliner, and I have an opening act who will play until twelve-thirty p.m.—a good friend of mine, Barry Nelson, from my hometown of Belfast. With his son Gary on bass, he'll play guitar and banjo and sing for the assembled throng that, even at this early hour is already half in the bag. At twelve-thirty, Barry will break his gear down, and I will set mine up. Then, as though prodded and jabbed by imaginary imps with little pitchforks, who cackle maliciously at my reluctance to perform, I'll take the stage and begin my annual day from hell.

I plan forty-minute sets with twenty-minute breaks, which should work out to twelve sets. At night's end, I should be soaked with sweat, reeking of second-hand cigarette smoke and croaking-hoarse. This is the plan, but of course, "The best-laid plans of mice and men gang aft agley," as Ulysses said to Penelope when she caught her drawers on the barbed-wire fence.

The audience, too, has its part to play in this spectacular *Commedia dell'Arte*. Almost the entire crowd will leave periodically, due to Paddy-whackery overload, or as we grizzled old hands call it— Hibernian satiety. They will be replaced by a fresh bunch who have been standing in the cold for hours clutching their $5 cover charge and telepathically imploring the "crowd-control technicians" to let them in. Once inside, they will be able to shoehorn themselves like sardines into the milling mass, drink overpriced green beer, eat ersatz Irish victuals, and mix a metaphor or two. This maneuver is known in the pub-biz as "turnover," and has the fervid approval of all bar owners.

So, I will perform two sets of songs and jokes, and when the audience has changed, I will perform the same two sets for the next shift, and the shift after that. Essentially, I'll do the same two sets six times. This way, I won't have to wrack my brains to come up with twelve sets of different songs. Brilliant! In theory, this is how it's supposed to work, but some things usually force me to alter the day's game plan.

Like some folks deciding to stay all day.

When they hear me repeat a song, they'll yell, "Hey! You sang that one earlier! What'sa matter? Losin' your memory?"

Or requests.

I'll sing a request for a customer—"When Irish Eyes Are Smiling," and five minutes later, someone who wasn't listening when I did it the first time will request it again. I'll say, "Sorry, I just did that one a few minutes ago." And he'll reply, "Well, I didn't hear it. Do it again!"

If I don't sing it again, he'll bitch and moan about how he waited for hours in the goddamn cold to pay $5 to come in here and pay another $5 for a goddamn beer and another $5 for a goddamn bowl of lousy stew, and the least I can do is sing his goddamn song for him.

So to keep the peace, I'll start to sing it for him, whereupon the first person who requested the song will shout, "Hey! You sang that one earlier! What'sa matter? You only know one goddamn song? I didn't pay $5 to hear you sing the same goddamn thing over and over again all goddamn day!"

Then we'll have the sloppy drunk who leaves his beer on the rail in front of the stage (Remember, there are no tables), and as sure as God made little green Brussels sprouts, this guy will tip it over onto the monitor speaker and microphone cables. Without a word of apology, he'll turn around and muscle his way through the crowd, back to a beer station, buy a couple more cups of beer, and return to the front of the stage, where he'll go through the whole routine again.

So this is the St. Patrick's Day scenario that's unreeling in my head, causing me to feel as though there's a tractor-trailer in my lane bearing down on me, and there's not a damn thing I can do about it. As I drive down King Street in Alexandria, to the underground parking garage beneath Ireland's Own, I'm bracing myself mentally to make it through the day without getting into a row with some belligerent drunk who has the IQ of a Styrofoam bowl or getting the dreaded "green-beer sticky-wedgies." That's when your pants and underwear are so sodden from beer-spills that they work their way up between the cheeks of your arse and eventually take on all the characteristics of duct tape. Both sides of the duct-tape. At which point, something as simple as walking becomes fraught with peril.

When I get to St. Asaph Street, I'm surprised to see the entire square surrounded by police cars, roof racks ablaze with flashing red, white, and blue lights. All four streets on the block have been cordoned off by police officers standing guard by their vehicles. Cars are being waved off, but pedestrians are walking in and out freely.

I guess there has been a fire or a medical emergency in one of the stores close to Ireland's Own, and there's probably a fire engine and an ambulance on another street. This means I can't get to the parking garage, so I've got to search for an alternative parking spot and walk to the pub.

Great! A *real* crappy start to replace the imaginary crappy start to the day already conjured in my fevered brain.

There's a spot about six blocks away, so I grab it and park. I take a box of my cassettes in the hope that I'll sell a few over the course of the day, but there's little chance of that. When the once-a-year Paddy pays five bucks to get in and another five bucks for a goddamn beer and another five bucks for a goddamn bowl of lousy stew, he certainly is *not* going to pay ten bucks for one of my goddamn cassettes.

Fortunately, I was smart enough to leave my guitar in the pub last night; I didn't fancy having to tote it in its heavy, hard-shell case the six blocks to the gig. Like a condemned man walking his last mile, I make my way to the restaurant. My mood isn't improved by wise-ass strangers who see me, know who I am, and shout, "Dead man walking!"

As I get closer to the pub, it occurs to me that I don't see any smoke, and I don't hear sirens. The cop cars all have their lights going, but no sirens, and there are no signs of the pandemonium that accompanies a fire. No people running and shouting. In fact, it seems quite calm.

I turn left onto Cameron St., and there is a line of humanity snaking around the corner from North Royal Street, where Ireland's Own is located a mere thirty paces away. Clutching their $5 bills and shuffling to keep warm in the brisk March air. When I make the final right turn into Tavern Square and I.O.—that's when I see them. Standing on either side of the door, at the very head of the queue of customers, are two well-built young men in dark suits and sunglasses, speaking into their lapels.

"Good God," I think to myself. "On top of everything else that can go wrong—Mormons!"

I walk up to the head of the line to go in the door, but they block my path.

"Who are you, sir?"

"I'm Seamus Kennedy, the singer here. What's going on?"

No answer, just another question.

"What's in the box, sir?"

"My cassettes. I sell them during my show."

"Do not give one to the president."

"Hell, no. He can pay for one like everybody else."

One of them spoke into his lapels again. "He's here." Then he nodded at me. "Okay, sir. You can go in."

"Wait a minute—the president? *That* president? Of the United States?" Once inside, I realized that this was not going to be just another St. Patrick's Day. President Ronald Reagan was in the audience.

No political jokes today. And, shit, what if he knows that I voted Democrat in the election?

On the stage, Barry Nelson and his son were singing lustily for a packed house. To their right, on the other side of the stage rail—an area known as the Old Guard Corner—President Reagan and his good friend, columnist James J. Kilpatrick, sat at the only table in the whole place. Two old Irish-Americans having lunch and a couple of beers on St. Patrick's Day.

The Nelsons finished their set, and while they were breaking down their gear, I went to the upstairs storage area to get my guitar. To reach the elevator, I had to walk through the kitchen, where three Secret Service agents scrutinized the chef's every move. I'll bet they were making sure he was using real eye of newt and wool of bat, and not the generic stuff. Two more were guarding the elevator doors. I explained who I was and why I wanted to go upstairs, and one of them accompanied me, standing beside me while I took my guitar out of its case, tuned it, and came back down. Real casual-like, I tried to pump him for some information about the president's visit, but he was not the pump-able sort.

"Why, bless you, sir," he said in a delightful, fake brogue. "'Tis none o' your beeswax."

But he did tell me that a couple of the president's advance team came regularly to Ireland's Own, and that they enjoyed my shows so much that they wanted to bring the boss himself on St. Patrick's Day.

Well, I was flabbergasted, astonished, and pleased as punch all at once. Oh, yeah, proud as a peacock, too.

"No kidding! They brought the president to see me. Jeez, I'm honored. Who are they? Do I know them?"

"Why, bless you, sir," he declared with a little laugh. "If I tell you that, I'll have to kill ye. Ha-ha!"

Okay, then, no more questions. From the body language and the darting eyes of this fella and all the other Secret Service men, I guessed that none of them had been too keen on this excursion, and when I said, "Wow. Securing this place must be a logistical nightmare for you guys," he just nodded.

I came out of the kitchen, and with my guitar cradled carefully in my arms, I began to push my way through the crushing throng. Already it was loud, hot, and sweaty, as the crowd closed in around me, cups of green beer waving to and fro. It was like moving through quicksand. Where the hell is the Secret Service man? Isn't he supposed to clear a path through this mob for me? I'm playing for the president after all—his boss.

Oh, God, the president. Oh, God. Here. Today. To see me. Oh, God. Calm down. No pressure.

I went on the stage and closed the little gate behind me.

There he sat, not four feet away from me, enjoying a beer (in a real glass) and a bowl of stew (in a real bowl) with his buddy James J. (a real pal).

Plugging in my guitar and adjusting the volume, I strummed the chords to "Whiskey in the Jar" while I explained about the clapping procedure on the chorus. The regulars in the crowd knew exactly what to do, having been conditioned by my Chinese water-torture participation technique, and they got into it enthusiastically.

I can hear you now. "Seamus, how did they clap when they had no place to set their drinks?"

Funny you should ask.

Those who were near the stage-rail set their cups on it. Those who weren't had a slightly more difficult technique to master. Some would hold their cups by the rim between their teeth and clap, some would tuck their cups into an armpit, endeavoring to keep it as upright as possible and clap, some would hold the cup between their knees (again keeping it upright) and clap, but the clever ones held the cup in one hand and clapped the other hand with a partner who was doing the same thing. Regardless, there was a lot of spillage; hence the green-beer sticky-wedgies.

Now, I don't mind admitting that I was a little on the nervous side what with POTUS sitting so close to me and all, and I didn't want to look directly at the president, in case the Secret Service men misinter-preted my gaze and acted as Secret Service men do when they feel their boss is being stared at. It was all right for him to stare at me—ostensibly, that's why he was there—but I couldn't stare at him. So I decided to sneak the odd, sidelong glance to see if he was enjoying himself as the day wore on.

As I snuck my first glance of the afternoon, I was gob-smacked to see him smiling and clapping along with rest of the audience. Of course, *he* got to set his beer down on the only table in the place. It was easy for him! In his sober, dark suit, with his carefully coiffed hair and ruddy cheeks, he resembled everybody's grandpa having some fun at a family get-together.

James J. Kilpatrick, on the other hand, just grinned and nodded af-fably as his pint of Harp kicked in. One cool grandpa at the table was enough, and he wasn't going to compete with a master.

A few more songs and a few innocuous jokes, and the president was laughing and really getting into the spirit of the occasion with everyone else. I decided to do the notorious Unicorn song, during which the audi-ence makes hand gestures like mimes to indicate the animals listed in the chorus of the song. At this point, the owner of the pub, one Pat Troy, the pride of Kilcormac, Co. Offaly, usually comes on stage to lead the audi-ence in this unique form of sign language. He can work them to such a frenzy that the whole place strongly resembles three hundred people hav-ing a group seizure. When Pat is really cooking, I swear he's like a fundamentalist, old-time preacher at a tent-revival meeting full of singing, boozy sinners. Well, let me tell you, he was *on* today.

President Reagan and James J. Kilpatrick were moving their arms, doing the green alligators, the long-necked geese, and the rest of Shel Silverstein's menagerie, right along with the crowd, all of whom were just giddy with delight at the sight of the leader of the free world get-ting down and boogying with them.

As the last note of the song faded, Mr. Reagan received a huge round of applause, and Pat invited him to come on stage and say a few words. He stood up, and immediately the Secret Service were there to clear a path from his table through the cheering multitude to the stage. The crowd parted easily. You know, it wouldn't have killed the Secret Service guys to give me and my guitar a similar escort from the kitchen to the stage, would it?

I handed him my microphone, and I moved to one side while Pat Troy stood in the middle between us. I thought, "Ohmigod, the president is using my microphone. I'm never gonna use it again!" We both watched and listened raptly as he began, "First of all, a very great thank you to Pat Troy, the owner of this place. James J. Kilpatrick and I just thought we were coming over here for a St. Patrick's Day lunch. This was quite a surprise, but a very pleasant surprise. But I just want you to know I'm very leery about ethnic jokes now in my position. So the only ones I can tell are Irish."

I remembered that this was shortly after he caught a lot of flak for his faux pas during a sound-check for a radio broadcast, when he didn't realize that the mic was live, and he started joking about bombing the Soviet Union. "The bombing will commence in five minutes."

Now, he proceeded to do ten minutes of Irish stories.

"You know, my father told me when I was that high, that the Irish built the jails in this country, and then filled them."

The crowd loved it. Me, I was in thrall, standing up there with the president, who is doing a stand-up routine with *my* microphone. "On my trip to Ballyporeen, I went up on the Rock of Cashel, where St. Patrick erected the first cross in Ireland. And the young Irish guide who was showing me around took me through the cemetery, and he stopped beside one very ancient, large tombstone there. And the inscription on the tombstone read, 'Remember me as you pass by, for as you are, so once was I. And as I am, you too will be, so be content to follow me.' And that was too much for some Irishman of more recent vintage, who had scratched underneath, 'To follow you I am content. I wish I knew which way you went!'"

He had an old pro's delivery and timing, and the people lapped it up.

"Well, I thank you all for this, and a happy St. Patrick's Day to all of you. Why didn't I find this place seven years ago?"

Now, to this day I don't know what made me say it; perhaps it was the little imp with the pitchfork sitting on my shoulder, but I answered,

"That's because you were in the Eire Pub in Boston, that's why. Can't keep out of these damn places, can you?"

Oh, no! I just zinged the president! The Secret Service men will pounce on me and wrestle me to the floor. I'm dead meat. Thank God he's laughing, and so is the crowd.

Mr. Reagan was obviously familiar with the old showbiz adage—leave 'em wanting more. With flashbulbs popping all around, he turned to Pat and me, shook our hands, and said goodbye. As he was leaving, with a phalanx of Secret Service men around him, I leaned into the microphone. "Oh, Mr. President."

He turned and looked at me.

"Could you please send your waitress over, please?"

He held out his hands, and raised his eyebrows, puzzled.

I said, "She's got to clear off your table. We're expecting the Pope in five minutes!"

He threw back his head and laughed; everyone laughed, except the Secret Service detail. They didn't appreciate the unexpected delay in their exit procedure, or the possibility of bumping into the Papal entourage and having to duke it out with the Swiss Guard as they made their way to the door.

My dread of performing the rest of the day had vanished. I had a ball singing and joking and talking about "the visit" on my breaks with the folks who stuck around. My disgruntled mood had been dispelled by an avuncular old trouper who just happened to be the president of the United States, and whose gentle humor and cheerful disposition had brightened the day of all who had the good fortune to be in I.O. that afternoon. In fact, I was feeling downright gruntled. And as a performer, I had been impressed by his warmth, charm, and down-to-earth presence in a bar full of strangers.

A few days later, I received a package with the return address: The White House, 1600 Pennsylvania Ave. Washington DC. It contained a framed, signed photograph of the president shaking hands with me on stage in Ireland's Own, and a printed copy of the president's remarks, complete with my exchanges with him.

For once in my life, I was almost sorry I had voted Democrat.

GETTING SENTIMENTAL

Ships That Pass

Harry O'Donoghue

I've been performing in an Irish Pub called Tommy Condon's a few times a year for the last fifteen years. It's only a three-night gig, and because it's so close to home, I drive to and fro each night. Takes the guts of two hours each way, but that's no biggie for me. About forty-two miles north of Savannah, I turn off Interstate 95 onto SC Route 17, into the South Carolina low country, across the Combahee and Ashepoo rivers, and through the marsh and wetlands that fringe the Atlantic Ocean.

I generally leave my house late in the afternoon, so I have the pleasure of driving at what I consider the most beautiful time of the day—that brief period before twilight when the sun has almost set and burns with a fiery, otherworldly glow. Its last, golden rays hug the marsh and give the land a burnt orange color, a vivid contrast to the pink-blue sky that surrenders itself to each emerging star. No small wonder that older civilizations worshipped the sun.

This drive became special to me for another reason. About two miles from a little intersection known as Garden's Corner, there was a small caravan, or as they say in America, mobile home, to my left, sitting fifty yards or so off the road. What caught my eye one day was a little old black lady out in front with a garden hoe, busily tending to her small patch of land. Dunno why the scene struck a chord in me, it just did. It was the mid-eighties when I first noticed her. And from that moment on, whenever I made that journey, I looked for her.

She was always doing one thing or another in the front garden. Like the mobile home, it was a bit raggedy, but I was touched by her vigilance and tenderness towards it. I suppose it's the Irish in me. I see that same determination in my mother. I like to think I can see it in myself.

So one day, I gave a toot on the horn as I drove by. She looked up, smiled happily, and waved. I waved back. The pattern was set. From that moment on, whenever I made that trip, I would look for her, and honk and wave, and she'd smile and wave back. This went on for years. I thought of it as two spirits on separate paths, passing each other now and then, acknowledging each other with a wave. I looked forward to seeing her.

Then one day, she wasn't there. "Musta missed her," I thought. But she wasn't there the next time, either, or the next. The garden was overgrown, and weeds snaked up the side of the mobile home. There were no lights. It looked deserted.

I never saw her again, but I still smile and wave when I pass by, as I did last week. I'm sure she's moved on to the next journey, and maybe there are friends and family who have forgotten her. But I hope she knows there is an Irishman still out here who will never forget.

God bless you, dear, wherever you are.

ଔଚ

Me Ma and Totie Fields

Dennis O'Rourke

"I've been on a diet for two weeks, and all I've lost is two weeks."
Totie Fields

I sometimes do not understand why a particular performer is wildly successful, or why a certain song seems to be on everyone's lips. Both may seem mediocre, or at best, average. I'm downright mystified, and I confess to this bewilderment when I'm asked for my opinion of such things by friends and fans. You see, since I am in the music business, people assume I have insight into how things in show biz work, and why. I'm not so sure I do. It's one of those "The more I learn, the less I seem to know" kind of things. But there was a time when I wasn't a bit shy about expressing my assessment of most anything having to do with music, and I was often very likely to inveigh against some performer, show, or song. I'd do this in a droll voice, one laced snugly in sarcasm.

Mind you, I was not a heartless, mean-spirited prick. Actually, I was a very romantic and sentimental kid; that's partly what drew me to playing and writing music. But I had myself convinced that sometimes these qualities had to be concealed—that they could easily be construed as weakness. And the world I moved in was filled with people who had such great comebacks, put-downs, and witty one-liners that they rivaled

Oscar Wilde himself. To keep up with appearances, to stay in the game, I would give in to the dark side of me. And I have to admit, it was fun.

Nowadays, I just shrug when asked to explain the success of a pop star whose talent is suspect, or to comment on the popularity of the local band or pub singer. I'll say, "It's a big world with lots of people with different tastes." In response to a question about rap or hip-hop, I'll say, "It's a generation thing." To just about everything else, I'll mumble something about "marketing." I'm not always successful in holding back, but I try. The closest I get to a sardonic comment is when the academic in me refers to the book *Extraordinary Popular Delusions and the Madness of Crowds*, written by a fella named Charles Mackay in the mid-nineteenth century.

In any case, someone has to be truly bad, or have an act that relies on things vulgar or despicable before I say anything negative about him. This harkens back to a quiet lesson doled out on a warm afternoon in August 1978. It arrived courtesy of me ma and Totie Fields.

Totie Fields was a comedienne—a short, chubby little woman, brassy and loud, who appeared fairly often on the *Ed Sullivan Show* throughout the sixties. She was also a staple on daytime talk shows in the seventies like *Merv Griffin* and *Mike Douglas*. The line that opens this piece is a good representation of her humor. There was a lot of joking about marriage, as well. It was not my kind of stuff. Ma seemed to like her, though.

On this day, I was sitting in the kitchen eating a sandwich. I was two years into my career as an entertainer, and I was feeling pretty damn good about myself. Ma was at the other end of the table going through some bills. There was a small portable television—a little black and white—on the counter, tuned to the early news. The announcer solemnly intoned that the comedienne Totie Fields had died that day. She had been a diabetic, eventually losing her legs to the disease, but bravely weathering on, doing clubs and talk shows before succumbing to cancer. My mother watched and listened intently to the report. When it was done, she shook her head and said, "Oh, dear. What a shame."

The stage was set. I could commiserate, I could agree with Ma that it was a shame. What a tough break for a gutsy, spirited lady. Nah, I thought. This is too much. I can't agree with this. I've got to get tough. So, I did, and this time, I went way over the top with it. I grunted in disgust, and then arrogantly grumbled a few remarks centered on why I should care, why anyone should care that Totie Fields had died, or why it should be deemed so newsworthy. What did she have to do with anything that was really important in the great scheme of things? When I was done with this cruel and stupid tirade, I looked over at Ma. I waited for her reply.

"Oh, Dennis," she said at last. "Don't be so hard. She made a lot of people happy. She made a lot of people laugh." And there it was. She hadn't even looked up at me, but in a few words, quietly delivered almost in an offhand manner, my mother had taken the wind out of my sails, upset my apple cart, punctured my balloon, and held up a mirror in front of me, in which I could clearly see a young, insufferable horse's ass.

This hit me immediately and hard. I sat there speechless, shame reddening my cheeks. *She made a lot of people happy. She made a lot of people laugh.* The words sailed around my head. Ma was absolutely right. There were thousands of people out there, ordinary folk, who loved Totie Fields and tuned in to watch her. She struck a chord with them. She made them forget their troubles for just a little while, and isn't that what an entertainer is supposed to do? Where did I get off dismissing her like that just because *I* didn't like her humor?

Life can be an awful shit-storm for some of us on occasion. And I'm reminded of the grammar school nun who assured her little charges that life was a "vale of tears." We reach for something to help us get through it. We lose ourselves in a book, or buy a ticket to a movie. We go to a concert, buy some music. We turn on the television. Not everyone reaches for the same things. There's some who will go to a club to see a Totie Fields; others might come to a pub to hear an Irish entertainer.

I look back on all my years of performing, and I hope I've made some people laugh, made some people happy, even for just a little while. And I think, I hope, I pray that that might be just enough to get me into Heaven, where I'm sure I'll find me ma and Totie Fields.

DISTAFF

Meet the Wife

Dennis O'Rourke

They were a fun group—two couples in their late thirties and a solo guy about the same age. I sat with them on my breaks, and I drank some pints with them. We laughed a great deal. As they were leaving at the end of the evening, the solo guy, very drunk, pulled me aside and said, "You were great, man, just great. I'm going to bring my wife in tomorrow night to hear you."

This was at Liam's Irish Tavern.

Good as his word, there he was the next night at the same table, but he seemed to be alone. As I unpacked my guitar, he silently beckoned to me, indicating he had ordered us a drink and I should come over. So over I went, and sat down across from him. On the table between us sat a little covered bowl, an old piece of china. It had scotch tape over the top, holding the lid in place. The waitress set down two shots of whiskey, looked at the bowl, and cocked an eyebrow at me before she left.

He said, "I told you I was gonna bring my wife to hear you. Her name is Marjorie." I lifted my glass and said, "To Marjorie." He clinked his with mine, and we drank. I got up and played a set. He watched and listened, his hands cuddled around the bowl. When I took a break, I went to the bar and ordered two whiskeys, but he was gone by the time I got to the table.

The waitress came up beside me. She said, "Was that what I think it was?"

"Yes," I said. "I'm pretty sure it was."

◌

One Thanksgiving With the Wife

Frank Emerson

You know, my wife doesn't generally accompany me on the road. There are a couple of reasons for this. She has a job as the Director of Historical Resources in our town. As such, she is sort of the head honcho at the museums here and oversees the myriad programs that these institutions conduct. She's really good at it, too. I'm proud of her. But she puts in a lot of hours. Second, when she's able to string a few days off together, she doesn't much fancy spending them on the road with me, where she'll have to sit in a smoke-filled bar night after night.

Oh, don't get me wrong. She likes seeing and hearing me perform, all right, but not for nights on end. This especially comes home to her at the end of any given evening. My show is over, and she follows me into the bar where I'm being garrulous—having a couple of drinks and getting real intelligent and clever and bulletproof, and I start oozing good will. What a charmer. Well, instead of sitting there listening to all this, I think she'd rather have root canal work done. So it stands to reason that by way of these two factors, she doesn't come along often.

On those occasions when she does come with me, we've found that things work better if we try to make it somewhat special. Over the years, she has met some of my friends and enjoys most of them better than she does me—which is okay, since I enjoy most of them better than me, too. So there's solid ground right there. However, for 'peace in our time,' when she's with me, we try to do things in a bit of a different manner than my road trips are usually taken. This is a wise thing.

So anyway, at one time, Tommy Makem owned a pub in New York, and a nice one at that. They had a house soundman who was knowledgeable about the music and rode the board as you played. This ensured a good mix and sound quality. This was, and remains, a rare treat in Irish pubs. His place was in a good location, as well. I think it was W. 57th, off Lexington. (Anyway it was a street with a directional number off a street with a town's name.) I worked it a few times. One year, I was booked over Thanksgiving, with Thanksgiving itself off. It just so happened that my wife had a few days off at the same time. We figured that here was a chance for one of those spousal trip things.

We drove to Washington, DC, left the car at her sister's house, and took the train to New York. This strategy enabled us to avoid the hassles that certainly would have come about both inside and outside the car had we driven into Manhattan. We could both relax. A win-win situation.

We couldn't afford a first-class hotel, but we wanted something within striking distance of the pub. So we ended up in what I guess you'd call a second-class hotel. I'm not being obtuse. I mean it weren't a fleabag, but it sure weren't the Ritz. It was handy, though, somewhere around 42nd or 43rd or 44th Street—I forget. Near Times Square. And (and this is a big 'and') it was safe enough to satisfy my wife. Now my wife always checks the closets and under the bed for bad guys, and that's just in our own house. So since she gave it the thumbs up, you can be sure that the place was okay.

The gig at Makem's was going just fine, and she was enjoying being there, hearing me, meeting a few folks, and I was on pretty good behavior. Now comes Thanksgiving Day, and we're on our own in the Big Apple.

We wake up that morning, and after a small breakfast, venture out. Just over on 34th Street, the annual Macy's Thanksgiving Day Parade is getting under way. We decide to take it in. I'll tell you, it's pretty impressive. Lots of participants, lots of talent, lots of people. The spirit of the season abounds, and there is a genuine warm feeling all around; good thing, too, because the temperature would make Smokey the Bear start a fire. By God, it was cold. We stand it as long as we can.

We decide to walk back toward the hotel while giving some thought to where we're going to eat our Thanksgiving Dinner. Don't we pass right by the Algonquin. We stop. The Algonquin! The Round Table! The Rose Room! Dorothy Parker! Robert Benchley! Leave us go in—definitely!

We could get in all right, to the bar only, and that was all she wrote. The restaurant is booked solid for months. Hell, we probably couldn't have afforded it anyway. So we have a beer at the bar and peek into where we supposed the Round Table would be. It was all just fine, but a wave of sadness came over us when we realized that, of course, all of those fascinating people were long dead. Well, at least we'd walked and stood where they'd walked and stood. And I guess that was all right.

We resume our search for someplace to eat. We find a little pub, The Pig and—something—that was serving a Thanksgiving dinner. Good food, nothing fancy, and we get served by very pleasant folks. We talk about the city and our plans for the afternoon.

Some month or two before, we had bought tickets for the Rockettes at Radio City Music Hall. It was their Christmas show, a matinee—not something I would normally attend if it were just me. Nothing against it, I just wouldn't do it on my own. But this was different. This was a spousal thing. So we went. Much to my surprise, I enjoyed it. They were all terrific.

We leave the show feeling pretty good about things in general, and most importantly, about each other. Heading back toward the hotel, we round a corner in the theater district, and boom, there is the famous Sardi's. We figure, let's go in and hobnob with the Broadway-ites.

No problem getting in. No problem getting to the upstairs bar. I guess they're between rushes, and it is a holiday, after all. We walk around and gawk at all the caricatures of Broadway stars all over the walls.

We plunk down on a couple of stools at the end of the bar, still rubbernecking. Just a few other folks in conversation down at the other end. The bartender comes right over, introduces himself as Jack, and asks what we'd like. What I'd like is my face on one of the walls, but what I do is order drinks for my wife and myself, since I figure that's what he meant. He brings our drinks and starts a conversation with us. He's very friendly and seems interested in what we're doing in town. He tells us he lives in Red Hook and that he's originally from Dalmatia. I can't top that, so I tell him about us and that I'm performing at Makem's this week, and why doesn't he come by and have one on me. He says he just might do that and that the next round is on him. We tell him thanks and that when he's ready, we'll have the same again.

He excuses himself and goes to fix our drinks and talk with someone down the other end. We're figuring, jeez, these New Yorkers are okay by us. We're still ogling and pointing at the drawings on the walls. Jack comes back with the drinks just as a stocky, baldish, well dressed gent with a gimpy leg comes and stands next to us and calls out, "Jack, my usual, please." So Jack brings him the usual cocktail.

This fellow starts up a conversation with us, just like that. Says he doesn't get too many Irish musicians in the place. Asks how we like New York and so forth. I figure he's the manager, and that Jack has given him the skinny on us. He goes on and says that he's sort of in show business himself, on a part-time basis, that is.

"Oh?" I say.

"Oh, yes," says he, "and you've probably seen me in the movies."

"Oh?" I say again. I figure I'm holding up my end, giving him cues. I'm looking, but I don't know this guy.

"Yeah. Did you see that Peter O'Toole movie, *My Favorite Year?*"

"Sure. Great movie," I say.

"I was in that," he says.

I still can't place this guy. He senses this.

"You know the part where Peter O'Toole steals the police horse in Central Park and gallops away? Well, I was the cop holding the horse."

"It would have been quite a stretch if you'd told us you were the horse," I says. The guy laughs. My wife gives me a shot in the ribs.

"I'm sorry," I say. "I don't mean to be a wiseacre. No offense."

"Course not," says the guy. He then tells us of a few other films he's been in—*Julia*, *The Fortune Cookie*, and so on. Says he's got his SAG card. Just then, he catches sight of someone who's just come up the stairs behind us. He waves and shouts. "Be right with you, Colonel." I turn to look and see a bald-headed fellow in a suit heading toward the next room.

"Jack, give these folks their next round on me." Then to us, "You know the colonel, don't you?"

"The colonel?" asks my wife.

"Yeah, Colonel Klink—you know, from *Hogan's Heroes*. He's involved in a lot of stuff on Broadway right now. Nice guy. Wants to talk with me about something. He can wait a minute." We chat for a couple of more film credits, and he then says, "I gotta go talk to the colonel. Nice meeting you. Enjoy New York, and good luck at Makem's." And off he went.

Jack comes back with our drinks. He's smiling. "He doesn't do that a lot with people he doesn't know. I guess he likes you."

I ask, "Who is he, Jack? The manager?"

"No, not the manager. That's the man. That's Vincent Sardi."

How about that? Vincent Sardi—Junior, that is. Son of the original owner. Grew up in the business. From Queens. Enlisted in the US Marine Corps in World War II and left a leg in the Pacific. He rubs shoulders every day with a lot of famous, would-be famous, and past famous and powerful people. Everybody in the theater trade wants to catch his ear. And here he's a regular Joe. He's taken the time to make a couple of out-of-towners feel welcome. Good guy.

I suppose this whole thing doesn't have a lot to do with the music business, but it does point to the fact that had my wife not come along with me, none of what happened that day would have happened. I wouldn't have seen the Macy's parade, wouldn't have seen the Rockettes, wouldn't have gone in to the Algonquin, probably wouldn't have eaten much to speak of, and definitely wouldn't have met a Word War II hero/Broadway fixture. (I am quite certain that my wife was the real reason he stopped by in the first place. She is easy on the eyes, after all.)

What I probably would have done was go to some old bar and watch endless football games, drink drinks I probably didn't really want, and root for teams I didn't know with people I didn't know who were in the same position as myself (sort of hunched over a drink and an ashtray, listing first to starboard then to port), with nowhere else to go.

So maybe she's a good luck charm for me. I'd like to reciprocate one day. She certainly gets me to broaden my horizons when my natural predilections tend to narrow them.

BELFAST BEGINNINGS

East Winds from Belfast

Seamus Kennedy

I never intended to be a traveling folk entertainer, it's just something I fell into. In high school, I was a scholar-athlete and class clown. Languages were my specialty—Latin, French, Italian, Gaelic—with a smattering of English, and I had hoped to be an interpreter at the United Nations when I graduated from college. But as John Lennon so aptly observed, life is what happens while you are making other plans.

Whilst in high school, I became a member of a small folk combo called the East Winds. Played mandolin and a little rhythm guitar with Peter Kennedy (no relation), who was a great Bert Jansch-style picker, and lead vocalist/tambourinist Jim Higgins. We recorded Dominic Behan's song "Arkle," about the legendary Irish racehorse in 1965 or '66, with the "Leaving Of Liverpool" on the flip side, for Outlet records in Belfast. We were paid ten pounds each, with a crate of Guinness thrown in. As high schoolers, how could we possibly say no to such a deal?

Every time Arkle raced, Outlet did a big promotion with the single—a full-color photo on the cover (of the horse, not us!) with Pat Taaffe, the jockey, aboard. When Arkle fell and broke the pedal-bone in his foot, forcing him to retire, another big promo. When the horse finally died, yet another promotion, with his photo edged in black. Outlet sold a shitload of these singles every time the horse made the headlines.

Of course, the East Winds had broken up and left school by the time all of these promotions were in full swing, so we did not share in the profits.

And, God knows, we could have used the money. I remember breaking my mandolin pick (we called it a plectrum) at a gig one night, and because replacements were expensive in those far-off days, I had to use a collar stiffener from my shirt. I became adept at re-using broken strings, a skill that still stands me in good stead today, even though I can well afford new ones. If the string broke near the bridge-saddle, I would just remove the bridge-pin, thread the broken string through the

289

brass ball-end, tie a knot in it, poke it back through the bridge-hole, and replace the pin. No point using a new string if you didn't have to, you know.

Back then, when we played bars in some borderline areas, it was often hard to tell if we were in a Protestant pub or a Catholic one. So I learned the art (nowadays, it would be called a "survival skill") of reading the graffiti on the walls of the toilets. Some people could read tealeaves; some could read chicken entrails. I could read bathroom walls. For example, if there were a lot of "Fuck the Queen" calligraphy, we could do rebel songs all night long. If there were "Fuck the Pope" hieroglyphics, we'd do middle of the road, folky, non-Nationalist material. And if the graffiti had been painted over, we'd wing it and risk a kicking.

Aaahh, if I only knew then what I know now—what thirty-odd years of traveling and performing have taught me—I wouldn't have accidentally set my foot on that slippery downward slope of professional entertainment.

No, I'd have deliberately jumped on it and slid gleefully on my ass into the present.

കള്ള

Old Enemies

Seamus Kennedy

It was through hurling and Gaelic football that I first came to the US in 1970. Hurling is the fastest field-based ball sport in the world, and to the uninitiated eye, it looks like a violent hybrid of hockey and lacrosse with three-foot-long ash sticks (hurleys) swung vigorously at a small, leather ball in an effort to strike said ball past a goalkeeper into a goal net, or between the uprights of the goalposts, much like a field-goal in American football.

It is, in fact, an extremely skillful game with a premium on hand-eye coordination and fitness, and there is a lot of physical contact, both between players and between sticks and players, but remarkably very few serious injuries, considering the ferocity and speed with which the game is played.

Gaelic football, on the other hand (or foot), resembles a hybrid of rugby, soccer and Australian rules played on a field or pitch over one hundred yards long by seventy yards wide, with an H-shaped goalpost at either end. Just as in hurling, there are fifteen men to a side: a goalie, three fullbacks, three halfbacks, two mid-fielders, three half-forwards, and three full forwards. Unlike American football, there are no sissy, wussy pads or helmets worn; hence, more than a few players resemble hockey goalies before the advent of facemasks.

While growing up in the Nationalist/Catholic Falls Road section of Belfast in the 1950s and 60s, I developed an abiding love for Gaelic culture, music, sports, and language. I played Gaelic football and hurling, first at primary school, St. Teresa's, and then at grammar school, St. Mary's Christian Brothers, which was the first school from the North of Ireland to make it to the prestigious All-Ireland Colleges Hurling Final, 1968, played at the GAA Headquarters in Dublin—the hallowed Croke Park, where every Irish kid dreams of playing some day. Granted, it was the B division for schools from the less-talented hurling counties, such as Antrim, my home county, but we made it there, nonetheless, and it's one of the great thrills of my life to have played in that match.

While playing at St. Mary's between the ages of twelve and eighteen, I also played for a district club in the Falls area, which was named O'Donovan Rossa in honor of the great Irish patriot Jeremiah O'Donovan Rossa, from Rosscarbery, Co. Cork. It was founded in 1916, and celebrated its 85th anniversary in 2001.

Many of my fondest memories and strongest and oldest friendships were born while I played for the Rossa—and a few long-lasting rivalries.

As in any large community, rivalries can spring from such disparate sources as what street you came from, what school you went to, or what football team you supported—kind of like the Sharks and the Jets, without the dancing and all that singing about "Maria."

The Rossa, being one of the oldest and strongest teams in the district, had many rivals, like the Sarsfields from down the road, who were named for another great Irishman—Patrick Sarsfield—or lesser lights, like Dwyers, Davitts, Clonard, and St. Galls.

But our greatest rivals were a club from nearby Whiterock Road and the parish of St. John's, who were almost as old and powerful as the Rossa—St. John's, or as they were more commonly known, the Johnnies. While we had family dynasties of magnificent players who spanned several generations: the McDonalds—Seamus, Malachy, and Bartley; the Hamills—Sean, Liam, Eamonn, and Aidan, so did the Johnnies with the Gallaghers—Seamus, Henry, Eugene, and Mickey; and the Armstrongs—Pat, Dessie, and Gerry.

And we hated each other's guts.

For a start, our team jerseys were blue, with a broad gold band around the chest, and theirs were the same color blue with a white band around the chest. So, naturally enough, they insisted our gold band wasn't gold at all, but "yellow," indicating a lack of bravery on our part, while we in turn suggested that their white band was the color of chicken feathers, indicative of a white heart and cowardice.

Well, neither side would take these insults lying down, and so when we faced each other on the playing field, the latent hostilities frequently rose to the surface in the form of over-aggressive tackling. Let's face it—it sometimes became downright dirty and dangerous, with men trying to injure their opponents, and no one dared back down from a challenge, lest he be accused of cowardice by his own teammates. Grudges were held for decades, and occasionally it would spill over into street fighting after the games were long over. The rivalry was so intense that we wouldn't speak to each other. If we met on the street, there would be a curt nod of acknowledgement and no more; anything extra, such as "Hello," would be fraternizing with the enemy.

The only occasion a Rossa man and a Johnnies man would talk was if each were selected to play for the county team, which comprised the best players from all the teams in the county. But there would be no intimate tête-à-têtes, or revealing, sharing soul-baring conversation. That was reserved for the confessional on a Saturday night.

"Bless me, Father, for I have sinned. I deliberately split a Johnnies man with a hurley in the match yesterday. He got twenty stitches in the head."

To which the reply would usually be, "Never mind the medical report; did you win?"

We had deep philosophical discussions on the relationship between the clubs, along the lines of, "If you saw a Johnnies man drowning in quicksand, would you throw him a rope?" One of my more practical teammates had the ideal solution to this dilemma. "If he was one of their star players, no; if he was one of their weaker players, yes." Problem solved, conscience salved.

Incidentally, this seriously intense club rivalry is not restricted to Belfast. Indeed, clubs in the rural parishes in the rest of Ireland have ancient enmities that make ours seem like love-ins by comparison.

Now, for as long as Irish people have been immigrating to America, there have been Gaelic football and hurling clubs here, playing in league and championship matches every summer, and each major city with an Irish population has a team or two. Harry Boland's in Chicago, the Washington Gaels in DC. San Francisco, Cleveland, Buffalo, Philadelphia are all represented, but by far the most teams are in New York City, with just about every county in Ireland fielding a team. In fact, the All-Ireland Football Final in 1948 was played in the Polo Grounds at Coogan's Bluff, the famed home of the New York Giants baseball club.

When I was at university in Dublin in the late '60s and playing for my college team, UCD, I learned that New York teams would bring men out from Ireland to play for them in the summer league. Airfare, board, lodging, and a job were part of a very attractive package for a twenty-year-old student who wanted to go somewhere radically different from July to September. So, with my friend Sean Boylan, who won an All-Ireland Under-21 football medal with Antrim that year, I landed in New York.

We immediately latched on with the Waterford team, Sean becoming one of their star footballers, while I played hurling. The rivalries were not as intense as back home, although the games were just as hotly contested, but we'd go out for a few beers after the matches with our opponents. Any on-field animosity was dispelled after a few pints in a local hostelry, and few grudges were held.

I usually had my guitar at these post-match get-togethers, and I'd sing a few ballads and get the guys going in a bit of a sing-along. Gradually, I became known as a musician, and John McAleer, the gentleman who owned the bar to which we had repaired, offered me fifty dollars to perform on a couple of his off nights—Monday and Tuesday—in the hopes that my team mates would come to his fine establishment and spend lots of money on traditionally slow nights. Well, it worked, and I've been doing it ever since, firmly established in my chosen career as an Irish entertainer, traveling all over the United States, performing in pubs, clubs, festivals, and concerts. Entertaining is very much like prostitution; you start out doing it for nothing for a few friends, and the next thing you know, you're doing it for money for lots of people.

In 1990, my travels brought me to Seattle, where my friend John Callahan had booked me for a concert in the University Club, a lovely facility that bears more than a passing resemblance to an old English gentlemen's club, with plush leather armchairs, dark wood paneling, and fine food and beverages. A stage and a sound system were in place, and the show went over well with the assembled alumni, some of whom I even recruited for one of my pub tours of Ireland.

Following the performance, John suggested going to a nearby Irish pub called Kell's, up on Post Alley, for a pint of Guinness. With my arm thus twisted, we wended our way to Kell's and walked in. The place was about three-quarters full, and a two-piece band was playing a few songs on stage.

John and I moved to the end of the bar behind a man standing with one foot on the bar-rail, one elbow on the bar, and a pint in his hand, listening to the music. The barman came over to us, and I placed our order for two pints of stout.

The gentleman in front of us heard my accent, turned, and said, "Are you from Belfast?"

"I am," said I.

"What part of Belfast?" he asked.

Now, when people from Belfast meet anywhere in the world, this is where the verbal fencing begins. We are trying to discern whether someone is Protestant or Catholic, whether he or she is Unionist or Nationalist, and how to conduct the conversation according to the person's responses.

Basically, are we the same kind?

So there's thrust and parry, and a lot can be gleaned from seemingly simple answers. A Christian name alone can provide its owner's religious affiliation—Seamus, for example, is a traditionally Catholic name, as is Sean, Patrick, or Mickey. Winston, Mervyn, Trevor, or William usually denote a Protestant.

"What part of Belfast?" is an apparently innocent question that can provide a wealth of information to the inquisitor. The answer to this one can usually identify religious persuasion and political leanings, e.g. Falls Road = Catholic/Nationalist, whereas Shankill Road = Protestant/Unionist, with quite a few other locations providing equally good intelligence.

I grabbed the bull by the horns and said, "The Falls Road."

There, I said it. It's out in the open; let him deal with it how he may.

"So am I," he replied. Fair enough; we're from the same area.

"What part of the Falls?" I inquired. Okay, now we're getting down to specifics—streets and blocks.

"Whiterock Road," was his reply. "And yourself?"

"Just up the Glen Road. Seamus Kennedy's my name." I extended my hand.

He took it, shook it, and said, "Gerry Campbell."

"Are you 'Dodger' Campbell who played for the Johnnies back in the '60s?"

"I am," said he. "How do you know?"

"I played football and hurling against you. I'm a Rossa man."

"Are you Séimí Kennedy, the right-half forward?" he asked, using the Irish diminutive of my name, by which I was more commonly known.

"That's me."

"Well, fancy meeting you here of all places. What are you doing with yourself these days?"

I told him, and he told me what he was doing, and after a moment or two staring at each other to see how little we had changed in the intervening years, we shook hands again more warmly, and ordered up a couple of pints.

My friend John couldn't believe it.

"You two guys know each other. No shit! After all this time! No shit! What a small world!"

Dodger and I started recalling some of the epic blood and guts struggles between the Rossa and St. John's and basking in the memory of our glory days as all old, creaky, former athletes do, exaggerating our exploits to the point of mythology and elevating ourselves to the pantheon of Gaelic sporting deities.

We had finished the pints when John Callahan suggested going to another pub called Murphy's to check out the Irish band there. Dodger and I were quite content to stay there, recalling the old days, when John also mentioned that the pints were better in Murphy's. Well, that tipped the scales, so off we went.

As we entered Murphy's, the band was taking a break, so we bellied up to the bar and ordered three more pints. The guitar player from the band, a big redheaded young fella, heard us ordering and asked, "Are youse'uns from Belfast?"

The "youse'uns" gave him away. He was a Belfast man, too.

"What part are youse from?" Here we go again!

"Falls Road."

"Whiterock Road."

"Me, too."

"No shit!" yelled John Callahan.

"Are you a Johnnies man, too, like this glipe here?" I asked, indicating Dodger.

"I am. Liam Gallagher's the name."

Oh, no! One of the legendary Gallagher clan—St John's stalwarts for generations.

"This is Dodger Campbell; I'm Seamus Kennedy."

Handshakes and back claps all around.

Liam asked, "Are you *the* Dodger Campbell from those great teams back before my time?"

"I am," said Dodger, "and Seamus here's a Rossa man. We played against each other many moons ago."

"No shit!" said John Callahan. "I don't believe this! The three of you meeting here tonight! Unbelievable!"

Well, we talked and drank the night away, reminiscences flying like shrapnel, wallowing in an alcohol-induced nostalgia until we had to leave, with many promises to stay in touch.

Three months later, I was home in Belfast for a family visit, and I went to the Rossa clubhouse with my youngest brother, Gavin, who was still an active player on the Rossa hurling team. We were enjoying a couple of quiet pints in the lounge bar, catching up on family news, and I began to tell him about my travels around the US performing in various cities, when I remembered that night in Seattle.

"Here's an interesting wee story, Gavin," I said.

And I recounted meeting Dodger Campbell in Kell's and then meeting Liam Gallagher in Murphy's.

"Can you believe it?" I asked him. "Six thousand miles and thirty years away from the Falls, and I run into two Johnnies men in two different bars on the same night. What are the odds on that?"

He eyed me suspiciously and asked," You didn't talk to them, did you?"

PLAYING HURT, OR
NO GUTS, NO GLORY

The Splinter

Dennis O'Rourke

I 'll tell you a story about playing hurt.

I was living in South Florida and was asked by this agent with whom I had had previous dealings to do a gig at a joint some two hours from my home. It was a Saturday night fill-in for an entertainer who had a death in the family. I wasn't working that weekend, so I said, "Sure, why not; I'll do it." The money wasn't all that great, considering the travel involved, but I'd worked the gig a few times in the past, again, through this agent, and I fooled myself into thinking it was a good way to ingratiate myself to him. Quid pro quo, don't you know. That's how it's supposed to go, but it doesn't always, especially with some agents. Their memory banks service their own convenience. Especially this guy. Privately, I used to call him Sparky the Sphincter. In the end, I figured that when you get offered a bit of work, you take it. You might pick up a private party from some impressed member of the audience or another club owner will see you and you can by-pass the agent and his commission. And you might meet a woman.

The gig was easy enough, though it was more restaurant than pub. The live music was an afterthought. You could see that when you went into the joint during the day and looked around for a stage and Klieg lights. There were neither. In the evening, the staff would clear a small raised landing of its few two-top tables and chairs, and the entertainer would set up his equipment there. Right by the front door, where two chattering, giggly teenage hostesses stood—some cleavage, push-up bras, but otherwise anorexic little girls. People coming and going. Passers-by poking a nose in, looking, then leaving. Distractions everywhere. A noisy room with a high ceiling. The chairs pointed willy-nilly in every direction except the "stage." The bar immediately in front of you so that all you can see of the patrons seated there are their backs and spreading arses. In short, the all-too-usual bullshit.

I get up at the crack of noon on the Wednesday before the gig. I confess to being a bed-maker. Before I even put my lips to a cup of coffee, I make the bed. Years ago, I had purchased some furniture from a now-defunct company called This End Up. It was crate furniture built of Southern Georgia pine. Solid stuff. It looked more like it belonged in a cabin in the Montana woods than an apartment in South Florida, but I liked it. The bed was a king-sized platform. The mattress rested on two long sheets of some kind of particleboard.

I was feeling pretty damn good that day, and I was moving around briskly. I lifted the bottom of the mattress up enough to get my hands under it in order to tuck in the sheets. I shoved my hands, palms-up, under the mattress and immediately felt a stabbing, vicious pain in my left middle finger. I howled and jumped around the room like a cartoon character, holding my hand. Mighty leaps. Nureyev would have been impressed. I knew right then that I had done myself a serious injury. Blood was trickling out from under the nail. It seemed that with one vigorous thrust, I had contrived to drive a small shard of wood up under the fingernail. A splinter.

Over the next few hours I took eight or nine ibuprofen pills for the pain, to no avail. All the prescription painkiller bottles in my medicine chest were empty, fallen victim to recreational use. But the bleeding finally stopped, and when I examined it closely, I could see nothing under the nail. I figured that when I pulled my hand away, the splinter had remained in the wood. Well, something to be thankful for, anyway. (All together now: "Sure, it could have been worse.")

I picked up the guitar later that night. I couldn't bend the finger or press it down hard enough on the string to get the note. I began to fear the gig was in jeopardy, but I held off calling the agent. He was an excitable guy. He would have had a heart attack. There was probably no way he could get someone to replace me at that late date. But I reasoned that I had two days to heal. My recuperative powers had served me well in the past, and I had some hope they would come through for me again. They didn't.

On Friday afternoon, I was forced to call the agent and apprise him of my condition. "Oh, Jesus, Mary, and Joseph," he wailed. "You did what? How did you do that? Oh, Christ. Don't tell me this. This is the last thing I need to hear right now. I've got—" and then he proceeded to list all his troubles and woes. A litany of dread. When that was over, he began to plead. "Is there no way you can do this for me? I'm fucked if you can't. D'ya understand? Fucked. I've a contract to supply entertainment to these people. I know they're trying to weasel out of it. This is all the excuse they'll need to do that. Can you just show up and play a couple of twenty-minute sets? Can you do that much?"

"Listen," I said. "*You* don't understand. The nail is almost all black now, liable to drop off, and I can't bend the finger. How am I going to chord the guitar? How am I going to play?"

By that time I really didn't want to do this gig. We went 'round a bit, or rather, I listened in silence to more of his woes, until he finally wore me down, and I told him of an idea that had come to me that very morning.

"Well, I could try this: I can open tune the guitar and bar the frets with a good finger. Do just the three-chord stuff. I think I might get by with that."

A tremendous heave of relief soared through the phone, then dissolved into a series of unseemly sighs. Gratitude came in waves. Apparently, I had pulled him from the edge of an abyss. He was forever in my debt. And, by God, some of the greatest gigs to ever come down the pike were promised me.

Let me explain. You can tune the strings of a guitar by "open-tuning." Pick a key and tune the guitar so that when you hit the strings open, the chord in that key is there without your having to finger individual strings. Then you use one finger to bar the frets, and you get different chords. I picked the key of A and ran through a few songs, using a capo here and there. There are quite a few Irish songs that are only three or four chords anyway.

But all that went straight out the window when I got there. It was a great crowd—eager puppy faces, and they actually wanted to be entertained. I couldn't do that playing an open-tune all night, no matter how many times I changed the key using the capo. It just didn't sound right to me. And I was being denied over half of my play list—songs that required minors and sevenths and so on. My pride got me. So I wrapped a small band-aid as tightly as I could around the nail, leaving just the tip of my finger exposed so that I could feel the string. It hurt like all hell, but I resolved to ignore it. A couple of shots would have helped, but I had a ninety-mile drive home. I re-tuned and started up.

Well, I made it, played the whole bloody night, and did well. Packed up and drove home with the finger throbbing. The pain eased off a bit in the next few days, but was still there. I worked a club in Lauderdale the next weekend—Thursday through Saturday. Same approach. Tight band-aid. Gritting the teeth.

On Sunday morning, I went to the beach. The nail was black at the top, but growing out clear at the base. I felt pretty sure I wasn't going to lose it. Then it occurred to me that salt water might be the very thing I needed to cure whatever was raging under the nail.

Now, even though I sailed Merchant Marine for two years, I do not swim, at least not in the ocean. I love the sea, but I do not swim in it. When I am at the beach, standing knee-deep in the ocean, I look out at the bathers happily splashing around and the sun glinting off the water. Then I hear that music, those pulsing cellos. I can hear Robert Shaw singing, "Farewell and adieu to you fair Spanish ladies." I see the fin cutting through the water, and I scramble right back up on the sand. But I said my Hail Mary, stepped in amongst a crowd of splashing bathers (shark experts say there is safety in numbers), and let my hand trail in the water. I went in and out of the ocean several times that day, leaving my finger to soak five or ten minutes at a time.

I went home, and later that night, I examined the finger. I noted a small brown slice of gunk sticking out from under the top of the black nail, and knew immediately that the salt water had drawn it out. I found a pair of needle-nose pliers and took hold of the gunk and slowly pulled it all the way out. It was a splinter, more than half an inch long, and it had been there all week. I was astonished. I laid it out on top of the nail to see how long it was. It went over the cuticle. I had driven my finger so hard into it that it had not only gone all the way up the nail, but had buried itself in the flesh behind the nail. And I had played four gigs with it in there.

It quickly became a trophy. It was so big that I just had to wrap it up in some tissue, put it in my wallet, and every chance I had I would tell the story, and then dramatically produce the splinter. Groans and shrieks. I did this at the bar of O'Friel's several nights running. The splinter was pretty much deteriorated by then, and finally, my friend Leo Matkins convinced me that perhaps it was time to let this episode slip into the past. I went over to the wastebasket and dropped it in. We had a suitably celebratory drink in its honor.

The next time I had occasion to phone Sparky the Sphincter, I told him what I had done to myself. In my mind's eye, I could see him roll his eyes. Then he went past my tale of woe like a fart. He wasn't interested.

"Now what about these gigs you told me you'd get me for playing hurt?" I demanded.

"Ah," says he, in a solemn, troubled voice, "It's dead slow out there at the moment, and I've got other entertainers coming from Ireland that I've promised work. But don't worry, I have you in my mind, and I won't forget what you did for me, and—" And on he went. Quack, quack, fucking quack.

The finger healed, but because I had bent it over the string in the odd way that was demanded, a callus had grown under the tip of the nail. It hasn't gone away.

But I was proud in probably a boyish, even childish, way of all the gigs I had done playing hurt. So I carried the splinter around. Ah, a bit much, I suppose. But let me say this in my own defense—I knew a club owner years ago who did a similar act of "Hey, look what happened to me." He had survived an emergency gallstone operation, and the surgeon had presented him with the critters as a memento. They were a good size, too. This fella proceeded to put them in a little plastic bottle, and he would pull them out of his pocket whenever the mood struck him, show them to staff and customers alike. You can imagine the reactions. I believe in the end one of his waitresses got hold of the bottle, and in secret, gave it the heave-ho.

Maybe my showing off my splinter was childish, but at least I wasn't carrying around a bottle of gallstones and shaking them in people's faces like dice.

಄

Have a Cold? No, Thanks. Already Got the Big C. Nice of You to Ask, Though

Frank Emerson

Part One

This is kind of a hard thing to write about. But I guess I should address it. Just in case you didn't understand the title, I caught the cancer a while ago. I know that's not the normal way to put it, but as this plays out—you'll see that very little of the whole situation is particularly normal.

I was diagnosed in late October 2002. It came as a surprise to me. Not to make light of the thing, but I used to say that I drove way too fast to be worried about something like cancer. I figured what with life on the road and more than three decades in the bar rooms in a professional capacity, cancer would be the least of my worries. Something, or someone, else was much more likely to kill me. Well, obviously, I was wrong. What I really should have taken into account was the fact that I smoked cigarettes for over thirty-five years.

I found it a bit off the wall that the cancer that nailed me wasn't in the lungs or esophagus, which is where one would expect it to show up. Nope. Mine was bladder cancer. What is more: the doctors said it was directly attributable to the smoking. How about them apples? You could have knocked me over real easy. I mean I never stuck a cigarette anywhere near that neck of the woods. Not even trying to smuggle them. The medics said that had nothing to do with it. That might be a different kind of tobacco abuse, but it didn't apply here. I guess they knew what they were talking about, since I had it after all. So there you have it.

The treatment decided on was chemotherapy. There would be two three-month sessions, separated by an operation, which I refer to as "the Big Dig." It left me with a scar down my middle from stem to stern the size of Storrow Drive in Boston. This effectively destroyed any stomach muscles I ever enjoyed. Out would come my bladder, prostate, and a whole bunch of lymph nodes. The carvers would also muck about with my intestines. When I heard about this and all the stuff they would be taking out, I figured that afterward, if someone were to yell into my mouth, there would be an echo that would make history. But maybe that was just a panic thought.

The drugs that made up the chemotherapy treatment were very hard-hitting. This was the way I wanted it. In fact, for what it's worth, I insisted upon it. I wanted to attack this disease as aggressively as possible. The doctors agreed. I figured if the damned thing was going to give me the fight of my life, I should return the favor. To prepare, I was determined to do as much as possible not to let myself ebb either physically or mentally during the treatments prior to the operation, in the aftermath, or the follow-up treatments. Therefore, I started a heavy regimen of exercise—walking, the stationary bike, free weights, golf, and calisthenics. Consequently, my appetite—with a few exceptions right around treatment days when I felt really crummy—never diminished.

My stamina and strength held on pretty well. What with the steroids (which were part of the chemo drugs), the weight lifting, and the fact that I had quit smoking, I put on a few pounds. The MDs said that, in this case, it was a good thing.

Of course, it came to pass that I lost my hair—not that there was a whole lot there to begin with. But all of it was just gone with the wind. This included my beard, which had been a staple in my facial area for over a quarter-century and to which I had grown quite attached. All in all, I looked pretty pitiful: bullet headed, rather hollow eyed from the drugs, with wisps of a beard, which only made me look like what I needed was electrolysis. God, I was Gawdawful!

To top things off, during the months I was going through treatments, my mind pretty much went on a long trip to Coney Island, which is to say that mentally, I was a space cadet. I could carry on a conversation and remember none of it. I could not, of course, concentrate on learning new material or practicing. I recall, however, that one of my pet projects was to stare into space. I remember I used to like that quite a bit. I tried reading. I suppose I did a lot of that judging from the mound of at least three-dozen new titles I see piled on my desk. I am guessing I enjoyed them, too—judging from the dog-eared pages and the odd chili stain here and there. But I'll be damned if I can tell you, or me, for that matter, bugger-all about the plot of any one of them. I suppose the good thing to come of this is that now I'll be able to read them all again and enjoy them just as much as the first time around.

I know this may be belaboring the point, but I was a real mess. I have never been the prettiest of men, or the easiest to live with. At this point, however, I was definitely nobody's idea of any sort of dreamboat. My wife, Frances, certainly had her hands full and then some. Job from the Bible had nothing on her. I am planning to nominate her for sainthood while she's still around to enjoy it. I can do that, can't I?

At any rate, word got around the Irish/folk community that I was in a bad way. That they responded wonderfully would be a gross understatement. Besides the thoughts, prayers, and cards that came my way, Victor Power, in Savannah, Pat Garvey, in Gaithersburg, Maryland, and Danny O'Flaherty, in New Orleans all stepped up to the plate and organized what turned out to be extremely successful fund-raisers to help defray the medical expenses.

I won't go into too much detail, but people were very, very kind. A lot of money was raised. A whole lot of musicians donated time, talent, and money, as well. I will never be able to adequately express my thanks to all of the people involved. Suffice to say that the efforts of the communities on those occasions, the efforts of the musicians then and afterward, filling in for me, and the owners keeping performance slots open for me were well above and beyond the call of duty.

Anyways, as Pat Garvey would say, my treatments progressed. The months went by. I started to get more and more anxious about returning to work. Even Frances was getting into the act. She gave me absolutely no slack. When I would start to become particularly obnoxious or irritating, she would ask, "Don't you have to be somewhere? Like back on the road?"

Finally, and not exactly with the doctors' approval—but they weren't going to stop me—ten months after the initial diagnosis, I decided I'd had enough of the freeloading life. I don't mind admitting I was more nervous than somewhat at the prospect of getting back to it. I figured I looked horrible, and I wasn't sure how I was going to do along the lines of remembering things like music and lyrics, which tend to be fairly essential in the entertainment game.

I know I've written a lot about Kevin Barry's Pub, but that's where I've worked the most over my career, and I feel pretty safe there. So, Guadalcanal week, the first week in August, I opened up in this most comfortable of settings. I was decked out in a black shirt and trousers, two-toned black and white spectator shoes, and a black American Legion baseball cap. The cap was a concession of mine to keep the glare from my Mussolini-ish chrome dome from blinding the audience. Around my neck was a patriotic American tie. With the exception of the cap, this outfit has been my trademark for some time now.

The room was reasonably full, but it seemed that some people I had expected to see were missing. I figured this was really of no matter since I would probably be seeing them later on in the week.

I launched into "The Mary Ellen Carter," a song by Stan Rogers about perseverance in the face of adversity. I thought it would be appropriate in the light of my experience over the previous year.

Before you could say Jack Robinson, the doors opened, and about thirty-five people—men and women—came marching into the room clapping in time to the music. Not only that, mind you, but they were all decked out just like me! I don't think there was a patriotic tie or black shirt to be found in all of Savannah anymore. On top of that—who brings up the rear of this conga line but a television camera from the local news.

I didn't know what to say. I couldn't say anything. I sure as hell couldn't remember any lyrics. I vamped. Musically. Luckily, I remember how to do that. The people were laughing it up pretty good. Me? I was non-plussed. Finally I got my wits back about me. Still vamping, I stepped to the microphone and said, "Well, this is really something. I can't figure it out. Either all of these people go to my haberdasher, or there is a Viet Cong platoon somewhere that is plum out of black pajamas."

I then hit one final chorus of the song and ended it. From that point, the night went like gangbusters. There were a lot of musicians among my look-a-likes. They all got up on stage with me in a show of support and welcome back sentiment. We played the night away. It wasn't just something—it was something else. To top things off, they never even mentioned how ugly or different I looked—which is one way to get us into…

Part Two

Seamus Kennedy is a very talented old friend of mine from Belfast—"talented" and "old" being appropriate adjectives here. You probably know a fair amount about him from reading his stories in this book.

We go back in this business about thirty years. At one time, we lived in neighboring towns in Massachusetts. My son and his oldest son were born within a year of each other. Well, life goes on. I moved from there. Then Seamus moved from there to someplace else. The times we saw each other grew fewer.

The truth be told, most Irish/folk performers do not see a lot of each other unless they live in close proximity or are playing the same venue or festival. What it comes down to is that, generally, if you get a chance to see someone working, it means you are not working. Most likely, your paths will cross on the north and southbound lanes of I-95 or 75 or 81 in the middle of the night, and you'll never know it.

I have to mention that Seamus was one of those musicians who participated in a couple of the fundraisers thrown for me. He was very generous with his time, talent, money, and somewhat twisted sense of humor.

The last time I bumped into him was about three years ago, when we were both booked to perform at the Savannah Irish Festival. This was well before I got sick. At that point, I looked like my publicity photographs. Such was not the case now.

In February 2004, we were both booked again to play the Savannah Irish Festival. I was looking forward to seeing him and the other performers. I wanted to thank them for their kindness, and I looked forward to sharing the stage with them.

I was slated to perform the American National Anthem during the opening ceremonies, which would take place at about 11:30 in the morning on the Saturday, the fourteenth.

I arrived at the venue, the Savannah Civic Center, early in order get the lay of the land, warm up, and buy some tokens, which could be exchanged for food during the day. I bought two baggies of tokens. This cost me $20.

As 11:30 approached, I was standing to one side of the main stage, chatting with Jimmy Buttimer. Jimmy was the festival chairman—the head honcho. He was to make opening remarks and eventually introduce me.

While we were standing there, watching St. Vincent's Choir get ready, waiting for the color guard to get set, I looked out at the audience. Who do I see coming diagonally across the large hall, but Seamus Kennedy?

His eyes were darting all about—over and behind his glasses. His arms were pumping away, and behind his goatee, his jaw was grinding like he was chewing a wasp. This was a man on a mission. I stared. I couldn't help it. He looked ticked off about something. This did not make sense to me. The festival hadn't even started yet. What could have set him off so early? He was making a beeline for Jimmy. I just watched him come. I cut a glance over to Jimmy. He shot one back at me and muttered, "Uh-oh. What's this all about?"

Seamus arrived in front of us. He was concentrating real hard on Jimmy.

"Hey, Jim. Listen, where can I get some tokens for food? Maybe a sausage. I'm so hungry I'd eat my own shorts if there was any food value in them."

Now as much as that image might be disconcerting to both you and me, it is rather curious. It also made Seamus' point. Rather than let Jimmy reply that the token booth was about fifteen feet away from where we were standing, I reached in my pocket, pulled out a $10 bag of tokens and offered them up.

"Here you go, Shay."

"Ah, thanks very much. That's decent of you."

"No problem," says I

"So, listen, Jimmy," Seamus continued, "where can I—"

Seamus stopped short and did what used to be called a "triple take." Jackie Gleason would have added, "Homina, homina, homina." Milton Berle would have added, "I wuz—"

Seamus added none of that. His Belfast face lighted on me pretty good, and he let go one of the great belly laughs, such as I haven't heard in a long time. Finally, he got his breath back, opened his eyes, and said as Seamus would say—in fact did say, "Oh, fuck me! Fuck me! I didn't fucking recognize you, you fat fuck!"

Remember this is Seamus talking now—not me, heavens to Betsy. However, lest you get the wrong impression, let me explain. The whole thing was not meant maliciously. That word is used regularly as a noun, verb, adjective, adverb, gerund, and I don't know what all—very often in the same sentence. In this case, Seamus was just surprised all to heck and didn't know what to say, and so fell back on the tried and true.

In all honesty, though, I found his reference to my size smacking of just a bit of the kettle calling the pot black, since Seamus is no Twiggy himself.

He continued, "You used to be thinner. Now you're fatter! You used to have a beard. Now you don't! You used to have decent hair. Now look at you! Fuck! Frank!"

I have to make another point here in my own defense. Between the two of us, Seamus and I couldn't put together enough hair to clog a drain. This has nothing to do with the story. It's just something that needed to be said.

As he went through those statements, however, I recognized and old joke set up and couldn't resist.

"Well," said I, "that's all mighty interesting, but you must be mistaken. My name's Al."

Seamus didn't miss a beat. "Oh, changed you're name, too, I see. Well, fuck me. See you later then." And then off he went to buy some grub.

While all this was going on, Jimmy just stared and smiled. He turned to me. "What, may I ask, was all that about?"

"That, Jimmy, was vintage Bulldog Tavern. Savin Hill. The South Boston/Dorchester line. Circa 1973. It is also what helped to kill the last vestige of Vaudeville. Don't worry. He just had to get it out of his system. He'll be good to go as soon as he gets a sausage and a Guinness. So, are we all set for 'Oh, Say Can You See'?"

"All set," said Jim. Up he went to give the official welcome, introduce the color guard, the piper, St. Vincent's Choir, and me as the 12th annual Savannah Irish Festival got under way. I sure was proud to be there and thankful to be playing a part in it.

The way things stand with me right now, I seem to be doing okay. I've been off the smokes for about eighteen months. I'm still doing a lot of exercises. I'm feeling stronger at each performance. My last CAT scan was clear.

The way I figure, if I can grow a little hair, maybe drop a couple of pounds, wear some lifts—at the next festival, I might be able to con Seamus out of a $10 bag of tokens, and he won't know it's me. But it will be. Expletives be damned.

ဢ

The Checkout Girl With the Flu
Dennis O'Rourke

I was setting up the equipment in a club sometime ago, somewhere in New England, on a rainy, miserable Thursday afternoon. The music room was on the second floor of the building and was deserted at this hour, except for a waitress cleaning and readying the bar for the night. I was in the middle of a bad cold. She heard me coughing, sneezing, and grumbling, and she came over with a pot of hot tea, and urged me to sit down and take a breather. She waved off my warnings of possible contagion and sat down with me for a chat and a cup. It was of interest to her to know how entertainers were able to ignore the occasional malady, get on stage, and do the job. Waiting tables and slinging drinks, as she put it, was hard enough when she didn't feel particularly perky. But at least she didn't have to stand in front of an audience and entertain.

Indeed.

"Well," I told her, "in general, some folks, myself included, go to great lengths to avoid colds and flu. We religiously adhere to the standard, recommended rules of caution and prevention—we get plenty of sleep, exercise, eat fresh fruits and vegetables, and quaff bottles of water and citrus juices by the case. We double or triple our intake of Vitamin C. We wash our hands a dozen times a day, and we take care not to bring those hands, as scrubbed and sterile as they may be, anywhere near our mouths or noses. If the virus making the rounds is airborne, we do our best not to be too long in close proximity of those unforgivably careless about all of the above, and consequently allow themselves to 'come down with something.' We'll meet this person in the course of a day, inquire politely as to their well being, and when told, 'Oh, God, I've caught this awful cold,' we will immediately back away, throw our hands up defensively, and say, 'Well, don't give it to me,' as if the sufferer has some mystical power over the bug and can rein it in or cut it loose at will."

The waitress enjoyed this little recitation. I expanded my discourse.

"When an afflicted person visits my home without first informing me of their cloak of pestilence, I will do my best to cut their visit short, and after they are gone, I will bombard the air and anything they've touched with clouds of Lysol spray, paying particular attention to the doorknob."

"Lysol?" She raised an eyebrow.

"Indispensable," I said.

I went on to assure her that for an entertainer, getting on stage to do a show while doing battle with a cold or flu can be a Herculean endeavor of will and stamina. I hate it. A hangover can be treated with the judicial application of the hair of the dog. But a cold? The flu? I want to be at home in my bed, sipping herbal teas, catching up on my reading, and being ministered to by a loved one. The last place I want to be with my fever, stuffy nose, headache, and chills is in a smoky, noisy bar filled with healthy, robust revelers pounding on the tables and pouring gallons of Guinness down their gullets. I begrudge them their health and happiness. I sadly recall when I, too, had this joy in my heart and booze in my blood, and I begin to fear that this state of bliss will never again be mine. I want to tell them how sick I am, but I know I cannot. They don't want to hear it, and they don't care. I want them to understand just how mighty an effort it's going to be for me to get through the next four hours. This whine will not go down well with them or the club owner—*especially* the club owner. If he does not see a fresh shotgun wound anywhere on my body, he is unsympathetic.

When I privately confess my miserable condition to a fan or friend at the bar, looking for sympathy or commiseration, my heart will sink when they back up and say, "Well, don't give it to me." My mood darkens and sours even more. Then it's nine o'clock, and the stage beckons. I approach it as if it was a guillotine. Once up there, my fevered mind turns the happy faces at the foot of the stage to a crowd of toothless, drunken, French harpies holding up straw baskets to catch my head.

"Poor dear," she said. "But that's some imagination you've got."

For the entertainer, the singer, there is also the danger of an accompanying sore throat. How are you going to get past *that*? Robbie O'Connell once imparted a bit of advice to me during a discussion about the health perils of the road. You can sing and get through the night with a sore throat if, an hour before the show, you warm up the vocal chords with scales. Start low and soft and take your time. Massage the throat lightly with forefinger and thumb. Press a warm, wet towel over the affected area. To these perfectly sound suggestions I added one of my own—sing the songs in the first set in a lower key. Work your way up the ladder slowly.

"Sounds reasonable," she said.

"Robbie had added another tip," I told her. "Be careful what cold remedies you choose. Don't mix them. Forgetting this warning, I once medicated myself on stage with antihistamines, hot tea and lemon, and several belts of cognac. All of these contrived to make me feel like a new man. Pseudophedrine is like speed to me. I sailed still higher on the wings of Remy Marten, and in my drug-induced euphoria, I belted out the songs. In truth, I had dried up my throat and sinuses and then shredded my vocal chords by singing with the wild abandon of an eighteen-year-old garage rocker.

"I rose the next morning with the expected hangover, but when I tried to speak, nothing—absolutely nothing—came out. After several attempts, a single syllable emerged, or rather, cracked itself loose from the baked, desert driveway that was once my throat. It began in the key of A and flew up into a high C without any conscious effort from me. When I was finally able to cause some words to emerge, albeit in this uncontrollable, croaking cackle, I had to call and cancel a well paying gig that night—a frat party in Atlanta. Any attempt to sing would have brought serious, permanent injury to my vocal chords. I had to remain quiet for forty-eight hours."

"How much did you lose out on?"

"Four hundred bucks," I said.

She flinched.

"There's the rub," I said.

I have had to take the stage in less-than-ideal physical condition on countless occasions. Colds and flu be damned. I'll suck lozenges and gargle warm salt water between sets to ward off laryngitis. I will swill Vicks or Benadryl and pack my body with Ibuprofen. And why?

"The show must go on," my waitress said dramatically.

"Well, there is that, certainly. An audience has congregated to hear you perform. They may be your friends and fans. They want your music and your wit. They want to laugh, to have a good time. Sing, Dennis!" (I waited for her to acknowledge the Jack Benny-Dennis Day reference. Now there's a great metaphor for the relationship between a club owner and a performer! But she was too young.)

"Yes, the show must go on, and while I stand ready to pay homage to that tradition, I have to admit that my foremost reason for performing wounded is somewhat less noble. This is not an assured nine to five, forty-hour a week job. You take work where and when you can get it. There are no health benefits, and certainly no paid sick days. A club owner is not going to pay you for lying in a sick bed while paying another entertainer to take your place onstage. He who works gets paid."

My waitress nodded in agreement. In that regard, our jobs were exactly the same.

Given all this, it is of paramount importance for a singer to stay healthy. Vigilance is required. Beware the occasion of sin, as the nun once admonished. To that, I add, "Beware also the lair of the virus, which is the infected person, the air surrounding that person, and the things they touch."

She wanted an example, and I gave her one. "One conduit I long-suspected has been used by these pernicious, microscopic beasties to transfer themselves from one host to another is the supermarket checkout girl, who has a nasty cold or flu. She is going to be putting her diseased paws on every single item you have purchased and are about to bring into your home. If you allow this to happen, your only recourse is to submerge all the vegetables and fruits in water, wash them, and layer a coat of Lysol on all the canned goods before putting them away."

"Again with the Lysol? You spray Lysol on your groceries?" she said.

I nodded solemnly. Her eyes narrowed.

"But this is time consuming and not always effective. You must go back to the beginning and figure out a way to avoid the ailing checkout girl altogether."

"I'm all ears," she said.

"I will tell you how I handle this potentially ruinous encounter, and I have a feeling that if he was still alive, this would carry the Howard Hughes stamp of approval. When you have completed your shopping in the cold and flu season, park yourself and your cart at the rear of the longest line you can find. This will give you ample opportunity to observe the checkout girl. Watch her carefully for any symptoms—coughing, sniffling, and sneezing or blowing her nose. Noting any of these, you must immediately walk briskly to the next longest line. Begin your observations anew."

"Hadn't thought of that," she said.

"Keep in mind however, that the infectious checkout girl may be taking drugs that will prevent the symptoms from being apparent. You must be prepared for this possibility, and I recommend staying alert. Keep your ears open for any pleasantries exchanged between the customer and the checkout girl. Most customers will ask, 'How ya doing today?' Now, I have never met a person, checkout girls included, *with* a cold or flu, who will not immediately lay the ailment out for you in all its aching, feverish, phlegmy detail. If the checkout girl's reply is inaudible, strain to catch what the customer is saying. No person *without* a cold can resist consoling another who has. If you hear the customer offering the girl his own unfailing, miracle cure for colds, depart the line, pronto."

She nodded, impressed.

"But let us say the worst has happened. You've been fooled completely. You think your girl healthy until she has her hands on your broccoli, and then she suddenly rears her head back and unleashes a tremendous, watery sneeze, spraying spittle in all directions. As she wipes her nose with her sleeve and reaches for your carrots, you find yourself trembling with hope and prayer as you ask, 'Oh, dear. Bad allergies?' You will be horrified when you hear, 'I wish. No, I've got this flu that's going around. I was up all night throwing up, and I've had diarrhea all morning.'"

"I know that girl," my waitress hollered. "What do you do then?"

"Back up, take a deep breath and keep your wits about you. This is one of those emergencies that cell phones were made to handle. If you are a woman, reach into your purse and press the cell phone so it rings. If you are a man and carry it hooked to your belt, reach down and surreptitiously do the same. Look around you apologetically, put the phone to your ear, say, "Hello," and listen for a few seconds. Allow your face to gradually take on a look of deep concern while gazing at the folks in line behind you. Hold your hand up for silence. Then say in a loud voice, 'Yes, Mr. President. Yes, sir. I understand completely.' Wait a few beats, then say, "Yes, sir, I'll inform the secretary immediately, and I'll catch the next plane.'

"Mumble a distracted apology to the checkout girl, leave the contaminated groceries where they lie, and flee the store."

My waitress laughed and shook her head. "Very interesting," she said. She laughed, stood up, and pointed a finger. "You know," she continued, "I've learned over the years that you crowd, you pub entertainers, are a very strange bunch altogether."

She cleaned up our cups, went behind the bar, and began a loud rummage through the cabinets. I finished setting up. Twenty minutes later, I was on my way out the door, headed for the hotel to change. The audience would be here in a few short hours. I turned to wave goodbye, and found my waitress slowly walking around the room, winding her way through the tables. She held a can of Lysol high over her head, laying down a thick spray. She got up on the stage and turned to face me through the settling mist, aiming the can in my direction.

"You've a cold," she said with a big grin. "I have to think of myself and my customers. I don't want any of us exposed to your pernicious, microscopic beasties."

I was not the least offended. As a matter of fact, I gave her a thumbs up. Smart girl.

CB&

DOR: Have you ever lost your voice?

SK: I lost my voice one time when Tom O'Carroll and I were playing together; I had polyps on my vocal cords. I went to the doctor, and my voice was really raspy. I sounded like Ronnie Drew after he'd gargled with broken glass. That bad. And the doctor said, "Well, there's two things we can do. We can remove them surgically. Slice them off. Or you have to be quiet for three months. No talking. No singing. And you'll have to communicate by writing notes. And I immediately said, "Slice 'em off." Right. And he said, "Well, there's a four-week recovery period after that for the vocal cords to heal." So Tom and I contacted a fellow musician, a fella called Declan Hunt—the legendary Declan Hunt, who's back in Ireland now, and Dekkie was going to fill in for me. I was still going to play with Tom onstage, but I would just play guitar, mandolin, bodhrán, and stuff; I wasn't going to sing. Dekkie and Tom were going to do the singing. That way I would still have an income from the gigs. So I went in and had the polyps sliced off. It's not painful. There are no nerve endings in the vocal cords, so it doesn't hurt. But I was supposed to remain silent and write notes, which I did until the following week, when it was the first gig, where Dekkie was supposed to sing for me. So, I arrived at the gig, Tom arrived at the gig, and Declan didn't show up. Right? Tom normally sang just a few songs. He played the banjo and the mandolin, and sang back up on the choruses, but Tom didn't know a lot of our songs all the way through back then. He does now, of course! Well, we waited a half an hour; no sign of Dekkie. So I sang. Didn't affect me one bit. Sang clear as a bell. Wasn't raspy. And I just sang from then on. I just called Dekkie and said, "Don't need ya." And since then, from that night on, I just sang; it didn't bother me. I learned some vocal exercises from a singing teacher; learning to breathe from the diaphragm and project properly, and that really helps. So, I've never lost a night's work because of a sore throat.

CR80

Stoned on Stage

Dennis O'Rourke

John Vogt plays upright acoustic bass in Nashville. I call him the greatest bass player in the cosmos, and he has never made any effort to dissuade me of that opinion, or of giving it. Good paying club gigs in Nashville were difficult to find, still are, but we managed a few. The majority of them were at a four-star restaurant on Lower Broad called Merchant's. We'd work the downstairs bar a couple of weekends a month. We played some Irish, but mostly stuck to Folk and Country and some Rock. We were twice canceled because someone higher up wanted music more "classy" than what we were doing—original, esoteric guitar, jazz, and such. A few weeks after each of those occasions, I would get a call from the bar manager, a fan of ours, saying he had gotten us reinstated. When pressed, he revealed how he had achieved this no small feat. He took the numbers to the bean counters, and pointed out that when O'Rourke and Vogt performed, the bar made money. When the other groups were there, the cash register slumbered. But after a while, even this was not enough to save us from the ax. I cast about for somewhere else in town to work.

I used to frequent a joint in Bellevue called Natchez Trace, just a mile from my apartment. It was a nice family restaurant downstairs and a late night, drinking, shooting pool, and general raising hell room upstairs. Last call was at two-thirty am. Many's the night I would go to bed early, resolved not to venture out to dip myself in the bubbly and get up at the crack of noon with a construction site in my brain. I'd wake up at one in the morning, stare up at the ceiling fan in the dark, and argue with myself that I was really not missing anything; that sure, fun was to be had a short distance away, but I'd made it this far. In the end, I would usually get up. Correction. I *always* got up. I would return home at three in the morning, a great deal worse for the wear, because even though I had only a couple of hours, I would make a mighty effort to catch up, and I would succeed.

Charlie McCabe was the owner—a big, friendly fella with a sunny demeanor. He was enthusiastic when I broached the idea of John and I performing in the restaurant downstairs. There was no stage, so we set up in front of the plate glass window at the end of the room. All the folks who had come to see us at Merchant's were regulars there. Charlie was pleased, and so were we.

One Friday night, we had a good crowd that included two singer-songwriter acquaintances of mine who just happened to loath one another. Call them Frick and Frack. Bickering and snide comments comprised their discourse. Sometimes it was amusing to hear; others, it was just a pain in the ass. I would occasionally let one of them get up to play a song or two, and then, of course, if the other was there, I had to grant him the same privilege. Frick and Frack were present on this particular night.

I was seated on a bar stool, and John stood beside me with his bass. The night moved along pleasantly enough. Then in the middle of the third set, I began to experience a throbbing in my lower back. I resolved to ignore it even as it came on, it seemed, with teeth. I squirmed on the stool, trying to achieve some position to take the pressure off. Nothing worked. The pain grew. My face was hot. John looked at me.

"Dennis, I hate to tell you this, man, but you look awful."

I called a break and headed for the rest room. My face was a translucent white. Sweat rolled down my forehead. I stumbled upstairs to Charlie's office. He was sitting at his desk with a couple of friends. I made it to the middle of the room and collapsed. The pain was like a hot knife twisting around in my back. I flopped around on the floor like a freshly landed fish, again, trying to get into some position that would alleviate the pain. No go. I had never felt physical hurt like this. Charlie was up in alarm. One of his friends happened to be a physician's assistant. Her verdict was a kidney stone. She got on the phone to the emergency room at Vanderbilt Hospital and described my symptoms.

They helped me out to Charlie's car. They lowered the front seat to a reclining position, and I lay back, groaning, trembling, and shivering. I had gone from overheating to freezing. Charlie drove like a banshee. The street lamps I viewed from my supine view went by like subway tunnel lights. Charlie helped me into the ER. I was in no condition to talk, so he gave them what little information he had about me. They put me in a room. I tried to sit on the litter, but it was impossible. Charlie came in, and at one point I went down on my knees in front of him, imploring him to work some miracle. He was distressed. I crawled out of the room into the hall, where a couple of lab-coated doctors were standing. They backed away from me—made no effort to get me up or help me in any way. A nurse arrived. She and Charlie got me back on the litter. She produced a syringe, and the magic of Demerol charged through my veins. And the pain went away.

Charlie stood by me another hour before reluctantly taking his leave to get back to the pub. Another nurse came in and turned out the light. If someone had mentioned "kidney stone," I didn't hear them. If someone had said, "Drink water, and see if it will pass," I didn't hear that, either. So I ended up lying there all night in the semi-dark listening to the hospital pages. Early that morning, with a change of shift, a nurse came in and asked if it had passed. Had what passed? She gave me a strainer and a plastic urinal, and told me to go home and start drinking. She also informed me that Charlie McCabe had phoned three times in the night checking on me. He moved to the top of my Club Owners Hall of Fame.

Well, I had no way to get home, and I wasn't about to bother Charlie again. I called Don White, an Oklahoma country singer and writing partner, and he was there, pronto. I got home and fell asleep for a few hours. What woke me was the unknown whereabouts of my guitar and sound system. I called John Vogt.

"I've got your guitar, Dennis. Don't worry. Charlie's got your PA locked up in his office. And by the way, he paid us, too."

"But we didn't finish the night."

"That's what I told him, but he insisted."

Charlie McCabe moved out of the Hall of Fame into full-fledged sainthood. I bowed my head.

"Oh, and you'll find this amusing," John said. "After Charlie had hauled you off to the hospital, Frick and Frack got into an argument about which of them was going to finish the gig. They almost came to blows. Ended up taking turns onstage, trying to out-do each other. They used your guitar, but I kept an eye on them. It didn't take long for them to clear the room, anyway."

"Did you play with them?"

"Like Hell, I did."

Well, I drank water for a few days and finally went to a doctor, had the dye x-ray, and was told I had a stone so large it would never pass. I should not have been sent home. Lythotripsy was called for. The whole experience at Vanderbilt had been a bad one, and I was angry. Then they sent me a bill for a thousand or so dollars. I wrote them back, detailing everything that had gone on, and finished off with a sentence that contained the word "lawsuit." And that ended that. Every woman I've told this story to, dwelling on the level of excruciating pain involved, has come back with the same riposte: "You wimp. Now you've got a clue what childbirth feels like."

LATE NIGHTS AND
BIG IMAGINATIONS, OR IN THE
DARK NIGHT OF THE SOUL IT'S
ALWAYS THREE IN THE MORNING

The Exorcist

Seamus Kennedy

My colleagues and I writing this collection of stories have had our share of special and unforgettable moments, as well as some bizarre and horrific ones we'd really like to forget, but can't; like the memories of incredibly stupid things we did while drunk, which rise to the surface of our consciousness when we least expect them, to cause us mortal embarrassment and a visible cringe. This is one of those cringe-inducers.

Tom O'Carroll and I had been performing in Matt Kane's famous pub on 13th Street in Washington DC. It was in the early '70s and DC was a really enjoyable, lively city, with a superb nightlife wholeheartedly embraced and relished by those fun-loving young wastrels and roués of the Nixon administration. Ah, yes, I remember it well. Wilbur Mills, Fanne Fox (the Argentine Bombshell), and other youthful prodigals could have given the Great Gatsby, Daisy Buchanan, and that crowd a run for their money.

We had been booked into Matt's for a two-week run, Tuesday through Saturday, which left us free on the Sunday and Monday between the weeks.

Sunday was passed in luxurious indolence in the confines of our room in London Hall, an apartment building affectionately known as "Chez Kane," right across the street from Matt's pub. One-room efficiency apartments were leased on a weekly basis, and the room contained a pull-out sofa/bed, called a "Castro Convertible"—which I thought for years was a Cuban automobile, and a Murphy bed, which is a double bed folded up on springs and hidden in a closet. Just open the closet door and pull down the bed—voila!—nighty-night. In the morning, just push the bed up, close the closet door and voila!—a fake closet! As an Irishman, I suppose I should be offended by the name. Why couldn't it have been a "Shapiro bed," or a "MacTavish bed," or a "Gonzalez bed?" There was also a little two-ring electric cooker and a bathroom/shower stall, because even wandering Irish minstrels need to eat and wash sometime.

Tom was an ideal roommate with no disgusting habits (that I could discern), excellent personal hygiene, a very low snore quotient, fine taste in reading materials, and a willingness to jump in the shower with me and massage my shoulder muscles.

No, wait! I'm thinking of somebody else!

So we just idled away the Sunday, reading the *Washington Post* from cover to cover, stem to stern, A to Z, all sections. We watched a program or two on the old black and white TV set, which came with the room. We got all three VHF stations in Washington—this was before cable, mind you—and a couple of the UHF ones, and damn glad we were to have them, you smug, spoiled, consumer brat with your satellite dish and 700 channels from all over the world. You never had to stick a bent coat hanger with a ribbon of aluminum foil attached to it into the antenna receptacle in the futile hope of catching a glimpse of the George Allen Redskins led by Sonny Jurgenson through the snowy reception and audio static of a twenty-year-old Magnavox, did you? No, you didn't! So don't come whining to me about how tough things are for you now with the decline of the economy and your investment portfolios going into a tailspin, you la-di-da, candy-ass Yuppie wimps!

Sorry, I went away for a moment. It's okay; I'm back now. During our engagement at Matt Kane's, I had started reading the William Peter Blatty best-seller, *The Exorcist*, which subsequently was made into a blockbuster movie of the same name. Now, I was raised Catholic. Even better, I was raised Irish Catholic, so I had been exposed from an early age with stories of demonic possession and Satanic misdemeanors. The very concept of my body and mind in the control of a spirit other than Old Bushmills put the fear of God into me.

The very first one that I got in grade-school was the tale of the Gadarene swine in the Bible, where Jesus drove the evil spirits out of a possessed man into a herd of pigs, and they all galloped to their doom over a cliff or something. The man didn't jump with them, just the pigs, but the thought of all these unclean entities inhabiting a human being fascinated and terrified me.

The Irish Christian Brothers loved these stories, and they loved to frighten the piss out of prepubescent kids with them. Ostensibly, it was supposed to make us better Catholics by terrifying us so badly that we'd become daily communicants and pray furiously that we not succumb to "the devil and all his works and pomps," thereby opening the door to possession. And once the camel's nose is in the tent, well, you can imagine the rest.

The next one we got was the story of the Curé of Ars.

Jean Baptiste Vianney was the curate of the little village of Ars in France. He was such a good and holy man with a devotion to God, that the devil came and tried to win him over to the dark side by setting fire to his house and appearing in his room in the form of a big, black dog in the middle of the night and barking 'til all hours, so that the poor old Curé couldn't get any sleep and his health began to suffer. But he began to fast and pray and fight back, and eventually drove the devil back to the gates of Hell, where he belonged.

Then we were treated to narrations about exorcisms, and how special priests were selected to perform exorcisms and drive out devils and unclean spirits from unfortunate individuals who had inadvertently (or possibly advertently) created an opening in the spiritual tent-flap for the diabolical camel to stick his nose in. We were told how these priests prepared for the fight by fasting, praying, and training like a boxer for a title fight. They had to be strong, physically, as well as spiritually, for the battle they were about to enter, because the devil would use all the evil wiles at his command.

And there were instances, we were told, of a fine, big, healthy, 200-pound priest with a full head of black hair, reduced to a hollow-eyed, white-haired, 120-pound husk of his former self after just a two-day exorcism. Still others had become babbling raving lunatics.

The Brothers, most of whom were from rural Ireland, also told us great ghost stories, about the banshee—a spirit, usually a woman, who appears and wails and moans around a house when someone is about to die. This was a self-fulfilling prophecy. The person inside the house in the sickbed probably just thought he was sick until he heard the wailing and moaning; then he knew he was screwed. So he up and died.

The banshee could also appear in the form of black crows (not the musical group) or a strange black dog howling round the house of a sick person. This is the reason I keep a shotgun in my bedroom. If I'm in my sickbed, and I hear a dog barking or crows cawing outside, there'll be a mess of crow-and-dog burger all over my yard.

Anyway, these stories frightened seven shades of shite out of me as an impressionable kid and took root. And the nightmares…

I was intrigued, fascinated, repulsed, and scared because I believed, and I never shook that belief, even as an adult. I was drawn to tales of

322

the occult and the macabre, like Bram Stoker's Dracula, and other tales of vampires and werewolves because they held me in their icy thrall.

**

After Tom and I finished a night's work in Matt Kane's, we'd usually have a shift drink with the bartenders and waitresses, and then walk across the street to London Hall to retire for the evening.

Well, we didn't really retire. We'd have a couple more beers in the room, and sit up and read for a while, then we'd brush our teeth—I brushed Tom's and he brushed mine—and then we'd go to bed. Separate beds, one Castro, one Murphy. We'd read a bit more by the light of our bedside lamps and go to sleep.

Except, Tom didn't come back to the room with me every night. He had a few friends with musical tastes similar to his own, and most nights, he went with them to their house, where they would listen to records while incense burned, sip some wine, and stay up all night discussing the political intrigues of the day. This left me alone in the wee hours with The Exorcist.

Now, as long as Tom was *in* the room, I could read the story of the little girl who gradually became possessed by a demon and the priest who had to expel this evil spirit from her. But when Tom wasn't in the room, I'd try to read a little bit, realize I was by myself, and slam the book shut. The fact that the story took place in Georgetown, mere blocks away from the very room we were staying in served to intensify my fear. If I tried to sleep, I couldn't. I'd sit up with the light on, and reread the *Washington Post* from cover to cover.

Finally, when Tom came in at five or six in the morning, I'd be sitting up, wide awake, like a wife in curlers waiting for her drunken reprobate of a husband to come home. As he was performing his pre-sleep ablutions, I'd yell, "Where the hell were you 'til this hour of the morning?"

"Mmmmppphhh, mmmppbbblllff!" he would respond with his mouth full of toothbrush and Colgate. Then, he'd climb into bed, and literally, within seconds, he'd be fast asleep. Quickly, I'd grab the book and read a few more chapters. I couldn't help myself, it was an addiction.

I was addicted to fear and terror.

At about 8:30, with the morning sun streaming through the windows, I'd fall into a troubled sleep. It never occurred to me to take the book out into a park and read it on a bench in daylight. Oh, no. I had to read it late at night, in a rundown room in an old building probably haunted by the ghosts of all the people who had died there from the middle ages until the present.

One night, when Tom had gone off with his chums, I began to read a little more, telling myself, " It's only a story. It's only a story." The 75-watt bulb was somewhat deficient in the photon-department, and what little light it gave off cast eerie shadows on the walls and ceiling. I swore I could see spectral figures moving in them. Just then, I started to read a page where the devil began to speak in different voices through the little girl to the priest. One was a deep, rasping, man's voice coming from the child's mouth, saying things about the priest's innermost thoughts that the girl could not possibly have known. The pure evil of the moment caused the hair on the back of my neck to rise, and a chill crept over my body. I gave a convulsive shiver, and despite the warmth of the room, I felt cold. I stopped reading and listened intently.

Was that a creak I heard on the stairs just outside the room? My heart pounding, I put the book down on my lap and listened again. Silence, except for some late-night city noises from the window. I could hear the blood whooshing in my temples as I held my breath and resumed reading.

The door burst open!

"Ahh, Jesus!" I screamed as I dropped the book and pulled the covers over my head.

Tom came into the room carrying a pizza and a six-pack of beer.

"You bastard! You frightened the friggin' life outta me! Don't do that again!"

"I'm sorry. My hands were full," he said. "Do you want some pizza and beer?"

***

Eventually, I finished the book. I wound up taking it over to Matt Kane's during the day and reading it in a booth surrounded by beer-guzzling reporters and typesetters from the now-defunct *Washington Star*. I still got a thrill, but at least I wasn't terrified there.

"Hiya, Seamus," they'd say. "Whatcha readin' there? *The Exorcist,* eh? Any good?"

"Absolutely brilliant. I can't put it down."

Later, Tom and I went to a used-book store, one of our favorite activities while on the road, and browsed for a while.

"Seamus, here's one you'd like," said Tom, handing me a book.

I had to have it. So I bought it. You may have heard of it. *Hostage to the Devil: Twelve True Stories of Exorcisms by the Man Who Was There—Father Malachi Martin.*

The Shower Curtain

Dennis O'Rourke

She was a full-figured woman and a sweetheart. We met and chatted over the course of a three-night gig on the road somewhere around DC. On my last night, the both of us, heavily under the influence, decided to have a bit of a frolic at her apartment. I followed her there in my car. She cooked for us. We drank more. We tumbled into bed, but soon after some drunken fumbling and giggling, we were snoring into each other's faces.

I awoke a few hours later to answer a call of Nature. It was still dark. I rolled gingerly out of bed and immediately felt and heard the blacksmith warming up in my brain, signaling his intention to pound away at his anvil all day and all the way back to Boston. My mouth was a desert. My veins and arteries had become dried out plant stalks; my eyeballs, cracked marbles weighing a pound each. I made my way to the bathroom, naked, moaning and moving like an old, arthritic man. In the dark, I walked nose-first into the side of a door. I stifled a howl. Cupping the injured proboscis, I stumbled on and promptly whacked the two middle toes of my right foot into the iron leg of a table in the hall. (In these incidents, it's always the same foot, the same toes. I could hear the blacksmith chuckling.)

In the living room, I failed to see a glass coffee table and fell over it. Reaching for something stationary to break my fall, I managed to grab a vase of flowers from the middle of the table and bring it with me. I came down on my back, hugging the vase to my chest, water streaming over my face and flowers of indeterminate genus tickling my throbbing nose. There was no sound from the bedroom. She slept on.

My response at times such as these, alone or not, is to find humor somewhere in the thing. I've deemed it a better anodyne than cursing and railing at the heavens, which, for me at least, only results in more affliction being meted out by that merry prankster, the Lord God on High. So, still lying on my back, I brought the theme from *The Three Stooges* out and began to sing it. It seemed appropriate. Then I spoke a few of their trademark lines aloud: "Saaay! What's the matter with you?" "Oh, wise guy, huh?" "Hey, you! Airedale! Get over here!" And finally, the immortal, "Nyuck. Nyuck. Nyuck."

I got up from under the vase, placed it back on the table and returned as many of the flowers to it as I could find in the dark. Then I continued on to the bathroom. The light was on, and I staggered in. It was a bathroom with the ubiquitous ocean motif—a wicker basket full of seashells on the sink, the sink in the shape of a seashell; small, framed pictures of children playing by the seashore; all of this tightly engulfed by wallpaper featuring sailboats, seagulls, and lighthouses. And, of course, potpourri and scented candles to handle low tide when it arrived.

I poured a glass of water from the tap, and although the body function I was about to engage in does not require it for a male, I seated myself, glass in hand. I tossed the water back and sat there ruminating on life and death and my current, close proximity to the latter. I got up, poured more water, sat down, and tossed that glass back as well. The shower curtain hung over the outside of the tub and was pulled shut. It was within arm's length. It occurred to me that if I pulled it open, I might find a body. Wouldn't that be fun? I thought of this tender lass who had offered me her bed, and conjured up an image of her as a murderess, a harridan in a maiden's disguise who tempted traveling musicians into her home and then dispatched them with a long knife, storing them in the tub overnight to be chopped up the next day. Even now, she was stealthily making her way down the hall, clutching the knife, her satanic eyes ablaze. I looked at the shower curtain and heard those shrieking movie violins.

Then I sat there for a while and played with all of those absurd images—anything to take my mind off just how badly hung-over I was.

Since I would be seeking its healing powers in a few short hours anyway, I decided at last to relieve the suspense and have a look at the tub. I reached over and parted the curtain just enough to peer inside. I noted about two inches of standing water. Surprised and curious, I pushed the curtain farther and found three green-black, round shapes immersed in the water and three pair of blinking eyes staring back at me. I pulled the curtain shut and sat back. This had to be the early stages of *delirium tremens*. Either that, or my wild flight of fancy had taken me from *The Three Stooges* to a blood-hunting murderess, and from there to a bathtub full of giant turtles. Because that *was* three turtles I had just seen, wasn't it?

I looked again, and yes, there they were, looking back at me— wrinkled necks in full extension—dark, motionless, reptilian heads filled with the memory of thousands of years of evolution, and eyes, wary eyes, tensed, focused on mine. They were good-sized fellas, too, with shells about six inches wide. One began a slow advance toward me and made an effort to get up the side of the tub. After slipping back a couple of times, he gave up and returned to his former position. We all locked eyes once more. Did they want to be fed? Perhaps this was how she got rid of the evidence.

A few moments passed in idle fancy, and then my thoughts slowly returned to the state of my shattered body. More sleep was required, so I closed the curtain, got up, and made my way, very carefully, back to the bed and slipped in. I listened to the soft rise and fall of her rhythmic breathing. She didn't snore. I thought, I should marry this girl. Then I closed my eyes while familiar pop melodies played out in my head, and I took them into a dreamless sleep. Bacon and eggs awakened me a few hours later.

I sat up in bed. The blacksmith was still at work. While the clanging of his hammer and anvil had been dulled somewhat, there was no denying his presence. My shattered condition had been upgraded only to fragile. At times such as these, I often call to mind the words of the greatest party-maker of them all. Mr. Sinatra is reputed to have said, "I pity people who don't drink because when they get up in the morning, that's as good as they're going to feel all day." I worked in some thoughts of my own about death and rebirth, and then switched gears to formulate my plan of the day. It was simple enough. I had to acquire a gallon jug of water and hit the road, pronto. I had a gig that night in Boston.

I could hear my hostess singing in the kitchen. And then she came in soundlessly with a cup of coffee in her hand. She was fresh from the shower, clad in a white terry-cloth robe, her wet black hair wrapped up in a matching towel. She smiled beatifically, handed over the coffee and drew back the window drapes. Then she kissed me on the cheek and said, "Breakfast—whenever you're ready." She'd been in the bath, but said nothing about turtles. I said nothing about turtles. It had been a dream.

I got up at last, testing the air, getting my footing. I pulled on the pants and headed out to the kitchen. And there they were. No dream. I stepped over one and then another on my way to a chair. The third was under the table. She had given them the freedom of the road, and they were happily moving around the floor at full turtle-throttle. She sat down with me. We ate and made small talk. (Large talk was out of my reach.) The three shelled caballeros were not mentioned. I didn't ask about them because at that moment everything in that kitchen seemed perfectly natural. Everything fit.

I showered. The tub was sparkling clean. No standing water. No evidence of a turtle's lair. I dressed. We embraced. Would I like anything for the road? she asked. A sandwich? What I wanted was to get back into bed with her and accomplish what we had failed to do last night. In her arms, then, I discovered that there was still *some* life left in my body. But I had that gig, eight hours away. I mumbled something about water. She filled a large Mason jar from the tap and handed it over with gentle murmurs. Poor baby, she said. There was no, Call me. When are you back? Will you remember me? There was none of that, and that seemed to fit, too, for the both of us. And so off I went, out into the new day. I stowed the guitar in the trunk, got in the car, and placed the jar of water between my legs.

I concentrated on finding my way back to the Interstate. Once safely there, headed north, I replayed the events of the weekend. I thought about the lovely girl I had just left behind and her three caballeros, and because convoluted images are allowed, even encouraged in the hung-over mind, I imagined her then, seated at her kitchen table. And I saw this: Her shelled critters wearing sombreros, big straw ones, and sunglasses, and they were up on their hind legs, their green arms locked like the Rockettes, dancing in front of a small neon board that advertised "Larry, Moe, and Curly." And then I could hear my hostess joining in as they all sang:

"Me and you, and you and me
No matter how they toss the dice

It had to be
The only one for me is you, and you for me
So happy together!"
(G. Bonner – A. Gordon) Alley Music – Lieber-Stoller Songs

THE PRIVATE PARTY AND THE
PROFFERED ACCOMMODATION

Of Car Salesmen, Glaucoma and True Love

Dennis O'Rourke

I'll do private parties anytime I can. I did one in South Florida a few nights before Paddy's Day, the year of '05. They're usually easy and fun to do, and this one was no exception. It was Palm Beach County, a nice house in a gated community. I was to work seven to eleven. I set up in a corner out on the pool patio. The host was a genial fellow and his wife equally pleasant. He had invited some ninety guests. While the night was clear, the temperature was unseasonably cool. This kept most of the guests inside the house, but the host emerged periodically to assure me that I was being very well received. Warmed by wine and spirits, some braved the chill and sat at the tables in front of me. The night rolled on. I mixed the Irish music with pop tunes and some country. When the buffet was served, I took my place in line, shoveled in some bangers and mash, and then started what I assumed would be my last set at ten-fifteen. By this time, they'd loosened up, and as so often happens, finally decided to give their full attention to the music. They crowded around me, and I obliged by cranking up the sound system and belting out some rock and roll. The host was pleased. He leaned into my ear and whispered, "I know we said seven to eleven, and that's cool, but they're really having a good time. If you wanted to play a little longer, that would be fine with me."

No surprise here. I'd been expecting it. It happens all the time. The booze courses through the veins, lightens the head, and the inhibitions. The talk is loud, and the laughter is wild. We stand at the precipice of true revelry. Let's dive.

Let's sing.

Let's dance.

Where's the musician?

Well, I was getting a good paycheck for this, and I was being implored by several well-formed women to soldier on. But the hour was getting late, and I felt obliged to inform the host that it was my experience that eleven was the witching hour for outdoor parties, especially in a neighborhood as close-quartered as this. He brushed that aside.

"We had this last year, and there was no problem. The neighbors are cool."

I didn't tell him that I believed that somewhere, probably close by, lurked a very uncool neighbor who had vowed last year that this bacchanalian roar would be addressed should it happen again. I could see him right then hovering in a darkened room, peering through the curtains, cell phone in hand, looking at his watch and waiting. I offered to take the show inside, but the host wouldn't hear of it.

"Well, I'll be glad to play longer," I said. "I'm flattered. But don't be surprised, and don't blame me when the police show up."

Eleven o'clock arrived. I sang the *Midnight Special* and then launched into *What's Going On?* by Four Non-Blondes. The guests bellowed out the chorus. I had given an extra microphone to a lady standing beside me so that she might sing the chorus of *Amy*. A few bars into the song I saw two policeman emerge from the shadows of the back lawn and enter the screened-in pool area. I stopped the tune immediately. Groans and cries. I called their attention to the uniforms behind them. They all turned and the sound of revelry imploded as quickly as if it had been sucked up by a giant vacuum. There was a short meeting between the officers and the host. The cops left, and the host faced his guests with a stricken look. I had already put my guitar into its case.

Usually an appearance by the police does little to dampen spirits, to quiet things down, but this was a group easily intimidated. They dispersed in a matter of minutes, leaving the host even more crestfallen. He sat and watched me pack up my equipment, and I was careful not to lay any "I told you so's" on him. I thanked him, gratefully accepted a Tupperware full of bangers and mash from his wife and headed back to the hotel. I had occasion there to reflect on earlier private bashes, one in particular.

I wasn't so keen about working parties in the beginning. They were invariably on a weekend night, and back then, the money was lousy. Plus, a PA system was rarely called for. I'd worked hard to earn a stage and lights, and didn't want to go back to playing in a living room anytime soon.

I was working Liam's Irish Tavern in the late seventies. After the first set, the bartender handed me a scrap of paper with a name and phone number. The guy had called when I was onstage and wanted me to call back. He quickly came to the point. He wanted to hire me for a party he was throwing for his parent's fiftieth wedding anniversary. They were Irish-born, and he needed someone to do the music. I turned him down, saying I was booked on weekends and wouldn't be able to find anyone to sub for me for one night.

"This is on a Sunday night," he said.

"I'm still going to have to decline. Have you tried any of the other guys? I'd be happy to give you some names and numbers."

"No. We'd like you. My kids saw you at Liam's a few weeks ago, and they really liked you. They said you were great. We'd like you to do it."

I was not unmoved by the flattery, but still had no interest. He wouldn't give up. He begged me to give it some thought, and provided me with his work number as well. Turns out he was a car salesman at a big dealership just south of Boston. I told him, okay, I would think about it and get back to him. Truth be told, after I hung up I was resolved not to call him back at all. Just a few months prior, I had had an encounter with car salesmen that had left me filled with frightening impulses toward mayhem and murder, usually reserved for the Irish Christian Brothers who beat the hell out of me in high school.

I had been in an accident while driving in downtown Boston. Rolling through a green light, I was broadsided on the passenger side by a drunk kid. I escaped with just aches and pains, but the station wagon was a total loss, and because of the size of the PA speakers, I was forced to hunt another. Naturally, there was little to choose from at the used car dealerships I visited over the next few days. Apparently, a wave of mass-station wagon-hysteria, caused, no doubt, by the drinking water or alien intervention had recently swept the area, leaving the lots bare of anything worthwhile. In desperation, I allowed myself to be talked into putting down a $50 deposit on an old crate I had a bad feeling about from the get-go. That bad feeling was born out when I went to the bank for the loan and was told that I was being royally screwed. The price the salesman had quoted me was a thousand or so over the Blue Book price. The bank would be happy to give me a loan on anything I found that was in the ballpark.

I returned to the dealership and requested the return of my deposit. I was told that was not possible. I had made an agreement that if I did not accept the car, my deposit would not be returned. I recalled no such agreement. I howled in indignation. I followed the salesman into an office where we were joined by several of his co-workers. I paced the floor. I howled some more. They were silent, immovable. I mentioned the words integrity and morality and watched their stone faces sphinx-up further, even as the walls seemed to shiver. But it was futile. I was forced to leave without my fifty bucks. I ratcheted up my dislike for car salesmen to a fervent desire, a prayer for their own circle in Dante's Hell, and I entertained myself for weeks about just what horrors that might entail.

The very next night at Liam's, I got another call from the guy. He wasn't going to wait. He had to have an answer. I said, No. He blathered on again, about how good I was, and again, I was not unmoved. I finally asked him how much he was paying.

"Forty dollars."

"Forty dollars! Are you joking?"

"For only two hours," he said. "That's twenty dollars an hour. I don't make twenty an hour."

Of course not, I thought. You're making fifty an hour off desperate eejits like me. No, sir. I was going nowhere for forty dollars. He moved in with a different tack. His parents were old, fragile; one had cataracts, the other glaucoma. This was probably their last anniversary. I was weakening. Wouldn't I come and sing a few of the old Irish songs for them? Quack, quack, quack. And there'll be plenty of food, quack, quack, and drink. I collapsed. I told myself that I had to give in for the sake of the old folks. But mostly, I gave in because I knew he wouldn't. Forty bucks.

I drove out to his house on the appointed night. It was cold and sleet fell—another mystical night in Old New England. I rang the bell. The party was in subdued full swing, as fiftieth wedding anniversary celebrations generally are. Voices were on murmur-level, and the people huddled in groups of threes and fours. Adding the women's dresses and the men's suit coats and ties to the mix caused me to think that perhaps the old couple had shuffled off in the last few days, and I was to play at their wake. I walked into the living room, expecting to see them laid out in their Sundays on tables draped in green velvet with a white fringe.

The car salesman greeted me in a suit that would have done a carnival barker proud. After pumping my hand a few times, he directed me to a corner of the living room where an arm-less chair had been placed. He hovered as I unpacked the guitar and checked his watch.

"Well, we agreed on eight 'til ten. It's almost eight now. Uh, you said something about taking a break?"

"I did. Twenty minutes in the middle. Union rules."

His face betrayed a hint of his opinion of unions, but he merely grunted. I sat down and began to play. He stood back a few paces and watched intently, as if to assure himself that he was going to get his forty bucks' worth. Some heads turned, and there was a smattering of applause from a few of his guests. This seemed to make him anxious, and I was about to beckon to him and whisper that people cannot applaud with a drink in their hands, but he was whisked away by a woman seeking his aid in the kitchen. I picked my way through the Irish repertoire.

Performing in living rooms is difficult enough. You've got upholstery, curtains, and a rug. It becomes more difficult when there are groups of people standing right in front of you. The sound dies when it meets the first mighty rear-end, and there were plenty of those here. But gradually they parted, and I was a given a clear shot at the room. They stood on either side. Years later, I was given one of the best pieces of advice a performer can take to heart. My guitar player Leo Egan leaned into me one night at the beginning of a show and casually said, "Make them love you, Den." Well, I had no desire to make this particular crowd love me, but I was determined to give them my best and show the car salesman what a cheap prick he was. I would be so good they would love me and tell him so. "You're paying this man only forty dollars? Outrageous. You are a cad, sir. A low-life." He, in turn, would be bowled over by my professionalism and add a hefty tip to the measly forty dollars. Stranger things have happened. And so I did it. I won them over. I knocked them out. By break time, I was being heartily congratulated by people feeding on salted nuts, stalks of celery stuffed with cream cheese, and finally, roast beef sandwiches. The buffet was hardly worthy of fifty years of matrimony.

Finally, the moment arrived. The couple were led in, two frail, silver-haired teacups; bent and bowed, wearing large glasses with binocular size lenses. They were seated in the middle of the room. I played a couple of songs they had requested, and they beamed. Then I brought out my coup-de-tat. Tom Clancy had rendered a magnificent version of Willie Yeats' poem *Host of the Air,* captured on record in performance with his brothers and Tommy Makem. I had memorized it cold. Liam Clancy on another album had sung a beautiful ballad entitled *Eileen Aroon*. I loved it and had made it part of my repertoire. I had decided to combine the song and the poem. I began the song:

I know a valley fair, Eileen Aroon
I know a cottage there, Eileen Aroon
Far in that valley shade
I know a tender maid
Flower of the hazel glade, Eileen Aroon

The room was still. I sang the second verse and let the guitar ring on the last chord. Then I started the poem:

O'Driscoll drove with a song
The wild duck and the drake
And the tall and tufted reeds of a drear-heart lake
And he saw how the reeds grew dark
With the coming of night tide
And he dreamt of the long, dim hair
Of Brigid, his bride
Then he heard it high up in the air
A piper piping away
And never was piping so sad
And never was piping so gay

On I went, coping every nuance and inflection of Tom Clancy's rendition. I struck a chord on the guitar on the last word and began to sing the last verse of the song.

Youth will in time decay, Eileen Aroon
Beauty must fade away, Eileen Aroon
Castles are sacked in war
Chieftains are scattered far
Love is a fixed star, Eileen Aroon.

Truth is the "fixed star" in the song, but I had substituted "love" and set my eyes on the old couple as I sang it. And I did my best high swoon on the name Eileen Aroon, holding the note delicately before letting it dissolve into the last guitar chord. Mighty applause. Tears. The old couple trembled. I was pounded on the back. People were grasping the hands of the old couple. The car salesman was beaming.

I finished with a few up-tempos, got them clapping; a few uninspired efforts at a jig were made. Fini. The house was humming as I packed up. More congrats. The car salesman approached and took me by the arm and led me to the door. Now, I thought, comes the payoff.

"Well, that was just great," he said. "Unbelievable. Boy, oh, boy, you are so good, you really are. You made the party. Geez, you really know your business."

He pressed some bills into my hand and grabbed my arm. The door was open to the sleet and cold. I had the distinct impression that I was being given a subtle bum's-rush out the door.

"Thanks a lot," he said. "Careful driving home."

He closed the door. I stood on the silent porch. I set down the guitar, opened up my hand, and peeled the crumpled bills apart. By the light of the street lamp I counted a twenty, a ten, a five, and five ones.

Forty dollars.

ᏣᎦᏇᎠ

Monterey

Seamus Kennedy

One of the best things about being a traveling performer is the traveling. I love going to different places and meeting new people; singing, joking for fresh audiences, and making new acquaintances are bonuses in my chosen profession.

Of course, it helps if you like driving great distances and flying to far-off places as I do. An advantage to driving is that I have a lot of time to myself in the van, so I can listen to the CDs and tapes of other performers that I acquire on my peregrinations; this way, I can form additional favorites, add material to my repertoire, and steal comedy bits from my friends.

Driving also gives me the opportunity to come up with some original silly ideas of my own to try out on unsuspecting audiences. If the material works, I keep it, and if it tanks, I discard it.

For example, for years I sang a centuries-old Irish ballad—"The Bard of Armagh"—the melody of which has been adapted for use in many other songs, most notably the American Western classic, "The Streets of Laredo." Then I stopped doing it and dropped it from my song-bag for a while.

Well, recently I started singing it again, and I tied "the Bard" and "the Streets" into a little routine where I tell the audience, "You Americans are always stealing the melodies from our old Irish songs and sticking them on your songs." Then I'll sing "the Bard," and when I'm finished, I'll ask them to name the American song with the same melody. Someone will invariably shout, "The Streets of Laredo."

And now the bit of silliness that occurred to me while driving.

"The Streets of Laredo," as sung by Elmer Fudd:

As I walked out in the stweets of Wawedo,
As I walked out in Wawedo, one day;
I spied a young cowboy wapped up in white winen,
Wapped up in white winen, as cowd as the cway.

Sssshhh! Be vewwy, vewwy quiet. There's a wascawwy wabbit awound here somewhere.

You get the idea.

So driving is very enjoyable for me because I can learn new songs, come up with new jokes and routines, yodel, and pick my nose to my heart's content. Flying, on the other hand, is a different kind of pleasure.

I love to fly because I get to sleep. It doesn't matter what time of the day or night, early morning or red-eye, as soon as I've cleared security, boarded, and strapped myself in, I inflate my trusty little horse-collar pillow, open the in-flight magazine, and buzz through the crossword puzzle in about three minutes. Then I replace the magazine in the seat pocket in front of me, return my seatback and tray-table to their full and upright, locked positions, and give my full and undivided attention to the flight attendant as she lulls me to sleep with the safety instructions. It must be FAA regulations that flight crews speak in redundancies.

Recently, though, I've taken to wearing earplugs, as well, because the volume level of the aircraft intercom is roughly equivalent to that of a heavy-metal rock concert. I mean, when the captain comes on and says, in his comforting, reassuring avuncular tones, "Good morning, folks. My name is Charles Lindbergh; I'm your captain this morning, along with first officer Wilbur Wright—" and you leap screaming out of your seat, ripping the seatbelt from its mooring, to find yourself with your seatmates clinging to the ceiling by your fingernails and toes, that's an indication that the volume knob on the PA has been turned to eleven.

All major airlines, please take note.

***

I perform quite a few gigs in California each year, and one of my favorite spots is Monterey, on the Central Pacific coast. Monterey was immortalized by John Steinbeck in "Cannery Row," "Tortilla Flat," and my favorite, "Sweet Thursday." Although he was born in Salinas in 1902, a fertile agricultural area several miles from Monterey and the coast, he wrote vividly and humorously of the characters inhabiting the saloons and flophouses of one of the world's largest sardine fisheries, with its attendant canning factories and packing plants early in the first half of the 20th century.

By the 1950s, the sardines were pretty much fished out, and the canneries and plants fell into disrepair. As Steinbeck himself said, "The pearl-gray canneries of corrugated iron were silent and a pacing watchman was their only life." So Monterey began to revitalize itself as a tourist destination, cashing in on the Steinbeck stories with their wonderful cast of characters—Doc Ricketts, Mack, Whitey, Hazel and the boys, and Madam Dora Flood and her bordello, the Bear Flag, which, upon her death, passed to her sister Flora, who changed her name to Fauna.

Several of the canneries and packing-plants were gussied up and became trendy little shopping centers housing antique stores and restaurants with names like the Sardine Factory, the Cannery and the Tinnery, to attract an upscale class of visitor, one who has an excess of discretionary dollars. The fact that there are several world-class golf courses in the immediate vicinity helps, too. Courses such as Pebble Beach, Spanish Bay, Spyglass, Del Monte, Pacific Grove, Black Horse, and Bayonet can challenge even the most skilled golfers, amongst whom my name rarely appears.

A large packing plant, the Edgewater, right on the corner of Cannery Row and Prescott St., was leased in the early 1960s by one Dick O'Kane, entrepreneur and entertainer. He was a superb washboard player in a Dixieland jazz band, and he converted one side of the Edgewater packing plant into a huge, Roaring Twenties Chicago-style restaurant and bar, with a gangster/Capone motif, a 1920 flatbed Ford truck that became the bandstand, and waitresses in flapper dresses.

On the other side of the building, he installed an amusement arcade complete with a turn of the century, full-sized carousel and its ornately carved wooden animals, and an array of the most modern electronic games, mostly pinball, which became video games with the passing of time.

Prominently featured in the arcade was Dick's pride and joy, Professor Horace Q. Birdbrain, the chicken that was a champion Tic-Tac-Toe player. Seriously. He never lost.

For fifty cents, you got to play a real, live chicken a game of Tic-Tac-Toe, the grid on a glass window at the front of the chicken's cage, wired to light up with an X or an O when you or the professor pushed a button corresponding to the square in which you wanted to place your X or O.

Dick once told me, "That damned chicken has made me more damned money than all my other damned machines plus my damned restaurant put together!"

All I know is Professor Horace Q. Birdbrain kicked my ass every time I played him. The joint was a gold mine!

Of course, things change, and Dick was shrewd enough to change with them, unlike some restaurateurs, who will stick with a theme that has become outdated to the point of bankruptcy.

So when the winds of change started blowing, and the Roaring Twenties were no longer in vogue, Dick switched to a sports bar format with big-screen television sets all around the bar, tuned to ESPN or whatever station was showing a ball game. The amusement arcade remained the same, with the carousel firmly in place, and the video games updated.

And people still lined up to pay fifty cents apiece to be humiliated by a chicken.

The food and drinks in O' Kane's were of a consistently high quality and reasonably priced; in fact, he had the best happy-hour deal I've ever encountered. From 4:30 p.m. until 7:00 p.m. each day, Dick had a happy-hour menu that had people lined up around the block. For example, Tuesday was Cajun chicken day. For $2 you got a full half-chicken, Cajun-broiled, with mashed potatoes, gravy, a vegetable, a roll, and butter. On Wednesday, it was broiled fish—a large portion with mashed spuds or French fries, marinara sauce, and bread and butter for $2. Friday, for $1, it was roast beef *au* (or *sans*) *jus*, two heaping portions, freshly sliced from a huge steamship round on two crusty rolls, and the hottest horseradish I've ever had the pleasure of scorching my sinuses with—or all-you-can-eat spiced shrimp and cocktail sauce. All for a buck.

There must be a catch, I can hear you think.

There was.

Dick's business acumen told him that the money was to be made on the sale of drinks, not food. So all drinks were full price, not two-for-one, or half-priced, as most happy hours are, and you had to have at least one full-priced beverage with the happy-hour dinner. Most customers had more than one drink, hence, a very profitable happy hour.

This, then, was the situation when he hired me to perform in O'Kane's in 1990. He brought me in about four times a year to perform in his sports bar, and when I first saw all the TV sets tuned to sporting events, I was aghast.

"Dick, I don't think I can perform here with all the TVs on at the same time."

"Don't worry about that. I've got you on closed-circuit, which will be shown on all the sets in the pub and restaurant while you're on stage."

And he did. He set up a camera, which broadcast my image and sound to the furthest recesses of the building. There was no getting away from me! There was also a set right in my line of vision on the wall at the front of the bar, and no matter how I tried to avoid looking at it, my eyes were drawn to it.

It's fascinating to watch yourself on TV live. Unlike a mirror, where your image is reversed, so that if you move to your left your mirror image moves to its right, the TV image moves in the direction you are actually moving. So while I was singing, I'd move to my left, and watch my TV image move to its left as I was looking at it.

I was so mesmerized that on several occasions, I sang the same verse to a song four or five times while moving right and left, staring at the screen, thinking, "Wow, this is really cool!"

Some of the audience members realized what was happening, came to the stage, shook and slapped me, and yelled, "Seamus! Snap out of it! You're in a loop! Wake up!"

After that episode, I resolved not to watch myself on television ever again, even on tape.

***

It was a nice, busy Friday night after a full-house happy hour, with several large groups of conventioneers and business associates taking up quite a few tables.

The crowd was in a good, playful mood, participating in the silly bits, laughing at the jokes, and singing along with gusto, when directly across from the stage and under the TV set, which I was *not* looking at, the front door opened and two guys pushing bikes came in and started to make their way through the crowd to the back bar, manned by the incomparable Oyster Bill.

I immediately thought, "Oho! here's an opportunity for an amusing bit of diversion." So I stopped the song I was singing and announced that O'Kane's Pub had been officially declared a stop on the Tour de France, and that the first cyclists were arriving even as I spoke.

Then I said, "Gentlemen, you know, of course, that to register your times at this checkpoint, you actually have to ride your bikes through the pub."

Well, there was no room to move in the pub, it was so crowded; even the waitresses were having trouble getting through with their drink orders. The crowd began to laugh at the absurdity of my suggestion, but the lead cyclist did not find it in the least bit amusing. He appeared to be weaving a little as he pushed his way through the throng, and I got the uneasy feeling that this fella was drunk.

My uneasiness was confirmed when he screamed, "Fuck you, you asshole!" and lifting the bike over his head, tried to bull his way through the crowd to throw the bike at me.

Like most musicians in such a predicament, my uppermost thought is not one of self-preservation, but rather, instrument protection. I cuddled my guitar close to my body like a mother hen gathering her chicks beneath her wing and whimpered pathetically.

His buddy, with what turned out to be amazing prescience, turned around and quietly went back out with his bicycle. The bike-hurler surged three or four feet nearer to the stage through the sea of humanity, for a better shot, I suppose, before the head bartender, Tom Stewart, and a couple of stout hearts from the audience brought him down with a flying tackle. The bike fell harmlessly to the floor, where a group of off-duty Secret Service agents dived and covered it with their bodies. Then it was wheeled away to the door to await the arrival of its owner, who was being dismissed, thrashing and screaming, from the establishment. He struggled and kicked, lashing invective on the heads of all, as he was carried bodily outside and deposited unceremoniously on the sidewalk.

Unlike most drunks, and I speak from experience, instead of leaving to continue his revels at another bar, he tried to batter his way back inside, hurling dire imprecations hither and yon.

It was at this juncture that the services of the local constabulary were enlisted. The cops were there in minutes, and they gave the guy the opportunity to get his bike and go away peacefully, but no, he wanted to "go back inside and fight everybody in the goddamned place!"

The officers tried to restrain him, but he continued to struggle, and by then the police cars had multiplied like rabbits, and a dozen or so cops wrestled the chap into handcuffs and a police car, where he continued to vent his spleen at the world. They read him his rights and took him off for some rest and relaxation, as his friend turned to me and said, "Jeez, he's always doing this. I'll have to take his frigging bike home again."

I explained to one of the policemen that I felt somewhat responsible for the man's outburst with my mis-timed *bon mot*, and he explained that it wasn't my fault; the guy was known to the cops as a troublemaker when drunk. As we say at home, "A lovely lad when he's sober, but a right bollocks when he's pissed."

Apparently, this was part of his regular Friday night routine, and it was just my turn in the barrel when he came into O'Kane's. He'd spend the night in the local lock-up, get out the next day, pay the fine, come by the watering hole and apologize for his behavior, and then start all over again.

This particular night was recorded in the annals of O'Kane's lore as the Schwinn Toss, which some of the regulars thought should become part of the actual Tour de France, or in this case, Tour de Farce.

Myself, I think it should be an Olympic event.

***

Now, the canneries and packing plants aren't the only parts of Monterey to have been given a new lease on life with the changeover to tourism. Fisherman's Wharf #1, and Fisherman's Wharf #2 are the piers where the sardine fishing fleets returned with their catches. They were lined with old warehouses, fishermen's saloons, cafés, supply shacks and huts, which with renovation became shops, restaurants, and bars, to which tourists flock in the summer. There, kayaks and canoes can be rented to paddle out to see the kelp beds, sea otters, sea lions, and other marine life. The fleet of fishing-boats was replaced by large cabin cruisers for whale-watching trips on Monterey Bay and taking out groups of deep-sea anglers who prefer to use rod, reel, and a case of beer to catch their supper. When these modern-day Izaak Waltons return to the wharf after a few hours with a mild hangover, sun-burn, and an ice-chest full of dead fish, they can enjoy the spectacle of watching a professional fish disemboweler ply his trade as he expertly de-capitates, "cleans," and filets their catch.

But wait! That's not all!

As he guts the fish, he tosses the heads, tails, and innards to the wheeling, squealing gulls, brown pelicans, and the sea lions swimming 'round the boat. They know where the good stuff is, and they don't even have to work for it.

It's their very own sushi bar, with their very own sushi chef catering to their every whim, and they don't have to tip him!

Watching the seagulls spin in flight to catch a thrown salmon intes-tine is a sight no one should miss. Their flight-path and accuracy is the envy of every fighter pilot, and wait! there's more! Unlike fighter pi-lots, although I don't really know this for certain, seagulls can poop while they fly. Really. In mid-air! I've seen them do it.

The pelicans are quite comical when they catch a piscine entrail (I don't know how many more variants of "fish guts" I can come up with); when the tasty morsel enters the beak, it stretches like a rubber bag—the beak, not the tasty morsel—and the bird begins to maneuver

344

the delectable appetizer down its gullet in much the same way an ana-conda would swallow a capybara. Isn't nature wonderful, children?

The sea lions are so lithe and graceful, knifing through the water around the wharf, that it's easy to forget they weigh about 400 pounds. When a de-licious, big, severed fish head hits the water, they take off after it like a dog retrieving a stick. Fortunately for us, they don't jump onto the dock, drop the fish-head at the fish-disemboweler's feet, and bark for him to throw it again. No, they eat it. Then, and only then, do they bark for him to throw another one. Located on Fisherman's Wharf #2 is the London Bridge Pub and Eng-lish Tea Rooms, a cozy little British tavern with a splendid selection of beers and nostalgia-inducing Brit foodstuffs, such as fish and chips, bangers and mash, Yorkshire pudding, beans on toast, and a ploughman's lunch—that's several kinds of cheese with pickled onions, chutney, bread and butter, and a pint of ale. Yum!

It also has a very friendly owner and staff, who don't seem to mind disreputable Irish entertainers coming in to dine and mingle with the bar regulars, who are not at all put out by accounts of seagulls, peli-cans, sea lions, and fish guts. The bartender, Gordon, was a Brit who hated being called an Englishman; he insisted he was a Yorkshire man, and he had an eye for the ladies.

One of the most endearing fixtures in the place was a gent called George Eberl. In his early sixties, George came in every day for lunch and several (well, okay—many) glasses of red wine, holding forth with anyone on any topic under the sun. In other words, the kind of regular customer that most pubs love to have, to the point of drugging and kid-napping him from a rival establishment.

All subjects were grist for George's conversational mill, and he would discourse learnedly on politics, local, national, and international, religion, sports, science, and the declining quality of Monterey Bay fish-offal. (I did it!)

An erudite man, he had been a newspaper reporter and editor for over twenty years, and he had recently published a book on golf, which was his passion.

And now a shameless plug for George Eberl's book!

It's called "Golf Is a Good Walk Spoiled," and it recounts "bizarre and fascinating incidents involving decisions on the rules of golf." (Published 1992 by the Taylor Publishing Company, 1550 West Mock-ingbird Lane, Dallas, Texas 75235. ISBN 0-87833-791-1.)

He carried a tote bag containing nine or ten books around with him, selling them to folk he met in the pub, and he would autograph them at no extra charge. I first met him while we were enjoying luncheon at the bar of the London Bridge. We had exchanged a perfunctory nod, and a polite hello, when I noticed a copy of the book lying on the bar beside his empty wineglass. Of course, I didn't know he was the author.

"So you like golf then?" was my opening gambit.

"I do indeed," was his response.

"I play a little myself," I ventured, holding out my hand. "Seamus Kennedy's the name."

"I'm George Eberl, and I used to play, too," he replied, shaking my hand.

We then fell to discussing the recent collapse of Australian Greg Norman, who had lost to Englishman Nick Faldo in the Masters—one of the most embarrassing downfalls of a tournament leader in years.

"Norman went to pieces and choked," I said.

"Ah, but Faldo had been playing rock-steady all weekend, and when the collapse came, he was ready," he countered.

"True," says I.

George noticed his empty wine glass and looked over his reading spectacles on the end of his nose to see Gordon at the other end of the bar engaged in a tête-à-tête with a very attractive young blonde turista. He beckoned to get Gordon's attention, but to no avail.

"Gordon and his buttercups," he muttered *sotto voce*.

I then noticed the title of his book.

"'Golf is a good walk spoiled,'" I said. "George Bernard Shaw, I believe?"

"No," said he. "It's Mark Twain."

"I don't think so, George. I could swear that's a GBS quote. In fact, I'll bet you a glass of wine on it."

"Well, he must have said it well after Twain did, and I'll take that bet," he replied, and he opened the book to the page right after the foreword by C. Grant Spaeth, USGA president, with Twain's quote and attribution.

"You win," I said. "Another glass of red?"

We looked down to the end of the bar again to see Gordon in serious discussion—probably about quantum physics and their application to cocktail mixing—with the stunning young blonde. He was completely entranced, unaware of our presence. George lifted his glass and waved it gently in Gordon's direction, still getting no reaction.

"Where can I buy a copy of your book, George?" I asked.

"Right here. I carry a few copies with me wherever I go. It's a handy way to get a couple of bucks for pin money."

"Well, I'd like to buy one. How much?"

He responded, "Ten dollars. Would you like me sign it for you?"

I couldn't believe my good fortune. Meeting a famous golf author, having a few drinks and a stimulating conversation with him, and now I can purchase his book—hard cover—and have him sign it, all for the paltry sum of ten dollars. What a bargain!

I gave him the money, and he took a book from his bag, opened it to the flyleaf and wrote, " To Seamus, may all your golf walks be unspoiled—whether it was said by GB Shaw or Mark Twain. Cheers, George Eberl, April 12, 1994."

"Thank you very much, George," I said. "Now, let's seal this transaction with a drink. Let's get that glass of red for you."

He raised the empty glass once more, and looking towards the end of the bar, he waved gently. But Gordon was not to be distracted. He was probably inviting her for a Mediterranean cruise on his yacht, which was moored at Monte Carlo. George raised his eyes to heaven and said, "Excuse me." He got off his stool and walked around the corner toward the restrooms.

I picked up the book, read the dedication to me, by George (!), and began to leaf through it. I smiled at some of the anecdotes, anticipating a thoroughly enjoyable read. Just then, the telephone rang behind the bar. It rang five or six times before Gordon could pry himself away from his buttercup long enough to reach behind him and grope blindly for the phone, the whole time gazing raptly and unblinkingly into her baby blues, mouthing kissy-kissies at her.

"Hello, London Bridge Pub, Gordon speaking. What's that? I beg your pardon? A glass of red wine for George Eberl at the other end of the bar?"

Looking very sheepish and somewhat crestfallen, he brought a fresh glass of wine and set it down in front of George, who had just returned from around the corner, where the restrooms and the pay phone were located.

Dedicated with respect and affection to my friend, the late George Eberl.

CRW

Oh, by the Way...

Dennis O'Rourke

When I got into this full-time, back in the late seventies, it was not unusual to receive invitations to stay at the homes of folks recently met. I would arrive in a new town, set up the equipment at the club, and then head for the hotel room that had been reserved for me, or go in search of one myself. I would perform that night and make a few new friends and fans, and sometimes receive an invitation to forego the hotel and be their guest. There was always a spare room.

Now, these were people who truly loved Irish music and admired the entertainers. They were hospitable, generous people who jumped, it seemed, at the chance to put us up, to have a real performer—a minor celebrity, if you will—in their homes for a night or two. More often than not, I would politely turn these invitations down. I was uncomfortable at the thought of a strange house and bed and the ensuing glimpse into other people's private lives.

I was wary about bunking with families, especially if they had children, dogs, or both. As now, it was my habit to stay at the club after hours with the staff and imbibe a bit in the bubbly, to wind down before taking to bed around three or four. Sleeping till noon was a necessity. I did not fancy the idea of being awakened at seven or eight in the morning by breakfast smells, barks, children's yelps, and cheery morning chatter. Often, people trying very hard to be quiet will waken you with the effort. The tiptoeing and whispering, the occasional soft creak of a step can get you focused and awake. Loud noises are sometimes easier to ignore. I was also put off by the thought of the inevitable late-night trip to answer a call of Nature, proceeding down a darkened, unfamiliar hallway, possibly surprising a member of the household already in position in the bathroom.

Most folks understood my reluctance and did not press the issue. Others, however, would not take no for an answer. They promised to muzzle the dog if they had one and to tie up the children if they had any of those. There were a good few who were quite genuine in their desire, and sometimes I would relent and take them up on it, as long as I was reasonably certain it was not a spur of the moment invitation fueled by whiskey.

Of course, it would be incumbent upon me to sing a bit for them before bed. This was never suggested, but I knew better. Well, why not? I would think. What a perfect audience in a perfect venue—playing for folks who genuinely wanted to hear you, and doing it in their living room. I'd sing a few ballads, have a few more drinks, and not have to worry about car-weaving to a hotel. I could just weave-walk into the appointed room. Tipping the balance would be if the club was not picking up the hotel bill.

Once, in Portland, Maine, I took advantage of such an offer. They were a middle-aged couple with two kids in their early twenties. They stayed and applauded my whole show that first night and came back for the next two. They were quite delightful, all four of them, and made the offer so sincerely and repeatedly that I accepted on my last night, even though it was the living room couch I was offered. I was assured it was more than comfortable.

I followed them to their house outside Portland, near some farmland. Trees and fields. Country peace. A bit of an adventure, I thought. Something different.

We drank. I sang. The patriarch pulled out a beautiful sax and played a bit, and we had a good time 'til almost three. Then the big couch was made up for me—sheet, blanket, pillows—and they bade me goodnight. But before heading off to their own rooms, they all paused at the hall entrance. The matriarch stood with her hand on the light switch. "Oh, by the way," she said. "The railroad runs behind the house. We'll probably have one or two come by later. It's nothing. We sleep right through it." They all grinned. And then she hit the switch.

I fell asleep almost immediately, and my last thoughts were of how nice it would be to hear a train whistle far off in the night. And it wasn't long before that very pleasure was visited upon me. I awoke at the sound of the first blast. The romance of it all. I lay there thinking of the early sixties and the folk boom, and the guys who went to college for a couple of years and finished their education on the road, thumbing rides and hopping trains. Then they wrote songs. Eric Anderson, whom I much admired, came to mind.

"I'm going, my baby
I'm gonna leave you, pretty gal
For a train passed by

349

While you lay sleeping
I'll write you a letter
On a dusty boxcar wall."

Another blast of the whistle, closer this time. Then I heard the train itself, the big engine; all that power and beauty rushing toward me out of the night, perhaps on its way to Canada or somewhere far south of here, through the red clay of Georgia and into the Florida panhandle.

Was it my imagination or was the couch beginning to tremble? I sat up, pushed the pillow aside, and held the armrest. It *was* shaking, ever so slightly. The next whistle blast was closer and kicked my heart rate up a notch or two. I leaned over the couch and peered out the bay window. In the dark, through the trees, I could see a fierce, single shaft of white light coming from the right, pointed directly at the house and me. My reason told me that this could not be, but I looked at the living room floor, anyway, just in case tracks had magically appeared. I pushed the blanket aside and put my feet down on the hardwood floor. The floor was shaking. I stood up. I heard other things in the living room begin to shake. I walked over to an end table. It was shaking, too, as were the knick-knacks and framed pictures on it. I went back to the couch and looked out the window again. The light was gone. But right then there was an earsplitting blast from the whistle. I shot up from the couch, high-tailed it to the far end of the living room, and pressed my back against the wall. It, too, was shaking as if it were a living thing. I imagined the train bursting through the wall and cutting through the house like a knife. Then the engine was upon us. The house shook and seemed filled with the sound of a wild symphonic crescendo.

I continued to hug the wall, and listened while the cars rushed past with their clickety-clack. Finally I felt the wall relax behind me like a dog that had been trembling. Silence descended. I tiptoed back to the couch and looked out. I expected to see devastation out back; trees sliced through and ripped apart, the carcasses of dead deer, raccoons, and nocturnal dogs everywhere. The moonlight revealed nothing but pastoral landscape. I lay down again.

Ah, a little joke, I thought. How could anybody sleep through that? But the house was still. Maybe they really *had* become accustomed to it.

In the morning, we sat around a big table and had breakfast. "Yes," I told them, "I slept like a baby." I wasn't going to give them anything.

I caught Mom winking at her brood. Then she casually addressed me. "We had a pretty big train last night. Must have been three engines on it."

"Really?" I said. "I didn't hear a thing. Must've slept right through it."

Their collective eyes narrowed. They looked at each other and back at me. I concentrated on my scrambled eggs.

CHARACTERS ALONG THE WAY, OR UNUSUAL SUSPECTS

Glass Eyes and Golf Tees

Seamus Kennedy

Except for its acoustics, which really suck, Mullaney's Harp & Fiddle in the Strip District in Pittsburgh is a fine and friendly pub with an efficient staff and an appreciative group of hard-core regulars who enjoy the music and entertainment of folks like myself, Tom O'Carroll, Brendan's Voyage, Guaranteed Irish, Eugene Byrne, and a few big names they bring in for the occasional concert.

The Guinness pours well, and for people of the County Cork persuasion, there's Murphy's Stout. Resident Corkonian and bartender Declan makes sure *that* flows smoothly. Barman and manager Dave, a Pittsburgher by birth, keeps the IC and IC Light on hand and cold for the locals, and Rita from Derry, the Mother of all Waitresses, makes sure choice delicacies prepared by Matthew in the kitchen make it promptly to the customers who ordered them.

The cover charge is nominal, and performers usually play to a full house on the weekend. Reservations are a must at the Harp, or if you prefer, you can stand with the crowd at the bar.

It's pretty easy to work a full room. The crowd is there to hear the music and be entertained. They're in a good mood because it's the

weekend and they've put aside their cares and woes. Generally speaking, they're meeting us more than halfway in the goodtime department. Songs, jokes, witty and not-so-witty repartee, instrumentals—the Friday and Saturday crowds eat them up. Performers really enjoy working these audiences.

The tough ones are the slower nights—Tuesday, Wednesday, Thursday. There can be as few as a dozen people in the room; they might be happy hour holdovers, a few weary businessmen, or folks who have stopped in for a cocktail or two on the way to a hockey game. Their focus is not going to be the stage entertainment. We have to try a little harder to get their attention and hold it in order to keep some in the pub for a few more drinks. (It is a business, after all.)

If it's slow, the performers have to do something to keep themselves amused, as well. Trying out new songs or jokes, stringing old jokes together to come up with a little comedy routine, practicing a reel or a jig on the guitar—anything to avoid the appearance of ennui.

My own technique is to talk to the folks, to get a patter going on just about anything that comes into my head—the weather, politics, current events, insults. Just get them interested.

Well, it's a quiet Wednesday night in the Harp, but I do have a group of about two dozen young folks sitting at two tables in front of the stage. When I say young, I mean in their early twenties—a few of them are probably students at Duquesne University. They're ingesting delicious intoxicants and talking animatedly among themselves—not overly loud or obnoxious the way a group like this can sometimes be. I notice that one young man is blind. This lad, I think, will provide the perfect vehicle for me to gain their attention, entertain them, and ultimately win their approval and affection.

So I start telling blind jokes:

"Why do blind people never take up skydiving? It frightens the shit out of their dogs."

"How can a blind skydiver tell when he's about to hit the ground? The leash goes slack."

A couple of them laugh, and gradually the others stop talking and begin to listen.

"A blind man and his dog go into a department store. As soon as he gets through the door, he picks the dog up by the leash and starts swinging him round over his head. The manager comes over and says, 'May I help you, sir?' The blind guy says, 'No, I'm just looking around!'"

They're really laughing now. Especially the blind kid. So I sing a few songs, funny ones like "The Scotsman" and "Side by Side." I've got them. Time for an audience participation song or two. "Finnegan's Wake." If someone keeps clapping on the chorus after everyone else has stopped, he has to buy a round of drinks for the rest of his group. This one works. Then "The Moonshiner," a little ¾-time song where they clap once on the table and twice, pattycake, with a partner sitting across from them. The clapping gets more intricate as the song progresses.

The blind guy is gamely keeping up with the rest and having a ball. The set is over. I go to the bar, get a pint, and head to their table to say hello. They ask me to sit down and join them, which I'm happy to do. I

354

introduce myself to the blind guy—his name is Michael—and I ask if he minds the jokes.

"Not at all," he says, "In fact, I'll give you a couple for your routine. Did you hear about the blind man who wore his fingers to the bone trying to read a cheese grater?

"A blind man and his dog are waiting to cross the street. The dog lifts his leg and pees all over the guy's feet. The blind man reaches into his pocket, takes out a dog biscuit, and gives it to the dog. A stranger comes over and says, 'That's the most charitable thing I've ever seen. That dog deliberately peed on you, and here you are giving it a dog-biscuit.' The blind guy says, 'It's not charity. I'm just trying to find his head so I can kick him in the ass!'"

Two beauties. I file them away for future use. We swap a pair of glass eye jokes, and Michael mentions that he has two glass eyes. I ask if he can take them out, which he proceeds to do, grossing out everybody at the table but me. I'm enthralled. He dips one of them in his pint and pops it in his mouth, and the girls at the table squeal in disgust. "Ewwwwwwww! That's yucky! And gross! Eeeewwww!" This guy is brilliant!

Break over, time to get back on stage. A couple of songs, a couple of jokes, a couple of instrumentals, and I decide to do "The Unicorn," a song in which I teach the audience to mime the various animals named.

"Green alligators, long-necked geese,
Humpty-backed camels, and chimpanzees,
Cats and rats and elephants,
As sure as you're born,
The loveliest of them all was the unicorn."

I show them how to act out the animals, arms outstretched in front of the chest, moving up and down like an alligator's jaws; both hands up in the air, bent at right angles at the wrist, like a goose's neck and head, and so forth.

I see Michael asking one of the others, "What's Seamus doing?" because I'm demonstrating the motions, not describing them. So one of the girls takes his hands, and starts guiding him in the movements. He's into it.

Then I get silly.

I'd been playing golf that afternoon with Dave and Declan, so I have a couple of golf tees in my pocket. I decide to stick one of them up my nose. (I didn't say this was a class act.) I've done this on quite a few occasions, sometimes with a five-inch nail. It's a simple geek show trick that anyone with a nostril and a sinus can do, for heaven's sake. You simply tilt your head back, insert the nail into your nostril and gently push it all the way back into your sinus. It's not going anywhere near your brain, so you don't have to worry about that. But it's a great little attention-getter that can liven up the dullest dinner-party or soirée and cause a heave or two, even in the strongest stomach, especially if you pull your nostril over the nail head so that it can't be seen. Then you look at someone and say, "If I sneeze now, you're dead!"

Anyway, I slowly shove the golf tee into my nostril, gradually, until only the head is visible. The girls are squealing again and pretending to cover their eyes; the guys are laughing, and poor old Michael is saying, "What's he doing? What's he doing?"

I realize that this is distinctly unfair, and he deserves to be an equal participant in this showbiz extravaganza. So I call out, "Michael, I've a proposition for you. Come on up here on stage with me, and if you'll take out your glass eyes for the audience, I'll let you push the golf tee up my nose with your very own finger!"

Well, this is obviously an offer that no red-blooded, All-American blind guy can refuse. He stands up immediately, pushes his chair back, and allows one of the young ladies at the table to give him her arm and lead him to the stage to tumultuous applause and encouragement. "Go, Michael!"

I help him up, and he stands beside me, facing the audience. I insert the golf tee into my nostril about three-eighths of an inch or so and take his hand. He extends his index finger, and I place it on the head of the tee. The crowd is screaming hysterically.

"Now push gently."

And he does so, a little at a time, until all three and a half inches of the tee are in. His friends are doubled over. Then I pull the nostril down over it, and I let him run his finger over the little bump to assure him that it is, in fact, all the way in. Michael is giggling.

"Okay," I say. "Your turn."

He tilts his head slightly, rolls his eyelids back, and removes the glass eyes. The crowd is close to wetting themselves now. I believe there may have been a few involuntary squirts from the owners of bladders who were afraid to go to the bathroom in case they missed any part of this once-in-a-lifetime magic show. He holds the glass eyes up and displays them triumphantly, like a gladiator holding aloft a pair of heads severed from the shoulders of slightly less-skilled opponents. As in the Coliseum, the crowd roars its approval.

Then he drops one.

"Oh, shit!" he says as it hits the stage and bounces onto the floor and under a table. Pandemonium! His friends all rush forward, and hunker down in a search and rescue mission. It's nothing so small as a contact lens, so I know it's not going to take long to find. While they're occupied with the hunt, I turn to find Michael on his hands and knees, feeling around the stage.

"Michael," says I, "what the hell are you doing?"

"I'm looking for my goddamned eye."

A few moments later, the eye is recovered and returned to its rightful owner, who's relieved to have both headlights functioning again. Order is restored, Michael rejoins his pals at the table, and folk start breathing normally. This has been the highlight of the evening, I'm sure of that; nothing is going to top it, so I do a song to wind things up, and I bid the audience adieu, reminding them to tip their bartenders and waitresses.

And then, as I usually do last thing before I leave the stage, I say, "Please drive safely. I'd like to see all of you again."

And Michael stands up and hollers, "I will!"

∞

The Keys to the Kingdom
Robbie O'Connell

In the 1980s, Mick Moloney, Jimmy Keane, and I appeared several times on the nationally broadcast radio show Mountain Stage. It was recorded before a live audience in Charleston, West Virginia. On one of our repeat visits, the host, Larry Groce, had just introduced us when there was some kind of commotion in the audience. It was hard to see what was going on with the glare of the stage lights, but I could just make out a bearded man standing there talking. I figured it was a heckler, at first, but to my amazement, the man was invited up on stage. We were bewildered. He was introduced to us as the mayor of Charleston, who wished to make a presentation. A brief formal speech followed, and he then presented us with the keys to the city of Charleston. Why we should receive such an honor was a mystery to me, but being live on radio, we couldn't very well question it, so we graciously accepted. We discovered later that it was because we had recorded a reel Jimmy had written called the "Charleston Reel."

I can't remember much of what he said except for his final enigmatic words. "These keys will open the door to any bar in Charleston." The audience gave a big cheer, but I was still unsure of what it was all about. Wow! Did this mean free drinks? Was he insane, just kidding, or really naïve? You can't say something like that to a bunch of Irish musicians and expect to get away with it. What if we moved to Charleston and bankrupted the city? I can only assume that he thought we were gentlemen.

It was a Sunday afternoon, and the show finished around 5:30 p.m. We had a flight at 7:00 p.m., so as soon as the show finished, we rushed to the airport. On the way, we bemoaned the fact that we would not have a chance to test our keys at a local bar. The airport was almost deserted. Our flight appeared to be the final one of the evening. We raced to the departure gate only to discover that our plane had been delayed for at least an hour. There was nothing to do but wait, and we figured the airport bar was the best place for that.

We could see through the windows that the barman was alone, but we were dismayed to find the door locked. It was only 6:30 p.m., for Christ's sake. This was totally uncivilized and unfair. We had just done our day's work and were in need of a little relaxation. We banged on the door, but the barman ignored us. Annoyed, we pounded even louder. In a blinding flash of inspiration, someone suggested that we try the keys. We dug out our large golden keys and waved them in the air. Curiosity eventually overcame the barman, and he cautiously ventured towards the door. We motioned for him to open it. He stood undecided for a moment, and then he reluctantly opened it a crack.

"Sorry, guys, we're closed for the night."

"But you don't understand. The mayor just gave us these keys to the city and said that they would open the door to any bar in Charleston. Really, look!"

We held up the keys. He looked at us as though we were nuts. We quickly related the story of the mayor and his presentation at the Mountain Stage show, and to our great relief, he let us in. We killed an hour or so with our new buddy Joe, and had a few beers and a few laughs until our flight was called. When we asked for the check, Joe held up his hand and shook his head. He insisted we owed him nothing. He said he would send the bill to the mayor. Those keys really did work. We were amazed. We left him a big tip and dashed off to our gate.

A year or two later, we were back in Charleston to do the same show again. The first question we asked when we arrived was, "How's our friend the mayor?" There was an embarrassing silence and then someone said, "Well, at the moment, he's in jail."

"What? You're kidding, right?"

"No, he's really in jail. Something to do with selling cocaine."

"Wow! I guess he could use one of those keys now."

The more I thought about it, the more sense it made. It just figured that anyone who would give us the keys to their city would end up in jail.

⊂ℨ✄

What Goes Around...

Seamus Kennedy

When I'm in Pittsburgh performing at the Harp and Fiddle, one of my favorite things is going to the Strip District on a Saturday afternoon. The Strip District is really a misnomer, because it's not what you might think on first hearing the name. There are no dimly lit clubs with scantily clad young ladies writhing around poles or crawling on bearskin rugs to very loud music, which would cause every little capillary in your brain to calcify and explode instantly. Rather, it is a section of Penn Avenue from 22nd Street down to 15th Street, with stores and sidewalk vendors who cater to the tastes of just about every ethnic group in the way of comestibles, potables, and flea-market merchandise. Arabic, Asian, Irish, Italian, Hispanic, Slavic—all bases are covered.

Stores such as the Sunseri Bros., Jimmy and Nino, where you can purchase the finest quality Italian foods—bread, pasta, cheeses, virgin olive oil, spaghetti sauce, and much more from the old country. Primanti Bros., where their famous sandwiches are a sight to behold and a challenge to eat. For example, let's say you order a salami on rye with mustard, French-fries, and coleslaw; you get the fries and the coleslaw *in* the sandwich along with the salami and mustard. Don't ask. It's a Pittsburgh thing.

There's a Vietnamese restaurant which used to be called My Dung, but for some unfathomable reason the name was changed to Viet Pad. The food is exquisite. They serve a superb *pho*, a Vietnamese soup made of scalding beef broth with noodles, scallions, bean sprouts, and fresh chopped basil. Thin slices of raw beef are added to this heady potion, a few drops of hot pepper sauce splashed in; it is served with Vietnamese iced coffee. It doesn't get any better than that on a cold, blustery, November Saturday, I can assure you.

Outside the stores and restaurants, food vendors hawk their wares at stalls on the footpath, with Thai food—skewers of marinated chicken or beef, fried rice, and egg rolls—side by side with kielbasi, golubkis, and other Polish delicacies.

A lovely African-American lady called Miss Dilly sells the best barbecued ribs and chicken I have ever tasted, and that includes Memphis *and* Texas barbecue. She has her own secret recipe barbecue sauce with which she smothers racks of ribs that have been soaking in her equally secret marinade. Onto the sizzling grill they go, and forty minutes later, you walk away with the most delicious, mouth-watering rack of ribs you've ever had. Add a little collard greens and some of her homemade cornbread, and you could hibernate for the winter. In fact, you'd have to hibernate, because you can't get her ribs from December through April. No, sir (or ma'am). When the weather in Pittsburgh turns cold, Miss Dilly heads for the Bahamas.

Farther down the block is Wholey's Wholesale and Retail Food Market with fresh meat and fish. These people at Wholey's really know how to promote their shop. One day outside the store, they had a 15' great white shark, which had been caught a week or so before, off Montauk, Long Island. With it's maw lying open, exposing the multiple rows of serrated teeth, it scared the living bejeebers out of folks walking by. I think the scene would have been perfect if the theme from *Jaws* had been piped outside. *DOO-doo, DOO-doo, DOO-doo.*

They'd have been doing doo-doo in their britches.

Of course, not only fine foods are available on the Strip. Some stalls carry clothing, T-shirts, gloves, caps, and so forth, while still others sell used books, CDs, and tapes. It was at one of the latter that I happened to stop on my Saturday afternoon stroll, after I had just consumed a couple of Thai chicken kebabs with a spring roll and a Snapple. All was well with the world, and with a happy tummy and a sunny outlook, I just couldn't be angered.

Now, I always stop at used book and CD stalls to browse, because I never know what little gem I might unearth. A first edition of Dickens or maybe an original Shakespeare Folio. Aaaahhh, I can but dream. Or maybe a collection of Hank Williams' greatest hits, or possibly Hank Snow reciting the poems of Robert Service. Or who knows, Hank Thompson and the Brazos Valley Boys with the finest cry-in-your-beer honky-tonkin' songs, or even Hank Locklin's version of "Only the Heartaches." Anything recorded by anyone called Hank—but *not* Hank Jr.

So there I was, flipping idly through a box of used CDs, when the spine and the cover of one caught my attention. I flipped back a couple and lifted it out. No wonder I recognized it. It was one of my own CDs—"Seamus Kennedy in Concert."

Good heavens and great Scott, I thought. How can this be?

And there on the cover of the insert, in my handwriting, was the inscription "To Jimmy Grogan, all my best wishes, Seamus Kennedy." Jimmy Grogan is a part-time local singer of Irish songs in the Pittsburgh area, well known on the bar scene. Jimmy Grogan is not his real name. I have changed it to protect his identity. (His real name is Eddie O'Leary, and his address is 475 Mulberry Heights, Pittsburgh, PA 15202.)

I remembered the night I'd given it to him, when he'd come in to catch my show at Mullaney's Harp and Fiddle. We'd had a few drinks during my breaks, I'd answered some of his questions about the recording process, and I'd signed the CD for him—a little courtesy musicians do for one another. We chewed the fat a little more about gigs, owners, and PA equipment, and he left.

As I stood there, holding the autographed CD, I wondered what misfortune must have befallen Jimmy that I should find my recording in a used CD bin on a street-stall in the Strip District. He couldn't possibly have sold it, my gift, for base gain, could he? Unthinkable!

So I did what had to be done. I purchased the CD from the vendor and took it home. I removed the insert, and with my trusty black Sharpie, I wrote beside the original dedication:

"Dear Jimmy, So sorry to learn about the burglary and theft of your CD collection. With renewed best wishes, Seamus Kennedy."

And I mailed it to him.

CB&O

The O'Gradys

Frank Emerson

One of the advantages of being on the road is that you get to meet a lot of fine folks. Sometimes you know them just from the venues (read: bars), and your contact with them is limited to there. You share a lot of late-night chats after the gig. And you're over-served. And you attempt to solve:

1. All the problems that ever confronted the world
2. All the problems that confront the world now
3. All the problems that might confront the world in the future

And you pretty much accomplish these goals. And you swear besotted loyalty and mutual admiration. And dammit, you're sincere about it all. And the next morning, you're lucky if you can remember your own name, never mind theirs, or what was discussed.

Though this might be fulfilling in some respects, that fulfillment is, by and large, a fleeting thing. On the other hand, sometimes you're fortunate enough to make friendships with people who teach you something about stuff that matters—tangible intangibles, if you will, like family and kindness and altruism. Such were the O'Gradys. Tony O'Riordan used to crack that they were most of the nicest people that we knew.

Jack O'Grady was a big fellow from Queens, New York who in his youth attended a seminary and had a tryout with the Philadelphia Eagles, I'm not sure in which order. Anyway, he decided, or maybe it was decided for him, that neither was to be his life's work. He signed on with the US Treasury as a siderographer, sort of a designer/engraver, and among other things was instrumental in the birth of the two-dollar bill. Somewhere along the line, he met this real nice, real cute, real smart blonde from Roscommon named Elizabeth Sampey. Jack and Betty married and had eight kids.

Now, it's part of the nature of the music game that you find yourself working when everyone else is off. At times, this means over the holidays. You're away from family, appearing in a town not your own, with no one with whom to share the time. Thanksgiving, that wonderfully unique American holiday, can be a bit lonely when you're out on the road; for me, more so than Christmas.

Our first time in Washington, the O'Gradys took note that Tony and I would be at loose ends over Thanksgiving. Now, you'd think that with eight kids and all, their hands would be more than full, but they went ahead and opened their hearts and their home to two somewhat questionable characters they'd only recently met. After asking, "Are you sure?" and receiving an affirmative, we were only too happy to accept their invite.

We showed up with appropriate gifts—booze, a houseplant, some candy, and a pie. We also had our guitars with us. We didn't like to travel unarmed. Well, they laid on quite a spread. There was enough to feed a platoon, which between family, friends, drop-ins, and the two of us, there very nearly was. We ate, ate, drank, told stories, and laughed. Did we ever laugh; even their oldest boy Jimmy, who was then about sixteen or so. He'd had things a bit rough from the git-go. He was blind in one eye, deaf, had been born with a rheumatic heart or something like that, and might have had a couple of other things wrong we weren't immediately aware of. There was nothing wrong with his spirit, though. He wasn't supposed to see his first birthday, but he turned out to be more than up to the hand he'd been dealt. With the faith, determination, and unswerving love and devotion of his entire family, he beat the odds and was now studying art.

Well, when one of us cracked a joke, Betty or Jack would sign it for Jimmy, and he'd laugh in a sort of screech. He seemed to react more readily when Betty signed. (Some years later, Jack told me that he'd only recently discovered that he'd been signing incorrectly for some time. He realized that since his signs were a bit mixed up, Jimmy probably figured that his father was a bit on the slow side, or at the very least, did not have a particularly good command of English. Jimmy had been too polite to bring it up, since he didn't want to hurt his father's feelings.)

After the meal, we had a couple more drinks—our traditional dessert—and then broke out the guitars for a singsong. Neighbors came by, and everyone joined in. Some of the folks had their own party pieces. It was all real nice. At one point, I looked over and saw that Jimmy had his hand on the face of Tony's guitar as Tony was playing. Jimmy kept time by bouncing his knees, and every now and then, coming out with one of his sounds, more or less in time to the music.

Eventually, it was time to wrap things up. We started to make our goodbye's and say our thank yous. Betty came up to us and said she'd never seen Jimmy react to music like that, and no one had ever heard him try to sing. She thanked *us*! Before we could respond, Jack wrapped a big paw around each of us, laughed his big laugh and said that if Jimmy liked us, we must be okay. "Welcome to the family," he said. "Happy Thanksgiving."

We saw them fairly often over the next few years. It was always a warm and pleasant time. They even took to extending their hospitality to our girlfriends. I've long wondered if it was only after meeting the O'Grady's, spending time with them and seeing their relationship with me, that the girl who would become my wife figured that I wasn't the worst. One of these days, I'll have to thank them.

Note: I've since shown this story to my wife. She said the assumption I made about her feelings toward me and how she had arrived at them was right on the money. It's only now, some twenty-odd years later, that she felt she could tell me I'd been correct. And here, all this time, I really thought it was because I looked like Clark Gable.

Cﾞ80

Coastguard Bob

Seamus Kennedy

You know how some newcomers to a bar become regulars almost immediately and are accepted by the resident denizens as kindred spirits? Well, Coastguard Bob wasn't one of those. He was a goddamned nuisance right off the bat. Not a completely objectionable asshole, mind you—the type to get himself 86'd instantly by staff and patrons alike—no; rather, he was a pest—kind of like an annoying little brother who would say and do things to piss people off just to get attention. Things like yelling out the punch lines to all my jokes in a comedy routine two beats before I could say them, thereby spoiling the bit for me and the audience. And he did it just to get on my nerves, not out of malice. He was trying to make himself part of the fun going on around him, but he hadn't a clue how miserably he was failing at it. He'd whistle while waving dollar bills at the bartenders to humorously, so he thought, get their attention and endear himself to them for life.

There was a corner of the bar in Ireland's Own in Alexandria, VA that was essentially reserved for the regulars—Bacardi Mike, Benny C, Greg, Chip, and Old Half & Half—who were there every night of the week from eight until closing. The musicians performing at the place also hung out in the corner, which came to be known as the Viper's Pit. Coastguard Bob tried his damnedest to get these guys to like him and welcome him as one of their own, standing them rounds of drinks and generally pulling the "Hail fellow, well met" routine. But his boisterousness and bullshit torpedoed him, so they kept him at arm's length. Cordial, but not close. Oh, they'd accept his offer of drinks, all right—what good bar regular wouldn't?—but they'd never reciprocate, and they never admitted him to the inner circle.

They'd shoot the breeze with him and listen with feigned interest to his stories of heroic barroom brawls wherein he was always John Wayne, his tales of countless sexual conquests, and his oft-repeated contention that he had a manly ability to drink without getting drunk. Well, we never saw him in a fight, come in with a woman (or leave with one, for that matter), or drink more than two pints in a night. Consequently, when his back was turned or when he went to the head, all the guys would chorus, "What a bullshitter. What a dickweed."

One night, he was going on at length about this fabled capacity to hold his liquor, 'til he finally drove the boys to the breaking point. They'd had enough, and they demanded to know why it was no one had ever seen him drink more than two pints of beer at one sitting. Where and when, they wanted to know, did this mighty drinking take place?

Red-faced and rising to the bait, he called Tommy Casey, the bartender, and said, "Tommy, I bet you can't make me a drink that'll knock me on my ass."

"I don't know, Bob," Tommy replied. "I don't want to get in trouble. If you drive drunk after one of my concoctions, I could go to jail. It's *my* ass that would be on the line here, not yours."

"Don't worry about that, Tommy," said Bob. "If you make a drink that can knock me on my ass, I won't drive. I'll take a cab home. Fair enough?"

"Fair enough," said Tommy, and he turned his back to us and went to work at the bar like a mad scientist, pulling a bottle from this shelf, a bottle from that shelf, one from down here, one from up there—all different colors—and he poured a little from each into a cocktail shaker and gave it a vigorous shaking. We watched this process with keen interest. He poured the resulting mixture into a pint glass.

"Bob," he said. "You can only have one of these. There's a load of different liqueurs in this, and it's very strong. By the way, it's eight bucks."

Bob paid the eight dollars, tipped Tommy two dollars to showcase his largesse, and began to drink the cocktail. He took a mouthful and resumed the bullshit story he'd been telling before all of this started. We watched and waited. After a few minutes, he had half of it down, and he began to slur his words a bit. He shook his head as if to clear it.

"Tommy, this is good. What's in it?"

"Can't tell you, Bob. It's a trade secret."

Coastguard Bob drank some more, swaying like a reed in a gentle breeze, and said, "Whoooooo, boy! That's a beaut! But I gotta take a leak." And he went off to the bathroom, with a lovely little weave to his walk.

When he was safely out of earshot, we all asked in unison, "Tommy, what the hell is in that thing?"

"Lime juice, lemon juice, ginger ale, tonic water, Tabasco, grenadine, and a dash of Angostura Bitters."

"What? No alcohol?"

"Nope. Not a drop."

When Coastguard Bob returned, nobody said a word, but we nearly gave ourselves hernias trying not to laugh as he slowly got tipsier. Just as I headed back to the stage, I heard Bob demanding another pint of Tommy's secret concoction. At the end of my one-hour set I came back to the Viper's Pit to see how things were unfolding. The regulars were all tight-lipped, eyes bulging, veins standing out on their foreheads in the agony of repressed laughter.

"What happened?" I whispered when Bob had careened off to the head once more. Bacardi Mike said, "Right when you left, Bob asked Tommy for another one, and Tommy told him he'd make it, but he had to hand over his car keys. So he gave them to him. He just finished the second one now."

Coastguard Bob tottered back and said, "Tommy, you win. You made a drink that put me on my ass. I gotta go home. Will you call me a cab, please?"

The cab was duly summoned, Bob was placed therein and sent on his way. Then the laughing started. A veritable Vesuvius of mirth. Belly laughs, guffaws, chuckles, chortles, wheezing, and tears. High fives from each of us with Tommy Casey.

The next night, Bob came in and allowed as to how he got absolutely hammered on Tommy's invention, but didn't wake up with a hangover. Amazing. So he ordered another one. And another. At eight bucks a throw, plus tip. Again, he dutifully handed over his car keys and took a taxi home. The next night—more of the same. But this time, Tommy said, "You know, Bob, you're the only guy I've ever seen drink so many of these things. So I'm going name it in your honor. From tonight on, this is a Coastguard Cutter."

"A 'Coastguard Cutter'," Bob repeated proudly.

This scene replayed itself off and on for a few weeks until Coastguard Bob announced one night that he was being posted to Seattle. So we toasted his health and wished him well, bon voyage, and Godspeed. I told him about a fine Irish bar in Seattle called Kell's, where he would be made to feel as at home as he was in Ireland's Own—friendly regulars, good food and drink, and great Irish music.

And off he went.

Things returned to what passes for normal in the Viper's Pit. A month or so later, on a Friday night, I took my break at midnight and went over to the Pit. The usual suspects were there, blackguarding with Tommy and each other, when the phone rang. Tommy picked it up and put his finger in his other ear, the better to hear.

"Yeah, this is Tommy Casey. I can't hear you. You'll have to speak up. What's that? You're the bartender at Kell's Pub in Seattle?"

This immediately got our collective attention.

"There's some guy at the bar called Coastguard Bob? Say again? And what?"

We all leaned in.

"He wants *me* to tell *you* how to make a Coastguard Cutter?"

ദ്ധ

DOR: Have you ever had an obsessed fan in a pub? Somebody who might wait for you when you played a certain club—

SK: *(Laughs)*

DOR: Glaring at you or heckling you?

SK: I've never had them obsessed *bad* like that. I've had them obsessed *good*. And some people who follow me around and show up are bones and spoons and bodhrán players. There's one little fella from New England who used to follow Tom O'Carroll and me around with a penny whistle that he couldn't play, but he loved us, and he wanted to play with us. We always let him because, you know, he was harmless, but he really wasn't a whistle-player. Well, he wanted to play with us in the worst way, and the one tune he had learned was "The Rising of the Moon." But he could not play it right all the way through. So Tom and I got him up and let him play a couple of times. It was just dreadful. Then we learned the trick of cranking his mike up through the *monitor*, and turning it down in the *house*. So (Laughs) the house couldn't hear it, but he could. And there he was, playing along. It got so bad, though; he was coming in, and he wanted to play on other tunes. And we said, "No, we're not doing that in the key of D anymore. We're doing it in E flat." So he went out and bought an E flat whistle and came back. Then we said, "No, no. We're not doing it in E flat anymore. We're doing it in F. We're doing it in G." And he went and bought every key of every whistle until it looked like he had a quiver full of arrows. He'd follow us around, take one out, and play it, you know? It got ridiculous.

ଓଛ

The Old Bull

Dennis O'Rourke

The road can be a wonderful thing. There are women out there.

It's winter in New Hampshire. There's a foot of snow under a big yellow moon, but the pub is warm and inviting, and it's nearly full. We're all having a wonderful time. Midway through the second set, I spy a group coming through the door behind the audience. It's an older couple and two young women. The man and what I assume to be his wife are in their late sixties or so. The two other women are in their twenties. The man is standing in front of his little herd. He's a hulking fella, one of those guys that looks like a retired longshoreman. His massive shoulders are only a little stooped with age, and he has a big crop of unruly white hair.

As I sing, I watch as he admonishes the women to wait there for him, and then wends his way carefully through the crowded tables and into the middle of the room. He finds an empty table, and he adds a loose chair to the three already there. He looks slowly around him, surveying the assembled multitude. After a moment, he beckons with his hand, and the women dutifully trot towards him. He pulls out a chair for each and tucks them in, one at a time. One last look around, and the old bull sits down with his females.

I'm nearly choking. I can't wait to finish the song and tell the crowd what I've just observed. It's Nature. It's animal instinct. It's primal. It's evolution.

But I do it gently. It's not my intention to embarrass these folks. I have just seen this guy orchestrate a dance right out of Mother Nature. I want to heap praise on him, not laugh at him, and I have to manage it without getting the old bull pissed off at me.

First, I call the audience's attention to their table. Everyone looks. The women immediately get a little uncomfortable and smile nervously. The old bull fixes me with a dead stare. I hurry on. This has to be quick and sweet.

I relate what I've just seen to the audience. I tell them it's something out of Marlin Perkins' *Wild Kingdom*, a beautiful example of life in the wild translated to modern man. The male reconnoiters an area, in this case, a watering hole, while the females wait in the safety of the brush. When he's satisfied there is no danger, the male calls out and the females join him. (Mind you, I was careful to say "the male," rather than "the old bull.")

I ask the crowd if that protective and gallant behavior isn't worth a round of applause. Well, don't they give him a standing ovation. The women at his table join in, and the old bull's face is flush with pride and pleasure.

When I finished the set, I get myself a drink and head for their table. They are only too glad to welcome me. A chair is found, and I join them. They're a married couple and two grandnieces. The young women are up from North Carolina to do some skiing. They are both very pretty, especially the older one. They're bunking in a small lodge about a mile or so from the great-uncle's house. The great-uncle himself is still tickled by the ovation. His wife is beaming at him. The younger of the two women is munching pretzels. The older one is sipping wine and looking at me with lazy, hooded eyes. I've seen this look before—not often, but I've seen it. This is one sensual woman. She's interested, and by God, so am I.

They stay for the entire show, and I join them again after packing up the guitar. The old bull is a bit tipsy, but still on his toes. He's noticed the silent exchanges between me and the prettier of the grandnieces. He throws an arm around her, busses her on the cheek, and makes noises about "my girl," and then noticing the other's pout, he says, "My girls, both of them."

But when he's not looking, I'm getting a wink and a smile from *my girl*.

Well, it turns out they've come in one car. The old bull is going to drop them off at their lodge. We stand to say our good-byes. We shake hands. My girl slips me a balled-up napkin. I open it before they're out the door. It reads, "My sister is going to say she wants to stay the night at their house. Follow us. We're in a silver Caddy. When they drop me off, wait 'til they go, and come in."

I love this cloak and dagger stuff. I pull on my coat, count to ten, and I'm out the door. I hug the shadows along the building. I see them across the lot getting into their car. The old bull puts his wife in front and the girls in the back. He stands in front of his open door and looks around. I duck behind my car. He gets in his. I get in mine and follow at a discreet distance. After a mile or so, they make a left onto a small side road. There is a like road on the other side and I back up well within it, about twenty yards, and shut off my lights. In a few minutes, I see his headlights coming back. He pulls out into the main street and stops. Jaysus, I think. Am I far enough back he doesn't see me? Mother of God! The moon! He gets out of the car and looks around. His door is open. My window is down. I can hear his wife bawling at him to get back inside and take them home. One more look around, and he gets in. I listen as the sound of the big Caddy disappears in the frigid air.

I shoot across the street, skidding on some ice 'til I hit exposed dirt on the access road. I proceed slowly for about a hundred yards—the snow, the trees, and the moon all around me. The lodge presents itself, small, but beautifully constructed. A huge bay window in front. Up the steps and a breathless knock on the door. It opens, and I'm hauled inside where the celebration begins on the living room floor. We've been waiting nearly three hours for this. Moonlight blesses us through the big window, and as I place my hands on her "peachies," I can't resist a muted wolf-howl.

Even Mother Nature's implanted instinct can sometimes fail the grandest of old bulls.

TWO QUICKIES

A Rare Opportunity

Seamus Kennedy

It's not often that I get the chance to use the punch line from an old joke in a real-life situation. But the opportunity occurred one time when I was leading a group of American tourists on my annual pilgrimage to Ireland.

As well as performing full-time for a living, I also take tour groups to Ireland a couple of times a year to expose them to Irish culture, music, history, geography, Guinness, and of course, the people. Well, a few years back, we were in Galway for a couple of days, staying at the Imperial Hotel, right in Eyre Square, in the heart of the city. Great hotel and great craic altogether. We had just finished dinner in the hotel dining room, and I had made plans to take the group to one of the many singing pubs nearby, where I would sit in with the local musicians and play a few songs and tunes.

With my guitar over my shoulder, I was standing outside the front door of the hotel with a young fella from my group by the name of Jerome Murphy. Jerome was from Pittston, PA, it was his first time in Ireland, and like most Yanks of Irish heritage, he was having a blast.

We were chatting about this and that, waiting for the rest of the crew to join us so we could wend our merry way to the pub du jour, when a pigeon flew overhead and dropped a full load, which landed with a damp 'splat!' on Jerome's shoulder.

We looked at each other helplessly, and Jerome started feeling around in his trouser pockets for a handkerchief with which to remove the offending bomblet.

None was to hand.

He said to me, "Seamus, do you have a tissue on you?"

I pointed to the pigeon vanishing in the evening sky and replied, "Jerome, for heaven's sake, he's miles away by now."

⊗⊘

The Elf and the Talk Show Host

Dennis O'Rourke

Leo and I were working a restaurant out in the hinterlands. They asked us to promote the club and our show by appearing on a local TV program. The host was a tall, brassy, genial woman in her forties. We chatted a bit before the taping. She was wearing white pants and a white sweater. Below her waist, riding around her hips, was a low-slung silver belt which came together just above her nether region in the form of two hands joined.

"That's quite a belt you've got there," I said.

"Do you like it?" she said. "There's a little elf standing behind me."

"Well, if that's where his hands are, where is his nose?"

She cocked her head and smiled in such a way that I realized I had come perilously close to the abyss of bad taste. But she was a pro; she let it slide, and the taping went well. She asked a few good questions, and we did a couple of songs. When it was over, she shook our hands and strode from the set.

Leo observed that my remark might best have been kept to myself.

"Well, at least I had the good sense not to ask her the other question that occurred to me."

"And that was?"

"I was going to ask what happened to the elf when she sat down."

AUDIENCES

Viva Las Vegas

Seamus Kennedy

I think every performer, whether folk musician, jazz, rock, country, big band, or classical, would love to play Las Vegas at least once in his lifetime, just to say he'd done it.

Well, I did it.

In August 1999, my agent called to notify me that she had secured a week's booking in Wooloughan's Irish Pub in the resort at Summerlin, Las Vegas' newest luxury hotel, casino, and resort.

Las Vegas! Frank Sinatra, Dean Martin, Sammy Davis Jr., Peter Lawford, Joey Bishop. The Rat Pack! Count Basie, Elvis, Bob Hope, Bing Crosby, Johnny Carson, Kenny Rogers, Rich Little, John Denver. Legends, all. The greatest names in American showbiz had all played there. As well as Brendan Bowyer and the Big Eight Showband. From Ireland.

The money was right—travel expenses, food, accommodations were taken care of, and I was comped two rounds of golf at the resort's eighteen-hole championship course. I had never been to Las Vegas, never mind perform there, but I'll be honest—it was the complimentary rounds of golf that decided it for me.

A precedent had been already set—the great Brendan Bowyer, front man and lead singer for Ireland's top show band in the 1960s—the Royal Showband from Waterford—had been a staple at the old Stardust Hotel for many years with his outfit, the Big Eight. Brendan Bowyer, who had soared to number one on the Irish hit parade on many occasions with songs like "I Ran All the Way Home" and "The Hucklebuck," had persuaded the best musicians from other bands to leave the security of their jobs in Ireland and take a flier with him on being the headliners at a Las Vegas strip hotel and casino. And they had succeeded.

The fabulous Brendan Bowyer, who with the Royal Showband had sold out every dancehall in Ireland for God knows how many years and broken a lot of hearts when he decided to go for the gold and relocate to Glitter Gulch, USA. He also broke a lot of girls' hearts.

But as an Irish performer of note, he had paved the way for—me.

Yes, like Lenny Bruce, who had paved the way for all the comedians who wanted to say "fuck" in their acts, but didn't want to go to jail for doing so, Brendan Bowyer had done it so that I could. Sort of.

I landed at McCarran International Airport, and a Summerlin Resort air-conditioned limo was waiting to bring guitar, my golf clubs, suitcase, and me to the hotel. Good start.

At check-in, a pleasant and efficient assistant gave me the key to my room on the eighth floor. A most helpful bellhop brought my bags up to the room, opened the door, and ushered me inside. I tipped him, and I suspect I may have been slightly overgenerous because he dropped to his knees and licked my shoes, all the while intoning, "God bless you, sir. Thank you! Thank you! Anything else you require—anything—just call the front desk and ask for Mike! Got that, sir? Mike."

Then I looked around. My God, but this room was huge—and luxurious! It must have taken me fifteen minutes to walk from the door to the window. What a view. A panoramic vista of the Las Vegas skyline and the surrounding desert set against a cloudless, azure sky. And down there was the golf course—lush velvet fairways with little ovals and kidneys of white sand surrounding the green baize putting surfaces. Alongside the fairways, tall palm trees nodded their heads in approval.

A cherry wood king-sized bed with the most comfortable mattress I have ever bounced on. A matching cherry wood entertainment console with a 42" television, 190 cable channels, and a top-notch stereo radio/CD player with concealed speakers. There was a mini-bar with every conceivable primo drink from Sapphire gin and Stolichnaya vodka (plain and flavored) to Lagavulin single-malt Scotch and Bushmills Black Label. There were mixers, like sweet and dry Vermouth, and Angostura bitters, with jars of olives and maraschino cherries. All in miniatures! Yes! Someone was going to have dry martinis and Manhattans this week!

As I waited for the front desk to call and apologize for giving me the wrong room—that I was really supposed to be in broom storage in the basement with the janitor—I hung my clothes in the closet, which was as big as my bedroom at home. They looked really pathetic in one corner of that cavernous wardrobe, so I spread them out all over the place to make it look full. A shirt here, a pair of pants there; a tie here, another tie over there. I even put my socks and underwear on hangers to make the closet look like there was something in it—one sock per hanger.

Then I set out my shaving gear in the bathroom. The bathroom! It was like the shah of Persia's bathroom. Gold-plated fixtures everywhere. The sink faucets, (Sinks? There were four of them) the showerhead and stopper, the door handles, the heated towel racks, the toilet handle—all gold plated. Where the hell were a screwdriver and a wrench when I needed them? Hanging on the back of the door was a terry-cloth bathrobe—a thick, fluffy, warm, terry-cloth bathrobe; and the towels were equally thick, fluffy, and warm. I could already see that when it was time to leave, I was going to have great difficulty getting my suitcase closed.

Making my way down to the lounge where I'd be performing, I felt the first signs of sensory overload. Walking through the casino, my head reverberated with the sound of slot machines being force-fed quarters and regurgitating them occasionally. The flashing lights and ringing bells from thousands of one-armed bandits mingled with the music from the PA system to numb my senses. People cheering, shouting when someone hit a jackpot or a big hand in blackjack, added to the soaring crescendo. Madness! Why someone would sit for hours in front of a machine pumping coins into it in the hopes of a financial windfall when the mathematical odds were astronomically against them is beyond my ken. I don't know who said it, but it's true: Gambling is a tax on those who are bad at math. Well, the damned gelt-gulping automatons were getting none of my money—I can tell you that!

The lounge where I would perform was just outside the casino and off the main lobby of the hotel. It was very well appointed, and they'd obviously gone to a great deal of expense and trouble to create the appearance of an authentic Irish pub with its dark wood, faux thatching, and whitewashed interior walls.

No, seriously, it was very nicely done. But in a real Irish pub, the clientele was unlikely to be drinking very dry Stoli martinis, Manhattans, cosmopolitans, or Singapore slings. Nor would they be smoking Louisville slugger-sized Havana cigars. A pint of plain and twenty Afton would be more like it.

This place was an upscale Yuppie, cell-phone toting, nouveau-riche breeding-pit where the "elite meet to greet and eat" as they used to say in Duffy's tavern. It was a meat-market, where twenty-somethings with more money than sense came to scope out a possible brood-mare or stud. Hundred dollar bills flew 'round the place like confetti. The Chieftains and Van Morrison were blasting from the house PA system, which was one of the very best I'd ever seen. Top of the line speakers in every available nook and cranny, and there were plenty of crannies in this place.

The sound guys, Phil and Bill, came to meet me. Now was as good a time as any to set me up. They had a table and soundboard in a cranny near the stage, where my mic and direct box for my guitar were located. The stage had a four-foot-high rail around it with a bar on which customers could place their drinks, and there were nine or ten stools at this little bar. Good. I'd have an audience to work my up-close-and-personal magic on.

"Mr. Kennedy, we'll be doing sound for you tonight. Anything you need in the way of sound, we've got it. We'll set you up now, and Phil will run the board for you tonight," said Bill, or was it Phil. I did a quick one-two, one-two, and strummed a couple of chords on the guitar. It sounded fine to me.

"Okay, then, Phil," says I. "I'll see you at nine tonight." Or was it Bill?

Then I went back upstairs to perform my ablutions and change into the work duds. I had decided a nice leisurely dinner with a cocktail and a glass of wine at about six o'clock would be in order. So at ten past six, I was abluted, in full performance raiment and seated in one of the aforementioned crannies. I had a dry Tanqueray martini up with two olives as an aperitif, followed by a splendid filet mignon (medium-rare), garlic mashed potatoes with a side of asparagus, and a glass of very pleasant, but somewhat non-committal Pinot Grigio.

What? I hear you exclaim. White wine with red meat? Look, this is my story, so I can drink what I want with filet mignon.

Now I was ready for a stroll around the casino before taking the stage.

I was amazed at the number of people sitting mindlessly feeding coins into the slot machines. They all had the same glazed-over look, the automatic, almost reflexive motions—insert quarter, reach up, pull lever, repeat, ad nauseam or infinitum, whichever comes first. The only relief from the tedium of these actions was a pause to stub out a cigarette or light another one, or perhaps take a drink from an unending supply brought around by the omnipresent waitresses.

Okay, time to go to work.

Once on stage, it's all business with me. This is my workplace, and I'm about to start my job. I plugged the guitar in and gave Phil the nod. He turned down the stereo, turned up my mic, and I was off to the races.

I noticed, to my consternation, that the stage-rail bar was empty. There was no one upon whom to work my legendary up-close-and-personal magic. No matter, I'll get stuck in, and the crowd on the floor will join in. My usual starter, "Whiskey in the Jar" with the participatory clapping. Wait, something was amiss. No one was paying attention. No one was clapping. They were all congregated round the main bar, lashing cocktails into them and firing up stogies, and no one was paying a damn bit of heed to me. Maybe a few jokes would rope them in—a couple of sure-fire crowd pleasers:

O'Brien knocks on Murphy's door. "Murphy, are you coming down to the pub for a couple of pints?"

"I can't," says Murphy. "I've just started this jigsaw puzzle of a rooster. I wanna work on it."

O'Brien goes away on his own, but the next night he's back knocking on Murphy's door.

"Are you coming to the pub for a couple of pints?"

"No I'm still working on this jigsaw puzzle of a rooster."

The following night the same thing. "Murphy, are you coming down to the pub?"

"No." Murphy says, "I haven't finished this jigsaw of a rooster yet."

O'Brien walks into the house, looks down at the table and says, "Murphy, will you, for God's sake, put the Corn Flakes back in the box and come down to the pub with me!"

Nada. I was working to their backs. Their fronts were otherwise engaged in a schmooze-fest at the bar.

"What's the leading cause of death among lesbians? Hairballs!"

Nothing. I was performing for crickets, like in the old Bugs Bunny/Daffy Duck cartoon. I was dying a slow and ignominious death.

I tried fast songs, slow songs, funny songs, Irish songs, country songs. I just couldn't get their attention. I tried insulting them, but you can't insult people if they're not listening to you. Or as the old Irish Zen show biz paradox has it: "When an insult lands in a crowd of people, and they're not listening, does anyone care?" This has happened once or twice before in my thirty-three years of professional entertaining, and there's really nothing to do except play for myself and hope that somebody will hear something they like and start listening. So I began to do a few old, obscure Irish ballads I haven't sung in a long time, eyeballing the audience to see if anybody's noticing. Nope.

Near the end of the set, a drunk wobbled in and sat at the bar at the stage rail. He had a giant concoction in a martini glass and was waving a huge cigar around.

Great! I thought. Just what I need. A goddamn inebriated asshole in front of me waving cigar smoke in my face. Did Frank and Dean go through this? Did Sammy or Bing? Or Brendan Bowyer?

He was a tad unsteady on the stool and slurping the drink like a dog drinking from his bowl. Well, I thought to myself, he's a customer, and I owe it to him to try to entertain him. So I figured I'd try "The Irish Rover."

"Here's an up-tempo little Irish ditty about a ship that came over from Ireland many years ago with a most unusual cargo. If you feel like clapping along, join right in!"

In the year of Our Lord eighteen hundred and six,
We set sail from the coal quay of Cork,
We were sailing away with a cargo of bricks
For the grand City Hall in New York...

The guy stared at me through bleary eyes, weaved around on his stool, puffed his cigar, and took another huge gulp of his drink. No one else in the place was listening as I worked my way through the song.

I was into the last verse:

We had sailed seven years when the measles broke out,
And our ship lost her way in the fog.
And the whale of the crew was reduced down to two,
Just myself and the captain's oul' dog...

When the drunk suddenly made eye contact with me and said loudly, "Hey, buddy. Do you do any Sinatra?"

Well, I was so delighted to get a reaction, any reaction, that I began to nod my head madly in the affirmative, all the while continuing to sing the Irish Rover. I kept nodding and looking at him the whole time, for fear I'd lose the only audience I had.

Then the ship struck a rock (NOD, NOD)
Lord, what a shock (NOD,NOD)
And *nearly tumbled over* (NOD, NOD)
Turned nine times around (NOD, NOD, shit, I'd better go right into a Sinatra song, or I'll lose him)
And the poor old dog was drowned (NOD, NOD, Oh, God, which Sinatra song?)
*I'm the last of the Irish Rover*s
When somebody loves you,
It's no good unless he loves you all the way...

I went straight into "All the Way," with no stop between the songs, and I got him!

He sat enthralled through Sinatra's classic from his movie *The Joker's Wild*, and when I finished, he gave me a really enthusiastic round of applause.

"Thank you, very much, sir," I said, and he turned around to go back into the casino. He had gone only a few steps, when he stopped, turned back to me, and left a one hundred dollar bill on the stage bar.

"No. Thank you very much," he said, and walked out.

Finally, the week was over, and I was at the airport to fly home. There are slot machines everywhere in Las Vegas, even in the airport. I had checked all my luggage and was waiting at the gate to board my plane when I felt a couple of coins jingle in my pocket. I pulled out two quarters. What the hell, I didn't gamble the whole time I was at the casino, so I'd throw a couple of quarters into a slot machine. Just to say I'd done it. I put the first one in, pulled the handle, and watched the cherries and sevens roll by. Nothing. I put the second one in and pulled the handle. All of a sudden, bells and lights go off! Three cherries had lined up. I had won forty dollars. For the first time in my life, I had gambled and won!

Forty bucks! All in quarters.

Now, there's a lady with a money-cart who goes through the terminal changing coins into bills and vice versa, but she was way down the far end of the terminal, tending to some other winner's needs. And my flight was now boarding. No time to run down to the other end to have my winnings—my 160 quarters—changed into bills. I had to get on the plane. So I filled my pockets until they resembled Pony Express saddlebags and waddled my way on to the aircraft and home.

Thank you, Brendan Bowyer.

ఌ౪ఌ

STRAY CHAT/FRANK

DOR: With all of the material you do onstage—the songs, poems, the recitations—you're like a vaudeville act. Do you think you were born a hundred years too late?

FE: Oh, absolutely. Well, if not a hundred years too late, maybe twenty. I find I have more in common with a different generation than this one.

DOR: I've seen you perform in front of two people and two hundred. The size of the audience doesn't seem to matter—you are as intense with the two as the two hundred.

FE: Oh, I'm to respond to that?

DOR: Yes, please.

FE: Well, I figure they paid their buck, they deserve a show, and it doesn't matter if there's two hundred people or two. They paid to be entertained, and I'm gonna try to entertain them. That's all.

DOR: Where do you get the energy for that?

FE: Alcohol.

ఌ౪ఌ

Oh, Sister Josephine

Robbie O'Connell

I have found over the years that a well-chosen, spoken introduction can make or break a song. Certain songs, in particular the humorous ones, need to be set up properly, or the audience is likely to miss the point. It's as if they need to be told ahead of time that you expect them to laugh; they respond much better when prepped.

I started singing Jake Thackray's hilarious song "Sister Josephine," back in the 1970s, but it took me years to fine-tune the set-up so that the song did not misfire. It tells the story of a terrorist who, disguised as a nun, joins a convent to hide from the authorities. The humor lies in the ensuing havoc he creates among the nuns. Even though it was written about an event that took place in England, I found that if I set it in Ireland, it took on a whole new meaning because of the "Troubles." It is still one of the most requested songs in my repertoire, but performing it has, more than once, landed me in trouble.

Years ago, before I figured out the introduction, I sang "Sister Josephine" at the Black Rose, an Irish pub in downtown Boston. After a couple of verses, a hubbub erupted in the back of the room. I could not see what was going on, but the next thing I knew, some demented lady was charging the stage, swinging a large set of rosary beads and screaming that I was an evil blasphemer. I was sure it was a joke at first, but I gradually realized that she must have misunderstood the song and was really out to get me. I didn't know what to do. I just kept on singing and hoped the bar staff would intervene. She continued haranguing me from the front of the stage, insisting I should be ashamed to call myself Irish and that the raging fires of Hell would be too good for me. I was dumbfounded. It was the first time I'd ever been threatened by someone brandishing rosary beads, even though I had been taught by the Irish Christian Brothers, well-known masters of weapon improvisation. Luckily, there was a Bible nearby, and I hit her with it. Just kidding. The doorman quickly came to my rescue, and I survived the attack. I took a quick break and gulped down a pint of Guinness to calm my nerves. However, I couldn't help but wonder if "death by rosary beads" would have guaranteed me instant entry into Heaven.

On another occasion, I was booked for a concert at a township on the Jersey Shore that was heavily religious. The day before the show, I got an urgent message from the agent who had booked the show saying that the organizers of the event wanted me to sign an agreement stating that I would not sing "that song about the pregnant nun." Since I had never even heard a song about a pregnant nun, I refused to sign anything. But I knew damn well that they must have meant "Sister Josephine," even though there is no mention of pregnancy anywhere in it. On the night of the concert, I was sorely tempted to perform it, anyway. But fearing another attack by a misguided member of the audience wielding a heavy crucifix or some other religious paraphernalia, I chickened out.

The strange thing about "Sister Josephine" is that nuns themselves generally love it. I have frequently met women after a show that make a point of telling me they are nuns and loved the song. Although I must admit, this is sometimes accompanied by that "you naughty, naughty boy" look.

I used to play an annual concert in the Barn at the University of California in Riverside with Mick Moloney and Jimmy Keane. It was one of our favorite venues, with a very mixed audience, mostly from the locality. Prior to one show, just as we were about to go onstage, a middle-aged lady approached me.

"Are you going to sing 'Sister Josephine'? she inquired. Not sure whether she wanted me to say yes or no, I hedged and said we hadn't finalized the set list yet, so I wasn't sure.

"Oh, please sing it," she pleaded. "I'm a nun, and we heard you sing it here last year. We brought seventeen nuns along tonight just to hear that song, and one of them, our reverend mother, is a Sister Josephine. We also have five priests with us."

Despite the image in my head of being wrestled to the floor by a swat team of nuns, I agreed to sing it. They were dressed in ordinary clothes, but this being a community audience—everyone recognized them. Before I even finished the first line, the whole place erupted in laughter. They were rolling in the aisles at every verse and there was a thunderous ovation when I finished. The song had never gone over so well before. I thought I was set for life. I could see myself traveling around the country in a luxurious tour bus, doing the convent circuit and raking in a fortune.

When we returned the following year, I expected to find the place packed with nuns. I thought they would be lining up around the block. But, curiously, there wasn't a single nun or priest in attendance. I asked the organizer of the concert if there had been any negative feedback from the previous year, but she was unaware of any. I never did find out what happened. It is still a mystery. I can only conclude that the reverend mother, Sister Josephine, just like Queen Victoria, was "not amused."

ॐ

Bawdy in New Hampshire

Dennis O'Rourke

I was driven out of one pub by a clique of regulars. There was a chain hotel in Nashua, New Hampshire, and inside the lobby, they had built an imitation Irish cottage/bar complete with an imitation thatch roof. It was brand spanking new and kitschy in the way of the many other faux Irish pubs to follow. And, of course, there wasn't a stage or lights. But the money was good, and they put me up in the hotel. I could walk to work.

I played there a few times over a period of months and did well. My schedule had me away from the place for a while, and I was looking forward to returning. The gig began on a Wednesday night. There were a couple of young women in the audience who requested material I knew was vulgar, and vulgar material does not so much offend me as it bores me. I have only one risqué song in the repertoire, "Seven Drunken Nights," and I sang it for them. It wasn't enough. They wanted more. Miffed, they ignored me for the remainder of the night. I asked one of the staff what was up. Turns out a couple of entertainers who specialized in that kind of material had been in during my hiatus, and they had developed a following. (This was in the early eighties, when raw comedians and "shock jocks" had begun to emerge.) I knew one of these guys very well. He was a real character and a friend of mine. He had a regular gig at Liam's, and I frequently went to see him. No question—he could be outrageous; i.e., if he deemed it safe, given the tenor and size of the crowd, he would ask them if they had ever seen an Irish mushroom. He'd be sitting on a stool with the guitar across his lap. He'd pull the guitar away, and there would be a little, red, fleshy head sticking out over the top of his pants. It was his mickey.

On Thursday, the women were back with seven or eight friends. One of them had a shrieking laugh like a harpy. I groaned inwardly. It wasn't long before two of them approached me, again requesting this material. I tried to kid them out of it, but they were adamant. They dropped the names of the entertainers who played all this bawdy, raunchy stuff, and they demanded to know why I couldn't do the same.

"Well," say I, "It's not what I do. They do what they do, and I— Look. Why don't you let me do *my* show? You might enjoy it."

They turned their backs and walked away. I spent my breaks in the hotel room. On Friday night, there was a mob of them, some twenty people, loud and obnoxious. They sat right in front of me. The requests came up during the first set. I confessed to not knowing the songs. They grew more raucous. On my first break, I stood at the end of the bar. They sang the songs themselves, the harpy's voice like an ice pick in my ear. On my second break, I went to my hotel room and watched TV for twenty minutes. They ignored everything I did in the third set. I went to the room again on my last break. When I returned, I was stunned to find that they had turned their chairs around and put their backs to me. They were standing up, shouting and laughing at each other, pointedly ignoring me. It was a general uproar meant to provoke me. I bit the bullet. I said nothing. I just sang, and when the last set was over, I went to the bar and had several drinks before bed.

On Saturday night, the place was nearly empty—just a few couples and an occasional hotel resident wandering in and out. The bar staff felt sorry for me. I felt sorry for them. They weren't going to make any money that night. The regulars had made their statement. I was heartsick. I couldn't even bring myself to stay in the hotel that night. I got my check, packed my bags and equipment, and drove home. I never worked there again, and I still refuse to do that material.

CRBO

STRAY CHAT/SEAMUS

DOR: How about the audiences? There was respectful attention at the beginning.

SK: Yes, there was.

DOR: And now there's something entirely different.

SK: Well, I put that down to the television generation. TV has a lot to answer for. Some people go out and think they're in their own living room, and they think they can get up, go to the fridge, get something, come back, sit down, fart, scratch, belch, and start talking on the phone. They'll just walk across the front of who-ever's watching the performer. In your own house, you do that all the time, but not in public. There's a distinct lack of manners and graces among young people. They'll turn around and yell across rows of tables to one another.

DOR: How does that behavior affect your concentration?

SK: Well, because I've been doing it for such a long time, it really doesn't affect *my* concentration. I can still concentrate on a song. But, what I will see is one person, or a couple of people, annoying others who are trying to listen to me—that's when I intervene. Normally, if the whole audience is noisy, it doesn't bother me a bit. But if you've got a pocket of people who are trying to listen and pay attention, and you've got one idiot distracting them, that bothers me, and I will tear into the person making the noise, because I want these other people to hear me. And I usually say, "Hello. Excuse me. Hold on. I'm not background music. I am not a jukebox, you know. I do require a smidgen of attention from my audience. These people over here are trying to listen to me, and you are making it difficult for them." It can get nasty sometimes. But, you know, if it's just friendly heckling? No big deal.

છ૪૦

Conversation

Harry O'Donoghue

It had been a long night. I felt I had given a good performance, and judging by my product sales, the audience was in agreement. There were very few left in the room, and I was putting my guitar away when a couple approached me. He was tall, mid-fifties, and in decent shape, apart from the beer belly. She was several inches shorter and carrying a little more weight than she probably did in her prime. Income between one hundred and one hundred fifty thousand, I guestimated, and dressed accordingly.

He: "Great show."
She: "Wonderful, really wonderful. We had a wonderful time. You were wonderful."
Me: "T'anks."
He: "This is our first time to an Irish bar. We didn't know what to expect. It was great. Made our vacation."
She: "Oh, gosh, yes, this was wonderful. And we love Ireland. It's our dream to go someday, and maybe we will."
Me: "Yeah, you'd love it."
She: "We've read all about it. My Gawd, we even have relatives there."
Me: "Really? What part?"

She: "Cork County and Gallaway (sic), I think. I'm not sure. It was my great-grandfather who came to America—Pennsylvania in the eighteen hundreds."

He: "We're doing research to find out more."

Me: "Very nice."

She: "I just love the way you talk. It's soooo cute, that funny little accent. Say something—go on. I just love it."

He: "Don't embarrass the man. How did you come to Savannah?"

Me: "I drove."

She: "Oh, go on. You Irish with your funny little wit. So quaint."

Me: "Seriously, I lived in Philadelphia for about four years and I—"

She: "Philadelphia, Gawd. We live about an hour's drive west."

Me: "Small world."

She: "But why did you come here? Ireland is supposed to be beautiful. Why would you leave?"

Me: "Lots of reasons. Back in the late seventies, early eighties, things were—"

She: "It's beautiful and green. Everything is green, green, green. Why is it so green?"

Me: "Rains a lot."

She: "Oh, you Irish."

Me: "Anyway, in the eighties—"

He: "Plenty of Irish here in America, what with that famine thing and all."

Me: "There's millions claim Irish descent, but the Irish were coming to these shores long before the Great Hunger."

She: "Really?"

Me: "They came by road before the flood." (I borrowed that line from Danny Doyle.)

He: "That's very interesting."

Me: "Isn't it, though?"

He: "How long have you been here?"

Me: "Twenty-one years."

She: "Gawd. Will you ever go back?"

He: "To stay?"

Me: "Hard to say at this point. My family is—"

She: "Oh, look, Frank. He has CDs and tapes. Are these for sale?"

Me: "Uh, yes, they would be."

He: "How many do you have?"

Me: "Five. Two recorded live, two studio albums with original material, and a Christmas one with two of my colleagues."

She: "What's the difference?"

Me: "Different songs."

She: "Is this you?"

Me: "No, it's my younger brother. We couldn't find a good picture of me."

He: "Are they any good?"

Me: "No."

She: "Oh, there he goes again. So funny. You just crack me up."

He: "I see you have t-shirts and baseball caps with the same logo as the one on this CD. What is it?"

Me: "My logo."

He: "What does it mean?"

Me: "It's just some Celtic artwork I had done some time ago. I've been using it for about six years."

She: "It's very nice."

Me: "T'anks."

She: "Frank, we could get a hat for Tommy, a t-shirt for Jen, and a tape for us. We don't have a CD player, yet."

He: "That sounds fine. What's this?"

Me: "A copy of my newsletter and performance schedule with my website address and contact numbers."

He: "Absolutely fantastic. You have a website, as well. That's great. We have a computer, but we don't know how to use it, so we leave it for the kids."

Me: "No shit." (Okay, so I only thought that.)

She: "What do you think, Frank?"

He: "Will you be here tomorrow night?"

Me: "Yep."

He: "We'll come back for dinner and the show and get all the stuff then."

She: "Oh, yes, that's sounds wonderful, wonderful."

Me: "All the best."

And I watched them exit the pub and my life.

Cß80

Rocky Tops and Hairy Butts

Frank Emerson

In the heart of Five Points, which is in the heart of Columbia, South Carolina, sits Delaney's Music Pub and Eatery. That is what it says on a big sign over the double glass door. Under the name, on the same sign, is the proclamation: "Irish with an attitude." This phrase might seem redundant, particularly if you have ever run into guys from Hell's Kitchen in New York who have had a few pops. However, as you walk in this joint, you will receive a large "Hello" or "Hiya guys" from the bartenders. It is one of their duties to keep an eye peeled for fresh fish—that is to say, customers—and to welcome them warmly. So it would seem that the attitude mentioned on the sign is a pleasant one. Go figure.

Just inside the door, hung so you could not miss it was another sign, which enumerated the three, rules of the establishment. Recently, the sign was removed, as it was deemed no longer necessary. The rules remain however. They are as follows:

1.   Don't mess with the bald guys
2.   Have a good time, but behave yourself
3.   See rule number one

This bears explaining.

Delaney's is owned by two fellows, neither of whom is named Delaney. Maybe it's a family name, or maybe they just found it somewhere. It doesn't matter. They liked it. They used it. In fact, their names are Jeff Whitt and Joe Wilson, and they are bald. By choice. These are the bald guys mentioned in the rules. There might seem to be an implied warning in the rules. There is. It is revealed by the fact that Joe Wilson is more commonly known as "House" and Jeff is even bigger. In all honesty, however, the name "House" is a bit of an exaggeration. In reality, Joe is only about the size of a decent tool shed. Jeff—a one-car garage. To top everything off, they both sport well-trimmed moustaches and goatees. If you remember Anton LaVey, the founder of the Church of Satan, that is what they look like—only larger and in double. The interesting thing is that these fellows are two of the nicest guys you would ever want to meet—friendly, love to laugh, like music. But as the sign says: don't mess with the bald guys, if you are smart.

Now, Columbia is an armed forces town. The Army post, Fort Jackson, is located just out on the other side of the Interstate. Columbia is also a college town. The University of South Carolina is located right there, downtown. Five Points is a mustering place for soldiers and a whole lot of students. Although sometimes these two factions can be at odds, what brings them together are USC sports. Particularly football. The fans of USC Gamecocks are second to none in their enthusiasm and devotion. I like to think that this is because Lou Holtz, formerly of Notre Dame, is the head coach, but that's probably just me showing my parochialism. It is a fact that every bar in Five Points has a television on which athletic events are shown. Delaney's has four of them—two are normal living room-sized ones. The other two are the size of a drive-in theater screen. As a matter of fact, I think that's where they got them.

This whole story takes place on an autumn Saturday night. South Carolina is to face Tennessee at Tennessee in a late-starting game. It's going to be carried on local television. All the bars are packed with Gamecock nuts. This includes Delaney's Music Pub and Eatery.

I show up for my usual pre-show cocktail at about 8:00. The music is to start at 8:30. The place is packed to the gunwales with people in various states of intoxication. All eyes are riveted to the TV screens, where the Gamecocks and the Volunteers are having at it. Under the crowd's scrutiny, I put my guitar on stage and make my way to the bar.

Jeff comes out of the kitchen, where he is stationed tonight to handle the large volume of food. He greets me warmly.

"How are you, Frank? I guess you can see what's going on here."

"I'm fine, thanks, Jeff. And I sure can see what is going on here."

"Well, look, don't bother to start until after the game is over. It would be useless and probably dangerous. Particularly if we were to turn off the television."

"No problem," I said. "No problem at all."

"Good, then. Have a drink. Enjoy the game." Then he mops his forehead and goes back to do battle in front of the broiler and deep-fry machine.

I pass the next ninety minutes or so watching the game, having a couple of drinks, and jawing with the bartenders.

Eventually, the game winds down. Dark day in old Five Points, the boys from South Carolina are coming in second in a two-team event.

I'm getting myself set to go on stage—trying to figure out how I should open. Should I hit them with a big, strong come-all-ye? Should I do a lilting waltz? Should I do a rebel song? As I'm studying this problem, House approaches me. He is one of the bartenders on duty tonight. He twists open the cap on an airline-type nip bottle of very new Scotch and pours the contents into a rocks glass. He slides it over to me.

"Getting to be about that time, eh?" He has a peculiar look in his eye—mischievous, whimsical, even impish.

"Just about," I answered. "I think I'll give them five. Let them hit the bathroom and get settled in before I start."

"That's a good idea," says House.

"Yeah. It's too bad SC lost. It sure would be easier to face these people if they were happy."

"Yeah," he says. He is still smiling that odd half-smile. "I'll tell you one thing. You don't have a hair on your butt if you don't open with 'Rocky Top.'"

What this means in normal English is that I would be less than a man—a sissy Mary—if I do not start my show with the University of Tennessee fight song. The same University of Tennessee, which has just finished beating up the University of South Carolina. There are about 250 University of South Carolina fans right in front of the stage. They are angry and upset at the loss. They are also more than a little drunk. What House has come up with is a dare. Now I understand what the smile was all about.

I sip on my drink and nod to House. "Not a hair on my butt, huh?"

"Not a one," says House.

I sip on my drink again. "You know this could be a bit dangerous, don't you?"

"Of course, it could." He leans toward me. "No guts—no glory." House is a regular font of folk sayings tonight. None of which bode well for me.

"Let me have a top off on this drink." I turn and wend my way through the audience and up to the stage. I climb up and strap on my guitar. I turn on the sound system and the stage lights. I check my tuning. The crowd is oblivious to me. They are still wallowing in the heartbreak of gridiron defeat. I figure that maybe I have a fighting chance.

With no preamble whatsoever, House kills the television screens, and I slam into an introduction to this upbeat, bluegrass song that serves as Tennessee's fight song. Four bars later, I close my eyes, throw my head back, and start to wail:

"Wish that I was on old Rocky Top,
High in the Tennessee hills.
Ain't no smoggy smoke on Rocky Top
Ain't no telephone bills."

The song is sheer poetry. (Written by Felice and Boudleaux Bryant.) I am doing it okay. Sounding not bad at all. I can hear myself real well. Then I realize that the reason I can hear myself so well is that the crowd is not making a sound. I mean dead silence. I figure I'd best open my eyes and check them out.

People are frozen. They are stock still. All heads are turned toward me, staring, mouths agape. There is fire—real fire—and a hunger in their eyes. Now I know how the little lamb felt when he wandered into the local abattoir. I'm thinking that maybe this is not a good idea after all. Nobody says a word.

I stammer and try to make a joke out of it. "Oops—wrong song," I chuckle. "Heh, heh. My error. Let me start again."

Collectively, as if it was timed, the audience finds its voice. With a roar like a tsunami, I am hit with a chorus of people shouting "Boo!" in 250-part harmony. The force of the thing throws me backward from the microphone. I look to my right. Jeff has popped out of the kitchen, no doubt wondering, "What the hell was that?" He shoots a look to where House is stationed behind the bar. I do the same.

House is nowhere to be seen. Suddenly two hands appear over the back edge of the bar. Slowly, up comes House. He is as red as a lobster, shaking with laughter and nodding at me like a bobble-head doll. He is enjoying this whole scene like I don't know what. He starts applauding me and then rolls his hands round and round, like saying, "Keep going."

I do some quick thinking. What I should do is go into the South Carolina fight song to try to fix this situation, but I don't know the damned thing. I'm not sure anyone does. I vaguely recall hearing that it is set to the tune of "Hey Look Me Over" from the Broadway show, *Wildcat*, but this is no help.

In desperation, I start into "Nothing Could Be Finer Than To Be in Carolina." This does not work. They are still booing. It turns out that that song is about North Carolina, anyway, so it is no surprise that they are not pleased. I think and think. I take my last shot. I try to fake Neil Diamond's "Sweet Caroline." Well, Bingo! I don't know all the lyrics, but neither do they, except for the "Bum, bum, bum," which is in every chorus. They love it and shout it out each time it comes around, which it does a lot, since they have me keep playing it. I'm more than happy to do this since it means we now have a nice symbiotic thing going here. I'm making up lyrics left and right. Sometimes they rhyme, sometimes they don't. It doesn't matter, just as long as the "bum, bum, bum" keeps showing up. It keeps 'em happy.

This went on for a good while, and I was getting knackered. I'm trying to determine where to go from here when God intervenes. I break a string. Deliverance.

I look suitably disappointed as I announce that I have to take a break to hunt up a new string. I tell them that I will be back directly, and I encourage them to have another drink or two in the meantime.

I head over to the bar, where House, still chuckling and nodding, pours me a double and a Coca-Cola for himself.

I accept the drink and raise my glass. "Well, House, do you think I have a hair on my butt now?"

House raises his glass. "Man, more than that. You're an ape! Cheers."

We clink. We drink.

C*80

The Old Ball Game—a Play in One Act
Seamus Kennedy

Dramatis personae: Seamus Kennedy, an itinerant peddler of Gaelic musical diversions; Bobby O'Halloran, a concoctor and dispenser of liquid refreshments; Jim and Marie Twomey; and Bill and Nancy Doherty, an inebriated married couple; and Joe Siemanski, an aesthete and lover of all Celtic music.

Dramatis tempus: September 2000 AD.

Dramatis locus: A Hibernian hostelry aptly named the Bog Pub, in Scranton, Pennsylvania.

It's the third and last set of a busy Friday night, and Seamus Kennedy is on the small stage in the front window of the pub, performing for a still-enthusiastic, but slightly tipsy audience. The pub is a long, narrow room, with the bar running the length of the wall on the left side. There are about twenty-four occupied barstools, each of which is being capably served by Bobby O'Halloran. Between the barstools and the other wall, there are five tables, with four customers at each table.

In the small space between the stage and the end of the bar, there is one more table, at which are seated Jim Twomey and his wife Marie, and Bill Doherty and his wife Nancy. Just two feet beyond them, on the only stool at the end of the bar, facing the entertainer, sits Joe Siemanski.

Seamus: Thanks very much, folks. That was Dominic Behan's "Patriot Game." A great song. Right, what would you like to hear next?

Bobby: Sing "A Nation Once Again" and "The Parting Glass" so we can close up and go home!

Seamus: Good one, Bobby! Sorry, we have to stay here 'til the death. We're going down together.

Joe: (Holding aloft two of Seamus' CDs) Do "When the Boys Come Rolling Home."

Seamus: You mean that song on my CD "Let the Music Take You Home"? How's that for a subtle plug, folk? This astute gentleman has purchased some of my CDs, and he wants me to sing a song or two from them. Why, bless you, sir, I'd be glad to. (Sings the song, with the audience singing and clapping along.)

Joe: Thanks! Now can you do "A Walk in the Irish Rain"?

Seamus: Sorry, sir. It's one request per customer, and you've already used yours. Just kidding! (Audience laughs) Coming right up, sir. But before I do it, we're coming near the end of the night here in the Bog Pub, and I want to remind you folks to be nice to your bartender and waitress. They've been working very hard to get you into the condition in which you now find yourselves. They've taken care of you, so you take care of them. Okay, here we go. "A Walk in the Irish Rain." (Sings the song.) Applause.

Jim & Marie: Seamus, will you sing "Grandfather's Emigrant Eyes"?

Seamus: What's the magic word?

Marie: Please! Oh, please, pretty please.

Seamus: Well, since you asked so nicely, all right. (Sings the song.) Applause.

Suddenly, a blood-curdling scream rips through the background noise. (It gets everyone's attention.)

Joe: Aaaaaiiiggghheeeaaarrgghh! Let go! Let go!

Bill: (He has a death grip on Joe's testicles and is squeezing and twisting them.) You dirty bastard! You've been farting at my wife!

Joe: (In agony, standing on the rung of his barstool and stretching backwards in a vain attempt to pull free) I wasn't! I wasn't! I swear to God, I wasn't! No! No!

Nancy: Yes, you were, you filthy pig! You were, too—farting right in my face!

Joe: (Still screaming in pain) No, no! I wasn't! I was just sitting here.

Bobby: (Arriving from the other end of the bar.) What the hell's going on here? Stop it! Knock it off, you guys!

Bill: This dirty prick was farting right at my wife!

Nancy: He was! He was sitting right there on that stool farting right at my face.

Joe: (Writhing in torture) I wasn't! I wasn't! Let go of me, you asshole!

Seamus: (Aside to himself) Jeeze, I wish I could aim *mine* with such pinpoint accuracy.

Jim & Marie: (Jumping up and trying to pull Bill's arm away, unfortunately stretching Joe's scrotum, which is still in Bill's vise-like grasp) Let him go, Bill! The guy wasn't doing anything. Stop it! Let him go! Bill! Quit it, now.

Joe: Jesus! Stop pulling his arm away. He's still got hold of my nuts! Aaaaiiieeee!

Bobby: Okay, that's enough. Break it up, or I'm calling the cops.

(Finally, with a Herculean effort of body and mind, Joe wrenches free and turns away, sweating and pale. Panting like a dog in a locked car in July, he collapses on the bar and begins the dry heaves.)

Bill: Come on, you fucker! You want some more? I'll teach you! Fart at my wife, will you, you dirty bastard!

Bobby: Shut up, you! Stop it! Joe, you better get outta here. I'm gonna call the cops for this asshole.

Joe: (Regaining his breath) But I didn't do anything. I swear to God, Bobby, I didn't do anything. I don't know what these two crazy jerks are talking about!

Bill & Nancy: Oh, now we're crazy jerks, are we? Well, we'll show you!

(Bill lunges for Joe once more, but Bobby and Jim jumps between them and restrain Bill.)

Bobby: G'wan, Joe, get the fuck outta here. Come back tomorrow.

Joe: But I didn't do anything, Bobby. Honest to God, I didn't. I was just sitting there, and he grabbed me by the balls.

Bobby: I know, I know. Look, just get outta here now. I'll see you tomorrow.

Joe: Okay, okay. But I really didn't do anything. (Defeated, he leaves the bar.)

Bobby: You two—sit down and be quiet. (Yells at the top of his lungs.) Okay, folks, drink 'em up! Time to go! All right, let's go, people! Closin' time.

(Seamus takes his guitar off and places it on its stand. Then he turns 'round to turn off his amplifier. Throughout the pub, customers start swallowing their drinks and discussing the recent unpleasantness as they prepare to evacuate the premises in accordance with the law. Without warning, the door bursts open, and in rushes Joe. He makes a beeline for the end of the bar where he'd been sitting. Bill and Nancy leap to their feet, startled.)

Bill: Oh, so you're back for more, asshole!

Bobby: Joe! I told you to get outta here. Now!

Joe: (Yells as he dives for the bar) I forgot my CDs!

(He grabs the CDs and runs out as fast as he had come in.)

Seamus: God bless him. There's a man willing to suffer for my art.

Curtain.

CЗ8Ͻ

All The Confidence in the World
Harry O'Donoghue

All the confidence in the world. That's a great old saying, although I don't know anybody who has it. Most people lack confidence in one

398

way or another. I play music for a living, up on the stage, night after night, and it would be easy to think, "This guy has plenty of confidence to be able to stand there and do that. That's not necessarily the case. I think performers are blessed or cursed, depending on your point of view, with an unusual melding of bravado, creativity, a need to be accepted, ego, and a varying amount of confidence and talent. My own confidence level seems to have stabilized, and as I grow older, I find myself becoming more at ease with whom and what I am. I'm now aware that I probably won't set the world on fire, and I'm not likely to be the second Elvis. Know what? That's fine with me. I look at the man in the mirror, and I've come to like him. He's not a bad fellow, really. Of course, this was not always so. In my early years, I lacked conviction. I was a nervous wreck on stage, and like so many entertainers, I hated it when another musician came to see the show. It's widely known that some of those people come to criticize and belittle the band, not enjoy the show. Doesn't happen anymore; I just do what I do, and that's all that I do—take it or leave it. I have a vivid memory, however, of the night a bigwig musician came to see us perform. Way back when I lived in Philadelphia. God, it seems a lifetime ago.

It was a Friday night in February, and we were playing at McSorley's over in Ardmore. We were called Terra Nova at the time, and Trish and I were in the middle of our first set. We'd heard this guy was going to show up, but I kept praying he wouldn't. My performance was off, accordingly. Well, he arrived during our break, and when we took the stage again, my dexterity and powers of vocalization had diminished considerably, and it wasn't going well.

"What's wrong? Aitch, are you okay?"

"I'm fine, just a little nervous."

"A little? You're murderin' the bloody songs!"

"I can't help it with your man down there."

"For Christ's sake, will you wise up? Look, it's Friday night. If your man is so good, why doesn't he have his own fuckin' gig? Now, come on, let's show them what we can do."

Simple as that. Thanks, Trish.

Now, in all fairness, he really was a nice guy, we ended up friends, and to protect the innocent I won't mention his name. Of course, you can get some real pieces of work show up in the audience, as was this next case.

I was working the room at Kevin Barry's on a warm Saturday night. Please allow me to extrapolate. In show biz parlance, working the room basically means "winning over the audience," and it's meant to look easy. The average punter is thinking, "What a way to make a living, work a few hours a day singing, telling jokes and stories, and having a drink or two. Nothing to it." Well there *is* something to it. The audience is not privy to the countless hours of practicing, learning, and writing lyrics, memorizing jokes, stories, and the historic relevance of the material, and most importantly, perfecting the timing—that subtle pacing of a performance which makes it all flow together, which can only be learned by experience, by dying on stage, being a flop—whatever you want to call it. Hard lessons. So the next time you go to a live show and think, "It looks so easy," remember all the effort and hard work involved, and don't be fooled by the great illusion that is showbiz. Now then. I feel much better. Where were we? Oh, yes, I had announced the end of my first set and was giving my standard blurb about my available recordings, when I was interrupted by a chap who shouted, "Do you ever invite people up to sing?" Such was his volume I had no choice but to address the question on the microphone. "Yes, occasionally, if they're good."

"I'm very good."

"Okay, then, we'll sort it out during the break."

I stepped down from the stage as he got up from his table and walked over. He had a Roman nose, an all-American chiseled jaw, James Dean hair, selected strands of which fell down on his forehead like in the movies, and worst of all, he had me by at least six inches. He may even have had a Rolex watch adorning his wrist—the point being, he was, I begrudgingly admit, a fine specimen of manhood.

Anyway, he placed a condescending hand on my shoulder.

"You're okay, man."

"T'anks."

"I used to front a band, and it'd be cool if I could go on and sing one for my lady over there. Her and her friends'n me are out to raise hell in town tonight."

I looked over at the table, and there sat this staggeringly beautiful woman in a black halter-top t-shirt and tan mini-skirt who looked as if she had just walked off the set of a photo shoot at Cosmo magazine. Her long, auburn hair danced across her shoulders as she talked, and she would have been a vision to delight the senses were she not chewing gum in a most unattractive fashion, waving some sort of cigarillo around to help illustrate her conversation. Two words came to mind—trophy babe. The others at the table were hangers-on, happy to bask in the aura of these two beautiful people.

"Tell you what," say I in my thickest Irish accent. "Let me sell some tapes and CDs, have a word with some friends down the back, grab another bottle of water, get back up, do a couple of songs, and introduce you and away you go. Sound all right?"

"Huh?"

"Right enough; see you in a few."

"How's it goin'? For those who weren't here for the first show, good evening."

"Thanks. That was one of my own songs (had to get at least one original number in before I introduced this guy, just to let him know I was a serious musician myself. Who was I trying to convince?), and now, please welcome on stage—"

Strange to note that on my list of Things to Remember in Life, this guy's name doesn't show up, so not to spoil a good story let's just call him *Le Peacock*, and I assure you, if you saw this pompous clown, you'd agree the title fits quite well.

Up he steps on the stage, waves his hand like some foreign royal, and adjusts the microphone height to suit.

"Great, great; thanks, folks. Say, this guy's doing a fairly good job. Let's hear it for Mr. Donock here."

I purse my lips into what I hope is perceived as a smile. "Thanks, man." (Translation: "Fuck you, man.")

"Say, can I borrow the guitar?"

"Sure."

He took my guitar and held it by the neck—the neck, for God's sake, and let it hang down by his side. How dumb can you be—a precision stringed instrument, expensive, as well, and here's this clown (did I call him that before?) looking like he was auditioning for a B-list version of an Elvis movie. I could have choked him right there on the spot.

"I just want to say a few words before I begin."

"Fine," says I. "Let me stand by the door and make sure there's no feedback."

I listened to the first four words out of his mouth then headed up-stairs to have something for my nerves. I didn't need to see the posing and posturing this joker (better description, huh?) was about to get into. I was petrified for the health of my guitar, and if the truth be told, I needed a stiff drink to quench my mounting aggravation. On the way upstairs, I cautioned one of the wait staff, "Jen, keep an eye on your man there and give me a shout if I'm needed."

Now, have I mentioned that I play a left-handed guitar? No? Well, I do, and "does it make a difference?" you ask. Yes, it makes a differ-ence; it makes all the difference. Here's a quick guide:

Basically, there are six strings on the instrument running from high-est or thinnest on the bottom, to lowest or thickest on the top. On a left-handed model, this order is reversed so that the highest and lowest re-main on bottom and top respectively—still with me?

Should a right-handed player attempt to play a leftie guitar, he would find that the high string is on top while the bass or lowest string is down below. This, in effect, means all his chord shapes are wrong, as are all the scales—thus rendering the instrument exceedingly difficult, if not impossible to play. End of guide.

I settled in at the corner of the upstairs bar, and sure enough, only moments had passed when Jen came looking for me. She appeared to be in a panic. I called her over, and she told me I was urgently needed downstairs.

"Be right down, sweetie."

I got a refill and chatted for a few minutes with the bartender.

A few minutes can seem like a lifetime if you're standing on stage before a roomful of people and have nothing to offer. When I went back down, I bounded onto the stage to see what could possibly be wrong.

"What's wrong?" —wearing my most earnest expression.

"You never told me this guitar was left-handed."

"My God, I thought you knew. You sat for an hour during my first show. I was amazed there was another lefty in the audience."

"Yeah, well, there wasn't; I can't play this thing."

"I'm taking lessons, meeself. Whaddya do? T'anks, anyway."

"Right, thanks for nothing."

Surly, surly. Not at all a happy camper. He had less of a spring in his step going back to his table, but on the good side of things, his honey hadn't noticed a thing; she chatted all the way through his performance! I adjusted my mic back to its normal position and leaned in.

"Sorry for the mix up there, folks, but let's give him a big round of applause. It really was wonderful to have him on stage."

ぴ&

Lunatic Loose in Lima

Dennis O'Rourke

Back in the early 80s, I moved to Nashville. I had written an album of country-rock that I was fairly proud of, and decided to take a shot at flogging it there. I had tried selling the thing at the Irish gigs. People would pick one up and look at the titles. There was no "Black Velvet Band," no "Wild Rover," or "Danny Boy." "All original material," I would tell them. "Oh," they would reply. They'd pretend to be interested for another moment or two, thinking of a polite way to put it back down and return to their table. Trying to sell an album of country-rock in Irish bars speaks volumes about my marketing savvy. But by that time, I was writing quite a bit and proud of the songs. I sent a copy of a forty-five to some disc jockeys around New England, as well as to Bruce Bradley, a DJ who once worked WBZ in Boston, and was then on the air in New York. He wrote back immediately, a two-page letter that began, "Dear Dennis. Go to Nashville." And that was that.

It was a risky, some said—a foolish decision. Irish gigs were plentiful in the Northeast, and I was making decent money. But I wanted something bigger, something better. If I couldn't make it as a country artist (which I didn't), I resolved to become a songwriter.

I made the move, got a bartending job, and started pitching my songs on Music Row. The bars I worked allowed me to take a week or two off now and again to go back up north and work a gig, so I didn't let go of the Irish apron strings completely. I went up to O'Friels in Wilmington, Delaware a half-dozen times a year for the next four years. Seven hundred and fifty miles and fourteen hours each way. I got to know the scenery of the Shenandoah Valley pretty well.

In December of 1987, Randy Travis cut one of my songs, "Honky Tonk Moon," and when the album was released in July the following year, it was the first single. It spent three months climbing the charts and arrived at number one in early October. Those were heady days. I got out from behind the bar and pulled up a stool. But after a few months of fierce and relentless celebrating, I decided to go back to the Irish circuit—if nothing else, just to stay out of trouble.

I heard about a joint newly opened in Lima, Ohio. I booked a gig and drove up. Back then, Lima was in a terrible economic condition. The downtown area, where the new bar had been built, was a row of boarded-up retail stores. The city fathers were hoping that an Irish pub with entertainment would pump some life into the area by bringing people into town at night. The head of the Chamber of Commerce even took me to lunch.

It was a beautiful bar, and it started its run well. The place hummed at night. Of course, they had a jukebox filled with a lot of rock and roll, a little country, and two or three Irish records. Some of the crowd, mostly the younger people, would make a dash for it when I took a break. Van Halen would fill the room. When my twenty minutes was up, I would have the manager shut the box down, and while there was no outright groaning, I saw the disappointment in some faces.

Oh, they liked me all right, and they liked the usual suspects in Irish music—"The Unicorn," "Finnegan's Wake," and so forth. I decided to mix it up, to throw in some cover material of pop and rock. This seemed to please everyone, including management.

On my third night, I finished my set by announcing I would sing a song of mine that Randy Travis had recorded. Trying to be humble, I mumbled this, and not many people heard me. Down front was a table of girls in their early twenties, chattering away. (When I think about it now, it seems like the good old days. Why? Because they were just happily babbling amongst themselves then. Cell phones were rare. Now the kids come in, pull out their phones, and lay them down, like a gunslinger might lay out his Colt on a poker table. Or they immediately dial someone up for the regular fifteen-minute check-in.) I started the tune and looked down at the table, tickled to see one of the girls brighten and bounce up in her seat. I could clearly see her mouth the words, "Oh, this is my favorite song."

Well, I gave the tune the extra effort. I got down from the stage and went right over to her, beaming like a happy dad.

"Did I hear you say "Honky Tonk Moon" was your favorite song?"

"Oh, I love it. It's a great song. And I love Randy Travis."

"Well," says I, thrusting out my chest, "I have a surprise for you. I wrote it."

She laughed. "Oh, c'mon. Sure you did."

"No. I'm not kidding. I wrote it. I wrote 'Honky Tonk Moon.'"

Her smile disappeared. "No, you didn't."

I knelt down beside her. She backed away in her chair, apprehension beginning to show in her face.

"But I did. I wrote it." To my very great distress, I heard my voice coming out like a pleading whine. Her friends giggled and rolled their eyes. She turned away. I continued to insist, she continued to resist. Exasperated, I said, "Look. Have you got the album?"

"Of course, I do."

"Well, when you get home, look at the credits, and you'll see my name and my publishing company right beside the song."

I stood up and walked to the bar, thoroughly embarrassed. I found a waitress in back sneaking a cigarette, and I told her the story.

She said, "Well, I have the Travis album, and when I heard you were coming here, I looked up your name on it. That girl probably figures that if you really did write that song, what the hell are you doing playing Irish music, especially in a place like Lima?"

"I've got to keep working," I said. "Simple as that."

I went back up. The table at which the doubting Tomasina and her friends had sat was now occupied by a different group. It was a relief, really, not having them there. I was sure I had made a fool of myself. But after a few songs, I noticed that the girls had not left the bar; they had just relocated to the back of the room—way back in the room, close to the front entrance. It appeared they wanted nothing more to do with this seriously deluded entertainer and needed to be close to the door should he have a psychotic episode onstage.

❦

The Opening Act

Harry O'Donoghue

"Hello. Mr. Hand?"

"Uh-huh."

"Mr. Hand, Harry O'Donoghue here. You know my dad, Tom. He—"

"Tom's young fella. Jeez, how's he doin'?"

"Ah, he's grand. He said I should give you a ring. I'm playing in a group and thought maybe we could—"

"A group. Fair play. How many in it? What sort of stuff are you doin'?"

"Erm, there's three of us—myself and the girlfriend and Gerry Mulroy. We're doin' all kinds of material, from Christy Moore to James Taylor and the Eagles, a couple of Beatles ones and a lot of the Irish sing-alongy stuff. I thought if we got the chance, we could open for the Furey Brothers or Paddy Reilly sometime. The father said I might as well ask. Nothing ventured, nothing gained sort of thing."

"He's right, too. What about tomorrow night at the Old Sheeling Hotel. The Fureys are on, and you could do support. Eight o' clock okay?"

"What? Tomorrow night in Dublin? God. Eh, sure that'd be great."

"Are youse driving? You'll be okay to get there, yeah?"

"Yeah, I have a car. Thanks, thanks very much, Mr. Hand."

"Jim."

"Oh, okay. Eh, how much will we get?"

"Thirty-five quid. It's not a fortune, but you'll get the exposure, y'know?"

"Yeah, right enough. Thanks again. I'll see you tomorrow then."

"Grand."

Click

Thirty-five pounds, divided by three, less petrol money. I thought it'd be more, but still it was a good break.

Gerry was on his way to Wales for the weekend. I only just caught him going out the door.

"You can't go. We have a gig, opening for the Fureys in Dublin."

"How the hell did you manage that?"

"Never mind that. Are you in?"

"Sure."

We got lost going through Dublin, but arrived at the gig in good time. The stage manager was expecting us and asked if we'd be able to set up without disturbing the Furey brothers' guitars, flutes, pipes, and accordions already on stage. I assured him it wasn't a problem; we just had two guitars and a small keyboard. We could do our show, break down, and be off the stage in a matter of minutes. Our spot was thirty minutes, and there was no sign of the Fureys five minutes before we were due to start.

"The boys are doing an interview with RTE," says the stage guy, whose name was Benny. "It won't be a problem, don't worry. Do your show, and they'll be here before you're done."

"Okay," says I, beginning to sweat at the thought of going on.

"Right—you're on."

I opened with, "Good evening lazys an' gentemenn." That's how nervous I was. But we got through the set okay.

"And for our last number, before we hand you over to the fabulous Furey Brothers and Davey Arthur—"

"Thanks, thanks, very much. Goodnight."

Benny was waiting in the wings.

"The boys got held up. Out and do an encore."

"What?"

"Go on. They loved you. Give 'em another couple."

"Are you sure?"

"Yeah. Go back on."

So we did.

"Thanks, very much, all the best—goodnight."

Benny's waiting for us. "You'll have to do a few more. They're still not here."

"No way."

"C'mon, now. You have to help out."

"They'll eat us alive if we go back out there."

"Don't be stupid. Tell them there's a delay. Sing another couple, and it'll be fine."

"Ladies and—"

"Boo! Where the fuck are the Fureys? Boo! Boo! We want the Fureys! We want the Fureys! We want the Fureys!"

"Goodnight, goodnight, now; all the best." And we ran off the stage. Benny's waiting for us.

"Are you not doin' another few?"

"No."

"You have to."

"Not a chance."

"Look, there'll be trouble."

"There already is trouble."

"I'm telling you, get out there."

"You get fuckin' out there. We're not."

"You'll not get paid. I'll see to that."

"Shove it."

Welcome to show biz.

ACKNOWLEDGEMENTS

A tremendous debt of gratitude is owed my late friend, the song-writer C. Carson Parks and his wife Gail for their generosity, advice, and encouragement.

Kevin and Suzanne Jordahl were always there to answer a computer question and help me put new manuscripts together as the book grew.

Thanks to Edward Reardon for reading the stories as they came in and insisting from the beginning that this was a project that would fly.

And thanks to Peter Golden, my brother of a thousand years, for his infinite patience and sublime direction.

Dennis O'Rourke

AUTHORS (IN THEIR OWN WORDS)

Frank Emerson

Dublin's Frank Emerson was born too damned long ago to an Irish father and an Italian mother, which may have something to do with the nature of his mellow, non-volatile persona.

Having gained a semblance of a formal education, he tried his hand at various endeavors, including, but not limited to, the armed forces, the teamsters, short-order cook, grave digging, teaching, and acting. In the early seventies—the nineteen-seventies—he got into the folk/entertainment game. By his own admission, he has been keeping one step ahead of the talent police for over thirty years now. He considers himself lucky to be doing what he does for a living.

After a good deal of time in the Northeast, where his son, brother, sister-in-law, their children, and various cousins still brave the winters, Frank relocated to Washington, DC at the behest of the late publican, Matt Kane. It was there he was fortunate to meet his wife. A while later, the two moved to her hometown in bucolic Southwest Virginia.

Although he's on the road a lot, Frank is always happy and thankful to get back to his home in the rolling Appalachians. There he enjoys reading, writing songs and stories, practicing, playing golf, and spending time with his extended family on his wife's side, as well as his two Schnauzers. The latter are not related to him—although there is some physical resemblance.

www.frankemerson.com

Seamus Kennedy

Seamus was born in Belfast, Northern Ireland a few years after the war because he wanted to be near his mommy. The product of a mixed marriage—his father was male and his mother was female—he has been entertaining audiences all over the United States since 1971.

He studied languages (French and Italian, if you must know) at University College Dublin, but it was as an athlete that he arrived in New York in 1970. He had played Gaelic football and hurling (not to be confused with curling, the sport with big stones, ice, and brooms) at UCD and was one of the players the New York league brought from Ireland.

After the games, the team would repair to a Bronx pub to restore their tissues, and Seamus would drink beer, play guitar, and sing. Eventually the pub owner offered him a regular gig. Apparently, this was cheaper than supplying him with free beer.

He turned pro and formed a duo—the Beggarmen—with Tom O'Carroll in Boston. In '78, he went solo again and moved with his wife and two sons to Maryland in 1983.

Years of performing for Washington DC tourists led to some memorable gigs, including one in 1979 when he was selected to perform for Pope John Paul II at Trinity College in DC, and one in 1988 when he entertained President Ronald Reagan at Ireland's Own Pub in Alexandria, VA.

Well, we *think* he was entertained.

He now averages over 180 dates a year, including leading two tour groups annually to Ireland. He has recorded eleven albums and is currently at work on another.

Oh yes, he can order beer in five languages.

www.seamus-kennedy.com

Robbie O'Connell

Robbie was born in Waterford, Ireland and grew up in Carrick-on-Suir, Co. Tipperary, where his parents owned a small hotel. He began to play guitar and sing at age thirteen, and soon became a regular performer at the hotel's weekly folk concerts. He spent a year touring the folk clubs in England before enrolling at University College, Dublin, where he studied literature and philosophy. During those summers, Robbie worked as an entertainer in America, where he met his wife, Roxanne. In 1977, his celebrated uncles, the Clancy Brothers, asked him to join their group, and he subsequently recorded three albums with them. Two years later, he relocated to Franklin, Massachusetts. With the 1982 release of *Close to the Bone*, he established himself as a major solo artist. Still, he continued working and recording with other musicians, as well as the Clancy Brothers—among them, Mick Moloney and Jimmy Keane, and Eileen Ivers and Seamus Egan in the *Green Fields of America*. Three more critically acclaimed solo albums were released, one of which was voted the number one acoustic album of 1989 by WUMB in Boston. He participated in the live telecast of the tribute to Bob Dylan at Madison Square Garden in 1992. He has taught songwriting at several summer schools, including the Augusta Heritage Arts Workshop and Boston College. He also leads music and cultural tours of Ireland. He recently moved to Bristol, Rhode Island and is currently working on a new solo recording.

www.robbieoconnell.com

Harry O'Donoghue

Harry remembers having what he describes as a typically normal Irish childhood. "We were a close-knit, happy family, not a lot of money, but that didn't seem important." His dad constantly sang "mostly old show tunes and anthem-like songs. He fancied himself an Irish Al Jolson." Harry's education was forged by the not-so-delicate hands of the Christian Brothers, and he went on to become an electrician.

"My musical career got off to a late start at the age of twenty when I bought my first guitar, practiced until my fingers became blistered, and headed out, undaunted by the fact that I was terrible, to play some shows for the local branch of the Irish Wheelchair Association. A captive audience indeed, but great exposure!"

While working in Holland in '79, the group Terra Nova was formed. They were a popular opening act for the Fureys, the Wolfe Tones, and other touring artists, and the group first came to Philadelphia in May 1980. Within a month, they were performing in Southern California, and for the next two years traveled between California, Philadelphia, Ireland, and all points in between. Their first performance in Savannah was in April 1983.

"There were just two of us by then, and we made Savannah our new home. We recorded a second album in eighty-five and sold it to PolyGram Records, Ireland. Thought we were on our way, but it proved to be our swan song, and I found myself working as a solo act soon after."

413

Nowadays, Harry co-produces and hosts a weekly radio show for Georgia Public Broadcasting. He customizes and leads tour groups to Ireland annually and performs in concert at private events, festivals, clubs, singer/songwriter showcases, and on selected cruises with NCL. He has released nine albums thus far.

www.harryodonoghue.com

Dennis O'Rourke

Dennis was born in Dorchester, Massachusetts and grew up in the Irish enclave of South Boston. He was an altar boy in the final years of the Latin Mass and sang in the church choir of St. Theresa's in the "lace curtain" suburb of West Roxbury. This, he says, was his first taste of show business. He was taken by the variety of popular music available on the radio in the fifties, and eagerly embraced the folk boom of the early sixties, buying his first guitar at sixteen. In high school, he played in a rock and roll band until the arrival and success of the Clancy Brothers and Tommy Makem led him back to folk music. After three years in college and two sailing in the Merchant Marine, he moved to Ireland, living and working in Dublin for eighteen months.

Returning to Boston, he began his music career in earnest in 1976. To promote an album of original country-rock, he moved to Nashville, Tennessee in '82. While still performing in Irish pubs, he wrote and pitched country songs to established artists, finally achieving success in '88 when Randy Travis took one of his songs—"Honky Tonk Moon"— to number one. He continues to write and pitch songs to both country and jazz artists alike and is also at work on a collection of short fiction.

www.dennisorourke.com

414

Made in the USA
Lexington, KY
08 July 2012